Memory in a Time of Prose

Memory in a Time of Prose

Studies in Epistemology, Hebrew Scribalism, and the Biblical Past

DANIEL D. PIOSKE

OXFORD
UNIVERSITY PRESS

OXFORD
UNIVERSITY PRESS

Oxford University Press is a department of the University of Oxford. It furthers
the University's objective of excellence in research, scholarship, and education
by publishing worldwide. Oxford is a registered trade mark of Oxford University
Press in the UK and certain other countries.

Published in the United States of America by Oxford University Press
198 Madison Avenue, New York, NY 10016, United States of America.

© Oxford University Press 2018

Library of Congress Cataloging-in-Publication Data
Name: Pioske, Daniel D., 1982– author.
Title: Memory in a time of prose : studies in epistemology,
Hebrew scribalism, and the biblical past / Daniel D. Pioske.
Description: New York : Oxford University Press, 2018. |
Includes bibliographical references and index.
Identifiers: LCCN 2018012960 (print) | LCCN 2018029571 (ebook) |
ISBN 9780190649869 (updf) | ISBN 9780190649876 (epub) |
ISBN 9780190649852 (hardcover) | ISBN 9780190649883 (online content)
Subjects: LCSH: Bible. Old Testament—Historiography. | Bible.
Old Testament—Criticism, interpretation, etc. | Bible. Old Testment—Antiquities. |
Knowledge, Theory of (Religion) | David, King of Israel.
Classification: LCC BS1180 (ebook) |
LCC BS1180 .P56 2018 (print) | DDC 221.6/7—dc23
LC record available at https://lccn.loc.gov/2018012960

1 3 5 7 9 8 6 4 2

Printed by Sheridan Books, Inc., United States of America

To Chip Dobbs-Allsopp

Contents

Preface

ON THIS BOOK'S cover is a painting by the Dutch artist Aert de Gelder (1645–1727 CE), entitled "King David." The portrait carries a twofold resonance for the present study. In part, we find the image of an elderly David next to a document he is composing, an act well-attested within the biblical depiction of the king but problematized in the discussion that follows in its attempt to historicize the emergence of Hebrew prose writing in antiquity. Yet what is also featured in this portrait is a particular vision of the past, a vision that elides two and half millennia of history by depicting David as if he occupied the same world in which de Gelder lived. Untroubled by such anachronisms, de Gelder's work foregrounds a theme that will play out over the course of this book: how the past is conceived is shaped by the era in which it is thought.

Acknowledgments

IN A SEMINAR from what is now many years ago I was assigned Yosef Yerushalmi's moving and influential study, *Zakhor*. In the prologue to this work Yerushalmi describes a "paradox" that came to light through his historical research, a realization "... that although Judaism throughout the ages was absorbed with the meaning of history, historiography itself played at best an ancillary role among the Jews, and often no role at all; and, concomitantly, that while memory of the past was always a central component of Jewish experience, the historian was not its primary custodian" (*Zakhor*, xxxiv). The paradox of which Yerushalmi writes has stayed with me since, unable, as I have been, to escape the deep "misgivings" Yerushalmi lays bare over the course of his study. This book does not seek to resolve this paradox, but to speak into it further.

The work that follows came together over many years and with the support of many individuals, only some I am able to name here. But I begin where all things begin: with my wife, Suzette, and my daughters, Eve and Esther, who continually remind me with great persistence of the beauty of a world that exists outside of words on paper. With them I name here my mother, Starla, for her love and support throughout. In a work devoted to memory, I remember also my father, David, and of a life taken too early, and my grandmother, Marguerite, who succumbed to that disease that makes remembering impossible.

A book such as this does not come to be without the help of many in the academic community who took time out of their own lives and research to read, critique, and provide crucial insights into a study that is not theirs. So I offer my heartfelt thanks to Peter Altmann, Elizabeth Bloch-Smith, Simi Chavel, Chip Dobbs-Allsopp, Dan Fleming, Elaine James, Paul Kurtz, Mark Leuchter, Aren Maeir, Bernd Schipper, Mark S. Smith, Andrew Tobolowsky, Ian Wilson, and Jonathan Wylie for their comments on various chapters that follow. I would also like to thank the members of the Colloquium of Biblical and Ancient Near Easter Studies, led by Heather Dana Davis Parker and Heath Dewrell, and the steering committee of the Historiography and Hebrew Bible Program Unit within the Society of Biblical Literature, for their support and friendship throughout. Snippets of Chapter 2 appeared in a previous article published in the *Journal for the Study of the Old Testament* ("Material Culture and Making Visible: On the Portrayal of Philistine Gath in the Book of Samuel," *JSOT 42.2* [2018]) and a few elements from Chapter 4 appeared previously in an article published in the *Zeitschrift für die alttestamentliche Wissenschaft* ("Memory and its Materiality: The Case of Early Iron Age Khirbet Qeiyafa and Jerusalem," *ZAW* 127.1 [2015]: 78–95), and I thank these journals for their permission to draw on these studies here. I offer my warm thanks to Steve Wiggins, editor at Oxford University Press, for his shepherding of this book throughout its development.

I have the incredible good fortune of teaching within a collaborative, collegial, and above all supportive Department of Philosophy and Religious Studies at Georgia Southern University. I am particularly indebted to Dean Curtis Ricker of the College of Arts and Humanities and to the chair of my department, Karin Fry, for their continued support, and also to my friend and colleague, David Dudley, for his care and hospitality since our move south. The Zach Henderson Library has been nothing but helpful and generous during the research of this book, and I am indebted as well to Georgia Southern for travel funds that made this work possible.

This book is dedicated to my teacher, F.W. "Chip" Dobbs-Allsopp. Those familiar with Chip's work will find its imprint throughout the studies that follow. His scholarship is its model and his encouragement gave it life.

Savannah, Georgia

Abbreviations

AJA	*American Journal of Archaeology*
ANES	*Ancient Near Eastern Studies*
ARC	*Archaeology Review from Cambridge*
BA	*Biblical Archaeologist*
BAR	*Biblical Archaeology Review*
BASOR	*Bulleting of the American Schools of Oriental Research*
Bib	*Biblica*
BibInt	*Biblical Interpretation*
BN	*Biblische Notizen*
BthZ	*Berliner theologische Zeitschrift*
COS	*The Context of Scripture.* Edited by W. Hallo. 3 vols. Leiden: Brill, 1997–2002
Er-Isr	*Eretz-Israel*
ETL	*Ephemerides Theologicæ Louvanienses*
FGrHist	*Die Fragmente der griechischen Historiker.* Edited by F. Jacoby. Leiden: Brill, 1954–
HeBAI	*Hebrew Bible and Ancient Israel*
HTR	*Harvard Theological Review*
IEJ	*Israel Exploration Journal*
JANER	*Journal of Ancient Near Eastern Religions*
JANES	*Journal of Ancient Near Eastern Studies*
JAOS	*Journal of the American Oriental Society*
JBL	*Journal of Biblical Literature*
JESHO	*Journal of the Economic and Social History of the Orient*
JSOT	*Journal for the Study of the Old Testament*

KAI	*Kanaanäische und aramäische Inschriften.* Edited by H. Donner and W. Röllig. 5th ed. Wiesbaden, 2002
KTU	M. Dietrich, O. Loretz and J. Sanmartín. *Die keilalphabetischen Texte aus Ugarit: Einschliesslich der keilalphabetischen Texte ausserhalb Ugarits. Teil 1. Transkription.* Neukirchen-Vluyn: Neukirchener Verlag, 1976
NEA	*Near Eastern Archaeology*
NEAEHL	*New Encyclopedia of Archaeological Excavations in the Holy Land.* 4 vols. Edited by E. Stern. Jerusalem: Israel Exploration Society, 1993
OJA	*Oxford Journal of Archaeology*
Or	*Orientalia*
PEQ	*Palestine Exploration Quarterly*
PMLA	*Publications of the Modern Language Association*
PNAS	*Proceedings of the National Academy of Sciences*
RB	*Revue Biblique*
SJOT	*Scandinavian Journal of the Old Testament*
TA	*Tel Aviv*
UF	*Ugarit-Forschungen*
VT	*Vetus Testamentum*
ZAR	*Zeitschrift für altorientalische und biblische Rechtsgeschichte*
ZAW	*Zeitschrift für die alttestamentliche Wissenschaft*
ZDPV	*Zeitschrift des Deutschen Palästina-Vereins*

Memory in a Time of Prose

Introduction

MEMORY IN A TIME OF PROSE

*A common problematic, in fact, flows through the phenom-
enology of memory, the epistemology of history, and the hermeneutics of the historical condition: the problematic of the
representation of the past.[1]*

ONE OF THE great mysteries of the Hebrew Bible is how its stories about the
past came to be. When searching for clues that might offer some insights into
the creation of these writings, we are confronted at the outset by literature that
never discloses the dates of its composition or the settings in which its texts
emerged. The hope of circumventing this silence through the possibility of archaeological discovery, where the unearthing of a palace archive or corpus of
temple documents might reveal in situ instances of specific biblical texts, has
never been realized. The greatest archaeological find that pertains to the biblical writings is unquestionably the Dead Sea Scrolls, yet the earliest biblical
documents included among this cache (dated to ca. the mid-third century BCE[2])
were copies of what were likely preexisting manuscripts whose origins are still
unknown.

But the most serious impediment to our understanding of these stories' formation is the fact that their writers took no credit for them. Of those narratives
that form the focus of this work, not one text that recounts an occurrence from
Israel or Judah's past is accompanied by a signature or claim of authorship. This
omission is peculiar not only from the publication practices and perspectives of

---

1. P. Ricoeur, *Memory, History, Forgetting* (trans. by K. Blamey and D. Pellauer;
Chicago: University of Chicago Press, 2004), xvi.

2. F. Cross, "Palaeography and the Dead Sea Scrolls," in *The Dead Sea Scrolls After Fifty
Years: A Comprehensive Assessment*, vol. 1 (eds. P. Flint and J. VanderKam; Leiden: Brill,
1998), 379–402.

intellectual property common today, but also from the standpoint of the storytellers of the ancient Greek and Roman worlds to which we are also heirs.
So Herodotus can begin his famous work with the declaration: Ἡροδότου
Ἁλικαρνησσέος ἱστορίης ἀπόδεξις ἥδε ("Herodotus of Halicarnassus here displays
his inquiry. . . ." [Hdt. 1.1]).

By contrast, what we find in the narrative works of the Hebrew Bible are
anonymous, third person texts written by those whose identities are lost to history and, barring an unexpected archaeological discovery, will remain forever so.
A result of this anonymity was the rendering of written accounts that appear un-
mediated by any individual tethered to a particular time and place, stories voiced,
consequently, by a narrator who remains concealed and who is therefore ostensibly free from the restrictions imposed by a specific, identifiable point of view.[3]
Yet this sophisticated manner of storytelling also withholds important historical clues about the production of these texts. Within Herodotus's short opening
statement cited above, for example, three crucial pieces of information emerge
for the historian to consider: the name of the author (Herodotus), the author's
origin (Halicarnassus), and the type of account that is being put forward (an
"inquiry" or, as it is commonly translated, a *history*). Throughout his writings,
Herodotus even offers candid remarks as to where he obtained certain sources
(λόγοι) for his work and how he came to negotiate divergent or contradictory
reports from among them.

The stories told in the Hebrew Bible offer none of this information. Unable
to determine the precise personalities who contributed to these writings, scholars have long devoted themselves instead to what they can discern about how
the various biblical works were pieced together over time.[4] Through painstaking
analysis of the textual layers and seams that emerged during many generations
of activity, this approach to the biblical writings has helped to reveal the intricate manner by which this ancient collection of texts developed and the diverse
traditions that contributed to its formation. Even if the precise contours of the
sources behind these writings and the types of revisions made to them are still

---

3. R. Alter, *The Art of Biblical Narrative* (New York: Basic Books, 1981), 157–84. Cf. M.
Sternberg, *The Poetics of Biblical Narrative: Ideological Literature and the Drama of Reading*
(Bloomington: Indiana University Press, 1987), 84–128.

4. For introductory discussions on these matters, see O. Eißfeld, *The Old Testament: An
Introduction* (trans. P. R. Ackroyd; Oxford: Blackwell, 1965), 129–53; R. Kratz, *The
Composition of the Narrative Books of the Old Testament* (trans. J. Bowden; London: T&T
Clark, 2005), 1–5, 309–21; K. Schmid, *The Old Testament: A Literary History* (trans. L.
Maloney; Minneapolis: Fortress, 2012) 1–32; and R. Smend, "In the Wake of Wellhausen: The
Growth of a Literary-critical School and Its Varied Influence," in *The Hebrew Bible/Old
Testament: The History of Its Interpretation*, Vol. III/1 (ed. M. Saebø; Göttingen: Vandenhoeck
& Ruprecht, 2013), 472–92.

much debated, the lengthy process by which the biblical writers assembled and reworked the texts now enclosed within the Hebrew Bible has been demonstrated with great care and sophistication.

Dispelled through this research, accordingly, has been the image of the solitary biblical author composing finalized, lengthy works in a single lifetime, safeguarded after publication from further alterations and circulated for an audience who accessed them individually through private readings. In place of such ideas about authorship and literary production is our current appreciation of the Hebrew Bible as a composite and fluid text before its (late) canonization,[5] fashioned by numerous hands over the course of hundreds of years.[6] R. Alter, for example, lifts up the "elaborately layered nature" of biblical narrative and comments further:[7]

> A century of analytic scholarship has made powerful arguments to the effect that where we might naively imagine that we are reading a text, what we actually have is a constant stitching together of earlier texts drawn from divergent literary and sometimes oral traditions, with minor or major interventions by later editors in the form of glosses, connecting passages, conflations of sources, and so forth.

Undeterred, as Alter observes, from introducing revisions into older documents handed down to them and uninterested in claiming originality for what new compositions they may have achieved, the individuals who produced the writings of the Hebrew Bible operated under much different assumptions of authorship than current today.[8] For such reasons, an emphasis has come to be placed on the essential role played by a collection of unidentified scribes—what has been

---

5. So Carr, for example, observes that even in the Hasmonean period (164–63 BCE), "the books of the Hebrew Bible were still in a remarkable amount of flux at this time." D. Carr, *The Formation of the Hebrew Bible: A New Reconstruction* (Oxford: Oxford University Press, 2011), 153. Cf. Emanuel Tov, *Textual Criticism of the Hebrew Bible* (3rd ed.; Minneapolis: Fortress, 2012), 161–90.

6. W. Schniedewind, *How the Bible Became a Book: The Textualization of Ancient Israel* (Cambridge: Cambridge University Press, 2004), 1–34; D. Carr, *Writing on the Tablet of the Heart: Origins of Scripture and Literature* (New York: Oxford University Press, 2005), 3–16, 111–76; idem, *The Formation of the Hebrew Bible*, 3–11; K. van der Toorn, *Scribal Culture and the Making of the Hebrew Bible* (Cambridge: Harvard University Press, 2007), 1–50; E. Mroczek, *The Literary Imagination in Jewish Antiquity* (Oxford: Oxford University Press, 2016), 3–18.

7. R. Alter, *The Art of Biblical Narrative* (New York: Basic Books, 1981), 132.

8. So also Ulrich: "That is, each [biblical] book is the product not of a single author, such as Plato or Shakespeare, but of multiple, anonymous bards, sages, religious leaders, compilers, or tradents... the biblical books are constituted by earlier traditions being repeated, augmented, and reshaped by later authors, editors, or tradents, over the course of many centuries." E.

termed a "scribal culture"[9]—in the production and transmission of texts that came to be included within the biblical corpus.

By Hebrew scribalism, then, I mean a specific scribal tradition constituted by individuals who were demarcated from the vast majority of their contemporaries by being trained in the specific *craft* of writing and reading texts in the Hebrew language.[10] Artisans skilled in technologies of textuality,[11] these scribes were rarely the sole proprietors of the biblical documents we possess but were rather part of a wider, interconnected scribal craft tradition that generated, copied, and maintained texts held in common over time. The biblical writings were of course authored by individuals of great talent and creativity, but the terminology of "scribe" used in the following is one put forward to disabuse us of modern conceptions of authorship and book culture so as to be more sensitive to the wider ancient Near Eastern scribal milieu of which Hebrew scribes were also part. One of the great advancements made in recent biblical scholarship is a greater appreciation of the socio-historical circumstances in which Hebrew scribalism developed in antiquity, that is, the training, places of production, status, and function of scribes in the southern Levant, insights into which have been ascertained through more recent epigraphic finds from the region and from comparative considerations drawn from other scribal cultures in the ancient Near East.[12]

Ulrich, *The Dead Sea Scrolls and the Developmental Composition of the Bible* (Leiden: Brill, 2015), 2.

9. By scribal culture, van der Toorn writes of the "universe of these scribes: their social role and status, their training, the arts of their craft, their ways of thinking; in brief, scribal culture" (*Scribal Culture*, 8).

10. As discussed in Chapter 1, it is nevertheless important to note that the term "Hebrew" is a designation never used within the biblical writings to describe the language spoken and transcribed within it. Instead, this language is referred to as "Canaanite" (Isa. 19:18) or, in later texts, as "Yehudite" (Neh. 13:24). But by virtue of the millennia-long history in which the term Hebrew has been applied to the language of the Hebrew Bible, beginning with the Jewish writers behind the Mishnah in the third century CE, this study will do the same.

11. S. Sanders, *The Invention of Hebrew* (Champaign: University of Illinois Press, 2009), 130–36.

12. In addition to Van der Toorn and Sanders' works cited above, see, for example, A. Lemaire, *Les Écoles et la formation de la Bible dans l'ancien Isräel* (Fribourg: Éditions Universitaires, 1981); D. Jamieson-Drake, *Scribes and Schools in Monarchic Judah: A Socio-Archaeological Approach* (Sheffield: Almond Press, 1991); P. Davies, *Scribes and Schools: The Canonization of the Hebrew Scriptures* (Louisville: Westminster John Knox, 1998); E. Tov, *Scribal Practices and Approaches Reflected in Texts Found in the Judean Desert* (Leiden: Brill, 2004); R. Byrne, "The Refuge of Scribalism in Iron I Palestine," *BASOR* 345 (2007): 1–31; L. Perdue, ed., *Scribes, Sages, and Seers: The Sage in the Eastern Mediterranean World* (Göttingen: Vandenhoeck &

But questions about these scribes and the texts they composed remain. One uncertainty not addressed within approaches that focus on the stages of the Hebrew Bible's development is the character of the source material, written or oral, that the biblical scribes drew on in order to shape the stories that they eventually wrote down. This concern becomes more pointed with the widespread recognition that many of the biblical stories we now possess took shape long after the purported events they recount. Tales surrounding Samson's clashes against Philistine foes, Hannah's supplications at Shiloh, Saul's fall from grace, David's rise to power, Bath-Sheba's maneuvers to place her son on the throne—few historians today would argue that these are first-hand, eyewitness accounts of the incidents these texts describe. Yet if these stories were not contemporaneous reports, then a fundamental historical question comes to the fore: what did the biblical scribes *know* about the past referred to in their narratives? And how did they come to know it?

The intent of this book is to investigate such questions by focusing on a collection of biblical narratives that are set within the early Iron Age period (ca. 1175–830 BCE).[13] With the scribes behind these narratives writing many years, if not centuries, after the events their stories recount, this study examines what knowledge about the early Iron Age was available to them. The chief aim of this study, then, is to complement other historical approaches to the formation of the Hebrew Bible by focusing on the stories that its scribes devised in an effort to explore what information may have been conveyed to them about times previous to their own.

In short, the primary interest of this work is that of epistemology, or the sources, limits, and conditions of knowing that shaped the biblical narratives composed about the early Iron Age period. The immediate difficulty confronted in this pursuit is that the biblical writers never discuss how they formed their

---

Ruprecht, 2008); C. Rollston, *Writing and Literacy in the World of Ancient Israel: Epigraphic Evidence from the Iron Age* (Atlanta: Society of Biblical Literature, 2010), P. Davies and T. Römer, eds., *Writing the Bible: Scribes, Scribalism, and Script* (Durham: Acumen, 2013).

13. In terms of the archaeological record of the region, this timeframe would coincide with the Iron I–IIA periods. For considerations drawn for my dating of this period, and an overview of the debates surrounding Iron Age chronology in the southern Levant, see D. Frese and T. Levy, "The Four Pillars of the Iron Age Low Chronology," in *Historical Biblical Archaeology and the Future: The New Pragmatism* (ed. T. Levy; London: Equinox, 2010), 187–202; I. Finkelstein and E. Piasetzky, "The Iron Age Chronology Debate: Is the Gap Narrowing?," *NEA* 74.1 (2011): 50–54; A. Mazar, "The Iron Age Chronology Debate: Is the Gap Narrowing? Another Viewpoint," *NEA* 74.2 (2011): 105–11; H. Katz and A. Faust, "The Chronology of the Iron IIA in Judah in Light of the Tel 'Eton Tomb C3 and Other Assemblages," *BASOR* 371 (2014): 103–27; Y. Asscher et al., "Absolute Dating of the Late Bronze Age to Iron Age Transition and the Appearance of Philistine Culture in Qubur el-Walaydah, Southern Levant," *Radiocarbon* 57.1 (2015): 77–97.

narratives or what source material they would have relied on for doing so. The substance of the putative sources they may have used, when they were accessed, or how they were incorporated into these scribes' writings all remain unknown to us. The obscurity of those who wrote these texts and the few traces they left behind about their craft only makes such questions more difficult to answer. However much we may desire to do so, we cannot, like studies of Thucydides or Berossus,[14] respond to such issues by focusing on the lives of particular biblical scribes in order to retrace the historical influences that contributed to the formation of their writings.

What is available to us however are the stories themselves. Embedded within these accounts are not only the literary seams and fractures that disclose important information as to the compositional history of the Hebrew Bible, but also a host of references to past phenomena—events, people, places, practices—that are said to have belonged to the era of the early Iron Age. These references are of utmost importance for the study at hand because they offer the opportunity to triangulate their claims with a wider constellation of archaeological evidence unearthed from the era in which the biblical stories are set, enabling us to examine the relationship between the past attested by these archaeological remains and that past represented within the biblical writings. Biblical allusions to the early Iron Age sites of Gath (Chapter 2) or Ziklag (Chapter 3), for example, invite us consider how these references resonate with what is known about these locations through the archaeological excavations carried out in their ruins.

Thus, even if we cannot identify the precise individuals who wrote these biblical texts or specify the dates in which they were composed, what is possible is to pursue an approach that juxtaposes the narrative world the biblical writings portray with an early Iron Age landscape made known through archaeological research. And what comes to light through this manner of investigation, I argue, are meaningful details concerning the past knowledge made available to Hebrew scribes through information handed down to them, including insights into the underlying frameworks and modes of knowing that would have made narrating a past in prose writing possible.

This historical interest in epistemology is explored in the following through a series of case studies that take up this comparative approach, each chapter focalized on particular biblical stories that occur during the centuries of the early Iron Age. My reason for restricting the present investigation to this period in

---

14. There is, for example, no study of a Hebrew scribe that parallels the seminal work of S. Hornblower, *Thucydides* (Baltimore: Johns Hopkins, 1987); or the recent collection of essays on Berossus in J. Haubold et al., eds., *The World of Berossus* (Wiesbaden: Harassowitz Verlag, 2013).

time arises in part from practical considerations. In light of the fact that the past narrated in the Hebrew Bible covers an era that stretches beyond two millennia, some limits are necessary in what can be covered within a work of this size and scope.

But the decision to limit this study to an early Iron Age past is also an attempt to be sensitive to the concerns of the biblical scribes themselves. For of all the eras that preoccupy those individuals behind the writing of the Hebrew Bible, it is the time of Israel and Judah's emergence as autonomous kingdoms during the early Iron Age period, of struggles against foreign foes and concerns over leadership and communal preservation, that receives the greatest amount of narrative space within the biblical corpus. To inquire into the early Iron Age is therefore to attend to that era which fascinated the biblical scribes most.

The questions this book seeks to address are therefore quite distinct from those works that attempt to demonstrate or refute the historicity of particular biblical claims made about the past. Nor does this study aspire to provide a critical reading of specific biblical passages so as to offer historical reconstructions of the rise of Israelite and Judahite political entities in the early Iron Age or the religious beliefs that may have been present in the region at this period in time. Instead, at the center of this study are the anonymous Hebrew scribes who, through methods and sources that are still mostly hidden from us, composed some of the most influential stories in the history of Western literature. This work's interest in the epistemological conditions that would have supported this storytelling is thus one attempt, among others that could be pursued, to better understand the scribal hands behind the shaping of this literature.

With these concerns in mind, the following study draws near in spirit to the pioneering work of H. Gunkel and H. Greßmann at the turn of the twentieth century. Already incipient in the works of these scholars was an acute historical interest in the material the biblical scribes may have drawn on to form the narrative works that came to be included in the Hebrew Bible.[15] Departing from the dominant approaches of their time toward the compositional stages of biblical literature in antiquity, including J. Wellhausen's enormously influential analyses,[16]

---

15. For example, H. Gunkel, "Geschichtsschreibung im A.T.," in *Religion in Geschichte und Gegenwart*, vol. I (ed. H. Gunkel; Tübingen: Mohr, 1919–23): 1348–54; idem, "Geschichtsschreibung im A.T.," in *Religion in Geschichte und Gegenwart* (2nd ed.; Tübingen: Mohr, 1927), II: 1112–15; H. Greßmann, "The Oldest History Writing in Israel," in *Narrative and Novella in Samuel: Studies by Hugo Gressmann and Other Scholars 1906–1923* (trans. D. Orton; ed. D. Gunn; Sheffield: Sheffield Academic Press, 1991), 13–19.

16. For a review of the wider circumstances behind Gunkel's departure from Wellhausen, see now the incisive study of P. Kurtz, "Waiting at Nemi: Wellhausen, Gunkel, and the World behind their Work," *HTR* 109.4 (2016): 567–85. Cf. R. Smend, "Gunkel und Wellhausen,"

Gunkel and Greßmann sought instead to inquire into the presumptive sources that would have contributed toward the writings the biblical scribes later developed.[17] Even if their reconstructions of the historical settings in which these sources arose and the timeframe in which they were written down are not ones that will be followed here, the questions they posed about the precompositional material that contributed to the formation of the biblical narrative and, above all, their early insights into the importance of oral tradition and transmission on this corpus, are influences that will be felt throughout this work.

This book however moves beyond these early efforts by also building on a number of more recent studies of Hebrew scribalism that focus less on distinguishing the precise forms (saga, legend, report, etc.) these putative sources may have taken (*Formgeschichte*) or how they may have developed over time (*Überlieferungsgeschichte*) and more on the broader scribal contexts in which this source material came to be textualized. In addition to K. van der Toorn's important work on Hebrew scribal culture cited above, particular mention should be made in this vein of a series of investigations undertaken by D. Carr that point up the "oral-written interface"[18] that lay behind the biblical writings and whose scholarship, alongside other recent publications,[19] also foregrounds the essential role of memory

---

in *Hermann Gunkel (1862–1932)* (ed. E. Waschke; Neukirchen-Vluyn: Neukirchener Verlagsgesellschaft, 2013), 21–40.

17. For Gunkel's response to Wellhausen's critique of his method, see H. Gunkel, "Aus Wellhausen's neuesten apokalyptischen Forschungen. Einige principielle Eröterungen," *ZWT* 42 (1899): 581–611; Cf. idem, "Ziele und Methoden der Erklärung des Alten Testamentes," in *Reden und Aufsätze* (Göttingen: Vandenhoeck & Ruprecht, 1913), 11–29. For Greßmann, see H. Greßmann, "Die Aufgaben der alttestamentlichen Forschung" *ZAW* 24 (1924): 1–33. On this point, see again Kurtz, "Waiting at Nemi," 570–72.

18. Carr, *Tablet of the Heart*, 3–16; idem, *Formation of the Hebrew Bible*, 3–152. For further discussion of this theme and other scholarship on the topic, see Chapter 1 and its section on "Hebrew Prose: Comparative and Theoretical Issues."

19. The bibliography on memory is already vast within the sphere of Hebrew Bible scholarship, but for a sampling of different methods and perspectives, see J. van Oorschot, "Geschichte als Erinnerung und Wissenschaft—ein Beitrag zu ihrem Verhältnis," in *Erzählte Geschichte: Beiträge zur narrativen Kultur im alten Israel* (ed. R. Lux; Neukirchen-Vluyn: Neukirchner, 2000), 1–27; M. S. Smith, *The Memoirs of God: History, Memory, and the Experience of the Divine in Ancient Israel* (Minneapolis: Fortress Press, 2004); J. Gertz, "Konstruierte Erinnerung: Alttestamentlich Historiographie im Spiegel von Archäologie und literarhistorischer Kritik am Fallbeispiel des salomonischen Königtums," *BthZ* 21 (2004): 3–29; R. Hendel, *Remembering Abraham: Culture, Memory, and History in the Hebrew Bible* (Oxford: Oxford University Press, 2005); idem, "Cultural Memory," in *Reading Genesis: Ten Methods* (ed. R. Hendel; Cambridge: Cambridge University Press, 2010), 28–46; A. Leveen, *Memory and Tradition in the Book of Numbers* (Cambridge: Cambridge University Press, 2008); E. Ben Zvi, "On Social Memory and Identity Formation in Late Persian Yehud: A Historian's Viewpoint with a Focus on Prophetic Literature, Chronicles and the Dtr. Historical Collection," in *Texts, Contexts and Readings in Postexilic Literature*

within the scribal production of these texts.[20] In addition, a significant influence on the chapters that follow is the work of S. Sanders and his investigations into what the epigraphic record from the Late Bronze and Iron Age periods in the southern Levant can tell us about the early textualization of the Hebrew language in antiquity, including the remarkable decision made by Hebrew scribes, as Sanders draws out and details so well, to suddenly compose documents in their own local vernacular after centuries in which no scribe from the southern Levant had ever written his or her native language down.[21] Finally, the more recent work of F. W. Dobbs-Allsopp and his incisive study of what he terms an "informing orality" that conditioned how the biblical writings were developed and performed, whether in instances of poetry or in connection with forms of prose storytelling that sit at the center of this work, will be felt throughout the pages that follow.[22]

What separates this investigation from these important studies is its explicit interest in matters of epistemology and its turn toward more recent archaeological excavations in the southern Levant in order to address such concerns. A primary impetus for this work resides in the fact that we now have at our disposal an astonishing amount of new historical evidence pertaining to the ancient world of the southern Levant that was simply unavailable to scholars who came before. And this book argues that this new evidence matters for how we understand the knowledge drawn on by Hebrew scribes about an early Iron Age past and the

---

Explorations into Historiography and Identity Negotiation in Hebrew Bible and Related Texts (ed. L. Jonker; Tübingen: Mohr-Siebeck, 2011) 95–148; D. Pioske, *David's Jerusalem: Between Memory and History* (New York: Routledge, 2015), 8–62; I. Wilson, *Kingship and Memory in Ancient Judah* (New York: Oxford, 2017), 23–40.

20. Carr, *Formation of the Hebrew Bible*, 3–56; idem, "Orality, Textuality, and Memory: The State of Biblical Studies," in *Contextualizing Israel's Sacred Writings: Ancient Literacy, Orality, and Literary Production* (ed. B. Schmidt; Atlanta: SBL Press, 2015), 161–73.

21. S. Sanders, *Invention of Hebrew*; cf. idem, "Writing and Early Iron Age Israel: Before National Scripts, Beyond Nations and States," in *Literate Culture and Tenth-Century Canaan: The Tel Zayit Abecedary in Context* (eds. R. Tappy and P. K. McCarter; Winona Lake: Eisenbrauns, 2008), 97–112. For other important studies of scribalism in the ancient Near East that will have a bearing on the chapters that follow, see R. Williams, "Scribal Training in Ancient Egypt," *JAOS* 92 (1972): 214–21; J. M. Sasson, "On Idrimi and Šarruwa the Scribe" in *Studies on the Civilization and Culture of Nuzi and the Hurrians* (eds. M. A. Morrison and D. I. Owen; Winona Lake: Eisenbrauns, 1981), 309–24; E. Havelock, *The Muse Learns to Write: Reflections on Orality and Literacy from Antiquity to the Present* (New Haven: Yale University Press, 1986); Y. Cohen, *The Scribes and Scholars of the City of Emar in the Late Bronze Age* (Winona Lake: Eisenbrauns, 2009); R. Hawley, D. Pardee, and C. Roche-Hawley, "The Scribal Culture of Ugarit," *JANEH* 2.2 (2016): 229–67; S. Milstein, *Tracking the Master Scribe: Revision through Introduction in Biblical and Mesopotamian Literature* (Oxford: Oxford University Press, 2016).

22. F. W. Dobbs-Allsopp, *On Biblical Poetry* (New York: Oxford, 2015), 233–325.

epistemological assumptions that would have framed how this information was conceived and valued within the societies in which these scribes were active.

To cite an example: in the past fifteen years alone significant new excavation reports have been published on every major Iron Age Philistine center save one (Gaza).[23] In place of older conjectures about where the city of Gath was located and the reasons for its downfall, compelling evidence now identifies this ancient Philistine location with the site of Tell es-Safi and connects its destruction to Hazael of Damascus in the late ninth century BCE. In contrast to notions of a united and homogeneous Philistine society that worked in concert to control the coastal plain during the early Iron Age, a more nuanced understanding has emerged of the complex, and sometimes strained, interactions that occurred between Philistine city states composed of distinct and diverse populations. Against perspectives of sustained Philistine/Israelite antagonism in the twelfth to tenth centuries BCE, there is an increasing recognition of the fluid character of both ethnic identity and political borders during these centuries and an aware-ness of more pronounced moments of cultural exchange between communities who inhabited the coastal and highland regions of the southern Levant. Recent evidence from the southern Levant is consequently reshaping nearly every his-torical assumption held by past generations of historians who did not have access to this evidence.

Other studies could be cited. The City of David excavations in Jerusalem have produced six new volumes since the year 1990 on finds obtained under the initial direction of Y. Shiloh,[24] transforming our understanding of the early Iron Age status of this highland center in a manner that resists older notions of Jerusalem as a large, imperial capital city during the reigns of David and Solomon, but which also countervails more recent perspectives that deem this Jerusalem to have been a small village of little consequence. In addition to these reports, E. Mazar has published a number of volumes in the past decade that have offered controversial but nevertheless fascinating finds from the Iron I–IIA period that

---

23. M. Dothan and D. Ben-Shlomo, *Ashdod VI: Excavations of Areas H–K* (Jerusalem: Israel Antiquities Authority, 2005); T. Dothan, S. Gitin, and Y. Garfinkel, *Tel Miqne-Ekron Field IV Lower—The Elite Zone, The Iron Age I and IIC, The Early and Late Philistine Cities* (Winona Lake: Eisenbrauns, 2016); L. Stager, J. D. Schloen, and D. Master, eds., *Ashkelon 1: Introduction and Overview (1985–2006)* (Winona Lake: Eisenbrauns, 2008); A. Maeir, ed., *Tell es-Safi/Gath I: The 1996—2005 Seasons: Part 1: Text* (Wiesbaden: Harrassowitz Verlag, 2012).

24. For the most recent, which concludes with an overview of previous excavation reports, see A. de Groot and H. Bernick-Greenberg, *Excavations at the City of David 1978–1985 Directed by Yigal Shiloh. Vol. VIIA. Area E: Stratigraphy and Architecture* (Qedem 53. Jerusalem: Hebrew University, 2012).

include remains related to scribalism and the settlement's infrastructure,[25] and D. Ben-Ami has recently published the first volume of the renewed excavations in the Tyropoeon Valley that includes new insights into Jerusalem's western precincts during this time.[26] Even more, a spate of recent excavation reports have been published from early Iron Age sites unattested in the Hebrew Bible, including significant settlements that once existed at Khirbet Qeiyafa, Tel Rehov, and Khirbet en Nahas.[27] New excavations have also begun at the important site of Tell Abil el-Qameḥ (Abel Beth Maacah) in 2013,[28] and an early Iron Age temple complex was discovered in 2012 at the site of Tel Moza in 2012.[29] The list could go on.[30]

Recent epigraphic evidence recovered from southern Levant also impresses. In 2005 an abecedary was unearthed at the site of Tel Zayit that was dated to the late tenth century BCE by its excavator, demonstrating that an individual or individuals at this location possessed knowledge of an early linear alphabetic script that would have also been used, in time, to write out more lengthy documents in Hebrew.[31] This find can now be set alongside a remarkable collection of Iron I–IIA linear alphabetic inscriptions recovered only in the past two decades,

---

25. E. Mazar, *Preliminary Report on The City of David Excavations 2005 at the Visitors Center Area* (Jerusalem: Shalem Press, 2007); idem, *The Palace of King David: Excavations at the Summit of the City of David: Preliminary Report of Seasons 2005–2007* (Jerusalem: Shoham Academic Research and Publication, 2009); idem, *The Summit of the City of David Excavations 2005–2008*, Vol. I (Jerusalem: Shoham, 2015).

26. D. Ben-Ami, *Jerusalem: Excavations in the Tyropoeon Valley (Giv'ati Parking Lot)* (Jerusalem: Israel Antiquities Authority, 2013).

27. On the archaeological remains of these sites, see the extensive discussion in Chapter 4.

28. N. Panitz-Cohen, R. Mullins and R. Bonfil, "Northern Exposure: Launching Excavations at Tell Abil el-Qameḥ (Abel Beth Maacah)," *Strata* 31 (2013): 27–42.

29. S. Kisilevitz, "Ritual Finds from the Iron Age at Tel Motza," [Hebrew] in *New Studies in the Archaeology of Jerusalem and its Region VII* (eds. G. Stiebel et al.; Jerusalem, 2013): 38–46; idem, "The Iron IIA Judahite Temple at Tel Moza," *TA* 42 (2015): 147–64.

30. To cite only a few examples that are of consequence for this study, see now N. Panitz-Cohen and A. Mazar, eds., *Excavations at Tel Beth-Shean 1989–1996, Volume III: The 13th–11th Centuries BCE (Areas S and N)* (Jerusalem: Israel Exploration Society, 2009); Israel Finkelstein, David Ussishkin, and Eric Cline, *Megiddo V: The 2004–2008 Seasons*, Vols. I–III (Winona Lake: Eisenbrauns, 2013); and Shlomo Bunimovitz and Zvi Lederman, eds., *Tel Beth-Shemesh: A Border Community in Judah. Renewed Excavations 1990–2000* (2 vols.; Winona Lake: Eisenbrauns, 2016).

31. R. Tappy et al., "An Abecedary of the Mid-Tenth Century B.C.E. from the Judaean Shephelah," *BASOR* 344 (2006): 5–46.

including fascinating instances unearthed in such varied sites as Jerusalem, Beth-Shemesh, Khirbet Qeiyafa, Gath, and Tel Rehov.[32]

What this evidence offers are striking new vantage points by which to assess how the past depicted in the Hebrew Bible pertains to what we now know about the history of the early Iron Age through the material and epigraphic evidence that has been recovered. In part, this evidence offers ever more nuanced understandings of what features of an early Iron Age world were reflected or obscured within the texts the biblical scribes composed. But what this evidence also provides are insights into the types of knowledge that would have underpinned these biblical stories, the organization of which was often structured, I argue in the following, on information communicated by way of memory and word of mouth.

What the biblical scribes developed on the basis of this knowledge were prose stories of substantial length that were set in diverse geographies and amid many centuries in time. The appearance of prose writing among this scribal culture, then, has considerable historical import for the investigation that follows. By prose, I mean a specific form of writing distinct from verse, marked off by its close relationship to the style and genres of everyday speech patterns, including how we communicate stories colloquially to others about past events and experiences.[33] In contrast to the more pronounced artifice of verse, prose is unfinalized, open-ended, its form imposed, in the end, by margins and the edge of the page. Graphically, prose is thus distinguished by being written out continuously and in running format, with its line divided by practical considerations (the size of document) and not, as with the poetic line, by intentional ones. The decision by Hebrew scribes to narrate past stories in written prose and not through verse or other modes of written or verbal discourse, consequently, was a *sine qua non* development for the possibility of the storytelling familiar to us in the Hebrew Bible, not unlike the indebtedness of the great Ionian writers of the fifth century BCE to the rise of prose writing in their culture a century before.

Though commonplace today in a world saturated by prose texts, the exceptional character of Hebrew prose can be appreciated when we situate it historically. For as T. Linafelt observes, what "distinguishes biblical literature from

---

32. For a discussion of these epigraphic remains and their implications for this work, see the section in Chapter 1 on "Hebrew Prose: The Epigraphic Evidence."

33. Jeffrey Kittay and Wlad Godzich, *The Emergence of Prose: An Essay in Prosaics* (Minneapolis: University of Minnesota Press, 1987), 187–212. Cf. Northrup Frye, *Anatomy of Criticism: Four Essays* (Princeton: Princeton University Press, 1957), 263–67. So in a famous scene from Molière's *The Bourgeois Gentleman*, the clueless Monsieur Jourdain exclaims "Well, what do you know about that! These forty years now I've been speaking in prose without knowing it" (Act Two, Scene Four).

virtually all other ancient Near Eastern literature is that its extended narratives take the form of prose and not verse (or poetry)."[34] Indeed, what makes biblical storytelling so remarkable is that so few literary cultures in antiquity used this form of writing to tell stories about the past. Most narratives of this kind would have been performed by oral bards trained in the centuries-old craft of oral performance.[35] And when a past was put down in writing, the literary cultures of the eastern Mediterranean region used other means to do so: Homeric tales, to cite a famous instance, unfold in the sturdy rhythm of dactylic hexameter; the great Canaanite hero Danel has his story told by Ugaritic writers in epic verse form; and when a scribe recounts Idrimi of Alalakh's improbable rise to the throne in prose, this scribe chose not to write in a local West Semitic vernacular but in the international language of Akkadian, even though the scribe's knowledge of the cuneiform writing system used to compose this text was "inconsistent" and "idiosyncratic" at best.[36] Furthermore, when prose writing is suddenly harnessed for the first time among local vernacular languages in the Iron Age Levant (i.e., Aramaic, Moabite, Ammonite) to narrate a past, these texts, as Sanders observes, are almost always expressed in the first person voice of the ruler.[37] But the Hebrew scribes at the center of this study chose a different literary form: that of third person prose cast in their native Hebrew language.

To understand what knowledge about the past was available to these scribes also entails understanding something, then, about what led them to write in this particular way, and when. The aim of Chapter 1 is to attend to such concerns by examining the emergence of Hebrew prose writing in the Iron Age period. To do so, this study turns first to the epigraphic record from the southern Levant and then to instances of prose writing developed elsewhere among various literary cultures outside the Levant.[38] When coupled with theoretical considerations wed

---

34. Tod Linafelt, *The Hebrew Bible as Literature: A Very Short Introduction* (Oxford: Oxford University Press, 2016), 39. So also Kawashima: "Scholars have long noted that the prose narratives of the Hebrew Bible present us with something decisively new and unprecedented in ancient literature." R. Kawashima, *Biblical Narrative and the Death of the Rhapsode* (Bloomington: Indiana University Press, 2004), 4.

35. On this point, see the extensive discussion in Chapter 1.

36. E. Greenstein and D. Marcus, "The Akkadian Inscription of Idrimi," *JANES* 8 (1976): 59.

37. Sanders, *Invention of Hebrew*, 113–20.

38. E.g., J. Van Seters, *In Search of History: Historiography in the Ancient World and Origins of Biblical History* (New Haven: Yale, 1983), 55–208; S. Goldhill, *The Invention of Prose* (Oxford: Oxford University Press, 2002); J.-J. Glassner, *Mesopotamian Chronicles* (ed. B. Foster; Atlanta: SBL, 2004), 37–55; L. Kurke, "Plato, Aesop, and the Beginnings of Mimetic Prose," *Representations* 94 (2006): 6–52; J. Grethlein, "The Rise of Greek Historiography and the Invention of Prose," in *The Oxford History of Historical Writing: Volume I, Beginnings to AD 600* (eds. A. Feldherr and G. Hardy; Oxford: Oxford University Press, 2011), 148–70.

to the vernacularization of literature in antiquity and to the predominance of an older oral storytelling tradition in the region, the appearance of Hebrew prose, this chapter argues, was likely a rather belated event, emerging around the ninth century BCE—or roughly 1000 years after writing first appears in the eastern Mediterranean world.

With this rough *terminus post quem* for the establishment of Hebrew prose in mind, Chapter 1 then transitions toward a study of the epistemological under-pinnings of the source material that would have contributed to the prose stories told about the early Iron Age period in the Hebrew Bible, or an era that would have preceded the rise of Hebrew prose writing by a generation or more. The aim of this section, in short, is to historicize the possible forms of knowledge that would have been available to later Hebrew scribes who would have had few prose documents from the past in their possession. Following the work of M. Foucault, the intent of this section is to cast a spotlight on the *internal* conditions of know-ing that would have shaped these sources, this material's "configuration within a *space* of knowledge,"[39] so as to better appreciate how information about a past was conceptualized and sustained among the societies in which the biblical scribes were active. This manner of inquiry leads into the domains of oral tradition and the work of memory once more, in which past knowledge made available to the biblical scribes, I argue, would have been dependent on the possibilities of remembering. The conclusion of this chapter is then given over to how this "episteme" of memory, to borrow once again from Foucault,[40] may have influ-enced the written works about an early Iron Age past that found their way into the Hebrew Bible.

Chapters 2 through 4 of this book consist of three case studies that attempt to give flesh to the theoretical discussion put forward in Chapter 1. Each case study is devoted to what I argue is a different dynamic of how this episteme of memory is worked out within biblical stories set in an early Iron Age past. The intent of these chapters, accordingly, is to foreground distinct modes of remembering that would have contributed toward the stories told of an early Iron Age period, the dynamics of which were marked by a much different process of transmis-sion than source material handed down through lengthy narrative texts. Over against historical studies of memory in the ancient world that orient themselves synchronically or, conversely, to those works that accent either the preservative or revisionary character of a remembered past over time, each chapter of this work seeks to demonstrate a distinct process of remembering that would have

---

39. M. Foucault, *The Order of Things: An Archaeology of the Human Sciences* (London: Routledge, 2002 [1966]), xxiv.

40. Foucault, *Order of Things*, xxiv.

informed the source material drawn on by the biblical writers: those of resilience, entanglement, and forgetting.

Bound loosely to a historical past by their source material but untroubled by modern epistemological concerns rooted in a historicism birthed only in the past three centuries, what the biblical scribes developed through the knowledge available to them, this book contends, were prose works steeped in information derived from a remembered past. *Memory in a Time of Prose* is therefore an argument as much as it is the name of this book. The contention reflected in this volume's title is that there was a time in which Hebrew prose writing emerged in the ancient world of the southern Levant, a medium that, until the period in which such vernacular prose texts suddenly appeared in the region, had never before been used to tell stories about the past. At work in a world dominated by oral, living speech, much of the knowledge these scribes had available to them about the past were sources necessarily elicited from the memories communicated via word of mouth. The prose writings produced by these Hebrew scribes would therefore have been informed by a past sustained through oral storytelling that was rooted in the capacity to remember, just as modes of remembering within their society would be forever transformed by the introduction of the written word as an *aide-memoire*.

The intent of the following is to demonstrate how these frameworks for knowing the past, so different from our own, shaped the stories these scribes told. Embedded in the biblical stories investigated here, I conclude, are a spectrum of references to the early Iron Age period that find both moments of coherence and disconnect from the evidence recovered through modern methods of historical research. The various pasts represented within the stories the biblical scribes composed are thus seen to abide by a different set of assumptions as to what constitutes past knowledge in relation to our own, historical vantage point, stories informed by modes of retrospection whose recollections laid claim to a meaningful past but in a manner distinct from the knowledge generated within the historicism of "our modernity."[41]

---

41. Ricoeur, *Memory, History, Forgetting*, 305–14.

I

Hebrew Prose and Stories of an Early Iron Age Past

HISTORICAL AND EPISTEMOLOGICAL CONSIDERATIONS

We cannot trace the origins of ancient Israelite historical writing.
At a particular point it is there, and we already have it in its
fully developed form.[1]

HOWEVER HEBREW PROSE came to be, it arose in societies familiar with the written word but which nevertheless privileged the voice and the body as the media through which stories about the past were communicated. Recent studies on the formation of the Hebrew Bible have emphasized well that the biblical writings were created and consumed within predominantly oral contexts, shaped acoustically and circulated among those who would often experience these texts through the ear.[2] To be sure, biblical scholars had long recognized the influence

---

1. G. von Rad, "The Beginnings of Historical Writing in Ancient Israel," *The Problem of the Hexateuch and Other Essays* (trans. E. W. Dicken; London: SCM Press, 1964), 167.

2. For a number of important, recent works on the topic, see, for example, S. Niditch, *Oral World and Written Word: Ancient Israelite Literature* (Louisville: Westminster John Knox, 1996); F. Polak, "The Oral and the Written: Syntax, Stylistics, and the Development of Biblical Prose Narrative," *JANES* 26 (1998): 59–105; idem, "Book, Scribe, and Bard: Oral Discourse and Written Text in Recent Biblical Scholarship," *Prooftexts* 31 (2011): 118–40; W. Schniedewind, *How the Bible Became a Book: The Textualization of Ancient Israel* (Cambridge: Cambridge University Press, 2004), 1–23; D. Carr, *Writing on the Tablet of the Heart: Origins of Scripture and Literature* (New York: Oxford, 2005), 3–16; idem, *The Formation of the Hebrew Bible: A New Reconstruction* (Oxford: Oxford University Press, 2011), 3–12; idem, "Orality, Textuality *and* Memory: The State of Biblical Studies," in *Contextualizing Israel's Sacred Writings: Ancient Literacy, Orality, and Literary Production* (ed. B. Schmidt; Atlanta: SBL Press, 2015), 161–74; K. van der Toorn, *Scribal Culture and the Making of the Hebrew Bible* (Cambridge: Harvard University Press, 2007), 9–50;

of oral tradition and oral storytelling techniques on the formation of various biblical texts, particularly after the groundbreaking work of H. Gunkel in the early
twentieth century.[3] But the linear, developmental model adopted in these early
studies that advocated a stark division between an older, oral mindset and the
sudden appearance of a literate one (usually situated in the era of Solomon and
its "Enlightenment" during the tenth century BCE)[4] no longer holds.[5] Instead, it
is increasingly apparent that written and oral forms of discourse were continually
intertwined throughout the centuries in which the Hebrew Bible was composed,
with modes of textuality and orality shaping and being shaped by one another

---

R. Person, *The Deuteronomic School: History, Social Setting, and Literature* (Atlanta: SBL
Press, 2002), 83–102; idem, *The Deuteronomistic History and the Book of Chronicles: Scribal
Works in an Oral World* (Leiden: Brill, 2010), 41–68; R. Miller, *Oral Tradition in Ancient
Israel* (Eugene: Cascade Books, 2011), 40–58; F. W. Dobbs-Allsopp, *On Biblical Poetry*
(Oxford: Oxford University Press, 2015), esp. ch. 4, "An Informing Orality: Biblical Poetic
Style," 233–325.

3. So in particular the first sections of the introduction to Gunkel's third edition of his
work on Genesis, H. Gunkel, *Genesis* (3rd ed., Göttingen: Vandenhoeck & Ruprecht, 1910),
vii–lxxx; see also, idem, *Schöpfung und Chaos in Urzeit und Endzeit* (Göttingen: Vandenhoeck
and Ruprecht, 1895), 135–47. For a discussion of Gunkel and earlier approaches to orality
among biblical scholars, see especially R. Culley, "Oral Tradition and Biblical Studies," *Oral
Tradition* 1.1 (1986): 30–65; and D. Knight, *Rediscovering the Traditions of Ancient Israel* (3rd
ed.; Atlanta: SBL Press, 2006), 57–76.

4. So both Gunkel and Greßmann, in their influential studies [H. Gunkel,
"Geschichtsschreibung im A.T.," in *Religion in Geschichte und Gegenwart* (ed. H. Gunkel;
Tübingen: Mohr, 1919–23), I: 1348–54]; idem, "Geschichtsschreibung im A.T.," in *Religion
in Geschichte und Gegenwart* (2nd ed.; Tübingen: Mohr, 1927), II: 1112–15; H. Greßmann,
"The Oldest History Writing in Israel," in *Narrative and Novella in Samuel: Studies by Hugo
Gressmann and Other Scholars 1906–1923* [(trans. D. Orton; ed. D. Gunn; Sheffield: Sheffield
Academic Press, 1991), 13–19], posited a development over time by which the society of ancient Israel transitioned from an oral culture to one that produced written, historical narratives, the latter of which was occasioned by and produced in response to the formation of the
Israelite state. The link between state formation and textuality was then taken up and further
developed by von Rad who, in isolating the "Succession History" of 2 Sam 11–20 as the oldest
example of history writing in ancient Israel, commented: "There is no real difficulty at this
stage in relating this particular work to the age of Solomon, in which it undoubtedly took its
origin. Only in Solomon's era did the new order, which began in the time of David, develop
its cultural potential to touch every facet of human existence." Von Rad, "The Beginnings of
Historical Writing," 203.

5. For similar assumptions operative in other disciplines, and an important critique of them,
see M. Amodio, *Writing the Oral Tradition: Oral Poetics and Literate Culture in Medieval
England* (South Bend, Ind.: University of Notre Dame Press, 2004), 1–32; and H. Saussy, *The
Ethnography of Rhythm: Orality and its Technologies* (New York: Fordham University Press,
2016), 1–16.

among societies in which writing was known but oral communication pervasive and persistent.[6]

For historical insights into the writing of prose within an ancient society more accustomed to stories told through the spoken word,[7] the example of Thucydides is instructive because of his candid remarks on the topic. Compiling his work in exile about a conflict he had witnessed first hand, already in the opening line to the *Peloponnesian War* we find Thucydides placing a different emphasis on his history than what was found among earlier Greek writers: "θουκυδίδης Ἀθηναῖος ξυνέγραψε τὸν πόλεμον τῶν Πελοποννησιῶν καὶ Ἀθηναίων" ("Thucydides, an Athenian, has composed the war of the Peloponnesians and the Athenians. . . ." [Thuc. 1.1]). On the one hand, the decision to open the *Peloponnesian War* by announcing Thucydides's name and place of origin was a practice that conformed to those of previous Greek writers, emulating the older works of both Hecataeus (*FGrHist* 1F1) and Herodotus (Hdt. 1.1). Thucydides's prefatory use of the third person voice, replaced shortly thereafter by a switch to first person (Thuc. 1.1.3), also followed precedent.[8] But what is distinct about Thucydides's initial remarks is the verb he employs: ξυνέγραψε, a literal translation of which would read "brought together in writing."[9] This activity contrasts sharply with that of Herodotus,[10] who "displays" (ἀπόδεξις) his "inquiry" (ἱστορίης) with an eye toward performance and public recitation,[11] an act that was, according to

---

6. Carr remarks, for example, that his study self-consciously "builds on a stream of scholarship that emphasizes ways societies with writing often have an intricate interplay of orality and textuality, where written texts are intensely oral, while even exclusively oral texts are deeply affected by written culture." Carr, *Writing on the Tablet of the Heart*, 7.

7. On the predominantly oral context in which Thucydides was active, see A. Vatri, *Orality and Performance in Classical Attic Prose: A Linguistic Approach* (Oxford: Oxford University Press, 2016), 46–54, 68–69.

8. On the likelihood that the prefatory use of the third person voice—as found in Hecataeus, Herodotus, and Thucydides—was modeled on preexisting monumental inscriptions and derived from the language of display, see J. Svenbro, *Phrasikleia: An Anthropology of Reading in Ancient Greece* (tr. J. Lloyd; Ithaca: Cornell University Press, 1993), 149–66; J. Moles, "Ἀνάθημα καὶ κτῆμα: The Inscriptional Inheritance of Ancient Historiography," *Histos* 3 (1999): 44–53; E. Bakker, "The Making of History: Herodotus' Histories Apodexis," in *Brill's Companion to Herodotus* (ed. E. Bakker et al.; Leiden: Brill, 2002), 30–31.

9. Hecataeus does employ the verb "to write" [γράφω] in his opening statement, but this verb is both distinct from Thucydides's act of "bringing together in writing," and, more importantly, for Hecataeus the act of writing is preceded by an emphasis on oral speech ("Hecataeus of Miletus *speaks* [μυθεῖται] thus: I write in what follows as seems true to me. . . ." [*FGrHist* 1F1]).

10. On the polemical character of Thucydides's remarks with regard to Herodotus, see, for example, S. Hornblower, *A Commentary on Thucydides*, vol. I (Oxford: Clarendon, 1991), 5.

11. G. Nagy, "Herodotus the *Logios*," *Arethusa* 20 (1987): 175–84; Hornblower, *Commentary on Thucydides*, 61; R. Fowler, "Early *Historie* and Literacy," in *The Historian's Craft in the*

a number of ancient sources, carried out on different occasions by Herodotus himself.[12]

Thucydides takes a different tack. What is accented instead is the written quality of the account that follows, a point underscored throughout his history when Thucydides employs the same verb, ξυνέγραψε, eleven other times in his narrative in order to draw a particular year of the Peloponnesian War to a close, as one finds, for example, near the beginning of Book 3: "So ended this winter, and with it this fourth year of the war *composed* by Thucydides" (Thuc. 3.25).[13] Of interest, in this vein, is Thucydides's attempt to distance himself from expectations wed to public oral performance, where, in the great section on methodology found in the opening to his work, Thucydides cautions that his account may be "unpleasant to the ear" since his narrative was not intended as "a competitive piece that is listened to in the moment" (Thuc. 1.22).[14] Indeed, Thucydides's prose becomes so dense and unruly at various junctures that Dionysius of Halicarnassus, writing centuries later and as a historian himself, offers a lengthy discussion on how difficult Thucydides's work could be for readers to untangle and comprehend.[15]

Thucydides's account was nevertheless penned in a world dominated by oral discourse, as Thucydides's own comments very much indicate,[16] and it is necessary to resist the idea that Thucydides's statements were made with the intent of censoring oral performances of his text or excluding his work from an oral

---

Age of Herodotus (ed. N. Luraghi; Oxford: Oxford University Press, 2007), 108–109; R. Nicolai, "The Place of History in the Ancient World," in *A Companion to Greek and Roman Historiography*, vol. 1 (ed. J. Marincola; Malden: Blackwell, 2007), 23–25; For a more cautious assessment, see W. Johnson, "Oral Performance and the Composition of Herodotus' *Histories*," *Greek, Roman and Byzantine Studies* 35.3 (1994): 229–54.

12. For these sources, see J. E. Powell, *The History of Herodotus* (Cambridge: Cambridge University Press, 1939), 32–34; A. Momigliano "The Historians of the Classical World and their Audiences: Some Suggestions," in *Sesto contributo alla storia degli studi classici e del mondo antico*, vol. 1 (Roma: Edizioni di storia e letteratura, 1980), 366–68.

13. J. Morrison, "Memory, Time, and Writing: Oral and Literary Aspects of Thucydides' *History*," in *Oral Performance and its Context* (ed. C. J. Mackie; Leiden: Brill, 2004), 103. Cf. C. Darbo-Peschanski, "The Origin of Greek Historiography," in *A Companion to Greek and Roman Historiography*, vol. 1 (ed. J. Marincola; Malden: Blackwell, 2007), 32–35.

14. D. Shanske, *Thucydides and the Philosophical Origins of History* (Cambridge: Cambridge University Press, 2007), 19–20.

15. Dionysius of Halicarnassus, *Critical Essays*, I (trans. S. Usher; Cambridge: Harvard University Press, 1974), 513–15, 531–33. On the difficulties of Thucydides in terms of readability, see also Vatri, *Orality and Performance in Classical Attic Prose*, 254–58.

16. Morrison, "Memory, Time, and Writing," 95–96; Vatri, *Orality and Performance in Classical Attic Prose*, 68–69.

domain altogether.[17] Rather, what we find within Thucydides's remarks is an explanation, even an apology, for why his history may disappoint those accustomed to being captivated by works whose rhetoric sought to please those listening. Thucydides is after something different. Embedded within his reflections on method, Thucydides speaks of his desire to provide a more "exact" (ἀκρίβεια) rendering of the Peloponnesian War that distills a "clear understanding" (τὸ σαφὲς σκοπεῖν [Thuc. 1.22]) of what once occurred. Over against the poets prone to embellishment with their "exaggerations" and the orators who sought entertainment instead of truth in performances that, by virtue of their oral character, "could not be checked" (Thuc. 1.21), Thucydides grounds his work instead in the permanence of prose writing and the written word's availability to scrutiny and review.[18] Thucydides's composition is, as he famously terms it, a "possession forever" (κτῆμά τε ἐς αἰεὶ [Thuc. 1.22]).[19] An accent on the durative character of writing appears, in fact, again and again at key moments in Thucydides's text, such as in the story of Nicias's letter to the Athenians about the growing difficulties encountered in Sicily (Thuc. 7.11–15). Commenting on the incident, Thucydides observes that Nicias wrote down his letter rather than having its contents transmitted through the recollection of a messenger so as to avoid, "the incompetence in speaking, the failure of memory, or speaking to please the crowd" (Thuc. 7.8.2).

In light of this chapter's study of Hebrew prose, what is so interesting about Thucydides's emphasis on the written quality of his work is that he is compelled to emphasize it at all. Working a full two centuries after the initial appearance of Greek prose writings (which arose during the course of the sixth century BCE) and for an Athenian audience increasingly familiar with the written word,[20] the argument implicit in Thucydides's remarks—that there is something reliable and even distinctly true about written prose with regard to recounting a past—was

---

17. Hornblower suggests that parts of Thucydides work may have in fact been publicly performed at drinking parties or *symposiums*, though "of an admittedly high-brow sort." Hornblower, *Commentary*, 60–61.

18. J. Grethlein, "The Rise of Greek Historiography and the Invention of Prose," in *The Oxford History of Historical Writing: Volume I, Beginnings to AD 600* (eds. A. Feldherr and G. Hardy; Oxford: Oxford University Press, 2011), 155–65. On Plato's similar arguments against poetry and Plato's own turn to prose, see Eric Havelock, *Preface to Plato* (Cambridge: Belknap Press, 1963), 3–18, 276–311; idem, *The Muse Learns to Write: Reflections on Orality and Literacy from Antiquity to the Present* (New Haven: Yale University Press, 1986), 1–18. Cf. Leslie Kurke, "Plato, Aesop, and the Beginnings of Mimetic Prose," *Representations* 94 (2006): 6–52.

19. As Morrison points out, this term was likely of particular importance for a general in exile with little hope of publicly narrating his version of the war. Morrison, "Memory, Time, and Writing," 112.

20. Goldhill, *The Invention of Prose*, 10–11; Grethlein, "The Rise of Greek Historiography," 148–70; W. Harris, *Ancient Literacy* (Cambridge: Harvard University Press, 1991), 65–115.

one, it seems, that still had to be argued for during Thucydides's time, so persistent was an oral mindset and its attendant expectations with regard to narrating a past for others. The fact that such an argument was necessary receives some support from the sentiments recorded in the *Panegyric* (4.82) by the Athenian orator Isocrates around a decade after Thucydides had died (380 BCE).[21] In this work, Isocrates claims that none before him had done justice to the great events of the Persian War, though Herodotus's account had been in circulation for some sixty years and was certainly known in Athens when Isocrates was performing. Yet when Isocrates makes reference to those who were responsible in Athens for recounting stories about the great events and figures from former times, he identifies the role of the "poets and sophists," and not prose writers such as Herodotus or Isocrates's near contemporary and fellow citizen, Thucydides. "Even in the fourth century, after Herodotus and Thucydides," M. Finley remarks, "Athenian orators still clung to their traditional myths and their popular history, utterly indifferent to the new knowledge and new conceptions."[22]

Opinions such as those of Isocrates were therefore likely widespread. Though held in high esteem by later readers habituated to history written in prose, in the ancient Greek society in which Thucydides was active such storytelling was communicated principally through the spoken word.[23] R. Thomas calls attention, for example, to the persistent unease still present in Thucydides's Greek society toward written texts, including the fact that though Athens had begun the practice of creating official documents around 507 BCE, an archive would not be developed in the city for another century, and even then "politicians and historians did not make impressive use of its contents (nor were these particular well organized) till rather later."[24] Indeed, in the Athenian courts of this time oral testimony far outpaced documentary evidence in terms of importance.[25] But

---

21. So the example lifted up in J. Grethlein, "The Many Faces of the Past in Archaic and Classical Greece," in *Thinking, Recording, and Writing History in the Ancient World* (ed. K. Raaflaub; Malden: Wiley-Blackwell, 2014), 234.

22. M. Finley, "Myth, Memory, and History," *History and Theory* 4.3 (1965): 299.

23. Grethlein, "Faces of the Past," 234–55. Cf. B. Steinbock, *Social Memory in Athenian Public Discourse* (Ann Arbor: University of Michigan Press, 2013), 1–47.

24. R. Thomas, *Literacy and Orality in Ancient Greece* (Cambridge: Cambridge University Press, 1992), 96. Cf. idem, "Prose Performance Text: Epideixis and Written Publication in the Late Fifth and Early Fourth Centuries BCE," in *Written Texts and the Rise of Literate Culture in Ancient Greece* (ed. H. Yunis; Cambridge: Cambridge University Press, 2003), 162–88.

25. R. Thomas, *Oral Tradition and Written Record in Classical Athens* (Cambridge: Cambridge University Press, 1989), 41–43. Cf. Stephanie West, "Herodotus' Epigraphical Interests," *The Classical Quarterly* 35 (1985): 304–305.

perhaps the most famous example of this suspicion toward writing is expressed in another Athenian's work, Plato's *Phaedrus* (ca. 370 BCE), wherein Socrates recounts his well-known myth about the invention of writing, likening the written word to a *pharmakon* ([φάρμακον] *Phaedrus* 274ᵉ)—a deliberately ambiguous expression that can mean both remedy or poison.

The writings of Thucydides find importance for our investigation into the emergence of Hebrew prose, then, because it reminds us at the outset of this study that there was nothing natural or self-evident about the decision to narrate a past in prose writing in antiquity.[26] Today we are surrounded by prose texts everywhere in societies in which nearly everyone can read them, but this was not the case in the ancient world when literacy was much more restricted and oral traditions of storytelling more widespread. And even when a past came to be written down with great power and vision, as in the case of Thucydides, such prose texts did not immediately gain acceptance as the primary means of recounting or thinking about the past among those who had access to these writings. Narrative prose writing in the ancient world was an emergent phenomenon, often resisted in favor of other, more venerable means of oral discourse, and only gradually accepted as writing became more widely known within the societies that possessed it.[27] The early prose narratives that we possess from antiquity were the outcome, in this sense, of novel means of viewing both the world and the use of the written word, frequently precipitated by political and cultural developments never before encountered in the societies in which it arose.[28]

What also matters about Thucydides for this chapter's investigation are the sources on which he relied.[29] At work in a society predominantly oral in its

---

26. Grethlein, "Rise of Greek Historiography," 148–70.

27. So Havelock observes of ancient Greece that "while the last half of the fifth century begins to see the acceptance of prose as a viable means of publication, acceptance does not become complete until the fourth. This is three hundred years after the invention of the alphabet...." E. Havelock, *Prologue to Greek Literacy* (Cincinnati: University of Cincinnati Press, 1971), 59.

28. So a central argument from S. Pollock, *The Language of the Gods in the World of Men: Sanskrit, Culture, and Power in Premodern India* (Berkeley: University of California Press, 2006). Pollock comments: "Nowhere is the history of expressive, workly texts of literature and political discourse found to be coextensive with the history of a language. Literary silence is real, and it can be broken; and when it is broken, *something truly consequential in history is taking place.*" Ibid., 296–97 (my italics).

29. One need not accept Van Seters' conclusions pertaining to the date and formation of biblical prose (see my own remarks, for example, on the date of Hebrew prose below) to appreciate his careful analysis of the relationship between Greek and Hebrew prose traditions in terms of the sources used and the narrative form developed to recount a past among these two literary cultures. So Van Seters concludes: " . . .nothing in the literature of the Near East before the fourth century so closely resembles the biblical histories as the Greek prose histories." (p. 51). J. Van Seters, *In Search of History: Historiography in the Ancient World and the Origins of Biblical History* (New Haven: Yale University Press, 1983), 8–54.

methods of storytelling, the prose that Thucydides developed was an account derived primarily, and necessarily, from oral source material.[30] Prose texts penned
by other Greek authors of particular moments in the Peloponnesian conflict
simply did not exist for Thucydides to consult. For this reason, Thucydides,
so pointed in his attention toward the written word, is, as he himself observes
(Thuc. 1.22), highly dependent on oral informants for the telling of his story.[31]
Yet here, too, Thucydides follows in the wake of Herodotus, whose reliance on
oral sources—"at least five to one in favor of oral communication"—was equally
pronounced.[32] In a culture in which narrative prose texts were rare and oral storytelling traditions much more familiar, it could not be otherwise. Past knowledge
was mediated primarily through the spoken word and not the written one.

When reading the narrative prose works of the Hebrew Bible, the example of Thucydides encourages us therefore to be wary of our contemporary,
post-Gutenberg assumptions about the formation of these texts and their reception. Like Thucydides and those Greek writers who preceded him, the biblical
scribes at the center of this study were not modern historians cloistered in libraries and animated by troves of older written texts;[33] nor were the prose writings
these scribes produced ubiquitous and readily available for private readings by
individuals in silence and isolation.[34] The prose that one reads in the Hebrew
Bible interfaced throughout its development with forms of orality, had antecedents located in oral narrative traditions, and were likely composed with a preference
for oral sources even when written documents were available.[35]

---

30. P. J. Rhodes, "Documents and the Greek Historians," in *A Companion to Greek and Roman Historiography*, vol. 1 (ed. J. Marincola; Malden: Blackwell, 2007), 56–60.

31. Thomas, *Oral Tradition*, 235–36; R. Nicolai, "Thucydides' Archaeology: Between Epic and Oral Traditions," in *The Historian's Craft in the Age of Herodotus* (ed. N. Luraghi; Oxford: Oxford University Press, 2001), 263–85.

32. K. H. Waters, *Herodotus the Historian: His Problems, Methods, and Originality* (2nd ed.; London: Routledge, 2014), 76. On Herodotus and Thucydides's sources, see also A. Momigliano, "Historiography on Written Tradition and Historiography on Oral Tradition," in *Studies in Historiography* (London: Weidenfeld & Nicolson, 1966), 211–20; O. Murray, "Herodotus and Oral History," and "Herodotus and Oral History Reconsidered," in *The Historian's Craft in the Age of Herodotus* (ed. N. Luraghi; Oxford: Oxford University Press, 2001), 16–44, 314–25.

33. Van Seters, *In Search of History*, 195–99

34. On this point, see especially Van der Toorn, *Scribal Culture*, 27–50.

35. So, at least, the case for early Greek writers, as detailed in Momigliano's influential article on the topic, but a point likely resonant for early scribal cultures that lived in predominantly oral societies unaccustomed to archives or archival research. Momigliano, "Historiography," 215–17. Cf. West, "Herodotus' Epigraphical Interests," 304–305.

What this means for the studies that follow is that the prose produced by Hebrew scribes in antiquity was also influenced by an "informing orality" that F. W. Dobbs-Allsopp has discerned within the production and reception of written biblical poetry. Dobbs-Allsopp comments:[36]

> . . . the management of knowledge and its verbalization in ancient Israel and Judah was dominantly and prominently oral, communicated in speech, face-to-face, embodied. The world of the Bible and the world in which the Bible took shape was a thoroughgoing oral world. Even in the midst of ever increasing literacy and the emergence of a (more) textual culture, as in Israel and Judah throughout the Iron Age, orality can still be expected to circumscribe, shape, and orient these new written modalities.

The "thoroughgoing oral world" in which biblical prose narratives were similarly produced was a world, consequently, in which many of the biblical stories would have been composed more for aural consumption than for individual reading, created, disseminated, and performed for audiences accustomed to experiencing these stories principally through the human voice.[37] This point cannot be lost from view in the discussion that follows. The narrative prose of the Hebrew Bible was influenced by expectations and conventions wed to older traditions of oral storytelling, just as the texts these scribes composed would have helped frame and contribute to oral performances within the societies in which these writings were developed.[38]

The questions these observations raise are ones that sit at the center of this book. If Hebrew prose writing was a particular historical and cultural phenomenon that emerged over a certain period in time in antiquity, and if many of these prose writings were derived ultimately from oral tradition and shaped in response to oral storytelling techniques, then a series of pressing historical issues comes into view: what information, for example, was available to the

---

36. Dobbs-Allsopp, *On Biblical Poetry*, 233–34.

37. On the influence of oral tradition on biblical narrative more broadly, see Polak, "The Oral and the Written," 59–105; Miller, *Oral Tradition*, 68–113; Susan Niditch, "Hebrew Bible and Oral Literature: Misconceptions and New Directions," in *The Interface of Orality and Writing: Speaking, Seeing, Writing in the Shaping of New Genres* (eds. A. Weissenrieder and R. Coote; Tübingen: Mohr Siebeck, 2015), 13–17; Dobbs-Allsopp, *On Biblical Poetry*, 243–46; R. Person, "Biblical Historiography as Traditional History," in *The Oxford Handbook of Biblical Narrative* (ed. D. Fewell; Oxford: Oxford University Press, 2016), 73–83. For more pointed discussion, see comments below.

38. Carr, *Writing on the Tablet*, 7; Niditch, "Hebrew Bible and Oral Literature," 6–18; R. Miller, "The Performance of Oral Tradition in Ancient Israel," *Contextualizing Israel's Sacred Writings: Ancient Literacy, Orality, and Literary Production* (ed. B. Schmidt; Atlanta: SBL, 2015), 175–82.

biblical scribes for the stories they told about a past that preceded their own time by a generation or more? On what basis did they construct their accounts when older written texts were limited and rarely sought after as repositories of past knowledge? How do we theorize the information conveyed though the written stories these scribes eventually developed about former eras and happenings?

Such are the questions that guide this work. Before responding with the studies in the chapters that follow, however, a number of preliminary considerations must be addressed. The first issue that presents itself is the general timeframe in which a written Hebrew prose tradition arose in ancient Israel and Judah. In contrast to the observation of von Rad that is quoted in the epigraph to this chapter, the argument put forward in the following is that, some seven decades after von Rad's seminal investigation, we now possess evidence that helps us situate the emergence of Hebrew prose within an approximate period in time. Once a *terminus post quem* for the development of Hebrew prose is established, a clearer understanding of the sources that would have contributed to various biblical narratives can come into focus.

The second movement of this chapter is then given over to the character of this source material and, more specifically, to the epistemological underpinnings that would have supported the information included within it. The contention is made here that a preponderance of sources available to Hebrew scribes about the early Iron Age past (ca. 1175—830 BCE) would have been those derived from oral tradition. As a consequence, the knowledge conveyed through this source material and the mechanisms by which it was communicated would have been rooted in the cultural memories maintained by residents of the southern Levant over time. The conclusion to this chapter then takes up certain epistemological implications connected to this insight, a phenomenon that throughout this work is characterized as "memory in a time of prose."

The Emergence of Hebrew Prose: Historical Considerations

Hebrew Prose: Attributes

The prose found in the Hebrew Bible is distinguished by a number of features. The first is that these texts were written out in a linear alphabetic script[39] and

---

39. J. Naveh, *Early History of the Alphabet: An Introduction to West Semitic Epigraphy and Palaeography* (Jerusalem: Magnes, 1997), 53–124; C. Rollston, *Writing and Literacy in the World of Ancient Israel: Epigraphic Evidence from the Iron Age* (Atlanta: SBL Press, 2010), 11–19; G. Hamilton, "Reconceptualizing the Periods of Early Alphabetic Scripts," in *An Eye*

composed predominantly in Hebrew,[40] a West Semitic language used by a modest number of individuals in the ancient world who occupied regions in the southern Levant.[41] The term "Hebrew," as used in this study, thus refers to a local language once spoken and written out in antiquity (distinct from modern Hebrew spoken today) and not to a particular ethnic group, population, or territory. The Hebrew scribes at the center of our investigation may or may not have considered themselves to be "Hebrew," but the language they used within their texts derives from this West Semitic dialect. Spoken within a limited geographical area and among a population more often conquered than active in conquering, Hebrew never became an imperial or "cosmopolitan" language, to adopt S. Pollock's terminology,[42] such as was the case with Akkadian, Aramaic, or Greek, that were widely dispersed across the Near East and adopted by those whose mother tongue differed from that used by the empire of the time. When Hebrew was written down outside the territories of the southern Levant, it was done so by those who could trace their lineage to communities who had once arrived from this region.[43]

Another feature of biblical Hebrew prose is that it offers lengthy accounts about the past by narrating former affairs through forms of emplotment and by drawing on a distinct collection of literary conventions to do so.[44] Such

---

for Form: Epigraphic Essays in Honor of Frank Moore Cross (eds. J. Hackett and W. Aufrecht, eds.; Winona Lake: Eisenbrauns, 2014), 39–49.

40. Another language found in the prose writing of the Hebrew Bible is Aramaic, as present, for example, in Ezra 4:8–6:18; 7:12–26 and Dan 2:4b—7:28. The stories of an early Iron Age past at the center of this study, however, are written in Hebrew.

41. J. Huehnegard and J. Hackett, "The Hebrew and Aramaic Languages," in *The Biblical World*, Vol. II (ed. J. Barton; London: Routledge, 2002), 3–24.

42. On the notion of "cosmopolitan" languages, see S. Pollock, "The Cosmopolitan Vernacular," *The Journal of Asian Studies* 57.1 (1998): 6–37; idem, *The Language of the Gods*, 10–18, 75–114. On the use of Pollock's work within the sphere of the ancient Near East, see the seminal studies of S. Sanders, "What was the Alphabet For? The Rise of Written Vernaculars and the Making of Israelite National Literature," *Maarav* 11.1 (2004): 25–56; idem, *The Invention of Hebrew* (Champaign: University of Illinois Press, 2009), 1–11, 36–41.

43. Schniedewind, *A Social History of Hebrew: Its Origins Through the Rabbinic Period* (New Haven: Yale University Press, 2013), 126–38.

44. On this understanding of narrative and emplotment, see especially H. White, *Metahistory: The Historical Imagination in Nineteenth-Century Europe* (Baltimore: Johns Hopkins Press, 1975), 7–11; P. Ricoeur, *Time and Narrative*, vol. I (trans. K. McLaughlin and D. Pellauer; Chicago: University of Chicago Press, 1984), 52–90. Cf. T. Linafelt, *The Hebrew Bible as Literature: A Very Short Introduction* (Oxford: Oxford University Press, 2016), 27–49.

elements include thematic recurrences and allusion, frequent instances of dialogue between characters, the manipulation of narrative time (i.e., the adoption of a narrative preterite, the use of deictic markers, forms of analepsis and
prolepsis, representation of simultaneous events), and storytellers adept at
drawing attention to "a genuine inner life" of their characters, both human
and divine, by gesturing toward but leaving largely inaccessible the thoughts
and motivations of these protagonists.[45] A fine example of this prose tradition, here marked by dialogue and focalized on the nebulous, inner workings
of its leading character, is found in a scene that depicts David's confrontation
with his servants after the death of his firstborn child with Bathsheba (2 Sam.
12:20–23 [MT]):

ויקם דוד מהארץ וירחץ ויסך ויחלף שמלתו ויבא בית יהוה וישתחו ויבא אל ביתו וישאל
וישימו לו לחם ויאכל ויאמרו עבדיו אליו מה הדבר הזה אשר עשיתה בעבור הילד חי
צמת ותבך וכאשר מת הילד קמת ותאכל לחם: ויאמר בעוד הילד חי צמתי ואבכה כי
אמרתי מי יודע יחנני יהוה וחי הילד: ועתה מת למה זה אני צם האוכל להשיבו עוד אני
הלך אליו והוא לא ישוב אלי

Then David arose from the ground, washed, anointed himself, and
changed his clothes. He entered into the temple of Yahweh and worshipped, and then he went to his own house. When he asked, they placed
food before him and he ate. Then his servants said to him, "What is
this thing that you have done? While the child was alive you fasted and
wept. But when the child died, you arose and ate food." He said, "While
the child was still alive, I fasted and wept; for I said, 'Who knows? The
LORD may be gracious to me, and the child may live.' And now he is dead.
Why should I fast? Can I bring him back? I am going to him, but he will not
return to me."

What is David thinking and feeling in this scene? What guilt does he bear for the
loss of this son? What resentments does he harbor toward the deity responsible for
the child's death? We do not know, but it is precisely in not revealing these thoughts

---

45. Linafelt, *Hebrew Bible as Literature*, 31. On these literary features, see also E. Auerbach,
Mimesis: The Representation of Reality in Western Literature (Princeton: Princeton University
Press, 1953), 3–23; M. Sternberg, *The Poetics of Biblical Narrative: Ideological Literature and the
Drama of Reading* (Bloomington: Indiana University Press, 1987), 58–185, 264–341; R. Alter,
The Art of Biblical Narrative (2nd ed.; New York: Basic Books, 2011), 221–36; R. Kawashima,
Biblical Narrative and the Death of the Rhapsode (Bloomington: Indiana University Press,
2004), 1–16, 63–76, 125–60.

and emotions that biblical prose "forces the reader to negotiate the many possible ways of imagining the characters' inner lives."[46]

The prose we find in the Bible is not, then, the terse king lists or brief accounts one reads in the royal inscriptions or annals of Mesopotamia,[47] but instead draws nearer in form to certain Egyptian prose stories, such as Sinuhe (COS 1.38) and Wen-Amun (COS 1.41), and in plotlines and themes to a wide collection of literature from the ancient Near East, including epic material (e.g., Kirta [COS 1.102] and Aqhat [COS 1.103]),[48] commemorative writings (e.g., Tel Dan Stele [COS 2.39]), royal apology (e.g., The Apology of Hattušili III [COS 1.77]),[49] (pseudo-) autobiography (e.g., Idrimi [COS 1.148]; Birth Legend of Sargon [COS 1.133]), law,[50] and chronicles (e.g., Babylonian Chronicle [COS 1.137]), among other instances.[51] There is little doubt that the narrative prose of the Hebrew Bible is heir to this rich repertoire of older literature from the ancient Near East. Yet in comparison to these more venerable writings, what we perceive in the Hebrew prose tradition of the Bible is a

---

46. Linafelt, *Hebrew Bible as Literature*, 36.

47. A. K. Grayson, "Assyria and Babylonia," *Or* 49.2 (1980): 140–94; Van Seters, *In Search of History*, 55–76. J.-J. Glassner, *Mesopotamian Chronicles* (Atlanta: SBL Press, 2004), 37–53; C. Waerzeggers, "The Babylonian Chronicles: Classification and Provenance," *JNES* 71 (2012): 285–98.

48. J. Greenfield, "The Hebrew Bible and Canaanite Literature," in *The Literary Guide to the Bible* (ed. R. Alter and F. Kermode; Cambridge: Harvard University Press, 1987), 545–60; S. Parker, *The Pre-Biblical Narrative Tradition: Essays on the Ugaritic Poems* Keret *and* Aqhat (Atlanta: Scholars Press, 1989).

49. H. Hoffner, "Propaganda and Political Justification in Hittite Historiography," in *Unity and Diversity: Essays in the History, Literature, and Religion of the Ancient Near East* (ed. H. Goedicke and J. J. M. Roberts; Baltimore: The Johns Hopkins University Press, 1975), 49–62; H. Tadmor, "Autobiographical Apology in the Royal Assyrian Literature," in *History, Historiography and Interpretation* (ed. H. Tadmor and M. Weinfeld; Jerusalem: Magnes, 1983), 36–57. A. Knapp, *Royal Apologetic in the Ancient Near East* (Atlanta: SBL Press, 2015), 161–276.

50. S. Chavel, "*'Oracular Novellae'* and Biblical Historiography: Through the Lens of Law and Narrative," *Clio* 39 (2009): 1–27; idem, *Oracular Law and Priestly Historiography in the Torah* (Tübingen: Mohr Siebeck, 2014), esp. 257–70.

51. Van Seters, *In Search of History*, 354–62; D. Damrosch, *The Narrative Covenant: Transformations of Genre in the Growth of Biblical Literature* (San Francisco: Harper & Row, 1987), 51–143, 298–326; E. Greenstein, "On the Genesis of Biblical Prose Narrative," *Prooftexts* 8.3 (1988): 349–50; M. Smith, "Biblical Narrative Between Ugaritic and Akkadian Literature: Part I: Ugarit and the Bible," *RB* 114.1 (2007): 5–29; idem, "Biblical Narrative Between Ugaritic and Akkadian Literature: Part II: Mesopotamian Impact on Biblical Narrative," *RB* 114.2 (2007): 189–207; A. Rainey, "The Northwest Semitic Literary Repertoire and its Acquaintances by Judean Writers," *Maarav* 15.2 (2010): 193–206.

depth of characterization and complexity of narrative technique "that must astonish anyone familiar with the literatures of ancient Egypt and Mesopotamia."[52]

In addition to its use of a vernacular language and its narrative qualities, what also sets apart biblical prose from other prominent ancient Near Eastern writings, such as the Egyptian story of Wen-Amun or the Akkadian Birth Legend of Sargon, is that it narrates a past through an anonymous third person voice.[53] To be sure, the use of the third person is found in other texts from the ancient Near East, such as in the Hittite "Deeds of Šuppiluliuma I" (COS 1.74), the fluctuations between first and third person discourse in a few royal inscriptions from Assyria and, from the eighth century BCE onward, the dominant use of the third person in the Babylonian Chronicle Series.[54] But it nevertheless remains a remarkable feature of biblical narrative that it recounts a varied past inclusive of both royal and non-royal agents almost exclusively in the third person voice, with the anonymity of the biblical narrators forming a striking contrast not only to those Greek historians such as Herodotus and Thucydides, but also in comparison to the first person discourse that dominates many royal genres of prose writing from Mesopotamia.[55]

The point of such observations is not to suggest a particular genealogy of biblical prose in an effort to establish *how* it came to be, but rather to identify certain features of this Hebrew prose tradition so as to better understand *when* it emerged. That is, what is sought here are considerations that help us to situate the rise of Hebrew prose at a proximate period in time by attending to those traits identified above—the adoption of a linear alphabetic script, the use of a vernacular language, its collection of narrative traits, and, finally, the employment of third person discourse—in an effort to investigate when this specific form of writing, over against other categories and possibilities, initially appeared in the ancient world of the southern Levant. For although storytelling is natural and a

---

52. Greenstein, "On the Genesis," 347. So also the assessment of Damrosch ("In a small country, in a society younger and less prosperous than the great cultures of Egypt and Mesopotamia, literary composition reached a degree of power and beauty previously unknown in the Near East" [Damrosch, *The Narrative Covenant*, 1]) and Kawashima ("Scholars have long noted that the prose narratives of the Hebrew Bible present us with something decisively new and unprecedented in ancient literature . . . anticipating in striking ways the modern novelist's craft" [Kawashima, *Biblical Narrative*, 4]).

53. On this point, see Kawashima's sophisticated analysis of "the disappearance of the speaking subject from the language of narration" [p. 37] within biblical Hebrew prose in Kawashima, *Biblical Narrative*, 35–76.

54. Grayson, "Assyria and Babylonia," 165–67, 173–75; Van Seters, *In Search*, 62, 79–92.

55. Van Seters, *In Search*, 55–78, 92–99; P. Machinist, "The Voice of the Historian in the Ancient Near Eastern and Mediterranean World," *Interpretation* 57.2 (2003): 117–37.

phenomenon of everyday language,[56] the following intends to show that *writing down* prose stories about past events is not, but is rather a specific development that materializes at distinct moments in history depending on the literary culture examined.[57] There is, in short, "a time in which prose appears."[58]

Hebrew Prose: The Epigraphic Evidence

With this more modest question of *when?* in view, we start with the epigraphic evidence. First, it is important to underscore that writing existed in the Levant for many centuries before the appearance of any Hebrew prose text. Epigraphic remains from the region attest to the production of both hieroglyphic and syllabic cuneiform documents throughout the second millennium BCE that were written in the cosmopolitan languages of Egyptian and Babylonian, including instances produced by local scribes trained in the methods and materials necessary to generate such writings.[59] Even if most residents of the region were unable to read and compose such documents, the written word was nevertheless known in the Levant by at least the Middle Bronze Age II period (ca. 2000–1550 BCE) and was used by local scribes and the larger empires they served from this time forward. Canaanite inhabitants of the Levant who spoke in dialects that were forerunners to Iron Age Hebrew would have been familiar with writing, therefore, but chose not to produce texts that reflected their own local languages.[60]

This situation changed as the Late Bronze Age came to a close. As Sanders details, at the coastal city of Ugarit, in north Syria, the alphabet was adapted to a cuneiform writing system during the thirteenth century BCE and was suddenly used to compose a varied collection of literature in a local vernacular language

---

56. M. Bakhtin, *Speech Genres and Other Late Essays* (trans. V. McGee; eds. C. Emerson and M. Holquist; Austin: University of Texas Press, 1986), 60–102; P. Ricoeur, *Time and Narrative*, vol. 3 (trans. K. Blamey and D. Pellauer; Chicago: University of Chicago Press, 1988), 244–49.

57. So a central argument in J. Kittay and W. Godzich, *The Emergence of Prose: An Essay in Prosaics* (Minneapolis: University of Minnesota Press, 1987). See especially pp. ix–xiii.

58. Ibid., ix.

59. W. Moran, "The Syrian Scribe of the Jerusalem Amarna Letters," in *Amarna Studies: Collected Writings* (eds., J. Heuhnergard and S. Izre'el; Winona Lake: Eisenbrauns, 2003): 259–74; W. Horowitz, T. Oshima, and S. Sanders, *Cuneiform in Canaan: Cuneiform Sources from the Land of Israel in Ancient Times* (Jerusalem: Israel Exploration Society, 2006); R. Byrne, "The Refuge of Scribalism in Iron I Palestine," *BASOR* 345 (2007): 1–12; Schniedewind, *A Social History of Hebrew*, 31–48.

60. Sanders, *Invention*, 76–77; I. Shai and J. Uziel, "The Whys and Why Nots of Writing: Literacy and Illiteracy in the Southern Levant During the Bronze Ages," *Kaskal* 7 (2010): 67–83; Schniedewind, *A Social History*, 47–48.

(Ugaritic) that had never been written down before.[61] And during this era residents of the southern Levant also began to inscribe objects in local languages with greater frequency using a distinct linear, alphabetic script tradition.[62] By this time the technology of alphabetic writing was quite old, with early prototypes dating back to 1900 BCE, if not earlier.[63] But the production of alphabetic texts had long remained limited to a sparse clientele of local craftsmen and merchants who worked mostly on the periphery of the empires they inhabited.[64] Official scribes employed within the administrations of Canaanite city states never adopted alphabetic writing, but instead wrote out their texts in the dominant prestige script tradition of the Middle and Late Bronze Ages, syllabic cuneiform. But with the collapse of the Late Bronze Age palatial society in the southern Levant the scribal infrastructure for cuneiform writing also disintegrated. Left in its wake was the old linear alphabetic script that, because it had never been tied to the political economy or high culture of the Late Bronze Age, persisted after this moment of social upheaval.[65] With the advent of the Iron Age period (ca. 1175 BCE) cuneiform writing all but disappears from the southern Levant while instances of linear alphabetic texts gradually increase, with this script tradition being adopted by

---

61. Sanders, "What was the Alphabet For?," 25–56; idem, *Invention*, 36–58. C. and R. Hawley also observe that the adoption of a local alphabetic script, use of a vernacular language, and the omission of a genealogy ("son of X") for scribes who wrote in cuneiform alphabetic at Ugarit—all distinct from scribes who wrote in the more distinguished Mesopotamian cuneiform traditions at the site—suggest that these scribes were "affirming their *independence*, affirming the fact that they and their work represent *not continuity* but instead a *profound rupture* with previous scholarly tradition." C. Roche-Hawley and Richard Hawley, "An Essay on Scribal Families, Tradition, and Innovation in Thirteenth-Century Ugarit," in *Beyond Hatti: A Tribute to Gary Beckman* (eds. B. Collins and P. Michalowski; Atlanta: Lockwood Press, 2013), 262.

62. Sanders, *Invention*, 99–101; Rollston, *Writing and Literacy*, 15–16, 19–24; I. Finkelstein and B. Sass, "West Semitic Alphabetic Inscriptions, Late Bronze II to Iron IIA: Archeological Context, Distribution and Chronology," *HeBAI* 2 (2013): 153–56; Schniedewind, *A Social History*, 63–64; O. Goldwasser, "From the Iconic to the Linear—The Egyptian Scribes of Lachish and the Modification of the Early Alphabet in the Late Bronze Age," in *Alphabets, Texts and Artifacts in the Ancient Near East: Studies Presented to Benjamin Sass* (eds. I. Finkelstein et al.; Paris: Van Dieren, 2017), 118–60.

63. G. Hamilton, "Reconceptualizing the Periods of Early Alphabetic Scripts"; idem, "Two Methodological Issues Concerning the Expanded Collection of Early Alphabetic Texts," in *Epigraphy, Philology, and the Hebrew Bible: Methodological Perspectives on Philological & Comparative Study of the Hebrew Bible in Honor of Jo Ann Hackett* (eds. J. Hutton and A. Rubin; Atlanta: SBL, 2015) 127–56; Goldwasser, "From Iconic to Linear," 134–47.

64. Sanders, *Invention*, 49; Shai and Uziel, "Whys and Why Nots," 75; Schniedewind, *A Social History*, 34–36.

65. Sanders, *Invention*, 106–108; Byrne, "The Refuge of Scribalism," 1–31; Schniedewind, *How the Bible Became a Book*, 56–57.

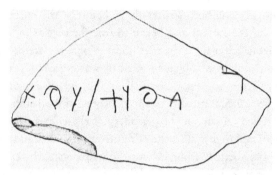

FIGURE 1.1 Tell es-Safi Sherd, Early Iron Age Period (Drawing by Author).

local Iron Age residents in the southern Levant and by leaders of the more northern Phoenician city states that had survived the destabilizing end to the Late Bronze Age era.

Examples of texts written in a linear alphabetic script and in local languages from the twelfth to tenth centuries BCE are modest but significant, and stem from a number of distinct regions in the southern Levant. In and around the Shephelah instances include the Tell es-Safi Sherd from Gath (See Figure 1.1.),[66] the Ba'al Sherd[67] and ostracon[68] from Beth-Shemesh, the Gezer Calendar (KAI 182), a broken inscription from Lachish,[69] an abecedary from Tel Zayit,[70] and two recent epigraphs produced from excavations at Khirbet Qeiyafa.[71]

In the Judean highlands a late eleventh/tenth century BCE inscription was found on a pithos jar in the Ophel area of Jerusalem,[72] and a few miles southwest

66. A. Maeir et al., "A Late Iron Age I/Early Iron Age II Old Canaanite Inscription from Tell es-Safi/Gath, Israel: Palaeography, Dating, and Historical-Cultural Significance," *BASOR* 351 (2008): 39–71.

67. P. Kyle McCarter et al., "An Archaic Ba'l Inscription from Tel Beth-Shemesh," *TA* 38 (2011): 179–93.

68. E. Grant, "Découverte épigraphique à Beth šémèš," *RB* 39 (1930): 401–2; F. M. Cross, *Leaves from an Epigrapher's Notebook: Collected Papers in Hebrew and West Semitic Paleography and Epigraphy.* (Winona Lake.: Eisenbrauns, 2003), 324–25.

69. B. Sass et al., "The Lachish Jar Sherd: An Early Alphabetic Inscription Discovered in 2014," *BASOR* 374 (2015): 233–45.

70. R. Tappy et al. "An Abecedary of the Mid-Tenth Century B.C.E. from the Judaean Shephelah," *BASOR* 344 (2006): 5–46.

71. H. Misgav, Y. Garfinkel, and S. Ganor, "The Ostracon," in *Khirbet Qeiyafa: Vol I. Excavation Report 2007–2008* (Y. Garfinkel and S. Ganor, eds.; Jerusalem: Israel Exploration Society, 2009): 243–57; Y. Garfinkel et al., "The 'Išba'al Inscription from Khirbet Qeiyafa," *BASOR* 373 (2015): 217–33.

72. E. Mazar et al., "An Inscribed Pithos from the Ophel, Jerusalem," *IEJ* 63.1 (2013): 39–49.

of the city a four letter inscription from around 1000 BCE was incised on a pot-sherd recovered from a tomb near Manaḥat.[73] Further to the north an additional inscription was produced from excavations at Khirbet Raddana,[74] while a fine inscribed bowl from Kefar Veradim[75] and three brief inscriptions were unearthed at Tel Rehov.[76] In addition to these finds an assemblage of unprovenanced incised arrowheads[77] from this era have been recovered and a number of royal inscrip-tions were also located at the city of Byblos on the Phoenician coast (e.g. KAI 1, 4, 5, 6, 7).[78]

The historian must wait another one hundred years, however, before more lengthy alphabetic texts emerge in the epigraphic record from the southern Levant. C. Rollston's important work on this corpus demonstrates that only in the late ninth to eighth centuries BCE do scribes residing in the kingdoms of Israel and Judah begin to standardize their alphabetic script in terms of a common morphology, orthography, and numbering system (termed the "Old Hebrew" script tradition), thus differentiating it from its Early Alphabetic antecedents and from other regional scripts that also develop during this time (i.e., Moabite, Ammonite, Edomite). Such evidence, Rollston observes, suggests that around this era (ca. late ninth century BCE, late Iron IIA/early IIB period) there was suddenly incentive for local scribes to write out their texts in a more consistent script,[79] a development motivated, perhaps, from growing state administrative

---

73. L. Stager, "An Inscribed Potsherd from the Eleventh Century," *BASOR* 194 (1969): 45–52.

74. J. Callaway and R. Cooley, "Salvage Excavation at Raddana, in Bireh," *BASOR* 201 (1971): 9–19.

75. Y. Alexandre, "A Canaanite-Early Phoenician Inscribed Bronze Bowl in an Iron Age IIA–B Burial Cave at Kefar Veradim, Northern Israel," *Maarav* 13 (2006): 7–41.

76. S. Aḥituv and A. Mazar, "The Inscriptions from Tel Rehov and Their Contribution to the Study of Script and Writing during the Iron Age IIA," in *"See, I will bring a scroll recount-ing what befell me" (Ps 40:8): Epigraphy and Daily Life from the Bible to the Talmud Dedicated to the Memory of Professor Hanan Eshel* (E. Eshel and Y. Levin, eds.; Göttingen: Vandenhoeck & Ruprecht, 2014): 39–68.

77. See Appendix A of F. M. Cross, "The Arrow of Suwar, Retainer of 'Abday," in *Leaves from an Epigrapher's Notebook*, 195–202.

78. For a discussion of these Phoenician inscriptions, see A. Lemaire, "Levantine Literacy ca. 1000–750 BCE," in *Contextualizing Israel's Sacred Writings: Ancient Literacy, Orality, and Literary Production* (ed. B. Schmidt; Atlanta: SBL Press, 2015), 11–15.

79. C. Rollston, "Scribal Education in Ancient Israel: The Old Hebrew Epigraphic Evidence," *BASOR* 344 (2006): 47–74; idem, *Writing and Literacy*, 92–113; idem, "Scribal Education During the First Temple Period: Epigraphic and Biblical Evidence," in *Contextualizing Israel's Sacred Writings: Ancient Literacy, Orality, and Literary Production* (ed. B. Schmidt; Atlanta: SBL Press, 2015), 84–101.

interest in the scribal profession as the young kingdoms of Israel and Judah matured during the course of the ninth century BCE,[80] but which may have also been shaped indirectly in a more decentralized fashion through the influence of regional trade networks and increased commerce as economies throughout the eastern Mediterranean recovered after the collapse of the Late Bronze Age palatial society.[81] What is more certain is that following this standardization process the rate of textual production in the southern Levant increases noticeably, with writings composed in local Hebrew dialects appearing with much greater frequency, by a more varied range of individuals, and within a broader collection of genres than ever before during the eighth to sixth centuries BCE.[82]

What this epigraphic evidence suggests, then, is that for the Iron I–IIA periods (ca. 1175–830 BCE) textual production in the southern Levant was more limited.[83] When texts do appear during this era they are conspicuous for their inconsistency in terms of letter forms, stances, and formatting,[84] suggesting that writing at this time was localized and somewhat restricted, more the province of disconnected, regional scribes who plied their trade independently for those petty rulers and other clientele who had the means and inclination to hire them. These were not state-sponsored scribes supported through a well-developed and interconnected scribal apparatus. As Sanders and R. Byrne detail in their separate studies, inscriptions from the Iron I–IIA periods reveal few state administrative concerns (records of commodities, tax receipts, diplomatic letters, etc.), but most often take the form of scribal exercises that kept the scribal craft alive or texts written onto objects of possession for those who could afford the services of those able to write.[85]

What is absent from this corpus of Iron I–IIA inscriptions, consequently, is key: narrative prose writing. In fact, no alphabetic text that narrates a past through prose has been recovered from this era anywhere in the eastern Mediterranean world. To locate such a text, we must wait once again until the late ninth century

---

80. Rollston, "Scribal Education," 74; idem, *Writing and Literacy,* 112–13. This perspective is supported by the first appearance of administrative texts from Israel and Judah, namely, the Samaria and Arad ostraca.

81. So the important argument of Sanders, *Invention*, 130–33.

82. Naveh, *Early History of the Alphabet*, 69–78; Carr, *Writing on the Tablet of the Heart*, 164–73; Sanders, *Invention*, 136–55; Schniedewind, *A Social History*, 99–125.

83. Naveh, *Early History*, 70; Sanders, *Invention*, 108–13; Byrne, "Refuge," 22–23.

84. Hamilton, "Periods of Early Alphabetic Scripts," 39–50.

85. As Byrne observes, it appears that the survival of scribalism during this era "ironically hinged on its own irrelevance, i.e., in its relevance to those who could afford the *luxury.*" Byrne, "Refuge," 23. Cf. Sanders, *Invention*, 108–13.

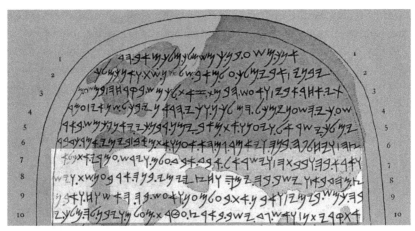

FIGURE 1.2 Mesha Inscription, ninth century BCE, lines 7–10 highlighted (Picture: Public Domain).

BCE when instances of narrative prose emerge for the first time in the form of royal monumental inscriptions.[86] In locations as varied as modern day Jordan (the Mesha Stele [KAI 181]), northern Israel (the Tel Dan Inscription [KAI 310]), and north Syria (Zakkur Inscription, [KAI 202]), local rulers began to forge royal steles that rehearsed past accomplishments in vernacular languages and in narrative prose form. A passage from the Mesha Stele, written around 830 BCE (See Figure 1.2.),[87] offers a fine example of this phenomenon (KAI 181: 7b–10):

> Now Omri had taken possession of a[ll the (8) la]nd of Medeba and he dwelled in it during his days and half the days of his son—forty years—but Chemosh restored (9) it in my days. So I rebuilt Baal-Me'on and I constructed a reservoir in it. And then I rebui[lt] (10) Qiryaten. Now the men of Gad had dwelled in land of Ataroth from ancient times. . . .

Apparent in these lines are narrative features that expand the possibilities of linear alphabetic writing beyond brief texts that name objects or mark items of possession. Instead, what we find in the Mesha Stele is an extended prose text that recounts a past in a local vernacular language (Moabite) never before written

---

86. N. Na'aman, "Royal Inscriptions and the Histories of Joash and Ahaz, Kings of Judah," *VT* 48 (1998): 333–35; idem, "Three Notes on the Aramaic Inscription from Tel Dan," *IEJ* 50 (2000): 92–104; Sanders, *Invention*, 120–22.

87. A. Lemaire, "La stèle de Mésha et l'histoire de l'ancien Israël." *Storia e tradizioni di Israele: scritti in anore di J. Alberto Soggin* (eds. D. Garrone and F. Israel; Brescia: Paidcill, 1991), 146–47.

down, detailing former events and achievements for a presumptive audience who, from the perspective of its royal patron, might be persuaded by its claims.[88] Abruptly, one thousand years after the invention of the alphabet, the Mesha Stele offers the first tangible instance of alphabetic writing being used for the purposes of narrating putative affairs from a past through prose. In terms of form (vernacular, narrative prose writing in a linear alphabetic script) and content (stories about past occurrences), this Moabite monument—alongside those other royal steles that appeared during this time in the Levant[89]—provides the earliest analogue to what is present in the narrative prose works of the Hebrew Bible.[90] Epigraphically speaking, the ninth century BCE marks the birth of vernacular, narrative prose writing in the Levant.

The first (non-biblical) Hebrew prose text appears around one hundred years later. Displayed beneath ground in a water channel hewed out from the bedrock below Jerusalem, the Siloam Inscription was written around the late eighth century BCE, most likely during the reign of Hezekiah at a moment when the Judahite capital was preparing itself for Assyrian siege.(See Figure 1.3.)[91] The inscription details how, at the end of the tunneling project, workers reached one another on the channel's completion (KAI 189: 2b–5):

> . . . and there was heard the voice of a man calling out to his co-worker, for there was a fissure in the rock on the right and [on the left]. And on the day of the breakthrough the stonecutters struck, each one to meet his co-worker, pick against [p]ick. And then the waters flowed from the spring to the pool for twelve hundred cubits.

What is striking about the Siloam Inscription for this chapter's investigation is that it offers concrete evidence of a distinct Hebrew prose tradition "very close"

---

88. Bruce Routledge, "The Politics of Mesha: Segmented Identities and State Formation in Iron Age Moab," *JESHO* 43 (2000): 221–56; Sanders, *Invention*, 114.

89. Max Miller, "The Moabite Stone as a Memorial Stela," *PEQ* 106.1 (1974): 9–18, Na'aman, "Three Notes," 120–22; Douglas Green, *"I Undertook Great Works": The Ideology of Domestic Achievements in West Semitic Royal Inscriptions* (Tübingen: Mohr Siebeck, 2010), 89–284.

90. On the relationship between the Mesha Inscription and biblical prose, see F. Polak, "The Discourse Structure of the Mesha Inscription: 'I-Style,' Intonation Units, and Oral Performance" in *Marbeh Hokmah: Studies in the Bible and the Ancient Near East in Loving Memory of Victor Avigdor Hurowitz* (eds. S. Yona et al; Winona Lake: Eisenbrauns, 2015), 407–27.

91. R. Hendel, "The Date of the Siloam Inscription: A Rejoinder to Rogerson and Davies," *BA* 59 (1996): 233–37; J. Hackett et al., "Defusing Pseudo-Scholarship: The Siloam Inscription Ain't Hasmonean," *BAR* 23 (1997): 41–50, 68; G. Rendsburg and W. Schniedewind, "The Siloam Tunnel Inscription: Historical and Linguistic Perspectives," *IEJ* 60.2 (2010): 188–203.

FIGURE 1.3 Siloam Inscription eighth century BCE, lines 2–5 highlighted (Picture: Public Domain).

to instances of biblical prose.[92] For in contrast to the Mesha Stele and its proud first person declarations—"I am Mesha. . . . I constructed. . . . I rebuilt"—the Siloam text draws nearer to a biblical prose tradition by representing a past through third person discourse: ". . . and there was heard the voice of a man calling out to his co-worker. . . ." Here we come across the anonymous voice also used among the biblical storytellers who, in contrast to the rulers of the ancient Near East or the historians of Greece, refuse to enter themselves into the stories they tell.

By the end of the eighth century BCE the Siloam Inscriptions makes it apparent that a Hebrew prose tradition had become common enough to narrate details of past construction measures carried out by local craftsmen in an inscription that few would have seen. It is likely, then, that Hebrew scribes at this time also had the skill and ability to develop prose narratives akin to those now found in the Hebrew Bible. If the Mesha Stele provides evidence that local scribes from the Levant could produce narrative, vernacular prose texts by the late ninth century BCE, the Siloam Inscription demonstrates that a Hebrew prose tradition was familiar and mundane enough to record public works projects in Jerusalem—without reference to any royal patron—a century later. Considering that Mesha controlled a territory that was for two generations under Israel's control and whose scribal infrastructure was quite similar to its Cisjordanian counterparts, it can be surmised that rulers in Samaria (and most probably Jerusalem)

---

92. F. W. Dobbs-Allsopp et al., *Hebrew Inscriptions: Texts from the Biblical Period of the Monarchy with Concordance* (New Haven: Yale University Press, 2005), 500.

would have also had the capacity to sponsor scribal works similar to Mesha's in an era contemporary with, if not somewhat antecedent, to him.[93] The Siloam Inscription attests to the fact that this putative vernacular prose tradition was well-established a century later. In light of these finds, the epigraphic record would suggest that a rough *terminus post quem* for the rise of vernacular, narrative prose writing in the southern Levant should then be situated sometime in the ninth century BCE. The late Iron Age (Iron IIB–IIC, ca. 830–586 BCE) demarcates itself from the early Iron Age (Iron I–IIA, ca. 1175–830 BCE), epigraphically speaking, as being the time in which a Hebrew prose tradition was established.

Hebrew Prose: Comparative and Theoretical Issues

The epigraphic evidence surveyed above has the benefit of coming to us unedited and fixed to an approximate date on the basis of paleographic and/or stratigraphic considerations, something our biblical texts do not. The historical import of these inscriptions for our study of the rise of Hebrew prose writing is therefore substantial. Nevertheless, the epigraphic evidence must be taken with due caution for an investigation into an era in which papyrus scrolls and other perishable material were likely the most frequent means used by Hebrew scribes to convey the written word.[94] Texts lettered on durable surfaces such as potsherds and weapons and stone should not, then, be taken as the maximum extent of writing during this time. The argument that our epigraphic texts do not provide warrant to discount the emergence of vernacular Hebrew prose tradition in a time earlier than the ninth century BCE cannot be fully deflected. Even more,

---

93. No royal monumental inscription from Israel or Judah has been recovered, but fragments of four extant inscriptions may have been derived from former royal display inscriptions. For Samaria, see S. A. Birnbaum, "The Inscriptions," in *Samaria-Sebaste III: The Objects from Samaria* (eds. S. Crowfoot et al.; London: Palestine Exploration Fund, 1957), 33–34. For three such inscriptions from Jerusalem, see M. Ben-Dov, "A Fragmentary First Temple Period Hebrew Inscription from the Ophel," in *Ancient Jerusalem Revealed* (ed. H. Geva; Jerusalem: Israel Exploration Society, 1994), 73–75; F. M. Cross, "A Fragment of a Monumental Inscription from the City of David," *IEJ* 51 (2001): 44–47; and R. Reich and E. Shukron, "A Fragmentary Palaeo-Hebrew Inscription from the City of David, Jerusalem," *IEJ* 58 (2008): 48–50.

94. A. Millard, "In Praise of Ancient Scribes," *BA* 45.3 (1983): 143–53; idem, "Only Fragments of the Past: The Role of Accident in Our Knowledge of the Ancient Near East," in *Writing and Ancient Near Eastern Society: Papers in Honour of Alan Millard* (Berlin: de Gruyter, 2005): 301–19; and idem, "Scripts and Their Uses in the Twelfth–Tenth Centuries B.C.E." in *The Ancient Near East in the Twelfth–Tenth Centuries* B.C.E. (eds. G. Galil et al.; Münster: Ugarit, 2012): 405–12; R. Kratz, *Historical and Biblical Israel: The History,*

conclusions drawn from epigraphic evidence will always remain vulnerable to the possibilities of further archaeological discovery in the years ahead.

But what lends further support to this perspective of the gradual and somewhat belated emergence of Hebrew prose are comparative and theoretical considerations wed to the rise of prose writing among other literary cultures in antiquity. The example of Thucydides is once again of some consequence. Greek writers possessed knowledge of an alphabetic script by at least the eighth century BCE via their contact with the Phoenicians. And to the best of our knowledge the Homeric epics were written down not long thereafter.[95] Yet during this era of increasing textual production no Greek author penned a prose text: Hesiod's *Works and Days* is a farmer's almanac written out in poetic form; the writings of Thales and Parmenides, developed a century later, are philosophy rendered in verse.[96] Only in the mid-sixth century BCE, in fact, some two hundred years after the Homeric epics were first textualized, do Greek prose writings begin to appear among a small collection of Ionian writers (e.g., Anaximander and Hecataeus of Miletus, Charon of Lampsacus).[97] And still two hundred years after the appearance of these first Greek prose documents (i.e., fourth century BCE)—and a full four hundred years after the introduction of alphabetic writing to the region (eighth century BCE)—Thucydides's *Peloponnesian War* could still be viewed with some skepticism because this past was written in prose and not catered toward oral recitation.

Thucydides is not an outlier. Over and over again, among a vast range of literary cultures spread out in different geographic locations and from different time periods, prose emerges late and long after the textualization of other forms of writing.[98] At Ugarit thousands of alphabetic cuneiform tablets have been recovered, including letters, legal documents, ritual material, and epics, many of which

Tradition, and Archives of Israel and Judah (trans. P. Kurtz; Oxford: Oxford University Press, 2016), 64–74; M. Richelle, "Elusive Scrolls: Could Any Hebrew Literature Have Been Written Prior to the 8th Century BCE?" *VT* 66 (2016): 1–39.

95. B. Powell, *Homer and the Origin of the Greek Alphabet* (Cambridge: Cambridge University Press, 1991), 219–37; idem, "Homer and Writing," in *A New Companion to Homer* (eds. I. Morris and B. Powell; Leiden: Brill, 1997), 3–33; Thomas, *Literacy and Orality in Ancient Greece*, 31–51.

96. C. Kahn, "Writing Philosophy: Prose and Poetry from Thales to Plato," in *Written Texts and the Rise of Literate Culture in Ancient Greece* (eds. H. Yunis; Cambridge: Cambridge University Press, 2003), 139–43.

97. i.e., around 550 BCE. See Kahn, "Writing Philosophy," 143; Goldhill, *The Invention of Prose*, 10–11; Grethlein, "The Rise of Greek Historiography," 148–70.

98. Kittay and Godzich, *The Emergence of Prose*, ix–xx.

find resonance with different biblical genres.[99] Yet not one text recounts events from an Ugaritic past through narrative prose writing. Nor has any other document written in a local language, for that matter, that has been recovered from the Levant before the Iron II period.[100] Moving west, A. Rodriguez Mayorgas observes that in Italy a Latin alphabet had been developed around the eighth century BCE, "but for reasons that still elude us the Romans did not feel the need to create what we now consider literary texts,"[101] and did not generate any prose writings about a Roman past until exposure to forms of Greek historiography led them to do so in the third century BCE.[102] G. Spiegel, to reach still further west and more recent in time, retraces, in a meticulous monograph-length study, how a vernacular prose tradition developed in France in the thirteenth century CE, after centuries in which French literature had been composed in Latin, as a *"product of a specific historical moment and situation* that endowed prose with a particular power for those who patronized, produced, and consumed works written in that discursive register."[103]

What these studies make clear is that there is nothing inescapable about the decision to represent a past in written prose form. Narrative prose works are commonplace today in a world "undeniably text centered,"[104] a world Kittay and Godzich term *après prose*, so dominant and familiar is this mode of writing to those of us who live within it.[105] In antiquity this familiarity with prose was not present. In many ancient societies prose writing never materialized. And when prose texts did appear in the ancient world, in nearly every instance it arrived late, centuries after a writing system was first introduced and adapted to a vernacular

---

99. See, for example, the collection published in Manfried Dietrich, Oswald Loretz, and Joaquín Sanmartín, eds., *The Cuneiform Alphabetic Texts: From Ugarit, Ras Ibn Hani, and Other Places* (2nd ed.; Münster: Ugarit-Verlag, 1995). On this point, see also Smith, "Biblical Narrative Between Ugaritic and Akkadian Literature. Part I," 22–29.

100. So M. Smith argues, with this evidence in view, that the genre of narrative prose historiography is not native to the Levant. Smith, "Biblical Narrative Between Ugaritic and Akkadian Literature. Part II," 189–207.

101. A. Rodriguez Mayorgas, "History and Memory in Roman Thinking about the Past: *Historia* and *Memoria* in Republican Literature," *Quaderni di Storia* 83 (2016): 51.

102. It is not surprising, from this perspective, that the first great history of Rome was written by a Greek, Polybius. F. W. Walbank, *A Historical Commentary on Polybius*, 3 vols. (Oxford: Clarendon Press, 1957–79).

103. G. Spiegel, *Romancing the Past: The Rise of Vernacular Prose Historiography in Thirteenth-Century France* (Berkeley: University of California Press, 1993), 2 (my italics).

104. Amodio, *Writing the Oral Tradition*, 2.

105. Kittay and Godzich, *Emergence of Prose*, xiii.

tongue. From a historical vantage point, Kittay and Godzich observe that what is so striking about an otherwise diverse collection of literary traditions is that there is "an epoch in each of these traditions in which there is no prose, and apparently never had been."[106]

Here the historical question of the emergence of Hebrew prose comes into focus. That is, what such comparative considerations underscore is that vernacular prose writing is most often a nascent form of written discourse actuated and developed over time through a constellation of influences that lead a literary culture to narrativize a past in prose rather than hymn it, poeticize it, or inscribe it in brief lists or terse annals.[107] Prose narration is not concomitant with production of written texts.[108] It is a significant feature of the historical evidence available that a literary culture's broad familiarity with writing, its adoption and development of a writing system, or even the composition of lengthy literary works are not predictive of prose. The production of tax receipts or treaties or high literary works such as *The Epic of Gilgamesh* tell us nothing, in fact, about the decision to narrate former affairs and happenings through vernacular prose writing. Mesopotamian scribes composed texts of great beauty and sophistication for nearly two thousand years before the Babylonian Chronicles appeared.[109]

The question we are after, then, is not *if* Iron Age scribes in the southern Levant could have written out narrative prose texts in vernacular Hebrew dialects.[110] Of course they could have. Rather, what we are asking is something more nuanced and specific. The question that concerns us here is when, more precisely, the cultural circumstances surrounding Hebrew scribalism prompted these ancient writers to begin to compose distinctly prose stories about the past after centuries in which their societies relied on other modes of communication

---

106. Ibid., ix.

107. Spiegel, *Romancing the Past*, 2–4.

108. Carr is certainly correct to point out that a "small-scale writing-education system does not preclude the creation of longer works," [Carr, *Writing*, 163 fn. 191], but the assumption that narrative prose documents, such as "narratives centering on figures like Jacob, Moses, and David" [p. 163], emerge seamlessly and quite early after the development of such a writing-education system fails to account for the comparative and theoretical considerations that suggest otherwise. For a similar critique, see Dobbs-Allsopp, *On Biblical Poetry*, 314–15.

109. e.g., T. Jacobsen, *The Harps that Once . . . : Sumerian Poetry in Translation* (New Haven: Yale University Press, 1987).

110. So the point registered in B. Schmidt, "Memorializing Conflict: Toward an Iron Age 'Shadow' History of Israel's Earliest Literature," in *Contextualizing Israel's Sacred Writings: Ancient Literacy, Orality, and Literary Production* (Atlanta: SBL Press, 2015), 109.

to do so. And this is an entirely different historical concern than that of the appropriation of the alphabet or the development of a consistent Hebrew script. Such occurrences are crucial because they allowed for the possibility of Hebrew prose, but Hebrew prose was not an immediate or necessary consequence of them.

The effort made by Hebrew scribes to narrate a past through prose writing is therefore no small matter. The fact that so few literary cultures pursued the possibility of writing out stories such as these in other local languages, despite the venerable scribal traditions in the Levant and the rich repertoire of literature produced in the ancient Near East, suggests that few cultures desired or had the incentive to do so. And though the biblical writings that we possess illustrate that Hebrew scribes did develop narrative prose stories about the past, two substantial deterrents would have long inhibited the production of such texts: first, the pressure exerted through the prestige of translocal, cosmopolitan literary works from the ancient Near East that long predated written Hebrew prose; and second, the influence of traditional modes of storytelling.

The world in which Hebrew prose emerged was a world in which syllabic cuneiform writing and the Akkadian language had long predominated. Bronze Age texts recovered from the southern Levant include a number of writings modeled on exemplars produced in Mesopotamia, such as scribal exercises (the Urra=ḫubullu fragment) recovered from Hazor,[111] a portion of a law code from the same location,[112] and a snippet of the *Epic of Gilgamesh* unearthed at Megiddo.[113] Sanders draws attention, for example, to how Bronze Age scribes who lived in the Levant produced documents based on Mesopotamian examples for at least five hundred years before writing down any text in a local vernacular language.[114] Documents fashioned during this era (ca. nineteenth to fourteenth centuries BCE) are instead written almost entirely in syllabic cuneiform, and most often express the international prestige language of the time, the Standard Babylonian dialect of Akkadian.[115] And the phenomenon Sanders points up is not surprising. When examining the writings from antiquity it is the languages

---

111. W. Horowitz et al., *Cuneiform in Canaan*, 74.

112. W. Horowitz, T. Oshima, and F. Vukosavovic, "Hazor 18: Fragments of a Cuneiform Law Collection from Hazor," *IEJ* 62.2 (2012): 158–76.

113. Horowitz et al., *Cuneiform in Canaan*, 102–104.

114. S. Sanders, "What was the Alphabet For," 44–47; idem, *Invention*, 81–88.

115. cf. P. Beaulieu, "Official and Vernacular Languages: The Shifting Sands of Imperial and Cultural Identities in First Millennium B.C. Mesopotamia," in *Margins of Writing, Origins of Culture* (ed. S. Sanders; Chicago: Oriental Institute of the University of Chicago, 2006), 190–92.

of empires, necessarily translocal so as to exert more uniform political and aesthetic claims on otherwise diverse linguistic populations, that dominate the textual landscape:[116] Akkadian, Aramaic, Greek and, later, Latin and Sanskrit are all disseminated by imperial powers and used to create literature by people in peripheral regions whose native languages were not those that appear in the texts they composed.

The Amarna Letters (fourteenth century BCE), Sanders observes further in his detailed investigation, offer a striking illustration of the influence exerted by such a cosmopolitan language in the southern Levant itself.[117] Composed by scribes who resided in Canaan and spoke forms of Canaanite ancestral to Hebrew, these letters, which were sent out to Pharaoh Akhenaten by vassals located in Canaan, were written in a script tradition and a vocabulary that derived from the Old Babylonian dialect of Akkadian.[118] But what is so fascinating about these documents is that they are often rendered with Canaanite grammatical features (i.e., prefixed and suffixed conjugations of Akkadian verbal forms) and made to conform to a Canaanite syntax (i.e., word order). [119] (See Figure 1.4.) The result are hybrid texts,[120] so to speak, that find such pronounced Canaanite interference on Akkadian forms that the language represented within these documents is often termed "Canaano-Akkadian."

Yet it is doubtful that anyone ever spoke this language. Rather, it is more likely that Canaanite scribes grafted their own local language onto Akkadian and thus "used Akkadian words, spelled in cuneiform, to write out Canaanite."[121] When reading these texts, scribes would have had to necessarily translate their documents into the language familiar to their audience since the unusual writing system employed in these letters did not conform to a language anyone could actually understand when voiced. So pervasive was Akkadian and the syllabic cuneiform tradition in Late Bronze Age Canaan, in other words, that Canaanite scribes encoded their own Canaanite language onto the only "writing" that made sense to them, cuneiform Akkadian.

---

116. Pollock, "Cosmopolitan Vernacular," 13.

117. Sanders, *Invention*, 80–88.

118. W. Moran, *The Amarna Letters* (Baltimore: Johns Hopkins Univ. Press, 1992), xviii–xxii,; A. Rainey, *Canaanite in the Amarna Tablets: A Linguistic Analysis of the Mixed Dialect Used by the Scribes from Canaan*, vol. 2 (Leiden: Brill, 1996), 1–16.

119. E. von Dassow, "Canaanite in Cuneiform," *JAOS* 124 (2004): 641–74. Cf. idem, "What Canaanite Cuneiformists Wrote: Review Article," *IEJ* 53.2 (2003): 196–217; Sanders, *Invention*, 81–88.

120. Rainey, *Canaanite*, vol. 2, 1.

121. Dassow, "Canaanite in Cuneiform," 642.

FIGURE 1.4 Amarna Letter 299 from Yapahu of Gezer. BM E29832 © Trustees of the British Museum (Picture).

The dominance of Akkadian and its syllabic cuneiform script tradition begins to subside however when a regional literature is produced for the first time in a local vernacular language over the course of the thirteenth century BCE at the city of Ugarit.[122] The great epics of Baal, Kirta, and Aqhat, among other writings, are literary works unlike anything created before in the Levant. But even this moment of impressive vernacular literary production is short-lived: Ugarit is destroyed, alongside other prominent locations and polities in the eastern Mediterranean, during the closing moments of the Late Bronze Age (ca. 1200 BCE). Vernacular writings do not appear again in the region for another three centuries. And then, quite suddenly, lengthy prose texts appear in Moabite, Aramaic, Phoenician, and Hebrew during the ninth century BCE.

What this evidence indicates is that vernacular literature in the Levant was neither common nor, for one thousand years, widespread. And this struggle for vernacular literature to take hold is a frequent theme found among other literary cultures situated in different geographies and timeframes. During what Pollock

122. Sanders, "What was the Alphabet For?," 42–47.

terms the "vernacular millennium," for example, an explosion of vernacular literature took place in a number of regions in both Europe and India around 1000 CE, eroding and eventually replacing the authority of Latin and Sanskrit through the composition of texts in languages such as French, English, Kannada, and Tamil.[123] But Pollock points out that this development was neither naïve nor inevitable. He comments:[124]

> Choices underlie the production of literary texts, whether vernacular or cosmopolitan, and in their interplay they constitute an intricate social phenomenon that necessarily comprises an element—however hard to capture—of cultural identity formation. Writing entails choosing a language (or, often, creating a language by the very production of texts), and thereby affiliating oneself with a particular vision of the world. While language choice itself is no small matter, choosing a language for literary text production most importantly implies affiliating with an existing socio-textual community, or summoning a potential community into being, and thus has defining social significations. But it has, equally, defining political significations, since the primary site of vernacular production everywhere at its commencement was the site of political power, namely, the royal court.

For the South Asian cultures at the center of Pollock's work the vernacularization process took on distinct regional overtones, but what is discerned among nearly all of these early vernacular writings is that a movement toward vernacular literature was a decision made with alternatives in view and political agendas in mind, and the choice made to produce vernacular literature was in some sense reflective of a new era of possibilities that appeared around the turn of the first millennium CE—increased trade and novel networks of exchange across Eurasia, the rise of nomadic empires in the Asian Steppe, the increasing presence and influence of Islam—that set the Indian subcontinent on a cultural and political trajectory never before realized.[125] The vernacular writings that suddenly materialized across the Indian subcontinent were not composed in a historical vacuum. Instead, throughout their textualization one finds again and again "a correlation

---

123. Sheldon Pollock, "India in the Vernacular Millennium: Literary Culture and Polity 1000–1500," *Daedalus* 127.3 (1998): 41–74; idem, "Cosmopolitan Vernacular," 6–37; idem, *Language of the Gods*, 19–29, 283–496.

124. Pollock, "India in the Vernacular Millennium," 46.

125. See Pollock's detailed reconstruction for not only South Asia but also Europe in *Language of the Gods*, 482–96.

between vernacular innovation and a re-configuration of the culture-power order."[126]

What stands out from Pollock's analysis is that the production of vernacular writings unfolds historically and by way of a host of social and cultural motivations. As Pollock puts it, "vernacular literary languages thus do not 'emerge' like buds or butterflies; they are made."[127] Vernacular texts such as those found in the Hebrew Bible do not then simply appear innocently and removed from the wider historical circumstances that envelop them. Rather, we find that vernacular writings such as these are willed into being. They are created by communities in response to previous political orders and more cosmopolitan literatures that no longer exert the power they once did or exert power in ways that invite the devising of texts in local languages that challenge, appropriate, or resist the dominant literary idiom of the time.[128] In France, G. Spiegel retraces how vernacular prose historiography arose among a concentrated clientele of aristocratic nobles dismayed by the increasing power of the monarch;[129] Dante's determination to write in a vernacular Italian, a decision explained at length in an entire tract devoted to the topic (*De vulgari eloquentia,* ca. 1300 CE), was inspired, at least in part, by a vision of uniting Italian lands within the Holy Roman Empire under one language that was distinct and removed from the Germanic polities to the north.[130] Sanders discerns a similar concoction of desires and provocations for the birth of vernacular literature—"an act of political will of an unprecedented sort"—at Ugarit and, later, Israel.[131]

What is also apparent from these studies is that the vernacularization process is often slow, resisted and antagonized by those who benefit from participation in more cosmopolitan literary cultures and the political powers from which often they derive. When vernacular writings on the topic of theology first appear at the University of Paris in 1210 CE, they are summarily set aflame.[132] The same fate awaits John Wycliffe's corpse two centuries later, dug up and incinerated due (in part) to his efforts in rendering the Vulgate into vernacular English. And for

---

126. Pollock, *Language of the Gods,* 336.

127. Pollock, "Cosmopolitan vernacular," 7.

128. Pollock, *Language of the Gods,* 468–81.

129. G. Spiegel, "*Pseudo-Turpin,* the Crisis of the Aristocracy and the Beginnings of Vernacular Prose Historiography in France," *Journal of Medieval History* 12.3 (1986): 207–23.

130. A. Gramsci, *Selections from Cultural Writings* (ed. D. Forgacs and G. Nowell-Smith; Cambridge: Harvard University Press, 1991) 187–88; Pollock, *Language of the Gods,* 464.

131. Sanders, "What was the Alphabet For?," 26; cf. idem, *Invention,* 47–75.

132. R. Olivier, *Holy Ignorance: When Religion and Culture Part Ways* (Oxford: Oxford University Press, 2014), 95–96.

causes more aligned with prestige than religious conviction, the first European philosophical tracts composed in vernacular French and English appear some four centuries after the bonfire at Paris in the seventeenth century CE—though such texts were quickly translated into Latin versions.[133]

For such reasons, gaps, frequently centuries in length, are found between the initial attempt to set down a local language in writing and the attempt to create lengthier, more sophisticated literary works in it. The adoption of a writing system and the possibility of writing out brief texts in a local vernacular—what Pollock terms "literization"—is seldom, if ever, coeval with the fashioning of texts beyond the mundane and everyday into a higher literary register—a practice Pollock describes as "literarization."[134] In the Kannada literature at the heart of Pollock's study there is a four-century divide between texts that appear in the Kannada language and the more stylized, high literary works later produced in this south Asian dialect[135]—or, roughly, the same interval between the first Greek alphabetic texts that emerge (eighth century BCE) and the prose of Thucydides (fourth century BCE). It should not surprise us, then, if roughly the same span appears to characterize the rise of linear alphabet writing in the southern Levant (thirteenth century BCE) and the emergence of vernacular prose (ninth century BCE) in the epigraphic record.

In addition to the influence exerted by imperial or cosmopolitan languages on the writings developed in the southern Levant, the second factor that would have impeded the development of Hebrew prose was the dominance of prevailing modes of traditional storytelling within the societies in which Hebrew scribes were active. There is little doubt that stories about the past were recounted by Hebrew speakers in the southern Levant long before the preparation of any prose text, transmitted and performed, as in many other oral societies throughout history, via the spoken word.[136] The oral cultures that sustained these ancient stories have long since disappeared. But we have traces of the influence of orality embedded throughout biblical prose, attesting, however obliquely, to its indebtedness to antecedent oral traditions and oral forms of storytelling.[137] Such instances include

---

133. Pollock, *Language of the Gods*, 473.

134. Ibid., 2–10.

135. Ibid., 336.

136. R. Finnegan, *Oral Literature in Africa* (London: Clarendon, 1970), 3–26, 305–464; Havelock, *Muse Learns to Write*, 63–78; J. Foley, *Traditional Oral Epic: The Odyssey, Beowulf, and the Serbo-Croatian Return Song* (Berkeley: University of California Press, 1990), 1–19.

137. U. Cassuto, "Israelite Epic," in *Biblical and Oriental Studies*, Vol. II (Jerusalem Magnes Press, 1973), 69–109; F. Cross, *From Epic to Canon: History and Literature in Ancient Israel* (Baltimore: Johns Hopkins University Press, 1998), 22–52; Niditch, *Oral World and Written*

the explicit foregrounding of the mouth and the ear within biblical narrative, as is evident in the well-known text from Deuteronomy 26: "You shall *answer* and you shall *say* before Yahweh your God, 'A wandering Aramean was my ancestor. He went down to Egypt as a foreigner, few in number, and there he became a great nation, powerful and numerous'" (Deut 26:5). In this account, as elsewhere in the biblical corpus (e.g. Exod. 13; Deut. 5, 10; Josh. 4, Judg. 6:13), the act of voicing a past takes precedence over any sense of reading or writing it down.[138]

The influence of orality on biblical prose is however much more widespread and subtle than what this example admits. Portrayals of individual and communal recitation, including lengthy speeches delivered about a collective past by leading figures (e.g., Josh. 24, 1 Sam. 12, 1 Kings 8), are but one technique used to construct a narrative world in which authority is often vested in what is spoken and heard: "Then the LORD said to Moses, 'I am going to come to you in a dense cloud *so that the people may hear when I speak with you and thus trust you ever after*'" (Exod. 19:9). Indeed, an underlying orality to biblical storytelling is quite pervasive: the citation of proverbial material (e.g. Gen. 10:9; 1 Sam. 19:24), the adoption of type-scenes and recurrence of narrative patterns (e.g., Gen. 1, 27; Exod. 2; Judg. 19, 1 Sam. 1),[139] phraseology and themes adapted from oral epic material,[140] and a syntax that lends itself, at moments, to the physiological demands of embodied oral performance (i.e., shorter noun strings, preference for parataxis, high frequency of finite verbal forms [e.g., Judg. 15:9–13; 2 Sam. 18:20–19:1; 2 Kings 6:1–7; 2 Kings 13:14–19)[141] are, among other traits,[142] indirect intimations

Word, 78–88, 108–109; idem, "Hebrew Bible and Oral Literature," 3–18; F. Polak, "Style is More than the Person: Sociolinguistics, Literary Culture and the Distinction Between Written and Oral Narrative," in *Biblical Hebrew: Studies in Chronology and Typology* (ed. I. Young; London: T&T Clark, 2003), 38–103; Dobbs-Allsopp, *On Biblical Poetry*, 233–47.

138. "Much biblical prose," Dobbs-Allsopps observes, "is acoustically shaped in no small part because it will still have 'listeners' as much in view as 'readers.'" Dobbs-Allsopp, *On Biblical Poetry*, 246.

139. D. Gunn, "Narrative Patterns and Oral Tradition in Judges and Samuel," *VT* 24 (1974): 286–317; E. Greenstein, "The Formation of the Biblical Narrative Corpus," *AJS Review* 15.2 (1990):165–78; Niditch, *Oral World*, 8–24; idem, "Hebrew bible and Oral Literature," 10–11; Alter, *Art of Biblical Narrative*, 55–78; van der Toorn, *Scribal Culture*, 14–16.

140. Cassuto, "Israelite Epic," 74–80; F. Polak, "Epic Formulas in Biblical Narrative: Frequency and Distribution," in *Actes du Second Colloque International "Bible et Informatique: Méthodes, Outils, Résultats" (Jérusalem 9–13 Juin 1988)* (eds. R. F. Poswick et al.; Geneva: Slatkine, 1989), 435–88; Greenstein, "Formation," 158–60; Niditch, *Oral World*, 17–24.

141. F. Polak, "The Oral and the Written," 59–105. Cf. Niditch, "Hebrew Bible and Oral Literature," 13–17; Dobbs-Allsopp, *On Biblical Poetry*, 243–46.

142. So, for example, commonly identified features such as the preservation of archaic references, a pronounced use of deixis, a predilection for epithets, or traits which express

of how Hebrew prose was shaped, to varying degrees, by an oral storytelling tradition once prominent in the southern Levant.

The point of drawing attention to this "oral aesthetic"[143] of biblical narrative for our purposes here is that it simply reminds us that early Hebrew prose emerged out of an oral milieu and had antecedents located, at least in part, in oral traditions. The prose produced during this time would have therefore taken root in a society in which oral stories and storytelling techniques were commonplace and familiar. For Hebrew prose to have gained traction in this context, accordingly, it would have had to find relevance and utility within a society accustomed to other, oral modes of recounting a past. The onset of Hebrew prose writing did not occasion the demise of the oral storyteller. As in other early scribal traditions,[144] there is little historical evidence of a "great divide" between orality and textuality in ancient Israel and Judah whereby writing came to replace oral communication as the primary means for disseminating cultural knowledge.[145] Instead, prose writing would have often been employed by ancient Hebrew scribes in the service of oral recitation and performance, just as oral habits and mindsets shaped the prose that was written down by these individuals.[146] Even generations after a Hebrew prose tradition had been well established, the Book of Jeremiah describes an episode when its prophet sends a scroll to Babylon so that it could be read aloud once before an audience and performatively destroyed (Jer. 51:59–64); in the Book of Ezekiel a divine order is given to consume a document so that Ezekiel can communicate

---

certain "metonymic" qualities inherent to what Foley terms "traditional referentiality." J. Foley, *Immanent Art: From Structure to Meaning in Traditional Oral Epic* (Bloomington, Ind.: Indiana University Press, 1991), 38–60; cf. Saussy, *Ethnography of Rhythm*, 156–72.

143. On the idea of an "oral aesthetic" behind traditional storytelling, see especially John Miles Foley, "Towards an Oral Aesthetic: A Response to Jesse Gellrich," *Philological Quarterly* 67 (1988): 477–78; idem, *Immanent Art*, 7–36. In terms of Hebrew scribalism, this idea was first taken up by Niditch [Niditch, *Oral World*, 10–12] and followed by others.

144. See, for example, the discussion in Amodio, *Writing the Oral Tradition*, 2–12; Thomas, *Oral Tradition and Written Record*, 9–10.

145. J. Foley, "Signs, Texts, and Oral Tradition," *Journal of Folklore Research* 33.1 (1996): 25–28; Niditch, *Oral World*, 4–6, 11–13; Raymond Person, "Scribe as Performer," *JBL* 117.4 (1998): 601–602; Carr, *Tablet of the Heart*, 4–8; Dobbs-Allsopp, *On Biblical Poetry*, 252–53.

146. Similarly, Vatri writes of Attic prose: "that the oral medium should come into play at some point in the history of a text and its use... may be envisaged for virtually all Attic prose texts at the time of their composition and/or (oral or written) publication." Vatri, *Orality and Performance in Classical Attic Prose*, 2. For the various contexts in which written texts were composed for explicitly oral performance (*hypokrisis*), see ibid., 37–100.

its contents by voicing them: ". . . eat this scroll, and go, *speak to the house of Israel*" (Ezek. 3:1). Such incidents, set in a time (ca. sixth century BCE) centuries subsequent to the appearance of a written Hebrew prose tradition in the southern Levant, thus reveal the tenacity of an oral mindset within this society and illustrate how written prose was still often used to support, and not displace, traditional forms of verbal communication at this time.

The preponderance of oral cues and expressions within biblical narrative makes some sense then as writings formed by Hebrew scribes who developed their writings with a sensitivity toward the needs of vocal rendition and aural reception.[147] A similar scribal interface between writing and orality is witnessed in other early scribal traditions. A. N. Doane, for example, in a study of incipient scribalism within Anglo-Saxon society, argues that the frequent reproduction of oral expressions and cues found in early Anglo-Saxon texts were the result of scribes who sought to "obey the somatic imperatives" the human voice imposed on works drawn from and composed for oral performance.[148] The attempt to mimic and reflect oral expressions within these documents, Doane contends, was thus one method used by these scribes to exercise their "communicative competence" within a culture that told stories principally through oral form.[149] Likewise, Thomas highlights a rich culture of *epideixis* (display performance) in Classical Athens where the language of the documents composed by scribes for these public recitations "seem roughly to replicate oral delivery."[150] The fourth century BCE rhetorician Alcidamas, Thomas points out, remarks that even those who wrote out texts did so with the goal of reproducing within their compositions the impromptu, verbal techniques of public performers because the speech of these orators was, in the end, simply more convincing.[151]

Such examples suggest that for Hebrew prose to have emerged it would have had to support and contribute toward the more venerable oral culture in which it arose. The residue of orality found within early prose writings from various scribal communities attests not only to the pronounced influence of oral forms of communication on these documents, but also to the "tenaciously persistent" oral culture and its concomitant expectations that subsisted even after prose writing had been introduced into a society.[152] In a series of important studies, Carr has documented

---

147. Person, "Scribe as Performer," 601–609.

148. A. N. Doane, "The Ethnography of Scribal Writing and Anglo-Saxon Poetry: Scribe as Performer," *Oral Tradition* 9.2 (1994): 423.

149. Doane, "Ethnography," 430–36.

150. Thomas, "Prose Performance Text," 180–81.

151. Ibid., 181.

152. Dobbs-Allsopp, *On Biblical Poetry*, 234.

how even later biblical scribes who had available a much richer assemblage of texts often still relied on memory and modes of orality to transmit and duplicate the written works under their care. "Students in a culture such as Israel's," Carr remarks, "learned the *written* tradition in *oral-performative* and *communal* contexts."[153] As in Classical Athens, then, where the performance of tragedies were supported by a secretary who read aloud the words of a particular written play so that it could be memorized by the performers who heard it,[154] written texts in ancient Israel and Judah were likely used as a means to sustain the transmission of cultural works but were not the primary means by which to access them.

The emergence of written narrative prose among an audience accustomed to oral modes of communication would therefore not have been immediate. The introduction of a new system of signification inherent to written prose was much more likely to have been slow and uneven in a society whose expectations were shaped by embodied oral storytelling and its means of reference, connected, as it was, to a host of spontaneous verbal and non-discursive gestures.[155] The richness and immediacy of oral performance, the possibilities available to the storyteller to anchor his or her account within a particular temporal and spatial context shared by those listening, the information derived from facial expressions and bodily movements, the common experience of hearing a tale together with others and responding to their reactions[156]—nearly all of these oral storytelling features are surrendered when a story is written down and detached from the storyteller's performance.[157] The jarring effect produced by a story rendered through written prose, lost to us who are so acclimatized to it, is that it somehow describes a world even when its storyteller is not bodily present.[158]

From this perspective, the failure of written narrative prose to develop among so many ancient literary cultures would demonstrate the resiliency of an oral culture of storytelling and the absence of a desire or catalyst to accommodate these verbal art forms to a new medium of prose texts. As Dobbs-Allsopp observes, "there is no inherent reason for oral art to ever be written down" since

---

153. Carr, *Formation*, 5 (italics original).

154. Thomas, *Oral Tradition*, 48–49.

155. Finnegan, *Oral Literature in Africa*, 373–88; W. Chafe, *Discourse, Consciousness and Time: The Flow and Displacement of Conscious Experience in Speaking and Writing* (Chicago: University of Chicago Press, 1994), 41–50, 82–136.

156. Kittay and Godzich, *Emergence of Prose*, xix, 17–23.

157. P. Zumthor and M. Engelhardt, "The Text and the Voice," *New Literary History* 16.1 (1984): 70; Saussy, *Ethnography of Rhythm*, 57–85.

158. W. Ong, *Orality and Literacy* (London: Routledge, 1982), 77–78, 99–101.

"its aboriginal medium is the human body and voice."[159] And when prose did appear among certain literary cultures, it took time for it to be admitted into the wider cultural repertoire of how past stories were transmitted and performed. Well into the sixteenth century CE, prose writings in England, A. Fox remarks, were infused with a "very 'oral' quality," so as to be read aloud among a population who, though literacy was on the rise, still preferred the experience of the voice to reading such texts in silence.[160] And Thomas observes of Athens that "even in the fourth century writing was only supplementary to oral transmission," with "documents new and comparatively unfamiliar. . . ."[161] Two hundred years after the publication of Hecataeus's great prose works (sixth century BCE), the contents of narrative documents found in the city of Thucydides and Plato were mostly "simple or inadequate without the oral or symbolic elements that accompanied them."[162]

We do not possess a collection of contemporaneous documents such as these from the southern Levant that intimate how vernacular prose writing was introduced or received. But we do know that there was a time, to draw from Kittay and Godzich's rich study, when Hebrew prose came to be. Whatever else they may be and however they might be read, the narrative prose stories now found in the Hebrew Bible are unquestionably cultural artifacts with histories as distinct as collared-rim jars or casemate walls. To be sure, the genealogy of these writings is less apparent than those cultural forms whose material remains have endured in the archaeological record in ways that ancient Hebrew manuscripts did not. Our evidence of the rise of Hebrew prose is admittedly limited to fragmented texts that have, often by chance, survived the vicissitudes of decomposition, erosion, or wanton destruction. Attempts to historicize the emergence of this prose tradition thus often run aground when postulating putative forerunners that have long since vanished or, more optimistically, remain buried.[163] We are not so fortunate as our colleagues who work to "discover some life" within a substantial collection of Anglo-Saxon or early medieval French manuscripts one thousand

159. Dobbs-Allsopp, *On Biblical Poetry*, 238–39.

160. A. Fox, *Oral and Literature Culture in England 1500–1700* (Oxford: Oxford University Press, 2000), 37. Cf. W. Ong, "Oral Residue in Tudor Prose Style," *PMLA* 80.3 (1965): 145–54.

161. Thomas, *Oral Tradition*, 60.

162. Ibid.

163. So Greenstein's caution in his review of Damrosch's *Narrative Covenant*: "Without a scrap of documentation from the contemporary period, it is impossible to trace the particulars of the Bible's early growth." Greenstein, "Genesis of Biblical Prose," 347.

years old.[164] Ours is a pursuit mostly devoid of manuscripts and mired in a past three thousand years in length.

Pointing up historical factors surrounding the vernacularization process or a Hebrew prose tradition's interface with older forms of oral storytelling cannot circumscribe and overcome this dearth of evidence. But such comparative and theoretical considerations are of historical significance because they caution against assumptions that would situate the appearance of Hebrew prose early, co-terminous with the adoption of linear alphabetic writing or the first appearance of a writing-education system in the Iron Age kingdoms of Israel or Judah. On the basis of these studies one can perhaps imagine writings from the early Iron Age that tally objects or name officials, poeticize the acts of heroes, or encode brief legal and ritual stipulations.[165] It is more difficult to envisage the production of narrative works such as those now found in the Hebrew Bible at this time.

The evidence at hand suggests, then, a period for the emergence of a native Hebrew prose tradition in an era other than the early Iron Age. And here we find that the Hebrew epigraphic remains recovered from the southern Levant square in significant ways with considerations drawn from comparative evidence of other ancient literary cultures and with theoretical discussions devoted to the rise of vernacular prose writing among societies dominated by more cosmopolitan traditions. Whether viewed from the angle provided from these epigraphs, factors wed to the vernacularization process, or issues surrounding the introduction of written prose into predominantly oral societies, such vantage points each suggest in turn that the development of Hebrew prose was a rather belated event, being established, I argue, near the dawn of the late Iron Age (Iron IIB–IIC, ca. 830 BCE–586 BCE).[166]

This *terminus post quem* for the emergence of Hebrew prose writing finds significance for our study because of the historical questions it allows us to pursue. For if the late Iron Age marks the beginning of a vernacular Hebrew prose tradition among scribes in the southern Levant, then we can be reasonably certain

---

164. Doane, "Ethnography," 422.

165. N. Na'aman, "Sources and Composition in the History of David," *The Origins of the Ancient Israelite States* (eds. V. Fritz and P. Davies; Sheffield: Sheffield University Press, 1996), 170–86; idem, "Three Notes on the Aramaic Inscription from Tel Dan," 96; Sanders, *Invention*, 106–13; Dietrich, *Early Monarchy*, 263–68; Schmid, *Literary History*, 63–68; Schniedewind, *How the Bible Became a Book*, 63; Schmidt, "Memorializing Conflict," 103–32.

166. For those who have reached similar conclusions through approaches different from that taken here, see, for example, Greenstein, "Formation," 162–63; Schniedewind, *How the Bible Became a Book*, 64–90; Smith, "Biblical Narrative, Part II," 201; Nadav Na'aman, "Saul, Benjamin, and the Emergence of 'Biblical Israel,' Part II," *ZAW* 121 (2009): 342–48; and Schmid, *Literary History*, 80–86.

that the biblical stories told about a time previous to this era—whenever these biblical texts were eventually written down and however they were brought together within a larger corpus of writings—were elicited from sources aside from older narrative texts produced during the early Iron Age. Of course, in light of the importance of an oral storytelling tradition throughout the first millennium BCE in the Levant, biblical stories told about later eras may have also been derived from sources other than older writings. But the biblical stories set in the early Iron Age afford us the opportunity to pursue the question of biblical source material in a more straightforward manner given the paucity of vernacular narrative literature in the Levant from this era. Establishing an approximate period for the emergence of a vernacular prose tradition in ancient Israel and Judah thus brings to the fore a question that carries our study into the realm of sources and their epistemological underpinnings: what did Hebrew scribes know about a past that preceded the rise of written prose?

Memory, Orality, Prose: Epistemological Considerations

The emergence of a vernacular Hebrew prose tradition in the late Iron Age indicates that stories written by Hebrew scribes about a past previous to this era were predicated primarily on sources other than older narrative prose texts. Extended prose documents set in a local Hebrew language would have been as rare in the southern Levant prior to the ninth century BCE, from this perspective, as was a local Greek prose tradition during Lycurgus's putative reforms at Sparta in the eighth century BCE or a Latin prose tradition during the founding of the Roman Republic in the sixth century BCE. Within each of these literary cultures there was "a time in which prose appears,"[167] and that time was often quite late and long after exposure to the written word.

Specific sources that were drawn on for the formation of biblical stories set in the early Iron Age period are, however, seldom identified and are never reproduced in any form within the Hebrew Bible itself. Further complicating our understanding of this source material is the anonymity of those scribes behind these narrative works and their reticence to inform us of how they crafted their stories and what information they may have used to do so. We have nothing in the Hebrew Bible that compares to those statements made by Herodotus (e.g., Hdt. 1.5, 1.95, 2.3) or Thucydides (Thuc. 1.22) regarding the sources consulted during the writing of their works or, for that matter, the interpretive method they

---

167. Kittay and Godzich, *Emergence of Prose*, ix.

used to adjudicate the claims of their source material. On this point, the gulf that separates Greek and Hebrew writers is substantial.[168]

Evidence embedded in various biblical stories nevertheless intimates that Hebrew scribes availed themselves of some source material for the composition of their accounts about an early Iron Age past. The primary indication of this dependence on sources is that a wide collection of biblical stories evinces an awareness of particular historical agents and affairs from the early Iron Age period that could have only been known to later writers if this information had been transmitted to them over time. The appearance of Philistine peoples in Canaan in the twelfth century BCE, an early Iron Age polity ruled over by the House of David, Pharaoh Shoshenq I's raid into the region in the late tenth century BCE, and Omride military prowess and political power at the beginning of the ninth century BCE, to cite some notable examples, are each attested in both biblical and extra-biblical sources from the ancient Near East.[169] The site of Shiloh functions as a significant early Iron Age highland settlement during that period in time when the Book of Samuel indicates its import, Hazor falls near the period in which Joshuu indicates it was destroyed, and the city of Gath flourishes when various biblical references describe it as an imposing Philistine center to the west of the highland regions. The stories told about an early Iron Age world in the Hebrew Bible do not appear, then, as a collection of fables constructed without reference to previous past realities. An acute interest in past affairs and individuals, grounded in historical time and a concrete geography, animates the stories surrounding the careers of Saul or David in ways quite distinct from that of the tale told of Gilgamesh's ferry ride across the Waters of Death.

Some of the source material consulted may have been derived from older texts. One finds within the biblical narrative, for example, references to other written works not included within its corpus, such as royal annals,[170] poetic verse and royal dirge (Josh. 10:13, 1 Sam. 1:18), and a "Scroll of the Wars of Yahweh" (Num. 21:14–15).[171]

---

168. So also E. Blum, "Historiography or Poetry? The Nature of the Hebrew Bible Prose Tradition," in *Memory in the Bible and Antiquity* (eds. S. Barton et al.; Tübingen: Mohr Siebeck, 2007), 25–46; Machinist, "Voice of the Historian," 117–37.

169. For an incisive discussion of the biblical narrative's relationship to foreign sources in the ancient Near East, see B. Halpern, "David Did It, Others Did Not: The Creation of Ancient Israel," in *The Bible and Radiocarbon Dating: Archaeology, Text, and Science* (London: Routledge, 2005), 424–37.

170. Thirty-four references are made to either the "Annals of the Kings of Judah" or "Annals of the Kings of Israel" in the books of 1st and 2nd Kings. The Chronicler adds two additional references: an "Annals of King David" (1 Chr. 27:24) and an "Annals of Jehu" (2 Chr. 20:34).

171. E. Greenstein, "What was the Book of Yashar?" *Maarav* 21.1–2 (2014): 25–35.

Such references suggest that some textual material may have been available for later scribes to consult, even if sporadically and in limited form, in order to develop their stories. In terms of annalistic material, it is important to point out however that the initial references to royal annals begin only with the late tenth century BCE reigns of Jeroboam I of Israel and Rehoboam of Judah according to the Bible itself (the "Scroll of the Annals of the Kings of Israel" [1 Kings 14:19] and the "Scroll of the Annals of the Kings of Judah" [1 Kings 14:29], respectively),[172] though a document is said to have descended from the time of Solomon (1 Kings 11:41). Nevertheless, there are no records of this sort linked to David, Saul, Samuel, or the various tribal leaders who are depicted by the biblical writers as their predecessors.

With these references to older texts, the historian must be mindful, however, of a tendency in the ancient world to name documents for rhetorical effect without a close reading of what these documents actually contained.[173] The footnote is a product of the modern world and its hyper-textual sensibility.[174] Nevertheless, our earlier observations on the increasing use of linear alphabetic writing in the southern Levant from the thirteenth century BCE forward means that the historian cannot rule out the possibility that brief lists of officials, matters of royal marriage and descent, regnal years, references to building projects, or short administrative records were passed down to later scribes from an earlier period in time.[175] The fact that Jerusalem endured for over a millennium in antiquity without being destroyed only adds to the possibility that older written texts persisted within its confines.[176]

---

172. Van Seters, *In Search of History*, 292–302.

173. K. Stott, *Why Did They Write This Way?: Reflections on References to Written Documents in the Hebrew Bible and Ancient Literature* (New York: T&T Clark, 2008), 52–60, 139–42; M. Leuchter, "The Sociolinguistic and Rhetorical Implications of the Source Citations in Kings" in *Soundings in Kings: Perspectives and Methods in Contemporary Scholarship* (eds. M. Leuchter and K. P. Adam; Minneapolis: Fortress, 2010), 119–34.

174. A. Grafton, *The Footnote: A Curious History* (Cambridge: Harvard University Press, 1997).

175. See discussion in Van Seters, *In Search of History*, 294–99; Nadav Na'aman, "Sources and Composition in the History of David," 171–73; idem, "Sources and Composition in the History of Solomon," in *The Age of Solomon: Scholarship at the Turn of the Millennium* (ed. L. Handy; Leiden: Brill, 1997), 76–77; W. Dietrich, *The Early Monarchy in Israel: The Tenth Century B.C.E.* (trans. J. Vette; Atlanta: SBL Press, 2007), 265–67; Pioske, "The Scribe of David," 163–88.

176. So Mazar: "since the city [Jerusalem] did not suffer any turmoil between the 10th and 7th centuries BCE. . . [o]ld inscriptions and other written texts, as well as oral transmission of information, could be preserved for centuries." A. Mazar, "Archaeology and the Biblical Narrative: The Case of the United Monarchy," in *One God—One Cult—One*

Information about a more remote past may also have been gleaned from experiences with more ancient locations and ruins. A. Alt theorized nearly a century ago that a number of biblical anecdotes were developed through an encounter with older remains in the region,[177] thus foregrounding the way in which a physical landscape could shape how past stories were created and transmitted over time in the southern Levant. In ancient Greece the influence of place was also pronounced on past storytelling, such as the in the opening of *The Peloponnesian War* when Thucydides investigates the remains of two older sites, Delos and Mycenae (Thuc. 1.8, 1.10), in order make determinations about these locations' status during a much more distant past.[178] Here Thucydides follows the practice established earlier by Herodotus who, according to his own account, was eager to frequent ruins during his travels abroad (e.g., Hdt. 2.125; 3.60). And some five hundred years after Herodotus, Pausanias, author of the *Periegesis*, details how he undertook an extensive journey throughout the Roman provinces on the Greek mainland, visiting local shrines and examining relics, in order to offer his own detailed account of how Greece appeared before it came under Roman control.[179]

References to older material remains in fact abound within the narrative writings of the Hebrew Bible, indicating their import for the scribes who composed these stories. Instances include stone memorials (Josh. 4:7, 7:26, 8:29), royal monuments (1 Sam. 15:12; 2 Sam. 8:3), commemorative pillars (Judg. 9:6; 2 Sam. 18:18), tombs (1 Sam. 10:2; 2 Kings 23:17), and venerable locations (2 Kings 19:25), including, in the case of 'Ai, a site whose very name means "the ruins" (Josh. 8:28). What is also of interest in this vein are the repetitive occurrences of the phrase "until this day" scattered throughout a wide collection of biblical stories in the books of Deuteronomy through Kings, cited, ostensibly, in order to draw attention to past phenomena that persisted into the time of the

---

Nation: Archaeological and Biblical Perspectives (eds. R. Kratz and H. Spieckermann; Berlin: De Gruyter, 2010), 46.

177. So Alt's theory of *"Ortsgebundenheit."* A. Alt, "Josua," in *Kleine Schriften zur Geschichte des Volkes Israel*, Vol. I (Munich: C. H. Beck, 1953), 182–92.

178. R. M. Cook, "Thucydides as Archaeologist," *The Annual of the British School at Athens* 50 (1955): 266–70; Hornblower, *Commentary*, 33–35.

179. J. Porter, "Ideals and Ruins: Pausanias, Longinus, and the Second Sophistic," in *Pausanias: Travel and Memory in Roman Greece* (eds. S. Alcock et al.; Oxford: Oxford University Press, 2001), 63–92; M. Pretzler, "Pausanias and Oral Tradition," *The Classical Quarterly* 55.1 (2005): 235–49; R. Osborne, "Relics and Remains in an Ancient Greek World Full of Anthropomorphic Gods," *Past and Present* 206 (2010): 56–72.

storyteller:[180] "The great stone by which they set down the ark of Yhwh is, until this day, in the field of Joshua of Beth-Shemesh" (1 Sam. 6:18). One can argue that this language is more rhetorical than reflective of an actual past reality experienced by the biblical scribes.[181] But such language usage, at the very least, presupposes an audience who might be persuaded by such claims with regard to more venerable objects and practices in the region, and thus an audience who were cognizant of older forms and phenomena that surrounded them. In the case of Jerusalem it appears that scribes were aware of more ancient features preserved in the city and made recourse to these older physical remains when constructing their stories about Jerusalem's past,[182] a point supported by the obscure reference in Nehemiah 12:37 wherein a procession passes by a "house of David" that would have been at least five centuries old by the time of those who walked by it. The detailed descriptions of terrain and towns and borderlands throughout these narratives indicate, furthermore, that the scribes who wrote them possessed a keen understanding of the Iron Age geography of the southern Levant.[183]

But for reasons reviewed above, the primary source material available to biblical scribes about an early Iron Age past would have been taken over from oral tradition.[184] Active in a society that possessed few older prose documents from this time (Iron I–IIA), the biblical scribes who began to compose narratives about the early Iron Age period would have necessarily derived most knowledge about this era from oral sayings and stories that had been in circulation for what was

---

180. B. Childs, "A Study of the Formula 'Until This Day,'" *JBL* 82 (1963): 279–92; J. Geoghegan, "'Until This Day' and the Preexilic Redaction of the Deuteronomistic History," *JBL* 122 (2003): 201–27

181. Van Seters, *In Search of History*, 49–50.

182. N. Na'aman, "Biblical and Historical Jerusalem in the Tenth and Fifth–Fourth Centuries BCE," *Bib* 93 (2012): 21–42; D. Pioske, "Memory and its Materiality: The Case of Early Iron Age Khirbet Qeiyafa and Jerusalem," *ZAW* 127.1 (2015): 78–95.

183. See, for example, the detailed study of Gaß in E. Gaß, *Die Ortsnamen des Richterbuchs in historischer und redaktioneller Perspektive* (Wiesbaden: Harrassowitz, 2005).

184. On the importance of oral source material for stories of an early Iron Age past in the Hebrew bible, see also Gunn, *The Story of King David*, 49–62; Van Seters, *In Search of History*, 51–52; N. Na'aman, "In Search of the Reality Behind the Account of David's Wars with Israel's Neighbours," *IEJ* 52.2 (2002): 215; idem, "Saul, Benjamin, and the Emergence of 'Biblical Israel,'" 342–48; Schniedewind, *How the Bible Became a Book*, 1–23; Dietrich, *Early Monarchy*, 264–67; I. Finkelstein, "Geographical and Historical Realities Behind the Earliest Layer in the David Story," *SJOT* 27.2 (2013): 133–35; J. Hutzli, "The Distinctness of the Samuel Narrative Tradition," in *Is Samuel Among the Deuteronomists? Current Views on the Place of Samuel in a Deuteronomistic History* (eds. C. Edenburg and J. Pakkala; Atlanta: SBL Press, 2013), 196–98.

perhaps a number of generations.[185] Consequently, as touched on previously, we find intimations of an oral mindset and idiom imprinted onto the prose stories these scribes developed. And even if some older texts such as brief royal records or diplomatic missives were preserved from the early Iron Age in Jerusalem or elsewhere, it is uncertain if any pre-Hellenistic scribe, Hebrew or otherwise, believed that such documentation superseded that of oral tradition in terms of importance for the stories they wanted to tell. As A. Momigliano observes, theirs was not a world in which archives of written texts held great cultural significance as a locus of information for developing stories about the past.[186] The directive to consult written records for information about a past not contained in the stories the biblical scribes decided to tell (1 Kings 14:19; 14:29; 15:7, 15:23, etc.) would be in keeping with this much wider cultural pattern of valuing knowledge other than that contained in written texts for insights into former times.

Foregrounding the importance of source material other than lengthy narrative texts for stories of an early Iron Age past is not a novel insight. Already in the work of Gunkel a century ago one finds an acute historical interest in the oral traditions that contributed to later biblical writings,[187] traditions that, in Gunkel's estimation, had not factored enough into scholarly studies on the formation of the Hebrew Bible. So Gunkel comments: "The world does not consist only of men [*sic*] who write books and those who copy them. Modern criticism has frequently overlooked the significance of oral tradition thus far and is all too prone to conclude a literary dependence at every point of contact between two writings."[188] And with Gunkel's student, H. Greßmann, this concern with past stories "transmitted only orally" is worked

---

185. So also for Herodotus and Thucydides, as emphasized in Rhodes, "Documents and the Greek Historians," 56–50; Waters, *Herodotus the Historian*, 76; Murray, "Herodotus and Oral History," 16–44. Cf. Nino Luraghi, "The Stories before the *Histories*: Folktale and Traditional Narrative in Herodotus," in *Herodotus: Volume I* (ed. R. Munson; Oxford: Oxford University Press, 2013), 87–112. For Thucydides, see Thomas, *Oral Tradition*, 235–36; Nicolai, "Thucydides," 263–85.

186. Momigliano, "Historiography," 216–17. Cf. Van Seters, *In Search of History*, 40–51, 195–99. As West notes, the cavalier manner in which Herodotus treats inscriptions—"more for ornament than for use"—again suggests an outlook that "belongs in many respects to a society in which literacy is simply an aid to oral communication." Stephanie West, "Herodotus' Epigraphical Interests," 304.

187. So a *locus classicus* from Gunkel's commentary on Genesis: "Consequently, we must first examine Genesis in the form in which it existed in oral tradition. If we want to understand the oral sayings we must depict the situation in which they appeared." Gunkel, *Genesis* (3rd ed.), xxxi.

188. H. Gunkel, *Schöpfung und Chaos*, 58 n. 2. I am indebted to P. Kurtz for this reference, and much else on matters of Gunkel. Cf. P. Kurtz, "Axes of Inquiry: The Problem of Form and Time in Wellhausen and Gunkel," *SJOT* 29.2 (2015): 247–95.

out even further beyond the material in Genesis, including those texts about the early Iron Age in Samuel and Kings where the boundary line between oral sayings and written, narrative works are deemed to be "fluid" at best.[189] Within the studies of both Gunkel and Greßmann, then, one finds an attempt to examine the preliterary background of the Hebrew Bible in such a way as to move beyond investigations devoted solely to the later compositional history of the biblical writings, analyzing instead the contours of the presumptive source material that may have contributed toward the production of these texts.[190] Research inspired by such interests have been frequent and highly influential among biblical scholarship, including studies pertaining to the possible socio-historical contexts (*Sitz im Leben*) in which this source material originated or the historical trajectory by which it developed and came to crystallize into textual form (*Überlieferungsgeschichte*).[191]

But what has received less attention is the question as to how past information conveyed through oral sources was made possible and, being possible, what type of past knowledge these traditions imparted. For in addition to mass literacy, exposure to ubiquitous textuality, and technologies of printing (books, journals, newspapers, internet) that exist today, what also separates us from the scribes behind the formation of the Hebrew Bible are deeply held epistemological assumptions about how genuine past knowledge is devised and constituted.[192] Thus, beyond the origin and development of the presumptive sources available to later biblical writers, what requires closer scrutiny are the particular

---

189. Greßmann, "Oldest History Writing," 13, 15.

190. With regard to Greßmann, see the programmatic article, "Die Aufgaben der alttestamentlichen Forschung" [*ZAW* 42 (1924): 1–33] and the remark, with an eye toward Wellhausen's past successes and a turn toward a new approach in the future, that "We require in our scholarship, therefore, not more literary-critical research but less." (p. 8). For Gunkel, see his reply to Wellhausen's criticism of his *Schöpfung und Chaos* in H. Gunkel, "Aus Wellhausen's neuesten apokalyptischen Forschungen. Einige principielle Erörterungen" *Zeitschrift für wissenschaftliche Theologie* 42 (1899): 581–611.

191. The literature on Gunkel's influence is vast, but for an overview see W. Baumgartner, "Zum 100. Geburtstag von Hermann Gunkel. Vortrag auf dem Alttestamentlerkongreß Bonn 1962," in *Congress Volume: Bonn 1962* (Leiden: Brill, 1963), 1–18; W. Klatt, *Hermann Gunkel: Zu seiner Theologie der Religionsgeschichte und der Entstehung der formgeschichtlichen Methode* (Göttingen: Vandenhoeck & Ruprecht, 1969), 261–71; Knight, *Rediscovering*, 17–25, 57–66; A. Campbell, "The Emergence of the Form-critical and Traditio-historical Approaches," in *Hebrew Bible/Old Testament: The History of Its Reception*, Vol. III/1 (ed. M. Saebø; Göttingen: Vandenhoeck & Ruprecht, 2015), 125–47.

192. Of course, as Schiffman writes (Z. Schiffman, *The Birth of the Past* [Baltimore: Johns Hopkins University Press, 2011], 277), "The historicist habit of mind has become so much the standard of common sense that we fail to see that it is itself a preconception." But a preconception it is, as Schiffmann's fine work details. On the emergence of a distinctive idea of historical knowledge in the modern era, including the methodological assumptions attendant

epistemic conditions that gave rise to this oral source material, the contingencies that would have further shaped this material's referential claims over time, and how the information communicated through such oral sayings were judged as meaningful within the period in which the biblical scribes were active.[193] How, in other words, do we theorize the past knowledge conveyed through an oral story-telling tradition that would have predominated before the emergence of written Hebrew prose in the southern Levant?

When such matters of epistemology have been pursued, they have often been curtailed by the tendency to frame this discussion with one concern in mind: namely, the historicity of the oral traditions investigated. What results, consequently, is a focus on external epistemological concerns, dis-connected from those once operative in antiquity and motivated instead by modern historicist interests whose chief aim is historical reconstructions of past (most often political or religious) realities.[194] E. Nielsen's important con-tribution to the precompositional background of various biblical texts takes pains to assert, for example, that these traditions were overwhelmingly conserv-ative in their transmission and should be understood, consequently, as histor-ically reliable from a modern viewpoint.[195] W. F. Albright, through the lens of epigraphic and archaeological finds, came to a similar assessment, finding much of the oral source material that he believed to lie behind the biblical writings to retain a high degree of historicity,[196] an appraisal that was, at moments, also

---

with its production, see especially M. Foucault, *The Order of Things* (London: Routledge, 2002 [1966]), 235–39; 400–406; M. de Certeau, *The Writing of History* (trans. T. Conley; New York: Columbia University Press, 1988), 56–114; P. Ricoeur, *Memory, History, Forgetting* (trans. K. Blamey and D. Pellauer; Chicago: University of Chicago Press, 2004), 293–313; R. Koselleck, *Futures Past: On the Semantics of Historical Time* (trans. K. Tribe; New York: Columbia University Press, 2004), 9–25, 192–204; and P. Fritzsche, *Stranded in the Present: Modern Time and the Melancholy of History* (Cambridge: Harvard University Press, 2004), 1–10, 201–19.

193. Foucault, *Order of Things*, xxiii–xxvi.

194. For a nuanced view of this topic from outside the field of biblical studies, see R. Finnegan, "A Note on Oral Tradition and Historical Evidence," *History and Theory* 9.2 (1970): 195–201.

195. E. Nielsen, *Oral Tradition: A Modern Problem in Old Testament Introduction* (London: SCM Press, 1954), esp. 18–38. On this point, Nielsen follows earlier Scandinavian scholarship, such as the perspective on oral tradition developed earlier by H. Nyberg in his influential study, "Das textkritische Problem des Alten Testaments, am Hoseabuche demon-striert," *ZAW* 52 (1934), 241–54, esp. 242–46. On this point, see also Knight, *Rediscovering*, 290–92.

196. W. F. Albright, *From Stone Age to Christianity* (Baltimore: Johns Hopkins University Press, 1957), 40–43.

followed by his students.[197] More recently, I. Provan et al. have affirmed and further developed this stance toward oral tradition.[198] But others have been less sanguine. Wellhausen, to cite an influential perspective, was quite skeptical of the historical value of the non-written sources that informed the biblical narrative,[199] an opinion with which Gunkel agreed in his attempt to demarcate the knowledge once expressed through an earlier oral storytelling tradition in ancient Israel from that of the proper scholarly (i.e., text-based, literate) work of the historian that arose later in Israel's history.[200] And many have followed suit in this vein, including G. Ahlström's cautious assessment of the historical character of verbal sayings[201] and N. Lemche's skepticism toward these traditions on the basis of the lack of controls available for such source material to remain stable and unchanged over time.[202]

The overriding concern of this stream of scholarly research is whether, or to what degree, the oral source material on which the biblical scribes depended preserved information that could be of value for modern historical pursuits. The importance of this issue is without question.[203] But limiting investigations into these putative sources by inquiring solely as to whether they may express (what we deem as) historically credible knowledge overlooks other, perhaps even more significant historical questions that we can ask of the biblical writings. For alongside efforts devoted to determining the modern historical value of the claims derived from an oral storytelling tradition in the ancient world of the southern Levant, it is also necessary to examine the more basic question as to how knowledge of a past was conceived of and sustained in a society of few written texts.

---

197. F. M. Cross, for example, also emphasized the importance of "actual historical memory," embedded in oral traditions, that Cross believed that the German school of Alt and his students failed to take seriously. See F. M. Cross, *Canaanite Myth and Hebrew Epic: Essays in the History of the Religion of Israel* (Cambridge: Harvard University Press, 1973), 83–89.

198. I. Provan et al., *A Biblical History of Israel* (Louisville: Westminster John Knox, 2003), 43–74 [esp. 57–59].

199. J. Wellhausen, *Prolegomena to the History of Israel* (New York, Meridian, 1961), 334–41.

200. Gunkel, *Genesis* (3rd ed.), viii–x.

201. G. Ahlström, "Oral and Written Transmission: Some Considerations," *HTR* 59.1 (1966): 69–81.

202. N. Lemche, "The Origin of the Israelite State: A Copenhagen Perspective on the Emergence of Critical Historical Studies of Ancient Israel in Recent Times," *SJOT* 12 (1998): 45–46.

203. J. Vansina, *Oral Tradition as History* (Madison: University of Wisconsin Press, 1985), 27–33; 186–204; Finnegan, "Oral Tradition and Historical Evidence," 195–201. From the field of biblical studies, see the epilogue to Miller's study ["Epilogue: Orality and Historicism"] in Miller, *Oral Tradition*, 114–20.

Forms of knowledge, regardless of their domain and who may hold to them, are not innate or transcendental. They are historical, a product of culture.[204]

As such, the very conditions of knowing that contributed to the creation of Hebrew prose needs to be historicized. Apart from those studies that assess what fragments of historical knowledge may be gleaned from ancient scribal works predicated on still older sources, what also necessitates critical attention is the question as to how the past knowledge communicated through these putative traditions was made possible or, said differently, how their "configurations within a *space* of knowledge"[205] once arose. What we are after in this sense is the attempt to situate, historically, the mechanisms and limits of knowing that shaped the source material available to ancient Hebrew scribes about an early Iron Age past and, in doing so, to take seriously the possibility that the information on which they relied, which they held to be true, was something distinct from our modern epistemic values pertaining to what constitutes historical knowledge. The aim of this historical approach, then, is to draw attention to how information about the past may have been constituted and organized by these ancient writers—i.e., the assumptions, beliefs, values, and practices that shaped what these ancient Hebrew scribes knew about the past they recounted through prose. What is sought through this manner of inquiry is something more than judgments as to whether ancient Hebrew scribes relied on proper or deficient sources when viewed from the vantage point of our modern epistemological commitments. We want to examine instead what modes of thought contributed to the information these sources contained.[206]

Such historical interests draw near to that of P. Veyne's penetrating study, *Did the Greeks Believe their Myths?*[207] Significant about this work for our purposes here is the manner in which Veyne calls attention to the epistemological "program" or, more evocatively, the "fishbowl" that enveloped particular ancient Greek thinkers at certain moments in time, limiting, though they could not perceive it themselves, the questions they asked about the past and the answers they provided.[208] Of historical interest to Veyne are precisely the conceptual

---

204. Foucault, *The Order of Things*, xii—xv; P. Veyne, *Foucault: His Thought, His Character* (trans. J. Lloyd; New York: Polity, 2010), 13–21.

205. Foucault, *Order of Things*, xxiv.

206. Or, as Pollock observes for the premodern Indian literary works at the center of his study: "What matters for me, in short, is making sense of *a historical form of consciousness* rather than attempting . . . to identify *a form of historical consciousness*" (italics original). Sheldon Pollock, "Pretextures of Time," *History and Theory* 46 (2007): 377.

207. P. Veyne, *Did the Greeks Believe in their Myths? An Essay on the Constitutive Imagination* (trans. P. Wissing; Chicago: University of Chicago Press, 1988).

208. Veyne, *Did the Greeks*, xii, 103–108. idem, *Foucault*, 13–21.

presuppositions about past knowledge that ancient Greek scholars brought
to the myths handed down to them. From the pre-Socratics to Pausanias one
thousand years later, the great writers from this tradition, Veyne argues, were
guided in their intellectual pursuits by cultural inferences about truth and reality that exerted enormous influence on how these thinkers approached the past
recounted in their society's mythological legends. The Greeks did believe in their
myths, Veyne observes, but it is the question as to how they believed—that is, the
epistemological frameworks and means of knowing that undergirded the stories
told of their culture's mythic past—that demands the historian's attention.[209]
Epistemic values must be historicized.[210]

Fascinating about this line of investigation is how Veyne is able to spotlight
particular epistemological commitments that informed how the Greeks thought
about their myths. There was a time, Veyne observes, when Homeric epic was
deemed to be an authentic account of a former age, even if this past occupied
an "earlier" time, before the current era, when the gods still involved themselves
in human affairs.[211] And then, during a rupture in this epistemological framework,[212] Plato suddenly declared that Homeric verse must not be admitted into
the city because it leads astray (Plat. *Rep.* 2.378^d) and Aristophanes forbade any
discussion of the "inventions of the ancients" when banqueting among friends.[213]
Aristotle and Thucydides, too, each in their own way, set out to rationalize
the Greek myths handed down to them, stripping Theseus, for example, of his
Minotaur-slaying feats and other fabulous acts so as to revise how Theseus's reign
in Athens' more ancient past was to be understood (Aristot. *Ath. Pol.* 41.2; Thuc.
2.15). What Veyne discerns among this collection of Greek thinkers, accordingly,
is a more critical attitude that suddenly arose toward their culture's traditional
myths, less susceptible to believing in the fantastic and less confident in the
truths contained within them. Homer, Strabo remarks in a striking passage indicative of this outlook, may have been familiar with the history of Pelias, but he
was quite ignorant (ἀνήκοος) of all that befell Jason once the Argo reached the

209. Veyne, *Did the Greeks*, 117–30.

210. "Far from being the most simple realistic experience," Veyne writes, "truth is the most
historical." Veyne, *Did the Greeks*, xi.

211. Ibid., 17–18.

212. Veyne's notion of an epistemological "rupture" is inherited from M. Foucault who, in
turn, was influenced by the work of his teacher, G. Bachelard, on this topic. See, for example,
G. Bachelard, *La formation de l'esprit scientifique: contribution à une psychanalyse de la connaissance objective* (Paris: J. Vrin, 2004), 15–27.

213. Veyne, *Did the Greeks*, 28, 61.

ocean (Strab. 1.2.38). "It was no longer possible," Veyne thus observes of this new era, "to believe in the supernatural in the old way."[214]

Yet what is of equal interest to Veyne is how this stance toward Greek myth experiences a rupture once more with the rise of the modern period. Now, suddenly, Aristotle and Thucydides's confidence in the reality of a Theseus, in spite of the mythical stories surrounding him, appeared naïve and even childish to those eighteenth century CE historians who sought the origins of Athenian society.[215] Cicero could ridicule those who believed Romulus was a semi-divine being birthed by a vestal virgin, but he did not doubt Romulus's existence, nor would any European thinker, for that matter, until the modern era and the rise of a form of historicism that abided by new epistemological assumptions with regard to the history of these legendary founding figures. What is deemed true knowledge of the past is never static, Veyne argues, but is instead contingent on a shared set of beliefs that establish the parameters by which this knowledge is organized and accepted as true. Or, as Veyne puts it in his provocative manner, "for what conforms to the program of truth in one society will be perceived as imposture or elucubration in another. A forger is a man working in the wrong century."[216]

Veyne's indebtedness to M. Foucault on these points is made explicit at the outset.[217] What we find in Veyne's project, in other words, is in some sense a working out of Foucault's notion of the episteme, applied, in this study, to how ancient Greeks thought about the past and the different "programs of truth" astir within different moments in Greek antiquity.[218] Foucault's own investigation into these issues was directed at a myriad of developments and disciplines, perhaps most famously in his study of what distinguished the conditions of modern thought that arose in the nineteenth century CE from the Classical and Renaissance periods that had come before. Foucault writes of his method:[219]

> ... such an analysis does not belong to the history of ideas or of science: it is rather an inquiry whose aim is to rediscover on what basis knowledge

---

214. Ibid., 46.

215. Veyne traces this moment to the essay by Bernard de Fontenelle, "De l'origine des fables" [1724], in which the idea is put forward that Greek myth may be complete fabrication. Ibid., 13–14, 133 fn. 23.

216. Ibid., 105.

217. Ibid., xii.

218. Within the sphere of biblical studies, Kawashima also draws on Foucault's notion of the episteme, but here directed to what Kawashima argues is the novelty of biblical religion in its ancient Near Eastern context. Kawashima, *Biblical Narrative*, 190–214.

219. Foucault, *Order of Things*, xxiii–xxiv.

and theory became possible; within what space of order knowledge was constituted; on the basis of what historical *a priori*, and in the element of what positivity, ideas could appear, sciences be established, experience be reflected in philosophies, rationalities be formed, only, perhaps, to dissolve and vanish soon afterwards.

Thus:

> ... what I am attempting to bring to light is the epistemological field, the *episteme* in which knowledge, envisaged apart from all criteria having reference to its rational value or to its objective forms, grounds its positivity and thereby manifests a history which is not that of its growing perfection, but rather that of its conditions of possibility.

What is revealed throughout Foucault's magisterial volume steeped in this "archaeology" of knowledge are those shared epistemological preconceptions, spread across an impressive array of thinkers and disciplines and geographies within Europe, that shaped, implicitly and most often unaware, how scientific study was undertaken and objects analyzed. Unbeknownst to those behind their creation, a guiding thread—a shared epistemological field in Foucault's parlance—bound together, to cite one example among many, the novel idea of labor within Smith's economic theory, the disintegration of Linneaus's classification system among biologists, and the loss among philologists of a belief in an original, primordial language once spoken by every early human, all of which, remarkably, take hold and are expounded upon in these very different disciplines during a brief period around the turn of the nineteenth century.[220]

Crucial about Foucault's work for both Veyne and for our study here is the idea of the historical *a priori* or "episteme," or the theory that a network of unconscious motivations, sensibilities, inferences, and values organize and enable the generation of knowledge (what Foucault terms its "positivities") within a particular culture at particular moments in time.[221] Knowledge itself is historically

---

220. "What came into being with Adam Smith, with the first philologists, with Jussieu, Vicq d'Azyr, or Lamarck," Foucault contends, "is a minuscule but absolutely essential displacement, which toppled the whole of Western thought: representation has lost the power to provide a foundation—with its own being, its own deployment and its power of doubling over on itself—for the links that can join its various elements together." Ibid., 259.

221. For studies of Foucault's epistemological theory, see D. Carroll, "The Subject of Archaeology or the Sovereignty of the Episteme," *Modern Language Notes* 93 (1978): 695–722; G. Gutting, *Michel Foucault's Archaeology of Scientific Reason* (Cambridge: Cambridge University Press, 1989), 139–260; T. Flynn, "Foucault's Mapping of History," in *A Cambridge*

contingent, Foucault's work argues, whether in the spheres of economics or natural history or, for our purposes, knowledge about the past, and when historicizing these epistemological frameworks one finds both lengthy spans of continuity in thought across centuries in time and momentary ruptures that invite new ways of viewing the world.[222] Z. Schiffman, whose historical analysis complements Foucault's insights so well, can thus detail the disparate conceptions of the past that motivated thinkers from Herodotus forward into the nineteenth century CE, demonstrating that "'the past' has a history, and not until it came into being could we have ideas about it, ideas that have gradually transformed it into an intellectual given."[223] For Foucault, the task then is to historicize forms of knowledge in this fashion so as to illustrate how older epistemes in previous epochs are framed and perpetuated before they give way to the crystallization of new epistemic outlooks. Much like Velasquez, therefore, who opens *The Order of Things* by stepping back from his canvas for a wider view of the portrait he is rendering, it is the historian, removed from the epistemological *a priori* of former eras, who has the distance necessary to see the lines and boundaries that once determined how specific modes of knowledge were realized in previous cultures.[224]

Veyne's mining of the epistemological foundations that supported belief in Greek myth offers an illustration of how historical research into an ancient episteme, more modest in its aims and more concentrated in its scope, might be applied to a particular culture in antiquity. The path paved by this work, then, is one where a similar set of questions can be pursued toward those prose stories developed by ancient Hebrew scribes, informed, as these biblical narratives are, by epistemological inferences and values as distinct and specific as the writings developed by their Greek counterparts. The task, then, is to inquire into the conditions by which past knowledge was made available to Hebrew scribes about the early Iron Age period.

Part of this historical work has already been undertaken. That is, in retracing the emergence of Hebrew prose tradition it has been shown that stories of an early Iron Age past would have been based on information conveyed principally through the spoken word. Consequently, we can posit that the epistemic values that informed the creation of these prose works were those shaped in response

---

Companion to Foucault (ed. G. Gutting; Cambridge: Cambridge University Press, 1994), 28–46; L. Alcoff, "Foucault's Normative Epistemology," in *A Companion to Foucault* (eds. C. Falzon et al.; New York: Wiley, 2013), 207–25.

222. Foucault, *Order of Things*, 55–56.

223. Schiffman, *Birth of the Past*, 277.

224. Foucault, *Order of Things*, 3–18.

to a predominantly oral culture that accessed and reflected on a common past by way of storytelling set in an oral mode, where traditional oral accounts were prized and presumed to offer significant cultural knowledge of former times. Information about a past gleaned from these oral traditions was certainly not static or homogeneous, and the effort made to address the constituting epistemic frameworks that supported their referential claims is not meant to suggest otherwise. Such source material was no doubt quite variable and multivalent, consisting of heroic tales, proverbs, family sagas, battle reports, riddles, and anecdotes, among other instances,[225] and originating from disparate geographical regions and kinship groups in the southern Levant with different, and at times, competing, interests in mind.

But in an era before the rise of Hebrew prose there is something unifying to the source material that descended from this era, epistemologically speaking, and that is the work of memory that circumscribed and sustained it. Derived from sources often steeped in oral traditions that had been passed on for generations, the biblical stories developed about an early Iron Age past would have been made possible through the capacity of these stories to be remembered, voiced aloud, and remembered once more. Information about former times was maintained, in short, in the memories of others. And what this means is that the exercise of memory and the knowledge elicited through it brings us closest to that epistemological "basis" or "field"—Foucault's episteme[226]—that enabled information about a past to be generated and passed down to later Hebrew scribes. The conditions of knowing a past, and its impediments, were deeply connected with the possibilities and limits of remembering.

Elsewhere I have attempted to articulate certain features of the "memory work" that would have contributed toward the narratives written out by Hebrew scribes in order to demarcate this mode of retrospection, at least in terms of its constituting epistemic values, from instances of historical research developed in the modern era.[227] Here it is worth accenting once more that what is understood by memory within this investigation is the "object-oriented character" of the effort to remember, that is, an understanding of memory as an intentional act separate from

---

225. Vansina, *Oral Tradition*, 13–26.

226. Foucault, *Order of Things*, xxiii.

227. Pioske, *David's Jerusalem*, 30–42, 263–65. For a further study of this theme, see idem, "Retracing a Remembered Past: Methodological Remarks on Memory, History, and the Hebrew Bible," *Bib Int* 23.3 (2015): 291–315; for another theoretically informed treatment of memory with regard to the formation of biblical narrative, see especially I. Wilson, *Kingship and Memory in Ancient Judah* (New York: Oxford, 2017), 23–40.

habitual or involuntary forms of recall that endeavors to return to or recover "what had earlier been seen, experienced, or learned."[228] This form of memory, then, is one exercised in the effort to "remember something,"[229] with that "something" consisting of events prior to the moment of recollection. Ricoeur comments:[230]

> the "thing" remembered is plainly identified with a singular, unrepeatable event, for example a given reading of a memorized text. Is this always the case? To be sure, as we shall say in conclusion, the memory-event is in a way paradigmatic, to the extent that it is the phenomenal equivalent of a physical event. The event is simply what happens. It takes place. It passes and occurs. It happens, it comes about. . . . On the phenomenological level, on which we have situated ourselves here, we say that we remember what we have done, experienced, or learned in a particular instance. . . .

Importantly, what is remembered through this act of recollection is not the antecedent event itself, captured precisely and rendered according to what once actually transpired during a particular past moment in time. The fragility of human memory, its vulnerability to manipulation and distortion and, above all, to forgetting, is well known.[231] As will be emphasized throughout this study, a remembered past is an impression of something that happened before, a form of representation that, as an impression, makes no claims of replication.[232]

But as a representation there is a dynamics to what is recalled through the work of memory, a dynamics that is fundamentally shaped by the cultural practices that contribute toward that which is remembered and recollected. It is a

---

228. Ricoeur, *Memory, History, Forgetting*, 22, 27. Within cognitive studies of memory, this would be construed as "declarative" or "episodic" memory. Cf. H. Eichenbaum, *The Cognitive Neuroscience of Memory: An Introduction* (2nd ed.; Oxford: Oxford University Press, 2012), 79–192; K. Michaelian, *Mental Time Travel: Episodic Memory and our Knowledge of a Personal Past* (Cambridge: MIT Press, 2016), 1–56.

229. Ricoeur, *Memory, History, Forgetting*, 22.

230. Ibid., 23.

231. On this point, see especially Ricoeur's observations in "The Exercise of Memory: Uses and Abuses," and "The Forgetting of Recollection: Uses and Abuses," in *Memory, History, Forgetting*, 56–92, 443–56.

232. So already Aristotle: "If there is in us something like an impression [τυπός] or mark [γραφή], why should the perception of this be memory of something else, but not of this itself? For when one exercises his memory this representation [πάθος] is what he considers and perceives." Aristotle, "On Memory and Recollection," 450[b]. For the great modern treatment of this idea, see the chapter entitled "On the Survival of Images" in H. Bergson, *Matter and Memory* (trans. N. Paul; New York: Zone, 1991 [1896]), 133–78.

dynamics, in short, rooted in memory's social character. Of course, memory is a product of individual consciousness and does not exist apart from it. But the great insight of M. Halbwachs at the beginning of the twentieth century was that the formation of individual memory occurs through the experience of particular social frameworks (*cadres sociaux*) that help to constitute and elicit these recollections, from early experiences in the family home to wanderings in public squares and to the encounters with the different groups and symbols that one happens upon within these social settings.[233] One's memories are supported—in Halbwachs's strong thesis, even enabled—through remembering with others.[234]

What this also signified for Halbwachs is that an individual's memories are something that extend beyond one's own past experiences to other memories attributed to an individual by other social groups of which they are part.[235] Our parents' memories, our grandparents' memories, the memories passed down through the generations, become our memories by virtue of being raised within a particular community and reared among the past stories recalled within it.[236] The circle then extends out further still to other, more distant communities within one's homeland and to other past moments in time, where specific cultural modes of remembrance—public storytelling, rituals, the shared experience of sacred sites, participation in commemorative ceremonies, the encounter with venerable images and landscapes[237]—serve to transmit and reinforce a past deemed significant by the larger society in which a particular individual is enmeshed.[238]

---

233. M. Halbwachs, *Les cadres sociaux de la mémoire* (2nd ed.; Paris: Presses Universitaires de France, 1952), esp. 146–77; idem, *La mémoire collective* (2nd ed.; Paris: Presses Universitaires de France, 1968), 1–17.

234. "Nous dirions volontiers que chaque mémoire individuelle est un point de vue sur la mémoire collective, que ce point de vue change suivant la place que j'y occupe, et que cette place elle-même change suivant les relations que j'entretiens avec d'autres milieux." Halbwachs, *La Mémoire Collective*, 33.

235. On the importance of the concept of "attribution" with regard to the formation of one's own memories, see especially Ricoeur, *Memory, History, Forgetting*, 93–132.

236. Halbwachs, *La mémoire collective*, 50–57.

237. J. Assmann, "Communicative and Cultural Memory," in *Cultural Memory Studies: An International and Interdisciplinary Handbook* (eds. A. Erll and A. Nünning; Berlin, New York 2008), 109–18; idem, *Religion and Cultural Memory: Ten Studies* (trans. R. Livingstone; Stanford: Stanford University Press, 2011), 1–31; A. Erll and A. Rigney, "Introduction: Cultural Memory and its Dynamics," in *Mediation, Remediation, and the Dynamics of Cultural Memory* (Berlin: De Gruyter, 2009), 1–14; from a cognitive perspective, see P. Boyer, "Cognitive Predispositions and Cultural Transmission," in *Memory in Mind and Culture* (eds. P. Boyer and J. Wertsch; Cambridge: Cambridge University Press, 2009), 288–320.

238. For a cognitive perspective on collective memory formation, see A. Coman et al., "Mnemonic convergence in social networks: The emergent properties of cognition at a collective level," *PNAS* 113.29 (2016): 8171–76.

Fundamental to the attribution of memories to an individual and their transmission over time, as Halbwachs already recognized, was the voice that communicated them.[239] The link between memory and orality is well-established.[240] From modern ethnographic studies to those directed toward societies in antiquity, one of the central tenets of investigations into oral tradition is that the stories told through it are those produced through the interaction between the storyteller and a reserve of cultural memories handed down to him or her.[241] At their core, D. Rubin comments in his study of the cognitive features of this oral/memory interface, "[o]ral traditions depend on human memory for their preservation," for "if a tradition is to survive, it must be stored in one person's memory and be passed to another person who is also capable of storing and retelling it."[242] The knowledge generated and transmitted through oral tradition can be understood therefore, as J. Vansina's influential study of orality emphasizes, as "information remembered."[243] The suspicion expressed toward the written word within Plato's *Phaedrus*, penned in a predominantly oral culture transitioning to greater text-dependence, gives teeth to precisely this theorized connection between memory and orality within such contexts: "Their trust in writing produced by external characters which are no part of themselves," Socrates's myth recounts "will discourage the use of their own memory within them" (Plat. *Phaed.* 275ᵃ).

Yet how, more precisely, memory conditions and supports the oral traditions recalled by the storyteller is of central importance. With regard to the Iron Age communities of the southern Levant, we have no access to the specific instances of orality that would have conveyed cultural memories over time since these

---

239. Halbwachs, *La mémoire collective*, 51.

240. See, for example, Ong, *Orality*, 56–69, 137–52; J. Goody, *The Interface Between the Written and the Oral* (Cambridge: Cambridge University Press, 1987), 86–109, 167–90; M. Innes, "Orality, Memory, and Literacy in Early Medieval Society," *Past & Present* 158 (1998): 3–36; D. Rubin, *Memory in Oral Traditions: A Cognitive Psychology of Epics, Ballads, and Counting-Out Rhymes* (New York: Oxford University Press, 1995); E. Casey, *Remembering: A Phenomenological Study* (2nd ed.; Bloomington: Indiana University Press, 2000), 119–21; Ricoeur, *Memory, History, Forgetting*, 162–81; Assmann, *Religion and Cultural Memory*, 101–21; Saussy, *Ethnography of Rhythm*, 63–85.

241. R. Finnegan, *Oral Traditions and the Verbal Arts: A Guide to Research Practices* (London: Routledge, 1992), 106–15; Rubin, *Memory in Oral Traditions*, 6–13; E. Minchin, *Homer and the Resources of Memory: Some Applications of Cognitive Theory to the Iliad and Odyssey* (Oxford: Oxford University Press, 2001), 1–31; J. Foley, "Memory in Oral Tradition," in *Performing the Gospel: Orality, Memory, and Mark* (eds. R. Horsely et al.; Minneapolis: Fortress, 2011), 83–96.

242. Rubin, *Memory*, 9–10.

243. So the theme pursued in Vansina, *Oral Tradition*, 148–85.

oral cultures have long since disappeared. But when turning to comparative evidence there is a strong sense that ancient Hebrew storytellers seldom produced such stories from the types of rote memorization often given prestige in societies accustomed to the memorization of written texts.[244] To be sure, the structure, themes, imagery, and key plotlines must be retained by a bard if the story performed is to be recognized and received by its audience. "What is known about the past," B. Schwartz comments with regard to the social arena in which these tales are presented, "limits what can be done with it interpretively."[245]

But in contrast to more succinct pieces of nonnarrative verse or proverbial material, comparative research indicates that those responsible for reciting lengthier oral narratives do not aim for word-for-word recollection. Rather, the stories told are more often the result of "a combination of composition and commemoration, of creation and memory,"[246] where "variability within limits" is the norm for what is recounted since such variability actually supports the cognitive process of remembering by releasing the storyteller from strict verbatim recall.[247] "The content of memory" for performers of oral tradition, H. Saussy observes, "is not a 'what' but a 'how,'" where the specific story recounted is actualized from a reserve of other possible iterations in view of host of strategic considerations having to do with audience, setting, and other social circumstances surrounding a specific performance.[248] What is recollected by a storyteller steeped in oral narrative traditions, accordingly, is not an account in which every word is recalled precisely from its previous performances, but rather the "recipe or strategy" of a story,[249] that is, the essential themes and characters and plotlines that are drawn on by the oral performer in order to make a story what it is upon every new hearing.

The fluidity of oral tradition steeped in memory reminds us that the knowledge retained and brought forth through it is something distinct from a past

---

244. Goody, *Interface*, 86–91; idem, "Memory in Oral Tradition," in *Memory* (eds. P. Fara and K. Patterson; Cambridge: Cambridge University Press, 1998), 76; Finnegan, *Oral Tradition and the Verbal Arts*, 108–109; Rubin, *Memory*, 6–7; Saussy, *Ethnography of Rhythm*, 70–73.

245. B. Schwartz, "Culture and Collective Memory: Comparative Perspectives," in *The Handbook of Cultural Sociology* (eds. J. Hall et al.; London: Routledge), 622.

246. This point was already made in A. Lord's *Singer of Tales* [Lord, *Singer of Tales* (Cambridge: Harvard University Press, 1960), 101–23], but has been reinforced through more recent ethnographic study. See, for example, Goody, *Interface*, 81.

247. Rubin, *Memory*, 6–7, 167–70.

248. Saussy, *Ethnography of Rhythm*, 70.

249. Ibid., 72.

preserved in narrative prose writing, calcified, as written prose becomes, within the materiality of documents that can be stored and passed on. And while the variability of oral tradition—what Saussy terms its "iterability"[250]—could appear as an epistemological deficiency from a modern, highly literate standpoint, to those located in predominantly oral cultures the restrictive, limiting features of the written word with regard to what could be remembered about a past—in which the scribe documents only one version of past over against the many others that could be recollected and voiced, with all their distinct emphases and details—is something that oral bards "would surely find distressing."[251] Nevertheless, with a writer such as Thucydides we find a particular shift in the assessment of oral tradition, in which the stories recalled within it did not afford the stability and accuracy Thucydides deemed necessary to recount great moments from the past. Whatever the motivations involved in the rise of Hebrew prose, the decision made to textualize a past by Hebrew scribes and not solely speak it would have therefore also marked a cultural shift in how past knowledge was stored and transmitted among the societies in which the biblical scribes were active.

But before this shift in mnemonic technique along the oral-written continuum, the predominantly oral source material available to the biblical scribes about an early Iron Age past would have been conditioned by different epistemic precepts, certain echoes and allusions to which are still embedded in the biblical writings. In addition, for example, to the variable, fluid character of the information communicated through oral stories derived from cultural memory, we can also surmise, on the basis of Halbwachs's work and those that have followed, that the knowledge imparted through these sources would have been marked by its collective character. Indirect evidence for this observation is attested to within the biblical narrative itself. A striking feature of the biblical language of retrospection, for example, is its collective quality. In some instances, the memories recalled are those of collective experiences from previous times: "Moses said to the people, 'Remember this day on which you came out of Egypt, out of the house of slavery'" (Exod. 13:3); "Remember the word that Moses the servant of the LORD commanded you. . . ." (Josh. 1:13); "I will utter enigmas from of old, things that we have heard and known, that our fathers have told us. . . ." (Ps. 78:2,9). But this language of memory also pertains to other spheres of social life,

---

250. Saussy defines a tradition's iterability as being "not a final result but only one exemplar in a series of recitations, and to be preserved it must be recomposed again and again, modularly, by members of the collective." Ibid., 72.

251. Ibid., 71.

such as rituals and festival ("Remember the Sabbath day and keep it holy" [Exod. 20:8]; "This day will be to you as one of remembrance; you shall celebrate it as a festival to the Lord" [Exod. 12:14]) or the commemoration of specific events ("So these stones shall be to the Israelites a memorial forever" [Josh. 4:7]; "So that day Achish gave him Ziklag; therefore Ziklag has belonged to the kings of Judah to this day" [1 Sam. 27:6]). Significantly, what is seldom attested to within these narratives are memories recounted by solitary individuals about their own, personal circumstances. The memoir will have to await the later era of Nehemiah.

What runs throughout this discourse of remembrance, then, is that it is addressed to a community who is instructed to recall a past held in common, thus offering one lens into how a past was maintained and transmitted along the conduits of oral tradition once vibrant in the communities of the southern Levant. Such injunctions conform, in fact, to an essential feature of cultural memory, whereby a shared past is reconstituted through repeated moments of social interaction and storytelling.[252] "Although individuals alone possess the capacity to remember the past," Schwartz observes, "they never do so singly; they do so with and against others situated in different groups and through the knowledge and symbols that predecessors and contemporaries transmit to them."[253] The knowledge engendered through such memories is, in this sense, participatory and self-enclosed, a result of attribution by a group and its appropriation by the individual who is a constituent member, "where the shared experience of the world rests upon a community of time as well as space."[254]

The communal element highlighted here is evident in both the anonymity of the biblical storyteller and the use of the third person voice to narrate stories of former times. For what is resisted through this narrative technique is precisely the more individualistic, analytic mode of inquiry undertaken by ancient Greek historians.[255] Nowhere among the biblical stories of the early Iron Age period, in other words, do we come across the persona of the author foregrounded in the stories themselves, able, even eager, to declare independence from established traditions and previous modes of knowing. So in a statement that has no equivalent

---

252. On the importance of repetition of shared memories for their retrieval among larger social groups, see H. Roediger et al., "The Role of Repeated Retrieval in Shaping Collective Memory," in *Memory in Mind and Culture* (eds. P. Boyer and J. Wertsch; Cambridge: Cambridge University Press, 2009), 138–70.

253. Schwartz, "Where There's Smoke, There's Fire: Memory and History," in *Memory and Identity in Ancient Judaism and Early Christianity: A Conversation with Barry Schwartz* (ed. T. Thatcher; Atlanta: SBL, 2014), 9.

254. Ricoeur, *Memory, History, Forgetting*, 130.

255. Cf. Blum, "Historiography or Poetry?," 28–35.

among the narrative works of the Hebrew Bible, Herodotus announces: "I have no intent of coming to judgment on this or that account. *But I will rely on my own knowledge* concerning who it was who first undertook unjust acts against the Greeks" (Hdt. 1.5.3).[256]

Rather than a past disclosed through the first person singular, biblical narrative is marked instead by the anonymous third person voice that recounts but does not stand outside of the past memories recounted,[257] evincing little interest toward appraising, through individual analysis, the knowledge communicated through the stories told.[258] In this sense, the biblical scribes draw near to those nameless oral storytellers whose task was not to author a work but to communicate and perform versions of it, more curators and purveyors of a remembered past than the solitary investigator who inquires into these stories so as to critique or affirm them.[259] Again, we find nothing in biblical narrative akin to Thucydides's complaint that the Athenians of his time too readily accept past traditions "untested" (ἀβασάνιστος [Thuc. 1.20]).

The authority and authenticity of biblical storytelling is not predicated on lone analysis. Instead, its significance is determined by a community who assent to its claims, a point further underscored when, here and there, the biblical storyteller does break out of the third person voice and gestures toward a broader collective through the use of the first and second person plural, thus evoking an "us" and a "you."[260] Such a technique creates a past that envelops the present context in which a story is voiced, eliding any sense of temporal distance so that future generations may hear these narratives as their own. Thus Moses, in a scene that takes place in a distant past, declares to the audience of the story: "Not with our ancestors did the LORD make this covenant, *but with us, who are all of us here alive today*" (Deut. 5:3). The anonymity behind biblical storytelling is consequently something akin to commonality, where the past recalled could be recounted by "anyone" since the knowledge

---

256. As Machinist observes, the first intimations we have of this "analytic-I" is with the later work of Ecclesiastes. Machinist, "Voice of the Historian," 133–35.

257. Even in the case of Deuteronomy where the first person voice is used throughout, such usage is posed through the convention of public oration, i.e., in these instances Moses is delivering a prolonged speech that occurs in the present moment. The larger story of Moses giving this speech is however couched within third-person narration.

258. Machinist, "Voice of the Historian," 136–37.

259. Blum, "Historiography," 33.

260. On this, see Sanders's perceptive comments in, *Invention*, 104.

conveyed is always in some sense present, and is always held in common with others.[261]

The specific settings within which these cultural memories were once voiced in ancient Israel and Judah were no doubt quite varied. Gunkel's romanticized notion of fireside, familial storytelling events during the winter months in ancient Israel rests on little actual evidence, even if kinship units were likely important conduits for the transmission of older oral stories.[262] But more concrete glimpses of the contexts of this storytelling tradition are found in certain passages of the Hebrew Bible, especially in liturgical (Deut. 5:26, 6:7; Ps. 106) and ceremonial settings (Deut. 31:28; 1 Sam. 11:14–12:18; Pss. 89, 106). Miller, moreover, highlights the distinct media and practices alluded to within the biblical corpus with regard to the performance of oral tradition, including musical instruments and dance.[263] What is also of interest from this perspective are those moments in biblical narrative when an assembly is gathered together in order to hear stories told of a common past. A notable instance is the scene depicted in Nehemiah 8 when those in Yehud arrive in Jerusalem to hear Ezra read aloud words from the "Torah of Moses." But we also find intimations of this public, collective storytelling tradition in other narrative works. Joshua, to cite a notable instance, is depicted as gathering all the tribes of Israel to Shechem so that he can recount a speech dominated by references to Israel's past (Josh. 24:1–13); Samuel does much the same to those assembled at Gilgal (1 Sam. 12:6–16), as does Solomon in his address during the dedication of the temple in Jerusalem (1 Kings 8:15–21). Such allusions are valuable not because of their historicity, but due to what they reveal about the cultural assumptions at work with regard to how a past was narrated and made known within the societies in which the biblical scribes wrote. Stories recalled about a past by biblical figures are in fact often staged, communicated orally within the context of certain places (the oak tree at Shechem, the altar at Gilgal, the temple of Jerusalem) and reinforced through particular responses made among an audience (public declarations, renewal ceremony of kingship, rituals enacted in the temple liturgy).

Such allusions also suggest that this knowledge was localized and reinforced through the experience of a physical landscape. Perhaps the clearest ancient

---

261. So Blum observes that these stories carry with them the assumption that their intended audience already "identify and agree with the narrator's presentation." Blum, "Historiography," 33.

262. Gunkel, *Genesis*, xxvii. Cf. Dobbs-Allsopp, *On Biblical Poetry*, 237.

263. R. Miller, "The Performance of Oral Tradition in Ancient Israel," in *Contextualizing Israel's Sacred Writings: Ancient Literacy, Orality, and Literary Production* (ed. B. Schmidt; Atlanta: SBL, 2015), 186–90.

example of the local character of oral tradition from antiquity is again found within Pausanias's account of his travels abroad where oral tales, sustained for many generations,[264] are cited throughout the *Periegesis* in order to render a more detailed portrait of the Greek mainland before it fell under Roman imperial control. We do not have evidence that the biblical scribes traveled and questioned in this manner, but what is apparent is that the stories told about the early Iron Age are ones specific to particular places: Gideon's encampment by the "Spring of Harod" (Judg. 7:1), Abimelech's coronation at the "oak which stood at Shechem" (Judg. 9:6), the placement of the ark in Kiriath-jearim at "the house of Abinadab on the hill" (1 Sam. 7:1), or David's flight to the "cave of Adullam" (1 Sam. 22:1) are but a few examples of a much wider phenomenon in which past stories are frequently associated with very specific terrain. The list of David's warriors (2 Sam. 23:8–39), with its numerous anecdotes and origins surrounding these fighters, are striking for the very reason that so many of these locations are never heard of again within the biblical corpus ("Hiddai from the Wadis of Gaash," "Shamah the Mountain Man"), suggesting that they were derived from somewhat more antiquated oral accounts that had nevertheless survived, and survived, at least in part, because of the landscape in which the memories behind these stories were connected.

The tangible features of the memories recalled is therefore evident in these examples, where particular landscapes or structures or objects form essential components of what is recounted within these stories. Again, such instances conform to what is expected of oral traditions rooted in memory since, as many studies have emphasized, we remember better when locating our memories in physical settings.[265] In a world of few written texts that would have aided the effort of recollection, moreover, the importance of the material means by which recall was supported would have been only more acute. With no images to turn to and written after the eyewitnesses to early Iron Age events had disappeared, it is likely that Hebrew scribes often drew on source material related to the landscapes and older material remains that surrounded them. (See Figure 1.5.)

---

264. Pretzler, in the epigram to her study, lifts up Pausanias's declaration that "What I am about to say has never been written down before, but is generally believed among the Athenians" (*Paus.* 1.23.2) [Pretzler, "Pausanias and Oral Tradition," 235].

265. So the groundbreaking work by F. Yates, *The Art of Memory* (London: Routledge, 1966). See also M. Halbwachs, *La Topographie légendaire des Évangiles en Terre sainte* (2nd ed.; Paris: Presses Universitaires de France, 2008), 117–57; E. Casey, *Remembering: A Phenomenological Study*, 181–215; Rubin, *Memory*, 57–59; C. Holtorf and H. Williams, "Landscapes and Memories," in *The Cambridge Companion to Historical Archaeology* (ed. D. Hicks; Cambridge: Cambridge University Press, 2006), 235–54.

FIGURE 1.5 Ruins of Iron Age Pillared Home from Megiddo, Looking East (Picture: Author).

The past knowledge sustained through oral storytelling in ancient Israel and Judah was also performative, as witnessed already within the allusions both to instruments and the ceremonial and ritual settings cited above.[266] Indeed, a hallmark of a past communicated through oral tradition is its performative character,[267] or the manner in which information is activated and enacted through the face-to-face, embodied exchange between one individual and another.[268] Foley accents the "kinetic, emergent, creative activity" that shapes how a past is recollected by oral storytellers, where access to a collection of past knowledge is made available not simply through speaking and hearing, but through the visceral experience of a story's performance.[269] What this

266. Miller, *Oral Tradition*, 98–113; idem, "Performance of Oral Tradition, 183–90.

267. Goody, *Interface*, xi–xii; 266–69; Foley, "Memory in Oral Tradition," 86–92; Rubin, *Memory*, 65–70; Saussy, *Ethnography of Rhythm*, 69–72.

268. E. Bakker, "Activation and Preservation: The Interdependence of Text and Performance in an Oral Tradition," *Oral Tradition* 8.1 (1993): 5–20; K. O'Brien O'Keeffe, "The Performative Body on the Oral-Literate Continuum: Old English Poetry," in *Teaching Oral Traditions* (ed. J. Foley; New York: MLA, 1998), 46–58.

269. Foley, "Memory," 84–92.

emphasis on performance also signifies is that the knowledge communicated through it is one which has an audience in view, both as recipients of these stories but also as participants in the storytelling process whose responses and feedback shape how the story takes form. In ancient Egypt, for example, evidence attests to the interaction between a storyteller and a royal audience whose assessment of the performer's story—through praise or jeers—molded its rendition.[270] The knowledge elicited through such storytelling is in this sense dialogical. Rubin points out that a story is remembered better during oral performance when an audience actively takes part in its production, making the story "theirs" inasmuch as it belongs to the one performing it.[271] The aim of recounting past stories for others, accordingly, is to make them memorable, and to do so the storyteller engages the audience through a host of verbal and non-verbal techniques, anchored within a particular place and time, that is made possible through a performance connected to the body, the voice, and the ear.

Lastly, for our purposes here it is important to underscore that the knowledge retained in memory and conveyed through the voice was most likely cumulative in nature. What is recalled through such performances, in other words, is not knowledge that has been produced through a form of inquiry that seeks to test past information, distill what is accurate, and retrieve what is true through the winnowing acts of critique. We do not find biblical scribes interviewing informants and comparing their testimonies so as to recover the more accurate deposition. Instead, virtually the opposite impulse appears present in these accounts, where biblical scribes tend to aggregate multiple versions of the same story into their narratives, thereby creating the oft-analyzed phenomenon of "doublets."[272] These doublets appear in a variety of texts: Saul is anointed king in Samuel's hometown (1 Sam. 10:1), for example, only to be made king once more in Mizpah (1 Sam. 10:24); Goliath is slain by David (1 Sam. 17:50) and then later by Elhanan (2 Sam. 21:19); tormented by an evil spirit, Saul attempts to impale David with his spear against a wall (1 Sam. 18:10–11) and then does so again shortly after under nearly identical circumstances (1 Sam. 19:9–10). A plausible explanation

---

270. D. Redford, "Scribe and Speaker," in *Writing and Speech in Israelite and Ancient Near Eastern Prophecies* (eds. E. Ben Zvi and M. Floyd; Atlanta: SBL, 2000), 187–88.

271. Rubin, *Memory*, 66. Cf. J. Pennebaker and A. Gonzales, "Making History: Social and Psychological Processes Underlying Collective Memory," in *Memory in Mind and Culture* (eds. P. Boyer and J. Wertsch; Cambridge: Cambridge University Press, 2009), 171–93.

272. See, e.g., B. Halpern, *The Constitution of the Monarchy in Israel* (Chico: Scholars Press, 1981), 150–71; E. Tov, *Textual Criticism of the Hebrew Bible* (2nd ed.; Minneapolis: Fortress, 2001), 241–43; Carr, *Formation*, 102–25.

for at least some of these doublets is that different (oral) sources of similar events were available to Hebrew scribes who valued the accumulation and preservation of these memories over a story's coherence, a move that was perhaps influenced by assumptions wed to storytelling rooted in orality or one made so as to allow future performances of these stories to adapt one story over against the other for the bard's own particular telling.[273]

What is also of interest about biblical narrative from this perspective is that even when written works are said to exist that could help refine the claims made among the sources available, these written works are referred to in such a way as to have little meaning for the stories the biblical scribes actually want to tell: "Now the rest of the acts of Rehoboam and all that he did, are they not written in the Book of the Annals of the Kings of Judah?" (1 Kings 14:29); "Now the rest of the acts of Baasha, what he did, and his power, are they not written in the Book of the Annals of the Kings of Israel?" (1 Kings 16:5). Instead of consulting these texts explicitly in order to give support to the past they recount, what has value for these writers appears to be information located elsewhere, often likely accessed through an oral tradition that had been transmitted over time by word of mouth: "Remember the days of old, consider the years long past; ask your father, and he will inform you; your elders, and they will tell you" (Deut. 32:7).

This was generational, residual knowledge. That is, what appears to be passed on within these sayings is the accumulation of older experiences, updated and made present within each successive generation who sought to make these past stories their own. It is knowledge, in short, that accrues. But as older memories aggregate within a stream of oral tradition, they often, by necessity, adapt and cohere to "new social and symbolic structures" within a community so that this remembered past retains its meaning and significance for those listening to a past they never experienced themselves,[274] or what Schwartz terms mnemonic techniques of "keying" and "framing."[275] What is represented through such stories, then, is a form of knowledge akin to the work of bricolage, or accounts imbued with a constellation of referents revised and reworked into new narrative forms

---

273. Cf. Miller, *Oral Tradition*, 69–70.

274. So, for example, Leuchter draws attention to "conventional mores" of political leadership surrounding older memories of Saul in 1 Samuel 9–11 that, among later audiences, were remembered in order to rethink the role of the Davidic monarchy. M. Leuchter, "The Rhetoric of Convention: The Foundational Saul Narratives (1 Sam 9–11) Reconsidered," *Journal of Religious History* 40.1 (2016): 3–19.

275. Schwartz, "Where there's Smoke," 15–17.

over time, in which "an assemblage of old beliefs coexists with the new, including old beliefs about the past itself."[276]

The past knowledge conveyed by way of memory and through word of mouth in the ancient Levant was no doubt far more complex and variegated than what these observations intimate. We are privy, in the end, to only those vestiges of an ancient epistemological framework reflected at moments within the biblical text itself and from those considerations taken over from comparative and theoretical study. But the advantage of attending to these features and taking them seriously, as Veyne's study of Greek myth illustrates so well, is that doing so encourages historical sensitivity to modes of knowledge production quite distinct from our own modern configurations, configurations that, whether we are aware of it or not, have been fundamentally shaped by modern historicist commitments.[277]

Positively stated, what results from these considerations of an "episteme of memory" at work in the ancient world of the southern Levant are insights into certain conditions that enabled knowledge of a past to be available to those Hebrew scribes who eventually used this material to develop their written prose accounts. Teased out from this analysis is, perhaps most significantly, the overriding fluidity and adaptability of past information made possible through memory and mediated through word of mouth. Even if distinct from our expectations of a stable and (relatively) unchanging collection of knowledge preserved in writing, the suppleness of oral tradition and the possibility of multiform renditions was likely an advantage for oral bards who devised their stories for particular performances within specific settings. Also significant about these epistemic features of orality/memory, with these circumstances in view, is its collective and cumulative character, where a reserve of cultural memories, often accrued over a number of generations and from distinct regions and times, are aggregated and made available for future iterations depending on the public and context in which these performances were realized. Against the individualism of the historian, these stories were produced most often dialogically, catered to the response of others and embodied and anchored in space. The information transmitted through memory and oral tradition can therefore be expected to be participatory, keyed to an audience and not presented for solitary analysis.

Foregrounding such qualities lays the groundwork for the case studies that follow, wherein an effort is made to examine more precisely how these

---

276. B. Schwartz, *Abraham Lincoln and the Forge of National Memory* (Chicago: University of Chicago Press, 2000), 301–302.

277. Foucault, *The Order of Things*, 238. Cf. Ibid., 235–39, 400–406.

epistemological considerations may have factored into the stories the biblical scribes wrote down. The intent of the subsequent chapters, then, is an attempt to take seriously the sentiments of R. Miller who, in his recent study of oral tradition in ancient Israel, writes that the "[t]he next avenue of research that lies before us" is that of the "interface" between the study of orality and memory as these lines of investigation pertain to the biblical writings.[278] For our purposes here, this manner of research is directed at a collection of stories of an early Iron Age world developed, I argue, by scribes who drew on information often gleaned from precisely this interface.

In drawing attention to these epistemic concerns it is important to note, in conclusion, that such considerations are not foreign to biblical scholarship. W. Dever, to cite a more recent instance, devotes a book-length study to fundamental questions that touch on the realm of epistemology, as made apparent in this monograph's title: *What Did the Biblical Writers Know and When Did They Know It?*[279] The parallels between the questions asked by Dever and those historical interests that run throughout this work are clear. With Dever's study, however, the principal epistemological interest is the degree to which the biblical stories about ancient Israel and Judah evince historical knowledge commensurate with, or at least beneficial to, the work of modern historians who seek to reconstruct the political or social realities of the Iron Age period. Dever's answer to the questions he poses—"they [the biblical scribes] knew a *lot*, and they knew it early"[280]—is a response that seeks to defend the historical integrity of the biblical narrative against those who think otherwise, especially those led astray by what Dever deems "postmodern" proclivities that contribute, in the end, to what he believes is the "aesthetic and moral devaluation" of the biblical corpus.[281] Here, an interest in epistemology is marshaled for reasons of apologetics and polemics.

The focus of this study is considerably different. The aim in this chapter and those that follow is not to defend or, conversely, to disparage, the referential claims of the biblical writings by way of recourse to their relationship to modern forms of historical thought. Rather, the intent is to investigate how the epistemic conditions that surrounded the production of prose writing in the southern Levant influenced the stories told by the biblical scribes. The result of this approach is

---

278. Miller, "Performance of Oral Tradition," 190.

279. W. Dever, *What Did the Biblical Writers Know and When Did They Know It?* (Grand Rapids: Eerdmans, 2001).

280. Dever, *What Did the Biblical Writers Know*, 295 (italics original).

281. Ibid., 296. For Dever's understanding of what he terms postmodernism, see pp. 246–55.

thus to bracket, at least for the moment, the question as to what the knowledge conveyed through these texts may contribute to modern historical reconstructions of the ancient world. The reason for such bracketing lies in the conviction that historical reconstructions that seek to utilize the biblical writings are better served by first having a sense of how the past was conceived of by the societies in which the biblical scribes were active, including the frameworks by which past knowledge was made possible and the mechanisms for how this knowledge was communicated over time.

From this perspective, what motivates this study is a concern much more akin to that expressed by E. Blum, who, in an incisive essay, develops the argument that behind the prose storytelling of Hebrew Bible lies a "different rationality," distinct and disconnected from both the guiding assumptions of how ancient Greek historians composed their works and the presuppositions that inform modern historical studies carried out today.[282] And, as Blum himself observes, this concern with a "different rationality" once operative among the ancient biblical writers reaches back once again to the work of von Rad who, toward the end of his life, reconsidered his famous, earlier treatment of the "Beginnings of History Writing in Ancient Israel" from decades before and arrived at somewhat different conclusions with regard to the particularity—what von Rad termed Israel's "own intellectual *schema*"—of how the past was framed and understood within the stories the biblical scribes told.[283] Gone from these later studies is von Rad's confidence in the grand "historical sense" so apparent in the "reliable documents" of ancient Israel;[284] instead, von Rad now comments, "the fact that these two views of history [biblical and modern] *are so divergent* is one of the most serious burdens imposed today" on scholarship of the Hebrew Bible.[285] In light of

---

282. Blum, "Historiography," 28. Cf. the earlier version of this essay where Blum iterates the same point: "Ebenso möglich ist jedoch eine Selbstspiegelung der Beschreibungskategorien in den biblischen/traditionalen Darstellung geschichtlicher Wirklichkeit, die selbst einer anderen 'Rationalität' folgen." Idem, "Historiographie oder Dichtung? Zur Eigenart alttestamentlicher Geschichtsüberlieferung," in *Das Alte Testament—Ein Geschichtsbuch?* (eds. E. Blum, W. Johnstone, and C. Markschies; Munich: Lit, 2005), 67. This point is also advanced, from a different perspective, by M. Smith, *The Memoirs of God: History, Memory, and the Experience of the Divine in Ancient Israel* (Minneapolis: Fortress, 2004), 131–32.

283. G. von Rad, *Old Testament Theology*, Vol. 2 (trans. D. M. G. Stalker; Louisville: Westminster John Knox, 1965), 427. For the longer discussion of this theme, see pp. 410–29.

284. von Rad, "Beginnings of Historical Writing," 166–68.

285. G. von Rad, *Old Testament Theology*, vol. 1 (trans. D. M. G. Stalker; Louisville: Westminster John Knox, 1962), 108. (my italics). B. Childs, in his own study of memory, comes quite near to von Rad's analysis of the distinction between biblical and modern conceptions of the past with an argument that the modern tools of historical research pursue different questions than

this reorientation toward the character of that past represented in these biblical stories, the challenge von Rad posed to subsequent generations of scholarship was to better recognize and appreciate this biblical schema of past knowledge "in all its otherness."[286]

This chapter has developed with von Rad's challenge in mind, endeavoring to chart the rise of Hebrew prose in antiquity and to examine the epistemological underpinnings that would have supported the stories the biblical scribes told. What has resulted from this pursuit are insights, I contend, into what Foucault termed an *episteme,* or the *a priori* presuppositions and conditions by which particular forms of knowledge are made possible among a culture, which, for our purposes here, have been connected to forms of past knowledge operative in the southern Levant that arose through the capacity to remember and which were communicated principally through word of mouth. What remains to be addressed is how these historical and epistemological considerations surrounding memory, orality, and prose writing matter for how specific stories told in the Hebrew Bible about an early Iron Age past took form. It is to these studies that we turn next.

---

those asked within the Hebrew Bible. Yet Child's own conclusion with regard to this divergence [B. Childs, *Memory and Tradition in Ancient Israel* (London: SCM Press, 1962), 88]—"Again, we maintain that there are no avenues to the history of which the Bible speaks except Scripture's own testimony to these events"—lacks any sense of the acute intellectual problems this stance poses, including ones that von Rad so earnestly raises, with Childs' comments effectively shielding, for theological reasons, the narrative world of the Hebrew Bible from historical analysis. For such reasons, the following study moves in a different direction from that taken by Child's investigation and toward the critical issues exposed by von Rad.

286. G. von Rad, "Offene Fragen im Umkreis einer Theologie des Alten Testaments," in *Gesammelte Studien zum Alten Testament,* vol. 2 (München: C. Kaiser, 1973), 299. Cited in Blum, "Historiography," 40.

2

Gath of the Philistines

THE RESILIENCE OF A REMEMBERED PAST

. . . we can understand how we recapture the past only by understanding how it is, in effect, preserved by our physical surroundings.[1]

IN THE FINAL scene of the Standard Version of *The Epic of Gilgamesh* (Tablet XI), Gilgamesh and his companion, Ur-Shanabi, return to the city of Uruk where the epic first began. Standing together before the fortifications of the site, Gilgamesh's final words in the epic are a series of exhortations directed toward the ramparts of the location he had once built and the precincts the city wall now enclosed. What is curious about these final commands, however, is that they had already been voiced once before at the very opening to the epic in Tablet I:[2]

> Go up. . . on to the wall of Uruk and walk around,
> Survey the foundation platform, inspect the brickwork!
> (See)if its brickwork is not kiln-fired brick,
> and if the Seven Sages did not lay its foundation!
> One *sār* is city, one *sār* is date grove, one *sār* is clay-pit, half a *sār* the
> Temple of Ishtar, three *sār* and a half (is) Uruk, (its) measurement.
> (I:18–23//XI:323–328)

The repetition of these lines at the beginning and end of *Gilgamesh* accords them a particular significance for the epic as a whole, forming, as they do, an inclusio to the tale recounted within it. What results from this narrative device,

1. Maurice Halbwachs, *La Mémoire Collective* (2nd ed.; Paris: Presses Universitaires de France, 1968), 146.

2. Translation taken from A. George, *The Babylonian Gilgamesh Epic: Introduction, Critical Edition, and Cuneiform Texts*, vol. I (Oxford: Oxford University Press, 2003), 725.

consequently, is a sophisticated framing technique, with the images of Uruk's monumental, fixed fortifications enclosing the many scenes of Gilgamesh's exploits abroad. And through this form of recurrence the audience of the work is invited to walk the walls of Uruk both prior to and after Gilgamesh's long quest, thus leaving us to ponder the meaning of Gilgamesh's great achievement as his story unfolds and later concludes.

There is something at stake, then, in these repeated requests to carefully examine Uruk's walls for the significance of Gilgamesh's story as a whole. What these lines might mean nevertheless remains open to differing interpretations. The great Sumeriologist T. Jacobsen found in the prologue of Tablet I and final lines of Tablet XI—both additions written onto an earlier edition of the epic—an attempt to evade the unresolved and unsettling problem of death that marked previous iterations of the story.[3] Consequently, the return to the walls of Uruk at the end of the Standard Version of the epic was in Jacobsen's estimation a rather stale, uninspired scene in which the hero had accepted his mortality and moved on, no longer troubled by a death he could not outpace. The tragic sensibility of the original epic had been lost, according to Jacobsen, to a romantic vision of far-away adventure, secret knowledge, and the enduring fame guaranteed by Uruk's monumental stature.

Others however have seen in Gilgamesh's final directives a more heroic sense of resistance against his looming mortality. On this reading, the tactile reality of Uruk offered a protest against the finality of death that Gilgamesh was forced to confront as his journey came to an end.[4] The repeated injunction to walk the walls of Uruk at the end of the epic was not, from this perspective, a sober acceptance of death but a challenge to it—a recognition that in circuiting Uruk's fortifications its builder would become present again "and in a form more durable than were his once exquisite body and spectacular acts."[5] The behest to carefully consider Uruk's fortifications could thus be understood as an appeal to remember its architect in the generations to come, a final plea voiced by the hero so as to claim a particular form of immortality at the precise moment when it appeared that such a quest had failed.

3. T. Jacobsen, "The Gilgamesh Epic: Romantic and Tragic Visions," in *Lingering Over Words: Studies in Ancient Near Eastern Literature in Honor of William L. Moran* (ed. T. Abusch et al., Atlanta: Scholars Press, 1990), 247–49.

4. W. Moran, "Gilgamesh," in *The Encyclopedia of Religion* (ed. M. Eliade; New York: MacMillan, 1987), 559; Jeffrey Tigay, *The Evolution of the Gilgamesh Epic* (Philadelphia: University of Pennsylvania Press, 1982), 149.

5. K. Dickson, "The Walls of Uruk: Iconicities in *Gilgamesh*," *JANER* 9.1 (2009): 31.

If the meaning of Gilgamesh's bidding to probe Uruk's walls resists any one interpretive lens for what its commands signify, what is nevertheless agreed upon by nearly all of its readers is that an acute narrative juxtaposition exists between the story of the hero's failed attempt at deathlessness and the invitation to survey Uruk's vast rampart once again. Whether borne of defiance in the face of death or an acceptance of it, Gilgamesh's commands regarding Uruk draw the audience's attention toward a permanence that Gilgamesh himself is unable to attain. Uruk's walls will outlast its legendary builder.

And they have. Since the early twentieth century the Deutsche Orient-Gesellschaft has been excavating the ancient city of Uruk (modern Warka), steadily revealing secrets long buried near the ancient concourse of the Euphrates River in what is today southern Iraq. It is now known that around 2900 BCE (the Early Dynastic I Period) a massive mud brick wall, 10 km in circumference, was built around an enormous city nearly 500 hectares in size (ca. 1200 acres) and which housed a population that approached fifty thousand.[6] Though Uruk would decline in size and status over the subsequent centuries, the remains of its fortifications nevertheless endured, as they still do to this day. (See Figure 2.1.) Thus, when *Gilgamesh* was being read in the courts of Neo-Assyrian emperors two thousand years after Uruk's walls had been built,[7] the rulers who heard of Gilgamesh's ancient exploits could still travel to the southern reaches of their empire and experience the ruins of the rampart credited to Gilgamesh's building efforts millennia before.[8]

Recognized already in the Standard Version of *Gilgamesh*, then, is what the later history of Uruk and the archaeology of its environs would attest: namely, that places persist, and with them traces of past phenomena that have been etched into their landscapes over time. For this reason, it is perhaps not

---

6. R. Boehmer, "Uruk-Warka," *The Oxford Encyclopedia of Archaeology in the Near East*, vol. 5 (ed. Eric Meyers; New York: Oxford University Press, 1997), 294–97. Van de Mieroop underscores the immensity of Uruk at this time, noting that the city was double the size of Athens after its expansion by Themistocles in the early fifth century BCE and nearly half the size of Rome at its height under the emperor Hadrian. M. Van de Mieroop, *The Ancient Mesopotamian City* (Oxford: Oxford University Press, 1997), 37.

7. Four copies of the Standard Version of the epic, for example, were found in the ruins of Ashurbanipal's library at Nineveh. For discussion, see A. George, *The Epic of Gilgamesh: A New Translation* (New York: Penguin, 1999), xxiii–xxiv.

8. Sargon II, for example, travelled to Uruk at the end of the eighth century BCE and claimed to rebuild the Eanna Temple housed within the ruins of the city. See G. Frame, *Rulers of Babylonia: From the Second Dynasty of Isin to the End of Assyrian Domination (1157–612 BC)* (Toronto: University of Toronto Press, 1995), B.6.22.6. On this point, see also R. McAdams and H. Nissen, *The Uruk Countryside: The Natural Setting of Urban Societies* (Chicago: University of Chicago Press, 1973), 55–57.

FIGURE 2.1   Ancient Uruk with City Wall in Foreground © Trustees of the British Museum (Picture).

surprising that in the Prologue to *Gilgamesh* the act of building Uruk's walls is coupled with the act of inscribing Gilgamesh's story on a "tablet of stone" (I: 9–12). Both undertakings reflect one another in their distinct use of material means, whether in writing on stone tablets or erecting brick ramparts, to preserve the past actions of the one who performed them. The explicit link established in these lines between tablet and city thus suggests an awareness that places, too, can be engraved with markings that call to mind former times. And, like tablets of stone, these inscribed landscapes can endure.

The intent of this chapter is to explore the epistemological implications of this insight concerning the duration of place for the Hebrew scribes at the center of this study. In a world in which forms of past representation common to us were scarce—internet searches, photographs, film footage, illustrations, volumes of texts carefully stored away in libraries and archives—a premise that animates this chapter's discussion is that places provided one of the few opportunities by which ancient communities in the southern Levant could encounter tangible evidence of times previous to their own. Past stories recounted within these communities could be enfleshed and animated, accordingly, from the material remains located in the places in which their stories were said to have occurred.[9]

---

9. So Aristotle's observation: "For place does not perish when things in it cease to be." Aristotle, *Physics* IV.1 (208b 35–209a 2).

Increasingly, an interest in the materiality of places and the depth of time re-vealed through them has been taken up by theorists in their investigations into how memories of a past form and persist within a society.[10] One of the most prominent of these voices, E. Casey, goes so far as to suggest that there is something inherent to places themselves that enable past recollections in ways unavailable to other means of remembrance. "By its very immobility," Casey remarks, "through the stolid con-creteness of things set within pathways and horizons—place acts to contain time itself."[11] Consequently, "what is contained in place is on its way to being well remem-bered. What is remembered is well grounded if it is remembered as being in a partic-ular place...."[12] With such observations, Casey joins an impressive array of thinkers who find in the material features of locations a particular form of endurance that lends itself to remembering over time.[13]

But what memories do places elicit and what knowledge about the past do these memories contain? The answer is not straightforward. If the cultural memo-ries of a community can be sustained over time by connecting to and being evoked by the material remains of meaningful sites, such memories are also vulnerable, as M. Halbwachs observed,[14] to the transformations that places undergo—whether in the appearance of new built environments, the slow decay of landscapes, or the de-struction and reconstruction of civic spaces and structures. The processes that un-dergird the preservation and disintegration of places are seldom uniform, nor are the modes of remembering that accompany them.

---

10. For further discussion of this point, see D. Pioske, "Memory and its Materiality: The Case of Early Iron Age Jerusalem and Khirbet Qeiyafa," *ZAW* 127.1 (2015): 78–95; idem, *David's Jerusalem: Between Memory and History* (New York: Routledge, 2015), 1–9.

11. E. Casey, *Remembering: A Phenomenological Study* (2nd ed.; Bloomington, Ind.: Indiana University Press, 2000), 214.

12. Casey, *Remembering*, 214–15.

13. For a short sampling, see Halbwachs, *La Mémoire Collective*, 130–67; idem, *La Topographie légendaire des Évangiles en Terre sainte: Étude de Mémoire Collective* (2nd ed.; Paris: Presses Universitaires de France, 2008); Gaston Bachelard, *The Poetics of Space* (Boston: Beacon Press, 1994), 7–10; E. Casey, *The Fate of Place: A Philosophical History* (Berkeley: University of California Press, 1997), 197–342; P. Ricoeur, *Memory, History, Forgetting* (trans. K. Blamey and D. Pellauer; Chicago: University of Chicago Press, 2004), 25–44; J. Malpas, *Place and Experience: A Philosophical Topography* (Cambridge: Cambridge University Press, 2007), 175–93; A. Jones, *Memory and Material Culture* (Cambridge: Cambridge University Press, 2007), esp. 1–26; Y. Hamilakis and J. Labanyi, "Introduction: Time, Materiality, and the Work of Memory," *History & Memory* 20.2 (2008): 5–17; J. Winter, "Sites of Memory," in *Memory: Histories, Theories, Debates* (eds. S. Radstone and B. Schwartz; New York: Fordham University Press, 2010), 312–24. Dariusz Gafijczuk, "Dwelling Within: The Inhabited Ruins of History," *History and Theory* 52 (2013): 149–70.

14. M. Halbwachs, *On Collective Memory* (ed. L. Coser. Chicago: University of Chicago Press, 1992), 183.

Yet it is a distinct feature of places in the ancient Near East that some sites endured over great lengths of time. For this reason, the historian must be sensitive to the *possibility* that memories from former times endured alongside the places to which they referred, supported and reinforced by the landscape to which these memories had become embedded. For every Mount Zion, misidentified in antiquity through memories that had become detached from the actual locations sought,[15] there is also a Karbala[16] or Kosovo Field[17] where memories of a past and the historian's object of study more closely coincide. The purpose of this chapter's investigation, then, in a manner distinct from those that follow, is to draw out and examine those modes of remembering more resistant to the revisions that are so common to a community's remembered past, and to consider how such memories may have influenced the source material available to the biblical scribes responsible for writing stories about a time more distant from their own.

The object of this chapter's study is the Iron Age site of Philistine Gath. The decision to explore this particular location arises from two considerations. First, Gath is referred to frequently and at key moments in the biblical stories recounted about the early Iron Age period. Within these narratives Gath often plays a significant role in the events that unfold, whether in its position as Goliath's hometown (1 Sam. 17:4), the location to which David seeks refuge in his flight from Saul (1 Sam. 21:10; 1 Sam. 27:2), or as the origin of a contingent of David's fighters that would support him throughout his life, including in the events that surround Absalom's coup (2 Sam. 15:18). There are nearly double the biblical references to this Philistine site, in fact, than to other settlements identified within the so-called Philistine pentapolis (Gaza, Ashkelon, Ashdod, and Ekron), including a number of anecdotes that leave the audience of these stories unsure as to whether Gath functions as a friend or foe to the biblical characters involved.[18]

The second reason for turning our attention toward Gath is that it was destroyed at a relatively early date (late ninth century BCE) in the Iron Age by

---

15. There was some confusion as to the location of "Mount Zion" already during the Greco-Roman period. It seems that Josephus, for example, identified Mount Zion, erroneously, as being located on the Western Hill in writings that descend from the first century CE (so Josephus in *Wars* V.4.1 and *Ant.* VII: 62–66), and was followed in this identification by Christian pilgrims during the early Byzantine period (so Jerome, *Vita Pauli* xlvi: 5).

16. S. Hyder, *Reliving Karbala: Martyrdom in South Asian Memory* (Oxford: Oxford University Press, 2006), 3–60.

17. V. Inglmundarson, "The Politics of Memory and the Reconstruction of Albanian National Identity in Postwar Kosovo," *History and Memory* 19.1 (2007): 95–123.

18. For a discussion of this theme, see D. Pioske, "Material Culture and Making Visible: On the Portrayal of Philistine Gath in the Book of Samuel," (forthcoming).

Hazael of Damascus.[19] The date of this destruction finds importance for this investigation not only because of the significant archaeological evidence preserved from the site, but also because this timeframe predates the era in which Hebrew scribes were actively developing vernacular, narrative prose accounts about their community's past. For this reason, it is unlikely that the scribes who made reference to Gath within their stories would have had access to first-hand, eyewitness information about the famed Philistine city that came to be razed by Hazael's army. Consequently, Gath provides a meaningful case study for exploring the epistemological underpinnings of the source material used by later Hebrew scribes to form prose accounts of early Iron Age events and figures.

To presage the discussion that follows, the argument put forward in this chapter is that the biblical writers possessed knowledge about Gath that was reflective of the location's early Iron Age past. The implications of this observation are far-reaching for the study at hand. If substantiated, what such references to Gath indicate is that the biblical scribes had access to source material that preserved information from an era that likely preceded them in time by decades, if not centuries. To pursue this line of investigation, we turn first to an examination of the literary representations of Gath now enclosed within the Hebrew Bible and, after this overview, we explore the archaeological evidence recovered from the ancient location (Tell es-Safi). This study then transitions into an analysis of the relationship between these literary and material traces connected to Gath, in which particular points of semblance are found to emerge. Such points of convergence surrounding the ancient site, I conclude, are suggestive of a particular dynamic that undergirded the transmission of past knowledge in the ancient world of the southern Levant: namely, one of resilience, with references to former times persisting in the memories recollected about them.

Philistine Gath in the Hebrew Bible: The Textual Evidence

Depictions of the Philistine city of Gath are some of the most intriguing of those that pertain to foreign locations in the Hebrew Bible. Yet before turning to these accounts it is important to differentiate Philistine Gath from other non-Philistine locations that also bear this name in the biblical record. "Gath" (גת) itself is a common West Semitic term designating an agricultural installation used for the

---

19. A. Maeir, "The Tell es Safi/Gath Archaeological Project 1996–2010: Introduction, Overview, and Synopsis of Results," in *Tell es Safi/Gath I: The 1996—2005 Seasons, Part I: Texts* (ed. A. Maeir; Ägypten und Altes Testament 69; Wiesbaden: Harrassowitz Verlag, 2012), 25–49.

processing of produce,[20] likely in conjunction with the pressing of grapes or olives.[21] Because such installations would have been rather ubiquitous in the vineyards and fields of the southern Levant (e.g., Judg. 6:11), one finds –*gath* attached to a number of locations in the Bible, including Gath-Hepher (Josh. 19:13; 2 Kings 14:25), Gath-Rimmon (Josh. 19:45; 21:24–25; 1 Chron. 6:69), Moresheth-Gath (Mic. 1:1), and the dual form of the name, common to toponyms in the southern Levant, Gittaim (2 Sam. 4:3; Neh. 11:33).[22]

Philistine Gath was a location distinct from these other biblical sites. The first reference to this particular city in the Hebrew Bible occurs in Joshua 11 where one reads of a race of giants, called the *Anakim*, who were pushed out of the highlands by Joshua's forces and who are said to have found refuge in the Philistine settlements of Gaza, Gath, and Ashdod (Josh. 11:22). Since the *Anakim* were inhabitants of the Cisjordanian highlands according to various biblical traditions (Num. 13:22, Deut. 9:2, Josh. 11:21), this population would have been likely considered by the biblical writers as native Canaanites who were driven westward by the invading Israelites, and who subsequently found refuge among the Philistine cities located in the coastal plain.

The second appearance of Gath in the Book of Joshua occurs in Joshua 13, a text that describes the land left unconquered by the Israelites in their movement through the southern Levant. Verses 2–3 of this chapter state:

> This is the land that still remains: all the regions of the Philistines, and all those of the Geshurites (from the Shihor, which is east of Egypt, northward to the boundary of Ekron, it is reckoned as Canaanite; there are five rulers of the Philistines, those of Gaza, Ashdod, Ashkelon, Gath, and Ekron). . . .

From these verses descends the biblical image, to be given more substance in later writings, of a Philistine "pentapolis," or a political body comprised of five autonomous city states that acted in concert with one another in order to promote and defend the interests of an area of Canaan controlled by Philistine peoples.[23]

---

20. *HALOT*, 206.

21. Schniedewind argues, on the basis of Ugaritic and Akkadian evidence, that a נת referred to more than just a press, but rather "a fortified complex where agricultural products were brought for processing and storage." W. Schniedewind, "The Geopolitical History of Philistine Gath," *BASOR* 309 (1998): 71–72.

22. For Bronze Age references to various Gaths in the region, see A. Rainey, "Publish it Not as Gath," *IEJ* 54.1 (2004): 100–104.

23. P. Machinist, "Biblical Traditions: The Philistines and Israelite History," in *The Sea Peoples and Their World: A Reassessment* (ed. E. Oren; Philadelphia: University of Pennsylvania Press, 2000), 57–58.

What Gath is not, accordingly, is Israelite, either in terms of population or territory. Within these initial references to Gath what becomes apparent, then, is the foreign character of this location. Whether in its role as the haven for the *Anakim* or its inclusion alongside other Philistine cities unconquered by the Israelites, Gath is positioned beyond the periphery of the Israelite tribes, a site and population quintessentially "Other" from whom the biblical scribes consider their audience to be.[24] (See Figure 2.2.)

Themes of foreignness in the Book of Joshua become matters of outright hostility in the Book of Samuel. War erupts between Philistine and Israelite forces in the area between Aphek and Ebenezer in 1 Samuel 4, at which time the Israelites are defeated and the ark of Yahweh is carried to the Philistine center of Ashdod. Having brought destruction and disease to the location on its arrival, the leaders of the Philistines assemble and those of Gath agree to house the war palladium in their city (1 Sam. 5:8). There, too, a great panic breaks out when tumors are found on the young and old men of the site, and the ark is subsequently sent north to Ekron (1 Sam. 5:9–10) before being returned to the Israelites along with compensation for the five Philistine city states involved (1 Sam. 6:4, 17). In 1 Samuel 7, Philistine encroachments beyond the "border of Israel" (1 Sam. 7:13) are further abated by Samuel's efforts and Yahweh's intervention, with the towns and territory once seized by the Philistines now recovered by Israel "from Ekron to Gath" (1 Sam. 7:14). The reclamation of this area by Israelite forces suggests that previous to this episode the Philistines were understood to have extended their control eastward into the northern foothills (Shephelah) and neighboring highland regions, and thus had successfully infiltrated territory considered Israelite by the biblical writers.[25]

Disputes over territory between the Israelites and Philistines continue in the Book of Samuel. Within these conflicts the inhabitants of Gath often play a prominent role, perhaps because the location was positioned, alongside Ekron, as the most inland, eastward settlement of the Philistine city states, and thus abutted Israelite and Judahite holdings in the hill country.[26] Most famous of

---

24. Machinist, "Philistines," 67–69.

25. Y. Levin, "Philistine Gath in the Biblical Record," in *Tell es Safi/Gath I: The 1996—2005 Seasons, Part I: Texts* (ed. A. Maeir; Wiesbaden: Harrassowitz Verlag, 2012), 144.

26. For a discussion of this "border-land" region, see S. Bunimovitz and Z. Lederman, "The Archaeology of Border Communities: The Renewed Excavations at Beth Shemesh, Part I," *NEA* 72.3 (2009): 114–42; A. Faust, "From Regional Power to Peaceful Neighbor: Philistia in the Iron I-II Transition," *IEJ* 63.2 (2013): 174–204. On biblical storytelling that engaged this borderland region, see especially S. Weitzman, "The Samson Story as Border Fiction," *BibInt* 10.2 (2002): 158–74.

FIGURE 2.2 Map of Principal Philistine Cities Referred to in Hebrew Bible (Map: Author).

these skirmishes is that between David and Goliath of Gath (1 Sam. 17:4, 23), an immense warrior whose size evokes associations with the *Anakim* who had once found residence in Gath according to the Book of Joshua (Josh. 11). Again in this chapter animosity appears predicated on the control of land. Fought along the Elah Valley in the vicinity of Azekah and Socoh (1 Sam. 17:1–2), the combat the ensues between David and Goliath is presumably for jurisdiction over the strategic valley corridor that stretched below where goods and personnel flowed through the mountainous landscape. Once Goliath is killed and the Philistines routed, the latter are pursued "as far as Gath and the gates of Ekron" (1 Sam. 17:53) but, evidently, no further. In a manner that echoes 1 Samuel 7:14, the cities of Gath and Ekron once more form the boundary line that separates Israelite from Philistine lands, and no mention is made in the Book of Samuel of either Philistine sites being overtaken by Israelite forces.

It is Gath and the broader Philistine coalition, rather, who prove the aggressor in these early tales of conflict. Battles that take place at Ebenezer (1 Sam. 4), Mizpah (1 Sam. 7), Michmash (1 Sam. 13–14), Socoh and Azekah (1 Sam. 17), Keilah (1 Sam. 23.1–5), and Gilboa (1 Sam. 31) are conspicuous for their geographical pattern, with all activity being situated to the east of Gath in regions that will, in time, become home to the kingdoms of Israel and Judah. When highland groups are effective in resisting Philistine advances, the latter are pursued as far as "Gath and Ekron" but no further (1 Sam. 7:14; 17:52). Memories of the technological superiority of the Philistines (1 Sam. 13:19–22) are thus substantiated throughout these narratives in Samuel by memories of Philistine military superiority,[27] including the presence of Philistine garrisons in Geba (1 Sam. 13:3) and Bethlehem (2 Sam. 23:14) that were located in the very heart of Benjaminite and Judahite tribal lands.

Among the Philistines it is the inhabitants of Gath who are remembered as exhibiting particular military prowess. In a series of anecdotes written into one of the final chapters of the Book of Samuel (2 Sam. 21:15–21), reference is made to four different Gittite warriors who are termed ילידי הרפה, or "descendants of the Raphah" (2 Sam. 21:20). A common reading of this expression is to connect these Philistine champions with another race of giants referred to earlier in the biblical writings, the Rephaim[28] (Gen. 14:5, 15:20; Deut. 2:10–11, 3:11)—an interpretation buttressed by the impressive physical form of the four warriors described in this passage, including, once again, Goliath (2 Sam. 21:19). Such a view would understand "descendant" primarily as an ethnic designation, with these warriors connected to a particular group of people—the Rephaim—who resided in Gath and were noted for their physical form.[29]

---

27. Machinist, "Philistines," 57–59.

28. In the parallel texts of 1 Chronicles 20:4, 6, and 8 the spelling "Raphah" retains a final *aleph*, thus connecting these warriors to the Rephaim mentioned elsewhere in the biblical narrative. The loss of the final *aleph* in 2 Samuel 21 may be due to polemics (so Klein), or due to the Chronicler simply preserving an older spelling (as in other locations, i.e., Ishba'al v. Ishboshet in 1 Chron. 8:33 and 2 Sam. 2:8). For discussion, see P. K. McCarter, *II Samuel* (AB 9; Garden City: Doubleday, 1984), 451; R. Klein, *1 Chronicles: A Commentary* (Minneapolis: Fortress, 2006), 409; M. Smith, *Poetic Heroes: Literary Commemorations of Warriors and Warrior Culture in the Early Biblical World* (Grand Rapids: Eerdmans, 2014), 316–17.

29. S. R. Driver, *Notes on the Hebrew Text of the Books of Samuel* (Oxford: Clarendon, 1890), 353–54. G. Knoppers, *I Chronicles 10–29* (AB 12; New York: Doubleday, 2004), 732; R. Alter, *The David Story* (New York: W. W. Norton & Company, 1999), 333–35; B. Doak, *The Last of the*

Yet as a number of studies have argued, "descendant" (יְלִיד) in this passage could also mean "devotee," derived from the sense of someone adopted into or enslaved to a particular group.[30] This interpretation for the Philistine champions finds some support from West Semitic literary traditions recovered from Ugarit in which the Rephaim were represented as a collection of deceased, divinized warriors.[31] Among the votaries of these divine warriors, M. Smith points out, was the great hero Dan'il, who is named a *mt rp'i* or "man of Rp'i" throughout the Aqhat Epic (KTU 1.17 I 2, 17, 18, 35, 36, 37, 42; and eighteen other instances) in a manner that finds some resonance with the description of the Philistine fighters as "descendants of the Raphah" in 2 Samuel 21.[32] In light of these references to the Rephaim at Ugarit, the Philistine fighters connected to the Raphah in 2 Samuel 21 could be understood as those consecrated into a similar warrior cult of the Rephaim that was once located in Gath (so the "Raphah-in-Gath" of 2 Sam. 21:22).[33] On this view, the distinct martial abilities of the Gittite warriors named in these passages were linked to the powers given to them through the divinized dead, even if the great fighters of Gath are said to have fallen "by the hands of David and his servants" (2 Sam. 21:22)— including during one battle that occurs within the vicinity of Gath itself (2 Sam. 21:20–22).[34]

Rephaim: Conquest and Cataclysm in the Heroic Ages of Ancient Israel (Washington: Center for Hellenic Studies, 2012), 112–13.

30. F. Willesen, "The Philistine Corps of the Scimitar from Gath," *JSS* 3.4 (1958): 327–35; C. L'Heureux, "The *yᵉlîdê hārāpā*—a Cultic Association of Warriors," *BASOR* 221 (1976): 83–85; McCarter, *II Samuel*, 450–51.

31. So, for example, KTU 1.17 I–II; KTU 1.20–22, KTU 1.108; KTU 1.161.

32. Smith, *Heroes*, 314–21.

33. McCarter, *II Samuel*, 451. N. Na'aman, "The 'Conquest of Canaan' in the Book of Joshua and in History," in *From Nomadism to Monarchy: Archaeological and Historical Aspects of Early Israel* (eds. I. Finkelstein and N. Na'aman; Jerusalem: Israel Exploration Society, 1994), 241. Smith writes, "In view of the traditional West Semitic background of Rp'u and the Rephaim, it would appear that the Philistines in the area of Gath were known to have the local West Semitic warrior tradition associated with these figures, much as Philistines in Ashdod (1 Sam. 5:1–7; 1 Macc. 10:83–84) and elsewhere (Judg. 16:23; 1 Sam. 31:10) had adopted West Semitic deities, such as Dagan." Smith, *Heroes*, 318.

34. Maeir has recently argued that an inscription from Tell es-Safi/Gath bears the lexeme "rp'," thus attesting to the presence of a family of "Raphaim" at Gath—though this reading remains uncertain. See A. Maeir, "The Rephaim in Iron Age Philistia: Evidence of a Multi-Generational Family?" in *"Vom Leben umfangen": Ägypten, das Alte Testament und das Gespräch der Religionen Gedenkschrift für Manfred Görg* (eds. S. Wimmer and G. Gafus; Münster: Ugarit Verlag, 2014), 289–97.

With the appearance of David, however, the image of Gath in the Book of Samuel takes on a somewhat different hue. To be sure, David is credited with victories against Gittite combatants early in his career, including both Goliath (1 Sam. 17) and the Gittite "descendants of the Raphah" (2 Sam. 21:15–22). Nevertheless, throughout these narratives the city of Gath and its inhabitants also serve as a source of aid in times of distress, more friend than foe during David's rise to the throne. David's first encounter with the Philistine settlement occurs in his early escape from Saul in 1 Samuel 21. Having fled the sanctuary of Nob located just north of Jerusalem, it is recounted that David turns to the city of Gath for refuge (1 Sam. 21:10). Why David is drawn westward to this Philistine center is never explained by the storyteller, a silence that leaves David's motivations a matter of speculation—all the more so since David soon retreats south to the stronghold of Adullam and then east to the land of Moab (1 Sam. 22:1–3). The decision to enter into Gath is also striking considering David's reputation in battle against Philistine opponents (1 Sam. 18:7; 21:11; 29:5) and the revelation that he still carried the sword that beheaded Gath's great warrior (1 Sam. 21:9).

But the turn to Gath commences an association that will often benefit David within the remainder of the stories told in Samuel, even if the circumstances surrounding this alliance, as with so many of David's dealings in this literary work, are shrouded in ambiguity. The first reported encounter between David and Gath, in fact, indicates little of the value the location will provide David in the years to come. Accused of being a Philistine assailant and accorded the title "king of the land" by Achish's advisors, David soon fears for his life and feigns madness before the city's gate in order to orchestrate his escape (1 Sam. 21:14). The ploy is successful and David moves east to Adullam, gathering to him a band of discontents in a manner that closely resembles the stratagems undertaken by *Apiru* leaders of the region in the centuries before (1 Sam. 22:1–2).[35]

David's next encounter with Gath is, however, of an entirely different character, and most likely part of a different collection of traditions about David's rise to the throne than those present in 1 Samuel 21.[36] In 1 Samuel 27, David again

---

35. A. Alt, "Erwägungen Über die Landnahme der Israeliten in Palästina," in *Kleine Schriften zur Geschichte des Volkes Israel*, vol. I (Munich: C.H. Beck, 1953), 168–72; P. K. McCarter, "The Historical David," *Interpretation* 40.2 (1986): 121–22.

36. J. Grønbaek, *Die Geschichte vom Aufstieg Davids (1. Sam. 15–2. Sam. 5: Tradition und Komposition* (Copenhagen: Prostant Apud Munksgaard, 1971), 143–45; J. Vermeylen, *La Loi du Plus Fort: Histoire de la rédaction des récits davidiques de 1 Samuel 8 à 1 Rois 2* (Leuven: Leuven University Press, 2000), 134–35, 161–62; J. Hutton, *The Transjordanian Palimpsest: The Overwritten Texts of Personal Exile and Transformation in the Deuteronomistic History* (BZAW 396; Berlin: Walter de Gruyter, 2009), 271–75; J. Wright, *David, King of Israel, and Caleb in Biblical Memory* (Cambridge: Cambridge University Press, 2014), 33–35.

comes before the city of Gath, but this time with six hundred of his fighters in tow (1 Sam, 27:2). In this episode David receives little of the resistance he once received from Gath's inhabitants. Achish promptly offers refuge to David, his family, and his fighters on David's request (1 Sam, 27:3). After some time, David asks leave of the "royal city" (1 Sam, 27:5) and is granted the site of Ziklag to command, a settlement located somewhere along the southern reaches of Gath's dominion.[37] So pleased is the Gittite ruler with David's control of Gath's territory in the south that Achish requests David and his fighters to join him in battle against the Israelites, with the promise that David would soon be appointed to the vaunted position of royal bodyguard to the Philistine ruler (1 Sam, 28:1–2). David's response to this offer—"Very well, you will know what your servant can do" (1 Sam. 28:2)—is rich in ambiguity, resisting readings that would find in this statement a clear indication of David's loyalty to Saul and betrayal of Achish, or the reverse. But what is clear is that throughout this narrative episode both David and Achish benefit from David's activities at Ziklag[38] where the region is rid of forces hostile to both Philistine and highland populations, and that when we return to this scene after a brief interruption we find David and his men marching alongside of Achish's forces near Aphek. Achish's last recorded words to David in the Book of Samuel—"you have done well before me" (1 Sam. 29.10)[39]—need not be read, then, as the statement of a mistaken or befuddled ruler.

The special relationship forged between David and Gath in the Book of Samuel is not restricted to its ruler alone. In 2 Samuel 6, a story is told of how David transferred the ark of Yahweh from the town of Baale-Judah (Kiriath-Yearim), located on the western border of his realm, to Jerusalem. On the way trouble ensues and David decides to abandon the war palladium before entering the city. What is fascinating about the decision to do so with our concerns in mind, however, is that David stations the ark in the household of one who, of all the possible residences presumably available, was a Gittite (2 Sam. 6:10).[40] The ark resides

---

37. For an extensive discussion of this episode, see the treatment of 1 Samuel 27 and the location of Ziklag in Chapter 3 of this work.

38. The narrator of this episode, as noted especially by McCarter (P. K. McCarter, "The Apology of David," *JBL* 99.4 [1980]: 500–501), is careful to maintain that David did not strike any highland community while making raids in the south and deceived Achish in doing so (1 Sam. 27: 10–12). But as Jobling and Alter point out, Achish nevertheless benefitted from David's raids, both in terms of defense and spoil. D. Jobling, *1 Samuel* (Collegeville: Liturgical Press, 1998), 232–43; Alter, *David Story*, 169–70.

39. Here reading with the LXX[B] (ὅτι ἀγαθὸς σὺ ἐνώπιόν μου) given the loss of these statements due to haplography in the MT.

40. On the Philistine background of Obed-Edom, see N. Na'aman, "The Judahite Temple at Tel Moza near Jerusalem: The House of Obed-Edom?" *TA* 44 (2017): 3–13.

within the home of Obed-Edom of Gath outside of Jerusalem for three months until the abundance of blessings bestowed on the house's owner inclines David to retrieve the ark once more and finally install it in his royal center. In later tellings, Obed-Edom and his descendants come to be numbered among the Levites (1 Chr. 15–16, 26).

In 2 Samuel 15, another native of Gath plays a pivotal role in the story of David's life. This individual is Ittai, the leader of a mercenary force composed of Gittite soldiers who had joined David in Jerusalem.[41] Within the narratives devoted to Absalom's coup, Ittai emerges as a follower deeply loyal to David, undaunted by the rebellion against David and disinclined to return to Gath once Absalom had descended on the capital (2 Sam. 15:21–22). In the decisive battle of the Ephraim Forest where Absalom is defeated and David is restored to the throne (2 Sam. 18), it is Ittai, furthermore, who functions as one of three commanders of David's forces (2 Sam. 18:2), presumably overseeing the Gittite warriors who support David in the conflict. W. Dietrich observes that an "eerie analogy" thus emerges in the traditions surrounding David and the city of Gath within these scenes: where once David worked alongside Gath to defeat the House of Saul and the Israelites who supported it, now certain inhabitants of Gath have helped David defeat Absalom and the Israelites who sought to make Absalom king.[42] A possible partnership between Jerusalem and Gath is hinted at once more in 1 Kings 2:39–41 where Shimei, scion of the House of Saul, moves freely back and forth between Philistine and highland cities in an episode that allows Solomon to rid himself of one more Saulide descendant in a form of entrapment likely supported by leaders in Gath.

Depicted within these stories of David's life, accordingly, is a remarkable presentation of Philistine Gath given that those who are writing these stories do not hold the Philistines, broadly speaking, in high esteem. Nevertheless, in spite of the themes of enmity and otherness that surround the portrayal of the Philistines in these texts, the portrait of Gath is rendered with a somewhat different hue. On the one hand, Gath is differentiated from other Philistine city

41. On the similarities between the character of Ittai and David's earlier status as a leader of mercenary forces (also consisting of six hundred individuals), see N. Na'aman, "Ittai the Gittite," *BN* 94 (1998): 23–24.

42. W. Dietrich, "David and the Philistines: Literature and History" in *The Ancient Near East in the 12th–10th Centuries BCE: Culture and History* (eds. G. Galil et al.; Münster: Ugarit Verlag, 2012), 97. On the importance of the relationship between Gath and Jerusalem for David's reign, see already A. Alt, "Die Staatenbildung der Israeliten in Palästina," in *Kleine Schriften zur Geschichte des Volkes Israel, vol. II* (München: Beck, 1964), 57–58.

states as being of an elevated political status, with Achish named "king" (1 Sam. 21:10; 27:2) in contrast to the title of *seren* accorded to other Philistine leaders during this time (so 1 Sam. 5:8,11; 6:4,12,16,18; 29:2,6,7).[43] Gath's influence is also hinted at indirectly in these narratives through the martial capabilities exclusive to its warriors, whether in the famous figure of Goliath, Ittai and his mercenary force at Jerusalem, or the "descendants of the Raphah" described in 2 Samuel 21. Moreover, Gath's significance is intimated by the territory it controls, with boundaries extending, at least in certain moments of Samuel, from the eastern Shephelah to holdings in the far south along the Negev where Ziklag resides. Never does this territory come under Israelite/Judahite control in the stories surrounding David's rise to the throne, nor during the years when David rules from Jerusalem and extends his dominion from "Dan to Beersheba" (2 Sam. 24:2). Rather, it is David who often plays the part of vassal to Gath throughout these tales in a manner that drives the biblical scribes to take pains to assert that David was in fact a double agent, always loyal to the Israelite cause even when the circumstances may not have suggested it.[44]

One key to unraveling the ciphered character of David in the Book of Samuel appears to reside, then, in the city of Gath. Gath is a refuge (1 Sam. 27:1–4), a patron (1 Sam. 27:9–1 Sam. 28:2), and a vital component of the Philistine army that will occasion the deaths of central figures within the House of Saul, thereby setting the stage for David's emergence as leader of the highland regions (1 Sam. 29, 31). And, when David's kingship encounters its greatest crisis, it is once again Gittite fighters, housed in Jerusalem during this period (2 Sam. 15:18–22), who prove to be decisive in David's victory over Absalom and those Judahites and Israelites loyal to the prince. David's political fortunes within these narratives are acutely interwoven with Gath's, the success of each contingent, implicitly if not explicitly so, on the other. When reading between the lines of these stories it does not take a leap of the literary imagination to see a partnership between David and Achish, Jerusalem and Gath, that likely benefitted them both.[45]

Following the reference to Gath at the beginning of Solomon's reign in the anecdote surrounding the execution of Shimei, the Philistine city does not appear again in the biblical writings until over a hundred years have passed.

---

43. A. Rainey, "Syntax, Hermeneutics and History," *IEJ* 48 (1998): 243; V. Wagner, "Die סינירס der Philister und die Ältesten Israels," *ZAR* 14 (2008): 408–33; C. Edenburg, "Notes on the Origin of the Biblical Tradition Regarding Achish King of Gath," *VT* 61 (2011): 34–38.

44. P. K. McCarter, "The Apology of David."; B. Halpern, *David's Secret Demons: Messiah, Murderer, Traitor, King* (Grand Rapids: Eerdmans, 2001), 73–103.

45. Hertzberg, *I & II Samuel* (trans. J. Bowden. Philadelphia: Westminster, 1964), 213; Halpern, *David's Secret Demons*, 326–32; Dietrich, "David and the Philistines," 96–98.

In 2 Kings 12:18 (Eng. 12:17) the biblical writers provide a cursory statement observing that Hazael of Damascus had fought against Gath and captured it. The fact that Hazael is said to have attacked Gath and not Ekron is indicative, on the one hand, of Gath's enduring import within Philistine territory a century after Achish would have ruled. But this reference also suggests that Gath likely functioned as a crucial gateway into the highland regions and the capital of Jerusalem since it is to Jerusalem that Hazael turns next (2 Kings 12:18–19 [Eng. 12:17–18]).[46] 2 Chronicles 26:6 records, furthermore, that after Hazael's withdrawal from the region the city of Ashdod attempted to exercise control over Gath and Gath's domain—a move that, according to Chronicles, was quickly met by Uzziah of Judah in a battle or series of battles that led to Uzziah's control of northern Philistine territory.

In turning from Samuel-Kings and Chronicles to the prophetic corpus, two final references to Gath are worth mention. The first instance is found in Amos, a contemporary of Uzziah (Amos 1:1), who cites three cities of consequence—Calneh, Hamath, and Gath (Amos 6:2)—in a woe oracle delivered to leaders in Samaria and Jerusalem (Amos 6:1). In part, the reference to Gath within this passage finds importance for this investigation because the Philistine city is numbered among other prominent early Iron Age capitals found in the Levant. Calneh, identified with ancient Kunulua (Tell Ta'yinat),[47] was an impressive early Iron Age city located on the northern bend of the Orontes River near modern Antakya in southern Turkey;[48] Hamath (ancient Hama), situated in the central Orontes Valley, was also an important Aramean capital whose kingdom is referred to frequently in biblical (e.g., 2 Sam. 8:9; 2 Kings 14:28, 2 Kings 19:13) and Assyrian sources.[49] That Gath stands among these foreign sites

---

46. Schniedewind, "Geopolitical History," 74; Halpern, *David's Secret Demons,* 331.

47. P. Machinist, "Assyria and Its Image in the First Isaiah," *JAOS* 103.4 (1983): 719–37; N. Na'aman, "In Search of the Reality Behind the Account of David's Wars with Israel's Neighbours," *IEJ* 52.2 (2002): 211.

48. For recent surveys of early Iron Age remains recovered from the site, see T. Harrison, "Neo-Hittites in the 'Land of Palistin,': Renewed Excavations at Tell Ta'yinat on the Plain of Antioch," *NEA* 72.4 (2009): 174–89; idem, "Recent Discoveries at Tayinat (Ancient Kunulua/Calno) and their Biblical Implications," in *Congress Volume Munich 2003* (ed. C. Maeir; Leiden: Brill, 2014), 399–402.

49. On the kingdom of Hamath in the ninth century BCE, see E. Fugman, *Hama. Fouilles et recherches de la Fondation Carlsberg 1931-38 II: architecture des périodes pré-hellénistique* (Copenhagen: National Museum, 1958), 252–69; N. Na'aman, "Aribua and the Patina-Hamath Border," *Orientalia* 71.3 (2002): 291–95; D. Kahn, "The Kingdom of Arpad (Bit Agusi) and 'all Aram': International Relations in Northern Syria in the Ninth and Eighth Centuries BCE," *ANES* 44 (2007): 66–89.

testifies to the reputation it enjoyed, at least from the perspective of the audience of this prophetic text.

Yet the significance of this reference to Gath in Amos 6:2 can also be located in the fact that it provides evidence of the deep impression the Philistine city had left on the inhabitants of the southern Levant even after the city had been subjugated and destroyed. For what unites the three cities mentioned in Amos 6:2 is that each was conquered or in a state of decline as the ninth century BCE came to a close, or a generation before Amos would have appeared on the prophetic scene.[50] In light of their downfall, the cities referred to in this oracle thus appear to serve as a warning that even powerful royal centers in the region can come to an end—and thereby attesting, indirectly, to the stature accorded to Gath in the memories of those who were present after its defeat.

The second allusion to Gath occurs in Micah 1:10. In an echo of David's lament voiced over Saul and Jonathan in 2 Samuel 1:20, the phrase "Tell it not in Gath. . ." is repeated within a dirge composed for a roster of cities over which the prophet mourns. What is curious about this text is Gath's inclusion within it, as all other cities mentioned in Micah 1:8–16 are Judahite settlements situated securely in Judahite territory in the Shephelah region. Of course, this reference may be to a Gath otherwise unattested elsewhere in the biblical writings. But in light of the archaeological evidence recovered from Tell es-Safi (below), there is a sense that this reference to Gath was penned by those who, in the late eighth century BCE or after, now considered Gath to be a part of the Judahite realm.[51]

With these final references to Gath two key points crystallize for our consideration of the Philistine city and its presence among the writings of the Hebrew Bible. First, it is important to underscore that later Hebrew scribes, such as those behind the formation of Amos 6, were aware of the influence Gath had once wielded even though they were writing a generation or more after the city had been destroyed by Hazael. Second, the inclusion of Gath among a roster of otherwise Judahite settlements in Micah 1 offers one reason for why memories of Gath may have persisted into the time in which certain biblical writings were being formed: in the course of the eighth century BCE, as Hebrew prose writing began to flourish, Judah claimed Gath as its own.

---

50. Na'aman, "David's Wars," 210–12; A. Maeir, "The Historical Background and Dating of Amos VI 2: An Archaeological from Tell eṣ-Ṣâfî/Gath," *VT* 54.3 (2004): 319–34.

51. Levin, "Philistine Gath," 148.

Philistine Gath: The Archaeological Evidence

The location of Philistine Gath posed one of the great challenges to the historical geography of the southern Levant for those involved in this research in the nineteenth and twentieth centuries.[52] Proposals for the location of the Philistine settlement varied considerably during this time, including Albright's influential assessment that Gath was located at Tel Erani,[53] an idea that led to the hasty naming of the modern town located nearby, Qiryat Gath, in an area that proved to be quite removed from the ancient city's actual whereabouts. Further proposals for Gath's position stemmed from other major figures in the field, including B. Mazar's suggestion of Ras Abu Hamid just east of Ramla,[54] Wright's association of Gath with Tel Sera',[55] and Stager's identification of Gath with the remains at Tel Haror.[56]

It is now apparent that Philistine Gath was located at none of these sites. Instead, excavations carried out at Tell es-Safi in the past two decades have provided significant evidence that the ancient Philistine city was situated here on the southern bank of the Wadi Elah, roughly 45 km southwest of Jerusalem on the edge of where the Shephelah meets the coastal plain. In antiquity, Gath's position afforded it a number of advantages. In terms of transit and trade, Tell es-Safi occupied a key post on the local east-west route that passed through the Elah Valley, a corridor whose import resided in its capacity to allow traffic to move between the Mediterranean port at Ashkelon through Gath and into Jerusalem and the Central Benjamin Plateau.[57] (See Figure 2.3.)

In addition to geography, Tell es-Safi also benefitted from its location within the so-called Philistine alluvial basin that possessed both fertile soil and

---

52. So the quote from Anson Rainey that begins Schniedewind's discussion of the topic "Perhaps the most debated issue in Palestinian geography is the location of Philistine Gath." A. Rainey, "Gath of the Philistines," *Christian News from Israel* 17.2–3 (1966): 30. Cited in Schniedewind, "Philistine Gath," 69. For a brief overview of the numerous locations linked to Gath throughout the nineteenth and twentieth centuries, see A. Maeir, "History of Research: 1838–1996," in *Tell es Safi/Gath I: The 1996–2005 Seasons, Part I: Texts* (ed. A. Maeir; Wiesbaden: Harrassowitz Verlag, 2012), 100–101.

53. William F. Albright, "Contributions to the Historical Geography of 1922 Palestine," *Annual of the American School of Oriental Research in Jerusalem* 2–3 (1921–1922): 10–12.

54. B. Mazar, "Gath and Gittaim," *IEJ* 4 (1954): 231.

55. G. E. Wright, "Fresh Evidence for the Philistine Story," *BA* 29 (1966): 70–86.

56. L. Stager, "The Impact of the Sea Peoples," in *The Archaeology of Society in the Holy Land* (ed. T. E. Levy; New York: Facts on File, 1995), 343.

57. D. Dorsey, *The Roads and Highways of Ancient Israel* (Baltimore: Johns Hopkins, 1991), 189–91.

FIGURE 2.3 View of Elah Valley, Looking North from atop Tell es-Safi (Picture: Author).

adequate rainfall for intensive agricultural activity.[58] Given these conditions, a primary reason for the Philistine settlement at Gath was likely the area's agrarian resources. Yasur-Landau comments:[59]

> Bearing in mind the commonly accepted notion of the Philistines' aggressive, maritime nature, it may be surprising that fear of outside attack, by either Egyptians or others, and the need for access to sheltered harbors were not obvious considerations in choosing sites for settlement. Rather, the common factor of Tel Miqne/Ekron, Ashdod, Ashkelon, and Tell es-Safi/Gath is their position in the midst of considerable areas of arable land. Land, rather than sea, was the main resource that the Philistine migrants sought.

Perched atop an isolated hill and guarded by steep cliffs on its north and western flank, factors connected to defense, trade, and agriculture coalesced at Tell es-Safi/Gath in a manner that granted the location "all the natural advantages of a great city."[60] (See Figure 2.4.)

58. Schniedewind, "Geopolitical History," 70.

59. A. Yasur-Landau, *The Philistines and Aegean Migration at the End of the Late Bronze Age* (Cambridge: Cambridge University Press, 2010), 288.

60. Schniedewind, "Geopolitical History," 70.

FIGURE 2.4 View from atop Tell es-Safi, Looking Northwest (Picture: Author).

For such reasons, Tell es-Safi was settled and fortified already in the Early Bronze Age III period (ca. 2700–2200 BCE). Encompassing an area of around 24 ha at this time, the city stood as one of the largest urban entities in the region and included a centralized administrative system and bureaucracy.[61] At the end of the EB III period, however, Gath entered into a period of decline. The site would recover during the Middle Bronze Age IIB period (ca. 1750–1600 BCE), but functioned throughout this era as the smaller counterpart to the more impressive MBA site of Tel Miqne/Ekron located 8 km to the north.[62]

Centuries later, Gath once more rose to prominence as a Canaanite city state. Found among a corpus of letters exchanged between Pharaoh and Pharaoh's Canaanite vassals (El Amarna Letters, fourteenth century BCE) were eleven texts sent out originally from Gath (Akk. *Gimtu*) that offered insight into the political authority Gath exercised in the southern Levant during the Late Bronze Age.[63] In one letter the ruler of Gath, Shuwardata, writes of the difficulties he encountered during the rebellion of thirty towns under his control (EA 283), hinting at the

61. I. Shai et al., "The Early Bronze Age Remains at Tell es Safi /Gath: An Interim Report," *TA* 41 (2014): 20–49; I. Shai et al., "The Early Bronze Age Fortifications at Tell es-Safi/Gath, Israel," *PEQ* 148.1 (2016): 42–58.

62. A. Maeir and J. Uziel, "A Tale of Two Tells: A Comparative Perspective on Tel Miqne-Ekron and Tell es Safi/Gath in Light of Recent Archaeological Research," in *'Up to the Gates of Ekron:" Essays on the Archaeology and History of the Eastern Mediterranean in Honor of Seymour Gitin* (eds. S. Crawford et al.; Jerusalem: Israel Exploration Society, 2007), 31–32.

63. On the letters sent out from Gath, see Y. Goren, I. Finkelstein, and N. Na'aman, *Inscribed in Clay: Provenance Study of the Amarna Letters and other Ancient Near Eastern Texts* (Tel Aviv: Tel Aviv University Press, 2004), 283–86.

FIGURE 2.5 View of Excavation Areas A and E, Tell es-Safi (Picture: Author).

domain Gath once oversaw. Multiple LBA phases unearthed from Tell es-Safi, which now stood at an impressive 27 ha, attest to the image of the site found in these letters. Among the finds recovered were a substantial amount of Egyptian or Egyptianizing glyptics, two Hieratic inscriptions (in Areas E and F), and a large, well-crafted structure (Building 66323 in Area E)[64] that corresponds to other prominent public buildings located in contemporaneous LBA sites in the southern Levant.[65] (See Figure 2.5.) Such finds marry well with the picture of Gath found in the Amarna correspondence in which the Canaanite center appears as an important Egyptian vassal at turns allied with and hostile to other local Late Bronze Age city states in the region, such as Gezer, Lachish, and Jerusalem.[66]

Finds from Area E on the upper tell of site indicate that this precinct of the Canaanite city met some manner of violent end as the Late Bronze Age came to a close.[67] The most probable agents behind this takeover were the Philistines.

---

64. I. Shai et al., "Differentiating Between Public and Residential Buildings: A Case Study from Late Bronze Age II Tell es Safi/Gath," in *Household Archaeology in Ancient Israel and Beyond* (eds. A. Yasur-Landau et al.; Leiden: Brill, 2011), 107–31.

65. Maeir, "Introduction," 16–17; Maeir and Uziel, "Two Tells," 31–32.

66. N. Na'aman, "The Shephelah According to the Amarna Letters," in *The Fire Signals of Lachish: Studies in the Archaeology and History of Israel in the Late Bronze Age, Iron Age, and Persian Period in Honor of David Ussishkin* (eds. I. Finkelstein and N. Na'aman; Winona Lake: Eisenbrauns, 2011), 281–300; I. Finkelstein, "The Shephelah and Jerusalem's Western Border in the Amarna Period," *Ägypten und Levante* 24 (2014): 267–76.

67. A. Maeir, "Insights on the Philistine Culture and Related Issues: An Overview of 15 years of Work at Tell eṣ-Ṣafi/Gath," in *The Ancient Near East in the 12th–10th Centuries*

According to radiocarbon dates obtained from samples taken from Area A of the site, the appearance of Philistine peoples at Gath may have occurred already in the late thirteenth century BCE, or a generation before the emergence of Philistine material culture at Qubur el-Walaydah in the south and a century prior to such finds from Megiddo in the north.[68] How the transition from Canaanite to Philistine control of Gath unfolded during this period is uncertain, historically speaking. Maeir suggests that Philistine invaders may have "deposed the local Canaanite elites" of Gath while at the same time establishing themselves among the broader Canaanite population of the settlement, thus helping to explain why Gath suffered only a partial destruction—restricted to the elite enclave in Area E—when the Philistines appeared.[69] Yasur-Landau argues, however, for a less violent and more cooperative scenario in which Philistine immigrants and local Canaanite populations worked together in order to meet the challenges of uncertain economic and geopolitical circumstances that arose with the collapse of the Late Bronze Age palatial society in the region.[70] This perspective would offer another answer, then, to the question as to why locations such as Gath retained their Canaanite names and ample traces of Canaanite culture even after they came under Philistine control.[71]

With the advent of the Iron Age (Iron I), Gath became a Philistine center of considerable size and status. The sudden appearance of Mycenaean IIIC:1b pottery throughout Areas A and E and within domestic structures of Area F of the site[72]

BCE: *Culture and History* (eds. G. Galil et al.; Münster: Ugarit Verlag, 2012), 349–50; idem, "Introduction," 18.

68. Y. Asscher et al., "Radiocarbon Dating Shows an Early Appearance of Philistine Material Culture in Tell es Safi/Gath, Philistia," *Radiocarbon* 57.5 (2015): 1–26; Y. Asscher et al., "Absolute Dating of the Late Bronze to Iron Age Transition and the Appearance of Philistine Culture in Qubur el-Walaydah, Southern Levant," *Radiocarbon* 57.1 (2015): 77–97.

69. Maeir, "Introduction," 18; idem, "Philistine Culture," 350.

70. Yasur-Landau, *Philistines*, 287–94; idem, "The Role of the Canaanite Population in the Aegean Migration to the Southern Levant in the late Second Millennium BCE," in *Materiality and Social Practice: Transformative Capacities of Intercultural Encounters* (eds. J. Maran and P. Stockhammer; Oxford: Oxbow, 2012), 191–97.

71. S. Bunimovitz, "Sea Peoples in Cyprus and Israel: A Comparative Study of Immigration Processes," in *Mediterranean Peoples in Transition: Thirteenth to Early Tenth Centuries BCE: In Honor of Trude Dothan* (Jerusalem: Israel Exploration Society, 1998): 103–13; I. Shai, "Understanding Philistine Migration: City Names and Their Implications," *BASOR* 354 (2009): 21–23; G. Lehmann and H. Niemann, "When Did the Shephelah Become Judahite?" *TA* 41 (2014): 84.

72. A. Zukerman, "Iron Age I and Early Iron Age IIA Pottery," in *Tell es Safi/Gath I: The 1996–2005 Seasons, Part I: Texts* (ed. A. Maeir. Wiesbaden: Harrassowitz Verlag, 2012), 299–301; Maeir, "Introduction," 19.

provides evidence that residents of Gath possessed links to Aegean cultural wares, most likely in conjunction with the movement of Sea Peoples who had settled at Tell es-Safi and among other sites along the coastal plain. In light of the broad area in which such finds were recovered at Tell es-Safi—extending from Area A in the eastern reaches of the settlement to the far western sector of Area F—it is likely that the site was inhabited well beyond its upper tell and into the lower precincts of the city at this time,[73] with Uziel and Maeir estimating that the settlement once again reach ca. 23 ha during the Iron I period.[74] By way of comparison, Jerusalem stood at ca. 4 ha in the Iron I; Megiddo (Stratum VIIA) at 11 ha.[75]

In addition to the appearance of Philistine material culture at Gath during the LBA-Iron I transition, what is also of interest are developments that occurred in Gath's environs once Philistines began to settle at the site. Most important of these is the dramatic change in settlement patterns that define this era. Whereas in the Late Bronze Age the Shephelah region consisted of ca. twenty-four sites that ranged from large to middle-sized settlements with corresponding rural hinterlands, this number fell to only four settlements in the Iron I period (excluding Gath and Timnah, both Philistine sites), all of which were positioned on the very eastern edge of the Shephelah along the trough valley.[76] In the area surrounding Gath itself, survey results indicate that the region was almost entirely empty.[77] Nevertheless, the overall population of the Shephelah remained relatively stable due to the expansion of principal cities in

---

73. Maeir, "Introduction," 19; idem, "Insights," 353.

74. Joe Uziel and Aren Maeir, "Scratching the Surface at Gath: Implications of the Tell es-Safi/Gath Surface Survey," *TA* 32 (2005): 65–68; idem, "The Location, Size and Periods of Settlement at Tell es-Safi/Gath: The Surface Survey Results," in *Tell es Safi/Gath I: The 1996–2005 Seasons, Part I: Texts* (ed. A. Maeir. Wiesbaden: Harrassowitz Verlag, 2012), 173–82.

75. I. Finkelstein, "From City-States to States: Polity Dynamics in the 10th–9th Centuries BCE," in *Symbiosis, Symbolism, and the Power of the Past: Canaan, Ancient Israel, and Their Neighbors from the Late Bronze Age through Roman Palestine* (ed. W. Dever and S. Gitin; Winona Lake: Eisenbrauns, 2003), 76–77.

76. I. Finkelstein, "The Philistine countryside," *IEJ* 46 (1996): 225–42; A. Shavit, "Settlement Patterns of Philistine City-States," in *Bene Israel: Studies in the Archaeology of Israel and the Levant during the Bronze and Iron Ages in Honour of Israel Finkelstein* (eds. A. Fantalkin and A. Yasur-Landau; Leiden: Brill, 2008), 142–47; A. Faust and H. Katz, "Philistines, Israelites and Canaanites in the Southern Trough Valley during the Iron Age I," *Egypt and the Levant* 21 (2011): 231–47; A. Faust, "The Shephelah in the Iron Age: A New Look on the Settlement of Judah," *PEQ* 145.3 (2013): 204–208; Lehmann and Niemann, "Shephelah," 77–83.

77. I. Finkelstein, "The Philistine Settlements: When, Where and How Many," *The Sea Peoples and Their World. A Reassessment* (ed. E. Oren; Philadelphia: University of Pennsylvania, 2000), 170.

the area, suggesting that those who once lived in the countryside now resided in larger urban centers.[78] This decline in the number of settlements present in the Shephelah is all the more conspicuous in light of the fact that elsewhere in the southern Levant, particularly in the highlands, a significant number of new settlements emerged in the Iron I era that consisted of mostly small towns and rural villages.[79]

Such evidence gives rise to the question as to how and why the countryside was mostly abandoned in the Shephelah when other parts of the southern Levant witnessed an upsurge in settlement activity. The most plausible answer is that these developments were connected to the appearance of the Philistines at precisely this time. Having settled in former Canaanite centers, the Philistines, it appears, were involved in a process in which native Canaanite populations from rural areas of the Shephelah came to be relocated into the cities the Philistines now controlled.[80] Whether this relocation was forced or cooperative is unknown. But the result of this relocation was the creation of larger urban domains, such as Gath itself, that were composed of a rather heterogeneous population of Philistine and Canaanite peoples whose distinct identities and cultural interactions are manifest in the archaeological record.[81]

By the beginning of the tenth century BCE, or the Iron late I–IIA transitional period,[82] Gath embarked on its most important moment in antiquity. The

---

78. Finkelstein, "Philistine Settlements," 167–71; I. Shai, "The Political Organization of the Philistines," in *"I Will Speak the Riddles of Ancient Times:" Archaeological and Historical Studies in Honor of Amihai Mazar on the Occasion of His Sixtieth Birthday* (eds. A. Maeir and P. Miroschedji; Winona Lake: Eisenbrauns, 2006), 350–51.

79. I. Finkelstein, *The Archaeology of the Israelite Settlement* (trans. D. Saltz; Jerusalem: Israel Exploration Society, 1988), 330–56; idem, "Geographical and Historical Realities Behind the Earliest Layer of the David Story," *SJOT* 27.2 (2013): 145–46.

80. Shavit, "Settlement Patterns," 154–60; N. Na'aman, "Khirbet Qeiyafa in Context," *UF* 42 (2010): 503; S. Bunimovitz and Z. Lederman, "Canaanite Resistance: The Philistines and Beth-Shemesh—A Case Study from Iron Age I," *BASOR* 364 (2011): 37–51; Faust and Katz, "Philistines, Israelites, and Canaanites," 235–36.

81. So Yasur-Landau writes of the "astonishing fact" that "[i]n every house and assemblage in Ashkelon, Ashdod, and Ekron, local Canaanite pottery forms are found in large quantities, sometimes surpassing the quantity of locally-made Aegean pottery." Yasur-Landau, "Canaanite Population," 192. On the negotiation of foreign and local identity within Philistine Gath, see L. Hitchcock and A. Maeir, "Beyond Creolization and Hybridity: Entangled and Transcultural Identities in Philistia," *ARC* 28.1 (2013): 43–65; A. Maeir, "Philistine Gath after 20 Years: Regional perspectives on the Iron Age at Tell es-Safi/Gath," in *The Shephelah during the Iron Age: Recent Archaeological Studies* (eds. O. Lipschits and A. M. Maeir; Winona Lake: Eisenbrauns, 2017), 133–53.

82. Here, following the Modified Conventional Chronology of A. Mazar. See A. Mazar, "The Debate over the Chronology of the Iron Age in the Southern Levant: Its History, the

evidence at hand indicates that during this time Gath grew to an estimated 50 hectares (125 acres), making it one of the largest, if not the largest, city in the southern Levant.[83] By way of comparison, no other Philistine settlement surpassed 25 ha in the Iron IIA period, with most being considerably smaller; to the east, Jerusalem may have approached 12 ha in the Iron IIA period., or roughly one quarter of Gath's total settled area, and most highland sites were more modest still. Both the upper city of Gath, furthermore, and its expansive lower city appear to have been fortified by this era, with the recent unearthing of a monumental city gate again attesting to the city's prominence during a time in which few neighboring settlements could match Gath's size and defensive infrastructure.[84] (See Figure 2.6.) The sheer magnitude of Gath's dimensions in the tenth and ninth centuries BCE, from this perspective, is quite astonishing.[85]

How and why Gath developed as it did during this time nevertheless remains a mystery. Renewed Egyptian interest in the southern Levant in the late tenth century BCE has been identified as a potential agent behind the city's growth,[86] though evidence for a connection between Egypt and Gath is currently lacking. Another theory put forward is that the destruction of Khirbet Qeiyafa and the abandonment of Ekron at the beginning of the tenth century BCE offer a distinct set of clues as to Gath's rise: namely, that the leaders of Gath were responsible for both, and that the downfall of these important fortified cities to Gath's north and east allowed the Philistine city state to become the dominant polity in the region.[87]

Current Situation, and a Suggested Resolution," in *The Bible and Radiocarbon Dating* (eds. T. Highman and T. Levy; London: Equinox, 2005), 15–30; idem, "The Iron Age Chronology Debate: Is the Gap Narrowing?" *NEA* 74.2 (2011): 105–11; A. Faust, "The Chronology of Iron Age IIA in Judah in Light of the Tel 'Eton Tomb C3 and Other Assemblages," *BASOR* 371 (2014): 103–27.

83. Maeir, "Insights," 363.

84. Maeir dates the fortification of the lower city to the Iron IB (eleventh century BCE) period. Maeir, "Philistine Gath after 20 Years," 1141–47; idem, "Khirbet Qeiyafa in Its Regional Context: A View from Philistine Gath," in *Khirbet Qeiyafa in the Shephelah* (eds. S. Schroer and S. Münger; Fribourg: Academic Press, 2017), 61–71.

85. Maeir, "Introduction," 26–27; Aren Maeir, Louise Hitchcock, and Liora Kolska Horwitz "On the Constitution and Transformation of Philistine Identity," *OJA* 32.1 (2013), 23–24.

86. Finkelstein, "Geographical,"147.

87. Maeir and Uziel, "Two Tells," 37–38; Na'aman, "Khirbet Qeiyafa," 514–15. The excavators of Kh. Qeiyafa also suggest that the settlement may have been destroyed by Gath. Yosef Garfinkel and Saar Ganor, *Khirbet Qeiyafa Vol. I: Excavation Report 2007–2008* (Jerusalem: Israel Exploration Society, 2009), 4.

FIGURE 2.6 Tell es-Safi, Looking South, with Excavations of Gate Complex in Foreground (Picture: Author).

In keeping with this view, what is striking about Gath's rise at the outset of the Iron IIA period is that other settlements and regions within Philistia entered into a period of decline. Ashkelon[88] and, perhaps, Ashdod,[89] appear to be in a state of decline at the beginning of the tenth century BCE and the nearby Philistine city of Ekron is destroyed during this period,[90] with a number of smaller sites in Philistia also being abandoned.[91] Ekron's sudden collapse and the decline of other Philistine centers in the tenth century BCE would give credence, then, to the view that Gath may have expanded its influence at the expense of other Philistine city states.[92]

88. L. Stager, "Ashkelon, Tel," in *NEAEHL*, vol. 5 (ed. E. Stern; Jerusalem: Israel Exploration Society, 2008): 1584; A. Faust, "From Regional Power to Peaceful Neighbour," 179–80.

89. The character of Ashdod in the Iron IIA period (tenth to ninth centuries BCE) has been disputed. Finkelstein and Singer-Avitz assert that a gap in settlement activity was likely present during this time (I. Finkelstein and L. Singer-Avitz, "Ashdod Revisited," *TA* 28 (2001): 239–44). Ben-Shlomo argues against this viewpoint, but observes that the evidence is quite fragmentary for this era in Ashdod's existence. D. Ben-Shlomo, "Introduction," in *Ashdod VI. The Excavations at Areas H and K (1968–1969)* (Jerusalem: Israel Antiquities Authority, 2005), 1–9.

90. Seymour Gitin, "Philistia in Transition: The Tenth Century BCE and Beyond," in *Mediterranean Peoples in Transition: Thirteenth to Early Tenth Centuries BCE* (eds. S. Gitin et al.; Jerusalem: Israel Exploration Society, 1998), 167–73; Aren Maeir and Joe Uziel, "A Tale of Two Tells", 35–38.

91. A. Faust, "The Shephelah in the Iron Age" 210; idem, "Regional Power," 179–86.

92. Material culture from sites to Gath's south also evince an orientation toward Philistine culture during the Iron IIA period, perhaps in connection with Gath. See I. Finkelstein, B. Sass, and L. Singer-Avitz, "Writing in Iron IIA Philistia in the Light of Tel Zayit/Zeta Abecedary," *ZDPV* 124 (2008): 1–14; R. Tappy, "The Depositional History of Iron Age Tel Zayit: A Response to Finkelstein, Sass, and Singer-Avitz," *Er-Isr* 30 (2011): 127; I. Shai

At the very least, there are few archaeological reasons to maintain that Philistine city states always worked in concert and in one another's best interest.[93]

What is also of significance is that a number of important Judahite locations situated near the border of the Gittite realm are built at this time. In the late tenth/early ninth century BCE, the border settlement at Beth-Shemesh, for example, is purposely reconfigured as a large Judahite administrative center, replete with newly constructed fortifications, a water reservoir, and large public buildings.[94] Even more startlingly, the settlement at Lachish, once a substantial Late Bronze Age Canaanite city state and natural rival to Gath in the Shephelah region because of its close proximity (a short 15 km away), is nevertheless also rebuilt and refortified as a prominent Judahite "military city" (Level IV) sometime in the early ninth century BCE.[95] The result of the massive reconstruction efforts at Lachish was that "two of the most important cities in the southern part of the country existed and flourished side by side."[96] Thus, though the city of Gath grew and reached its apogee—in terms of size, population, and prosperity[97]—in the Iron IIA period, it did not appear to leverage its strategic location and considerable resources to inhibit or destroy the emerging polities that were adjacent to it on its eastern border during this time. Indeed, the development of Lachish by the kingdom of Judah leads N. Na'aman to go so far as to suggest that "throughout the late 10th-9th centuries BCE, peaceful relations exited between Judah and Gath" and that

---

et al., "The Iron Age Remains at Tel Nagila," *BASOR* 363 (2011): 38; E. Oren, "Sera', Tel," in *NEAEHL*, vol. 4 (ed. E. Stern; Jerusalem: Israel Exploration Society, 1993), 1329–35.

93. H. Niemann, "Neighbors and Foes, Rivals and Kin: Philistines, Shepheleans, Judeans between Geography and Economy, History and Theology," in *The Philistines and Other "Sea Peoples" in Text and Archaeology* (eds. A. Killebrew and G. Lehmann; Atlanta: SBL Press, 2013), 251–54; A. Maeir and L. Hitchcock, "'And the Canaanite was Then in the Land'? A Critical View of the 'Canaanite Enclave' in Iron I Southern Canaan," in *Alphabets, Texts and Artifacts in the Ancient Near East: Studies Presented to Benjamin Sass* (eds. I. Finkelstein et al.; Paris: Van Dieren, 2016), 219; Halpern, *David's Secret Demons*, 330–31.

94. Bunimovitz and Lederman, "Archaeology of Border Communities," 127–36.

95. D. Ussishkin, "A Synopsis of the Stratigraphical, Chronological and Historical Issues," in *The Renewed Archaeological Excavations at Lachish (1973–1994)*, vol. I (ed. D. Ussishkin; Tel Aviv: Tel Aviv University Press, 2004), 78–83; idem, "Gath, Lachish, and Jerusalem in the 9th Cent. B.C.E.—an Archaeological Reassessment," *ZDPV* 131.2 (2015): 134–39.

96. Ussishkin, "Gath, Lachish, and Jerusalem," 138.

97. Maeir, "Introduction," 26–27; Maeir, Hitchcock, and Horwitz "Constitution and Transformation," 23–24.

the refounding of Lachish likely "resulted from an agreement between the two kingdoms."[98]

The idea that an amicable, or at least nonbelligerent, relationship developed between Gath and the highland kingdom of Judah during the Iron IIA period receives further support from other archaeological considerations. I. Shai and A. Maeir, for example, have drawn attention to the presence of pre-LMLK storage jars within the Iron IIA Stratum A3 layer at Gath,[99] indicating that the city was actively involved in importing goods from its eastern highland neighbors in the tenth and ninth centuries BCE.[100] In addition, A. Maeir and E. Eshel have recently published an inscribed vessel, made of clay from the Jerusalem region, that was recovered from an Iron IIA temple in Gath and which may have been involved in cultic activity.[101] A common script tradition (linear, alphabetic writing in an Early Alphabetic script), in fact, was shared between early Iron Age locations in the Shephelah and highland regions, including epigraphs recovered from Gath and those unearthed at Beth-Shemesh and, further northeast, in Jerusalem, among other locations.[102] The much-documented trend throughout Philistia of particular Philistine cultural markers slowly disappearing through the adoption of local customs would also attest, from this perspective, to the influence of native,

---

98. N. Na'aman, "The Kingdom of Judah in the 9th century BCE: Text Analysis Versus Archaeological Research," *TA* 40 (2013): 264.

99. I. Shai and A. Maeir, "Pre-*LMLK* Jars: A New Class of Iron IIA Storage Jars," *TA* 30 (2003): 108–23; idem, "The Late Iron IIA Pottery Assemblage from Stratum A3," in *Tell es Safi/Gath I: The 1996–2005 Seasons, Part I: Texts* (ed. A. Maeir; Ägypten und Altes Testament 69; Wiesbaden: Harrassowitz Verlag, 2012), 347; I. Shai, "Philistia and the Philistines in the Iron IIA," *ZDPV* 127.2 (2011): 127.

100. Shai, "Philistia and the Philistines," 127. Cf. Maeir, "Introduction," 39. In the late Iron Age, Judah would also supply sites in Philistia with various goods, especially grain. See A. Faust and E. Weiss, "Judah, Philistia, and the Mediterranean World: Reconstructing the Economic System of the Seventh Century B.C.E.," *BASOR* 338 (2005): 71–92.

101. A. Maeir and E. Eshel, "Four Short Alphabetic Inscriptions from Late Iron Age IIa Tell es-Safi/Gath and their Implications for the Development of Literacy in Iron Age Philistia and Environs," in *"See, I will bring a scroll recounting what befell me" (Ps 40:8): Epigraphy and Daily Life from the Bible to the Talmud: Dedicated to the Memory of Professor Hanan Eshel* (Göttingen: Vandenhoeck & Ruprecht, 2014), 69–88.

102. G. Hamilton, "Reconceptualizing the Periods of Early Alphabetic Scripts," in *An Eye for Form: Epigraphic Essays in Honor of Frank Moore Cross* (eds. J. Hackett and W. Aufrecht; Winona Lake: Eisenbrauns, 2014), 39–49; Maeir et al., "A Late Iron Age I/Early Iron Age IIA Old Canaanite Inscription," 39–71; P. K. McCarter, S. Bunimovitz, and Z. Lederman, "An Archaic Ba'l Inscription from Tel Beth-Shemesh," *TA* 38 (2011): 179–93. E. Mazar, D. Ben-Shlomo, and S. Ahituv, "An Inscribed Pithos from the Ophel, Jerusalem," *IEJ* 63.1 (2013): 39–49.

southern Levantine culture and cultural traditions on populations descended from those who had once migrated to this region from elsewhere.[103]

The flow of economic and cultural exchange also however moved in the other, eastern direction. The adoption of Philistine wares at sites in the Shephelah[104] and the presence of Philistine cooking vessels at various highland locales indicate that Philistine ceramics were appropriated in regions to Gath's east, perhaps as material markers used to signal elite status or alliance with Philistine communities, but also through practices such as intermarriage.[105] In Jerusalem, the abundant amount of Nile Perch (and certain Mediterranean fish species) unearthed from its early Iron Age layers suggests that the highland center was actively involved in commerce that would have often flowed through Gath to the Mediterranean coast.[106] Figurines recovered recently from the Iron II temple at Tel Moza just outside of Jerusalem, furthermore, recall forms found among Philistine counterparts, which were likely influenced by Philistine exemplars;[107] and the "quite surprising" ceramic evidence of Late Philistine Decorated Ware [LPDW]) recently found in and around Jerusalem offers additional traces of Iron Age Philistine material culture in the highlands.[108]

---

103. B. Stone, "The Philistines and Acculturation: Culture Change and Ethnic Continuity in the Iron Age," *BASOR* 298 (1995): 7–32; J. Uziel, "The Development Process of Philistine Material Culture: Assimilation, Acculturation and Everything in Between," *Levant* 39 (2007): 165–73; Faust and Lev-Tov, "Constitution of Philistine Identity," 13–31; Hitchcock and Maeir, "Beyond Creolization," 51–74.

104. Garfinkel and Ganor, *Khirbet Qeiyafa: Vol. I*, 151–58; A. Faust, "The 'Philistine Tomb' at Tel 'Eton: Cultural Contact, Colonialism, and Local Responses in Iron Age Shephelah, Israel," *Journal of Anthropological Research* 71.2 (2015): 195–230.

105. D. Ben-Shlomo et al., "Cooking Identities: Aegean-Style Cooking Jugs and Cultural Interaction in Iron Age Philistia and Neighboring Regions," *AJA* 112.2 (2008): 225–46; D. Ben-Shlomo, "Food Preparation Habits and Cultural Interaction During the Late Bronze and Iron Age in Southern Israel," in *On Cooking Pots, Drinking Cups, Loomweights and Ethnicity in Bronze Age Cyprus and Neighbouring Regions* (eds. V. Karageorghis and O. Kouka; Nikosia: A. G. Leventis Foundation, 2011), 273–86.

106. W. Van Neer et al., "Fish Remains from Archaeological Sites as Indicators of Former Trade Connections in the Eastern Mediterranean" *Paléorient* 30.1 (2004): 101–47; B. Routledge, "A Fishy Business: The Inland Trade in Nile Perch (*Lates nil Soticus*) in the Early Iron Age Levant," in *Walls of the Prince: Egyptian Interactions with Southwest Asia in Antiquity* (eds. T. Harrison et al., Leiden: Brill, 2015), 212–33.

107. S. Kisilevitz, "The Iron IIA Judahite Temple at Tel Moza," *TA* 42.2 (2015): 156–58. Cf. D. Ben-Shlomo, "Petrographic Analysis of Iron Age IIA Figurines from the Ophel," in *The Ophel Excavations to the South of the Temple Mount, 2009–2013: Final Reports*, vol. 1 (ed. E. Mazar; Jerusalem: Shoham, 2015), 563–68.

108. A. Cohen-Weinberger, N. Szanton, and J. Uziel, "Ethnofabrics: Petrographic Analysis as a Tool for Illuminating Cultural Interactions and Trade Relations between Judah and Philistia during the Iron Age II," *BASOR* 377 (2017): 1–20.

The growing body of archaeological evidence pertaining to the multidirectional interactions and exchange between Gath and the highlands, including other instances,[109] indicates that if the early Iron Age period witnessed forms of boundary maintenance between Gittite and highland peoples,[110] it was also nevertheless an era of "ongoing interactions of a non-confrontational character between these cultures."[111]

Around the year 830 BCE the city of Gath was destroyed.[112] Evidence of a violent destruction has been recovered from throughout the site, with an 80 cm layer of ashen debris preserving the remnants of charred buildings, a large assemblage of complete ceramic vessels, and human remains.[113] The agent behind Gath's demise was Hazael of Damascus. Descending down onto Israel, Philistia, Judah and other polities in the southern Levant, Hazael embarked on a campaign in the late ninth century BCE to reorganize the region and include it within the Aramean empire he now controlled.[114] In addition to Gath, Hazael destroyed a number of northern Israelite sites and was also most likely behind the destruction of further settlements south of Gath, such as Tell el-Farah (South) and Tel Sera'.[115] Jerusalem and Judah were able to escape the violence, according to the biblical narrative, only through payment of ransom and the acceptance of vassalhood (2 Kings 12:18). What remained in the aftermath of Hazael's campaign was the great city of Gath reduced to mostly rubble, put to the torch by the Aramean

---

109. Hitchcock and Maeir, "Beyond Creolization and Hybridity," 43–65; B. David et al., "Disentangling Entangled Objects: Iron Age Inscriptions from Philistia as a Reflection of Cultural Processes," *IEJ* 65 (2015): 140–66; A. Maeir et al., "An Ivory Bowl from Early Iron Age Tell es-Safi/Gath (Israel): Manufacture, Meaning and Memory," *World Archaeology* 47.3 (2015): 414–38.

110. A. Faust, "Trade, Ideology, and Boundary Maintenance in Iron Age Israelite Society," in *A Holy Community* (eds. M. Parthuis and J. Schwartz; Leiden: Brill, 2006), 17–35.

111. Maeir et al., "Constitution," 25 (my italics).

112. Maeir dates this destruction to ca. 835/832 BCE. Maeir, "Introduction," 47–49.

113. D. Namdar et al., "The 9th Century BCE Destruction Layer at Tell es-Safi/Gath, Israel: Integrating Macro- and Microarchaeology," *Journal of Archaeological Science* 38.12 (2011): 3471–82.

114. A. Lemaire, "Hazaël de Damas, roi d'Aram," in *Marchands, Diplomates et Empereurs: Études sur la Civilisation Mésopotamienne Offertes à Paul Garelli* (eds. D. Charpand and F. Joannès; Paris: Éditions Recherche sur les Civilisations, 1991), 91–108; I. Finkelstein, *The Forgotten Kingdom: The Archaeology and History of the Northern Kingdom* (Atlanta: SBL Press, 2013), 124–27; H. Ghountas, *The Elisha-Hazael Paradigm and the Kingdom of Israel: The Politics of God in Ancient Syria-Palestine* (Routledge: New York, 2013), 20–80.

115. Lehmann and Niemann, "Shephelah," 88.

army after the location had been overrun and defeated. Remains from the con-flagration indicate that the heat from the fires that engulfed Gath reached 400 degrees Celsius.[116]

The era of Aramean domination in the southern Levant was nevertheless short-lived. After Hazael's death and the return of Damascus' foe, Assyria, to the region in 796 BCE, both Israel and Judah began to recover and prosper. Gath however did not. Though it appears that some structures in Gath remained standing after Hazael's campaign, wind-born sediments attached to the walls of various structures demonstrate that these buildings were left only partially standing and exposed to the elements, many having been abandoned for some time.[117] Skeletons unearthed beneath collapsed structures, a number found nearly intact, further suggest that those who survived the Aramean siege and onslaught did not return to bury the dead.[118] At the close of the ninth century BCE, Gath would have thus taken on a rather ghostly appearance, the vast city now laden with burnt-out homes and the decaying bodies of those who had not survived Hazael's offensive.

Around a hundred years after Gath had been destroyed the location began to be slowly resettled. Large swaths of the lower neighborhoods, such as Area D of the site, were, however, not inhabited, signifying that most of the new residents were confined to the former precincts of the upper city. What is of particular interest about this era is that the material culture left behind from these inhabit-ants reveals that they were most likely not Philistine, but rather affiliated with Judah.[119] Remains recovered from Area A (Stratum A2) and Area F (Stratums F7 and F8) include four-room homes and a ceramic repertoire that evinces a dis-tinct Judahite orientation, marking a conspicuous shift in the location's cultural orientation from the centuries before. The fact that Judahites now resided in the city in the late eighth century BCE would also suggest that the location had come under the control of the kingdom of Judah during this time, with most

---

116. Namdar et al., "Destruction Layer," 3480.

117. Namdar et al., "Destruction Layer," 3481; Maeir, "Introduction," 49; idem, "Insights," 393.

118. Namdar et al., "Destruction Layer," 3481; Maeir, "Introduction," 49, idem, "Philistia and the Judean Shephelah After Hazael: The Power Play Between the Philistines, Judeans and Assyrians in the 8th Century BCE in Light of the Excavations at Tell es-Safi/Gath," in *Disaster and Relief Management - Katastrophen und ihre Bewältigung* (ed. A. Berlejung; Tübingen: Mohr Siebeck, 2012), 245; idem, "Insights," 393.

119. Maeir, "Introduction," 49–51; idem, "Philistia and the Judean Shephelah," 246; idem, "Insights," 396; A. Zukerman and I. Shai, "'The Royal City of the Philistines' in the 'Azekah Inscription' and the History of Gath in the 8th Century BCE," *UF* 38 (2006): 730–31.

attributing the Judahite annexation of Gath to King Hezekiah.[120] But as with the great Philistine city of the Iron IIA period, so also the much more modest Gath of the Iron IIB era was brought to an end by way of military conquest. In 701 BCE, Sennacherib, ruler of the Assyrian Empire, marched through the Shephelah and laid waste to most of the cities of the region, Gath included.[121]

With Gath's destruction at the hands of the Assyrians the story of its Iron Age existence comes to a close. Few remains have been obtained from strata coterminous with the Iron IIC era (seventh to early sixth century BCE), and it is Ekron, now growing to an area of ca. 30 ha, that once again becomes the dominant city of the Shephelah in the time after Sennacherib's campaign. When biblical texts make reference to Philistine cities after the Iron IIB period, they consistently name four sites—Ashkelon, Ashdod, Gaza, and Ekron—with Gath never being included among them (e.g., Amos 1:8; Jer. 25:20; Zeph. 2:4; Zech. 9:5). When Nebuchadnezzar campaigned through the region at the end of the seventh century BCE and conquered Ashkelon, Ekron, and other settlements in the highlands and coastal plains, again no mention is made of Gath. The great city of the Philistines that dominated the southern Levant in the tenth and ninth centuries BCE would, in the end, never return to its former size and status after the Aramean conquest of the site. A few inhabitants find their way to Gath in the Persian Period, but little is left behind in terms of material culture.[122] Neither the Greeks nor the Romans rebuild the city, though the latter appear to have farmed over it.[123]

Gath and the Resilience of a Remembered Past

The archaeological remains recovered from Tell es-Safi find importance for this chapter's study because they offer a contemporary snapshot of how the city of Gath appeared in the early Iron Age period. The biblical texts that make reference

---

120. N. Na'aman, "Hezekiah's Fortified Cities and the LMLK Stamps," *BASOR* 261 (1986): 10–11; A. Fantalkin and I. Finkelstein, "The Sheshonq I Campaign and the 8th-Century BCE Earthquake-more on the Archaeology and History of the South in the Iron I–IIa," *TA* 33 (2006): 31; Maeir, "Insights," 398–401; idem, "Philistia and the Judean Shephelah," 247–51.

121. N. Na'aman, "Population Changes in Palestine Following Assyrian Deportations," *TA* 20 (1993): 104–24; I. Finkelstein, "The Archaeology of the Days of Manasseh," in *Scripture and Other Artifacts: Essays on the Bible and Archaeology in Honor of Philip J. King* (eds. Coogan et al., Louisville: Westminster, 1994), 169–87; Zukerman and Shai, "Royal City," 745–49; Maeir, "Introduction," 53–54.

122. Maeir, "Introduction," 56.

123. Ibid., 57.

to Gath do not offer such a perspective, but rather represent the end stage of a long process of composition and revising that extended well beyond the time in which Gath was an important Philistine city. But what is made possible through the material culture recovered from Tell es-Safi is the opportunity to examine what features of this early Iron Age city may have been refracted through the later literary images represented within writings now contained in the Hebrew Bible. And in bringing together the ancient archaeological and textual evidence pertaining to Gath we are able to ask a question that stands at the heart of this study: what did later Hebrew scribes know about the early Iron Age period?

Details pertaining to a race of giants who once inhabited Gath or a local outlaw feigning madness at its gate are not ones that can be pursued through this approach. But a broader collection of historical interests related to geography, culture, and politics are ones that can be explored. And when turning to these concerns certain points of semblance emerge between the material and textual evidence pertaining to Gath that have important implications for how we understand the type of knowledge passed on through the source material available to later biblical writers.

First, it is necessary to underscore that Gath's very appearance within texts of the Hebrew Bible is of historical significance for the study at hand. Destroyed at the end of the ninth century BCE and of little consequence in the centuries that followed, Philistine Gath is nevertheless referred to within the biblical writings, and prominently so. What these references to Gath demonstrate, accordingly, is that the biblical scribes had access to information that could have only descended from the early Iron Age period in light of the timeframe in which the Philistine settlement at Gath came to an end. Indeed, though the site appears to have come under some manner of Judahite influence in the mid-to-late eighth century BCE, Gath is nevertheless consistently recognized as a foreign, Philistine site of regional import before its fall to Hazael within a collection of biblical texts (e.g., Josh. 11, 13; 1 Sam. 5–7; 21, 27–31). And such references to Gath's Philistine background correspond well to the material culture recovered from the Iron I–IIA settlement, as detailed above, in which Gath is not only one of the largest cities of its time but is also distinguished by its distinct ceramic repertoire[124] and other instances of Philistine material culture, such as the presence of pebble hearths, public architecture, and evidence of pork consumption.[125] The references to Gath

---

124. Zukerman, "Iron Age I and Early Iron Age IIA Pottery," 265–312; Shai and Maeir, "The Late Iron IIA Pottery Assemblage," 313–64.

125. Maeir, "Introduction," 26–43; A. Maeir and L. Hitchcock, "Absence Makes the *Hearth* Grow Fonder: Searching for the Origins of the Philistine hearth," *Er-Isr* 30 (2011): 46–64; Maeir et al., "Constitution," 8–10, 17.

as an imposing Philistine settlement within biblical stories set in the early Iron Age period are not then a figment of the biblical storyteller's imagination, but connect, broadly speaking, to what is known about early Iron Age Gath from the archaeological record.

More about this settlement was known to the biblical scribes, however, than the *bruta facta* of its former existence and connection with Philistine populations, important as this awareness may be. The second feature to be observed is the general geographical setting in which the biblical writings situate Gath. On the one hand, this settlement is invariably linked to other Philistine city states in the books of Joshua and Samuel, with the latter positioning Gath somewhere near the Elah Valley and in close proximity to Ekron (Josh. 13:2–3; 1 Sam. 5, 17), a location that is now confirmed through the excavations carried out at Tell es-Safi. The depiction of Ekron and Gath together as Philistine cities of significance in these stories further buttresses this early Iron Age perspective.[126] For as the remains recovered from the two settlements indicate, in the thousand years that passed from the Middle Bronze Age to the end of the Iron Age, there was only one moment when both locations were of some size and status at the same time: the Iron I period, or the era in which the biblical writings indicate the importance of both.[127] The identification of Gath within a configuration of other Philistine city states, furthermore, can only reflect an Iron I–IIA landscape when Gath was a dominant Philistine settlement, as this portrayal would have made little sense to those situated in later eras when Gath was only a very modestly inhabited location.

What is also striking about the biblical references to Gath is the important role the site plays within stories crafted and revised long after the location ceased to exist as a dominating presence in the southern Levant. More than double the size of any highland settlement during the early Iron Age period and similar to the dimensions of Jerusalem at its height in the eighth to sixth centuries BCE (c. 50 ha), the startling size of Gath and the primacy it likely enjoyed as a Philistine center in the region are elements of the site also intimated throughout the biblical narratives that depict this era. An understanding of the magnitude of Gath's confines thus reframes how we understand the depiction of David's decision by the biblical writers, for example, to flee westward to Gath over against other

---

126. So Finkelstein argues that the allusion to both Ekron and Gath as significant cities "must preserve a 10th century memory—the last time when both Ekron and Gath were of significance." Finkelstein, "Geographical and Historical Realities, " 138 fn. 38.

127. Maeir and Uziel, "Two Tells," 29–42.

possible sites while evading Saul (1 Sam. 21, 27–28). The special status accorded to Gath in these narrative episodes makes some sense, in other words, in light of the material remains recovered from Tell es-Safi, including its massive early Iron Age gate complex, extensive fortifications, and rich cultural assemblage.[128] Of all the potential locations the biblical writers could have placed David in his flight from Saul, Gath was the one early Iron Age site in the southern Levant that would have offered the most protection and the most opportunities.

The image of a highland outlaw dwelling in Gath's confines also calls to mind the biblical references to those inhabitants of Gath who descend from different backgrounds than that of the Philistines. Included among these are groups affiliated with Canaanite populations, such as the *Anakim* (Josh. 11:22) and the "descendants of the Raphah" (2 Sam. 21:18–22), but also highland contingents, including not only David but also his fighters and their families who are all said to have lived within Gath for a significant period of time (1 Sam. 27:2–3). Regardless of the historical character of these particular references, what is significant about them is the recognition that Gath once housed a heterogeneous population that extended beyond Philistine groups, and that the borders that separated the Gittite realm from other political communities were quite fluid. Such a perspective finds importance for this chapter's study because Philistine material culture at Gath, like other Philistine centers in the Iron I–IIA period, exists side by side with an abundance of Canaanite and highland remains.[129] The fact that both Aegean and Canaanite motifs are found on kraters at Gath, that residents of this location depicted local Canaanite figures on their conoid seals, that the site adopted a form of linear alphabetic writing used elsewhere in the southern Levant, and that residents of Gath were influenced by other local cultural features (cultic, architectural, linguistic) are, each in turn, evidence that Gath housed populations from various cultural backgrounds and ethnicities.[130]

Instances of cultural exchange and influence between Gittites and other communities in its vicinity invite us as readers, furthermore, to attend to those moments of contact between Gittite and highland individuals within the biblical writings. In addition to David's stay in Gath with his family and his fighters

---

128. Maeir, "Introduction," 26–27; idem, "Philistine Gath after 20 Years," 139–42; Maeir and Hitchcock, "And the Canaanite," 211–19.

129. Yasur-Landau, *Philistines*, 287–94; idem, "Canaanite Population," 192; D. Master, "The Renewal of Trade at Iron Age I Ashkelon." *Er-Isr* 28 (2011): 111–22; Maeir et al, "An Ivory Bowl," 414–38.

130. Hitchcock and Maeir, "Beyond Creolization and Hybridity," 51–55; Davis et al., "Disentangling Entangled Objects," 140–66.

(1 Sam. 27:3), one can also point to Obed-Edom or Ittai, both Gittites according to the biblical narrative, who are depicted as having residences in or near Jerusalem (2 Sam. 6:10–12; 15:19–22). Such allusions need not, from this perspective, be understood as a subversive narrative portrayal by the biblical writers but in keeping with what was likely a common phenomenon throughout the early Iron Age period: namely, many occasions of non-violent interactions and more intimate relations between individuals from highland communities and inhabitants from Gath's domain in the Shephelah who traversed back and forth across these areas.[131] Scenes of highland peoples dwelling in Gath's confines or Gittites in Jerusalem are reasonable representations, then, with regard to those who would have resided in these communities in the early Iron Age given the material remains left behind of the heterogeneous populations at these locations. The absence of material evidence that would suggest outright hostility between Gath and highland communities, furthermore, makes it reasonable to infer that Gittites and individuals from the polities of Israel and Judah could coexist and likely did so for centuries, and that the biblical scribes were aware of such circumstances.

The broader geopolitical influence attributed to Gath by the biblical writers is also worthy of note. In the stories of David's flight from Saul, for example, the city of Gath is depicted as extending its reach to the far south and the site of Ziklag that was located somewhere near the Negev desert (1 Sam. 27). Before excavations were undertaken at Tell es-Safi a principal argument against its identification as Gath, in fact, was the observation that Tell es-Safi was located at too remote a distance in the north for it to have once controlled an area that included such faraway locales as Ziklag.[132] But in light of Gath's size and status during the Iron I–IIA period, it is now no longer difficult to envision a Gittite realm that encompassed the Shephelah region south to the Beer-Sheba Valley.[133] This

---

131. Weitzman's reading of the Samson narratives comes to a similar conclusion, with the Samson stories created, according to Weitzman's argument, to reinforce ideas of boundaries "because, apparently, these people did not draw clear boundaries themselves." S. Weitzman, "Crossing the Border with Samson: Beth-Shemesh and the Bible's Geographical Imagination," in *Tel Beth-Shemesh: A Border Community in Judah, Renewed Excavations 1990–2000: The Iron Age*, vol. I (eds. S. Bunimovitz and Z. Lederman; Tel Aviv: Emery and Claire Yass Publications, 2016), 266.

132. So both Albright's and Stager's rejection of Tell es-Safi on the grounds that it was located too far north from Ziklag. Albright, "Contributions," 10–12; Stager, "Forging an Identity," 162.

133. S. Bunimovitz and Z. Lederman, "Close Yet Apart: Diverse Cultural Dynamics at Iron Age Beth-Shemesh and Lachish," in *The Fire Signals of Lachish: Studies in the Archaeology and History of Israel in the Late Bronze Age, Iron Age, and Persian Period in Honor of David Ussishkin* (eds. I. Finkelstein and N. Na'aman; Winona Lake: Eisenbrauns, 2011), 36.

sphere of influence would have been made all the more possible by the fact that Ekron was destroyed at the start of the tenth century BCE, leaving Gath alone as a central city in the northern Shephelah, and that the city of Lachish, once a prominent Late Bronze Age city state and natural rival to Gath's south, was only rebuilt in the early-to-mid ninth century BCE. No other city of significance in the Shephelah, accordingly, would have stood between Gath and the Beer-Sheba Valley until the last moments of the Iron IIA period.[134]

An important point of continuity between the material remains of Tell es-Safi and the biblical portrait of Gath, then, is the authority Gath exerts in the biblical stories set in the centuries of the Iron I–IIA era. In part, this authority is represented through the character of Achish, a ruler who is depicted in a manner somewhat distinct from other Philistine leaders by being referred to as a king in contrast to the title of *seren* accorded to other Philistine leaders during this time (e.g., 1 Sam. 5.8,11; 6.4,12,16,18; 29.2,6,7),[135] and by being represented as a key military leader of the Philistine coalition (e.g., 1 Sam. 28:1–2; 1 Sam. 29). Whether Achish was a historical figure or, even more, a *primus inter pares* within a putative Philistine coalition[136] is something the archaeological record cannot determine. But what is evident is that with the beginning of the tenth century BCE Gath was in the process of becoming the primary Philistine power in the southern Levant at a moment when a number of other Philistine sites were entering into a period of decline.[137] Regardless of whether Achish existed, then, as the biblical narratives describe him, Gath certainly did, and it prevailed in a manner that dominated the surrounding region in the Iron IIA period.

The relationship between Achish and David in the Book of Samuel is also of interest from this vantage point, and perhaps redolent of a broader political alliance between Gath and Jerusalem during this period in time. Again, no archaeological finds can confirm or deny such an affiliation between these particular biblical characters. But what is present in the archaeological record is evidence of economic and cultural exchange between Gath and its eastern neighbors in the highlands.[138] Moreover, to date there is no indication of any outright hostility between Gath and highland communities to its east during the early Iron Age

---

134. Finkelstein, "Geographical and Historical Realities," 146.

135. Anson Rainey, "Syntax, Hermeneutics and History," *IEJ* 48 (1998): 243; Wagner, "Die סרנים der Philister und die Ältesten Israels"; Edenburg, "Notes on the Origin of the Biblical Tradition Regarding Achish King of Gath."

136. Rainey, "Syntax," 243; Na'aman, "David's Wars," 202; Shai, "Political Organization," 350.

137. Maeir et al., "Constitution," 26–27; Faust, "Regional Power," 179–86.

138. Ben-Shlomo et al., "Cooking Identities," 225–46; Maeir et al., "Constitution," 25.

period. Of course, malice, enmity, or resentments do not necessarily leave behind material markers in the archaeological record. But it is nevertheless striking that for a period of around three centuries we find no clear indication that forces from Gath ever attacked or destroyed a single location within the neighboring regions of Israel or Judah or, conversely, that it was attacked by individuals from these areas during this time.[139] Instead, large settlements such as Beth-Shemesh and Lachish are rebuilt along Gath's border by Judahite leaders who do not appear to fear any reprisals.

In light of such considerations it is significant that no mention is made in the books of Samuel or Kings that Israel or Judah ever conquered Gath or,[140] in the period after Saul, were even in tension with it. The negative archaeological evidence, so to speak, in which neither Gath nor Israelite/Judahite settlements along Gath's border evince traces of destruction in the Iron IIA period is of some historical significance,[141] then, given that the biblical texts are also silent about any antagonism between the two kingdoms erupting in the tenth and ninth centuries BCE. Rather, the archaeological evidence attests to the fact that Gath's rise in the Iron IIA period coincided with the founding of the House of David and the steady growth of this small kingdom to Gath's east.[142] The relationship depicted between David and various individuals from Gath (Achish, Obed-Edom, Ittai) in the Book of Samuel is, in this sense, once again suggestive.

The one moment of destruction that is identified in the Hebrew Bible is that of Hazael's conquest of Gath (2 Kings 12:18; cf. Amos 6:2). As detailed above, the archeological record offers vivid evidence of this event, with the city's conflagration and devastation demonstrated throughout the settlement during an

---

139. Maeir has also recently called attention to the relative paucity of "warfare-related material" from Gath's Iron I confines. Maeir, "Philistine Gath after 20 Years," 136.

140. In Chronicles, the parallel text to 2 Samuel 8:1 reads that David "took Gath and its daughter [villages]," which is the Chronicler's translation of a difficult term found in 2 Samuel 8:1, the מתג האמה. Given that the reference to Gath is an outcome of the Chronicler's attempting to make sense of a problematic term in the Chronicler's source material, the historical value of the reference to Gath here is quite negligible—a point reinforced by the archaeological evidence of Tell es-Safi. See S. Japhet, *I & II Chronicles: A Commentary* (Louisville: Westminster John Knox, 1993), 346; Levin, "Gath in the Bible," 145.

141. Na'aman, "Kingdom of Judah," 294; on the coexistence of the Judahite center of Lachish and Gath during the ninth century BCE, see again Ussishkin, "Gath, Lachish, and Jerusalem," 138.

142. Halpern makes this point explicit: "It is reasonable to suppose that David's irruption into Hebron and then Jerusalem and the assertion of his sovereignty over Israel represented a loss for Eqron, to Gath's benefit. . . . David likely allied not just with Gath, but also with pentapolis cities west of Eqron." Halpern, *David's Secret Demons*, 330.

era when Hazael sought to expand his empire from Damascus.[143] What is also of interest about Gath's status after Hazael's campaign however are those few biblical allusions that make reference to the location's Judahite affiliations in the eighth century BCE (Mic. 1:8; 2 Chron. 26:6). Over against past interpretations of these texts that have deemed them corrupt or as referring to a Gath other than the Philistine location,[144] the presence of Judahite material culture at Tell es-Safi from the Iron IIB period gives substance to the biblical perspective that Gath had, for a short period in time, come under Judahite control.[145] And when Gath declines further after Sennacherib's offensive in the Shephelah, so also does Gath disappear from biblical texts that allude to events after 701 BCE.

All told, a number of points of contact emerge within the constellation of textual and material traces that pertain to the city of Gath.[146] The purpose of drawing attention to these moments of convergence is not to argue for the historicity of the biblical portrayal. Rather, what matters about the relationship between these ancient textual references and Gath's material remains is what this relationship reveals about the sources available to those biblical writers who wrote and rewrote their narrative accounts about an early Iron Age past. And the frequency with which the biblical references to Gath resonate with what is known about the city through the archaeological record indicates that the stories told about this location in the Hebrew Bible were not the product of happenstance or chance reckonings. Instead, these moments of convergence must have been the outcome of information, transmitted to the biblical writers over time, that was reflective of the early Iron Age site of Gath itself.

Such findings bring us once more to the central question that lies at the heart of this work. What the archaeological evidence from Tell es-Safi illustrates is that the stories told about an early Iron Age past in the Hebrew Bible were predicated, at least in certain moments and with reference to certain places, on knowledge

---

143. Namdar, "Destruction Layer," 3480–81; Maeir, "Introduction," 49; idem, "Philistia and the Judean Shephelah," 244–45; idem, "Insights," 393.

144. Levin, "Philistine Gath," 147–48.

145. Maeir, "Introduction," 49–51; idem, "Philistia and the Judean Shephelah," 246; idem, "Insights," 396; Zukerman and Shai, "Royal City of the Philistines," 730–31.

146. Such a view would contrast with the earlier Finkelstein, who argued that the biblical depiction of the Philistines reflects a seventh century BCE reality (Israel Finkelstein, "The Philistines in the Bible: A Late-Monarchic Perspective," *JSOT* 27.2 (2002): 131–67) and draws near to the more recent Finkelstein, who does see pre-seventh-century historical material embedded in the biblical texts about the Philistines (Finkelstein, "Geographical and Historical Realities," 144–49). Cf. Maeir and Uziel, who are argue that the biblical texts regarding Gath were predicated on "concrete historical memory." Maeir and Uziel, "Two Tells," 34–35.

that descended from the early Iron Age period. In conjunction with those points raised in the previous chapter on the sources available to the biblical scribes, it cannot be discounted that these individuals had access to brief written references about Gath, including, perhaps, older documents that made mention of this neighboring Philistine polity. But many of the references to Gath—particularly with regard to the Iron I/early Iron II period (twelfth to tenth centuries BCE)— would have been dependent on an oral storytelling tradition that conveyed past knowledge by way of the memories recounted within it.[147]

Meaningful about the biblical references to Gath are two considerations for this chapter's investigation. First, references to Gath indicate that the biblical writings about the Philistine city were informed by source material that originated in the early Iron Age period. Second, the information contained in this source material demonstrates a particular resiliency to the effects of revision and forgetting so common to the dynamics of cultural memory within ancient (and modern) communities. A number of the anecdotes that informed the biblical accounts of Gath, it seems, endured for a number of generations—if not longer—until a loose collection of tales that involved Gath and various biblical events and figures crystallized into narrative prose form. Given the meager evidence we possess of the oral traditions and scribal practices that contributed to the shaping of texts about Gath in the Hebrew Bible, how and why this Philistine city was remembered with such tenacity remains something of a mystery. But what can be done to shed some light on this development is to briefly review other instances from antiquity in which a more remote past also endured and came to be textualized in later writings.

One can begin with the Hebrew Bible itself. A well-known instance includes the old memory of Philistine peoples descending from "Caphtor" within a diverse collection of texts that were written down no earlier than the eighth century BCE (Deut. 2:23; Jer. 47:3; Amos 9:7). This toponym, prevalent already in late second millennium BCE texts outside the Hebrew Bible, is likely to be identified with Crete or a broader geographical region in Crete's vicinity in the eastern Mediterranean region.[148] The significance of this biblical allusion to Caphtor is,

---

147. On the influence of oral tradition on these biblical narratives, see also Finkelstein, "Geographical and Historical Realities," 135; W. Dietrich, *The Early Monarchy in Israel: The Tenth Century B.C.E.* (trans. J. Vette; Atlanta: Society of Biblical Literature, 2007), 242–72; R. Person, "The Role of Memory in the Tradition Represented by the Deuteronomistic History and the Book of Chronicles," *Oral Tradition* 26.2 (2011): 537–50.

148. I. Singer, "The Philistines in the Bible: A Short Rejoinder to a New Perspective," in *The Philistines and Other "Sea Peoples" in Text and Archaeology* (eds. A. Killebrew and G. Lehmann; Atlanta: SBL Press, 2013), 21.

again, not in its historicity—the origins of the Philistines are much more complex and multifaceted than what a single location suggests. Rather, what is significant about this allusion is the widespread archaeological evidence that attests to a more general Aegean background of a number of groups that came to be identified with Philistine populations.[149] Biblical writers could have situated the Philistine homeland in any number of locations, and texts such as Genesis 11 illustrate how historically specious such references could be. But in the case of the Philistines older memories of an Aegean background endured within later textual traditions. Even more, a collection of early Iron Age cultural markers associated with this foreign background, as E. Bloch-Smith details, came to be embedded within later biblical writings concerned with constructing notions of Israelite ethnicity.[150] Considering the time frame in which such biblical texts were written down, the memory of an Aegean, non-native background to peoples affiliated with the Philistines would have had to persist for a number of centuries in the southern Levant.

Shiloh (Khirbet Seilun), situated ca. 17 km south of Shechem in the central hill country, offers another example from the Hebrew Bible. Portrayed prominently in biblical stories set in the Iron I period, Shiloh is identified as a place of tribal assembly and a location for an important Yahweh temple in a number of biblical texts (i.e., Josh. 18–22; Judg. 21; 1 Sam. 1, 4). Yet striking about Shiloh is that it is also referred to within the Book of Jeremiah (Jer. 7:12,14; 26:6, 9) as a site that symbolized divine judgment through its destruction long ago. When turning to the archaeological record of the settlement, it is clear that that Shiloh was in fact destroyed in the mid-to-late eleventh century BCE and not rebuilt again for another fifteen hundred years.[151] Accordingly, not only do the texts of Joshua, Judges, and Samuel that ascribe importance to Shiloh find resonance with Shiloh's position in eleventh century BCE even though they were written down after the Iron I period, but so also do the references to Shiloh's destruction in the distant past within the Book of Jeremiah. The references to Shiloh found

---

149. S. Sherratt, "The Ceramic Phenomenon of the 'Sea Peoples,': An Overview" in *The Philistines and Other 'Sea Peoples' in Text and Archaeology* (eds. A. Killebrew and G. Lehmann; Atlanta: SBL Press, 2013), 619–44; Stager, "Forging an Identity," 152–53; so also Singer writes that the "very preservation of the second-millennium B.C.E. term Kaptara in biblical Caphtor, the alleged origin of the Philistines, is suggestive for a long historical memory." Singer, "Philistines in the Bible," 21.

150. Elizabeth Bloch-Smith, "Israelite Ethnicity in Iron I: Archaeology Preserves What Is Remembered and What Is Forgotten in Israel's History," *JBL* 122.3 (2003): 401–25.

151. I. Finkelstein, S. Bumimovitz, and Z. Lederman, *Shiloh: The Archaeology of a Biblical Site* (Tel Aviv: Tel Aviv University, 1993), 383–89.

in Jeremiah, in fact, would not have been textualized until the late seventh century BCE at the earliest, or nearly *five centuries* after Shiloh had been destroyed.

More examples can be cited. Bethel, ca. 15 km south of Shiloh, is referred to frequently in the Books of Judges and Samuel (Judg. 20:18, 26; 21:2; 1 Sam. 7:16; 10:3) as a site of tribal politics and cultic celebration in stories that take place in the Iron I era. Archaeological remains from the location indicate that it was inhabited during this timeframe and likely functioned as a significant highland location in an era that witnessed an upsurge in settlement activity in the surrounding region.[152] Yet over against efforts to see these biblical references to Bethel as reflective of affairs that were actually taking place at the site in the much later Persian period, it appears that Bethel did not exist as an inhabited location in the Persian era.[153] It is much more probable, then, that references to Bethel's early Iron Age past were the product of older sources rather than later imaginings conceived of in light of Persian period realities.

The residue of a more remote past is found, in fact, within a number of biblical texts that were developed by Hebrew scribes at periods later in time. Examples are not restricted to a particular time and place, but rather stem from a wide chronological horizon and geographical region. These include faint Bronze Age allusions to geography and cult within the certain texts now found in the patriarchal narratives of Genesis and stories surrounding Shechem in the Book of Judges,[154] but also early Iron Age references to Hazor's destruction (Josh. 11) and the great temple once located at Shechem (Judg. 9:46, 49),[155] both attested to by archaeological evidence, and later Iron I reflections to sites in the Jezreel Valley (Taanach, Megiddo, Beth-shean) that remained Canaanite throughout this period in time (Josh. 13:2–6; Judg. 1:27–35).[156] (See Figure 2.7.)

---

152. I. Finkelstein and L. Singer-Avitz, "Reevaluating Bethel," *ZDPV* 125 (2009): 37–38.

153. Ibid., 45.

154. On Genesis, see R. Hendel, *Remembering Abraham: Culture, Memory, and History in the Hebrew Bible* (Oxford: Oxford University Press, 2005), 45–56; for Judges, see B. Benz, *The Land Before the Kingdom of Israel: A History of the Southern Levant and the People Who Populated It* (Winona Lake: Eisenbrauns, 2016), 303–65.

155. L. Stager, "The Shechem Temple: Where Abimelech Massacred a Thousand," *BAR* 29.4 (2003): 26–35, 66–69; E. Bloch-Smith, "A Stratified Account of Jephthah's Negotiations and Battle: Judges 11:12–33 from an Archaeological Perspective," *JBL* 134.2 (2015): 294–95.

156. So the examples raised in A. Mazar, "Archaeology and the Bible: Reflections on Historical Memory in the Deuteronomistic History," in *Congress Volume Munich 2013* (ed. C. Maeir; Leiden: Brill, 2014), 348–53. Cf. K. Van Bekkum, "Coexistence as Guilt: Iron I Memories in Judges 1," in *The Ancient Near East in the 12th–10th Centuries BCE* (eds. G. Galil et al.; Münster: Ugarit-Verlag, 2012), 525–47.

FIGURE 2.7 The Canaanite Gate of Megiddo (Picture: Author).

Tirzah, the old capital of Israel, is cited in the Song of Songs for its beauty in a manner that parallels the splendor of Jerusalem for the poet (Song 6:4). Yet, though once replete with a fine palace and patrician homes in the Iron IIA–B period,[157] Tirzah was nevertheless destroyed by the Assyrians and abandoned after the eighth century BCE, or around four centuries before Song of Songs was likely set down in writing.[158] Though ancient Near Eastern ideological conventions mandated that narrative accounts of royal conquest be embellished in order to promote the authority of its new ruler, the story of the acquisition of Jerusalem by David in 2 Samuel 5:6–9, to cite another instance, is strikingly spare. Here again, however, the biblical allusions to this event resonate with the archaeological evidence recovered from the late Iron I/early Iron IIA period in which Jerusalem was at most a modest highland stronghold.[159]

157. A. Chambon, "Far'ah, Tell el- (North)," in *NEAEHL*, II (ed. E. Stern; Jerusalem: Israel Exploration Society, 1993), 439–40.

158. F. W. Dobbs-Allsopp, *On Biblical Poetry* (New York: Oxford University Press, 2015), 484–85.

159. Pioske, *David's Jerusalem*, 223–33.

Such instances are not, however, restricted to the Hebrew Bible alone. Studies of Homer that compare its epic world with the ancient archaeological evidence recovered from the eastern Mediterranean region have found an "irreducible minimum" amount of references that are best connected to the Late Bronze era, even though the Homeric poems were not written down until five centuries later.[160] Such instances include allusions to chariotry, weaponry, and palatial architecture within these poems,[161] but also references to Troy itself—including the name Alexander as a leader of the location and the site's identification with the god Apollo, which are both indisputably rooted in a second millennium BCE context in light of Bronze Age documents that also make reference to these features of Troy.[162] Thucydides, whose opens his work by recounting various incidents from a more distant past, includes mention of the city of Corinth as the first Greek center to build the famed *trireme* ship in a time three centuries previous to Thucydides's own era (Thuc. 1.13). In contrast to Thucydides's historically spurious digressions about King Minos (Thuc. 1.4) or events related to the Trojan War (Thuc. 1.9) within these introductory remarks, traditions about Corinth's shipbuilding prowess, taken over from oral sayings ("the Corinthians *are said to have*. . . ."), have however been found to be generally reliable.[163]

Scholars of Icelandic saga have also drawn attention to fragments of a more remote past that came to be embedded within later textual traditions. Perhaps the most impressive example of this phenomenon stems from the work of Ari Thorgilsson (1067–1148 CE) and his book on the migration of Scandinavian peoples to Iceland (the *Íslendingabók*). Derived from a collection of earlier oral accounts, much of Thorgilsson's work has little to with any historical past. But a number of claims in the *Íslendingabók* have stood up to archaeological scrutiny, including Thorgilsson's dating of the initial arrival in Iceland to 870 CE, the fact that Icelandic communities were settled in the short span of sixty years, and that this settlement activity had a profound impact on Icelandic flora and

160. Susan Sherratt, "Homeric Epic and Contexts of Bardic Creation," in *Archaeology and Homeric Epic* (eds. S. Sherratt and J. Bennet; Oxford: Oxbow, 2016), 37–38.

161. O. Dickinson, "Homer, the Poet of the Dark Age," *Greece & Rome* 33.1 (1986): 29–30; S. Sherratt, "'Reading the Texts': Archaeology and the Homeric Question," *Antiquity* 64 (1990): 810–12.

162. M. Bachvarova, *From Hittite to Homer: The Anatolian Background of Ancient Greek Epic* (Cambridge: Cambridge University Press, 2016), 351–54.

163. J. Morrison et al., *The Athenian Trireme: The History and Reconstruction of the Ancient Greek Warship* (2nd ed.; Cambridge: Cambridge University Press, 2000), 27–28; S. Hornblower, *A Commentary on Thucydides*, vol. I (Oxford: Clarendon Press, 1991), 43.

fauna in the subsequent time period.[164] Such information, among other instances of similar moments of coherence between archaeological research and references embedded in these sagas,[165] would have been preserved through mechanisms of memory and oral transmission for roughly three centuries before these accounts were written down.

Though composed for purposes beyond those that animate modern works of historiography, references to a more distant past in texts composed in antiquity could nevertheless, at moments, retain connections to former eras and happenings. From scenes surrounding the raids of Myceneans on Egypt[166] to Berossus's account of Tarsus[167] to *Beowulf*'s description of pre-Christian north Germanic culture,[168] inlayed within written stories of former times are referential claims that connect more readily to the era in which a story is set than the later eras in which it was composed. Ancient communities, including the Hebrew scribes who are our focus here, were thus not completely severed from a past that preceded their own time—even if a mass of written texts from former eras were not in their possession.

The point of raising these examples from antiquity is not to treat them naively. References to the fish-man Oannes within Berossus's writings,[169] shape shifters in the Icelandic *Egil's Saga*,[170] the monster Grendel who haunts Beowulf

---

164. O. Vésteinsson, "Patterns of Settlement in Iceland: A Study in Prehistory", *Saga Book of the Viking Society for Northern Research* 25 (1998): 1–29; M. Cormack, "Fact and Fiction in the Icelandic Sagas," *History Compass* 5.1 (2007): 201–17.

165. See, for example, J. Byock et al., "A Viking-Age Valley in Iceland. The Mosfell Archaeological Project," *Medieval Archaeology*, 49 (2005): 195–218. J. Byock and D. Zori, "Viking Archaeology, Sagas, and Interdisciplinary Research in Iceland's Mosfell Valley," *Backdirt: Annual Review of the Cotsen Institute of Archaeology at UCLA* (2013): 124–41. On topic of sagas as historical source, see also J. Byock, *Viking Age Iceland* (New York: Penguin, 2001), 142–69.

166. J. Emanuel, "Cretan Lie and Historical Truth: Examining Odysseus' Raid on Egypt in its Late Bronze Age Context," in *Donum Natalicium Digitaliter Confectum Gregorio Nagy Septuagenario a Discipulis Collegis Familiaribus Oblatum* (eds. V. Bers et al.; Washington, D.C.: Center for Hellenic Studies, 2012), 1–41.

167. S. Dalley, "Sennacherib and Tarsus," *Anatolian Studies* 49 (1999): 73–80; cf. R. Bollinger, "Berossos and the Monuments: City Walls, Sanctuaries, Palaces and the Hanging Garden," in *The World of Berossos* (eds. J. Haubold et al.; Wiesbaden: Harossowitz, 2013), 140–41.

168. G. Russom, "Historicity and Anachronism in *Beowulf*," in *Epic and History* (eds. D. Konstan and K. Raaflaub; Malden: Wiley-Blackwell, 2009), 243–61.

169. G. Verbrugghe and J. Wickersham, *Berossus and Manetho, Introduced and Translated* (Ann Arbor: University of Michigan Press, 2001), 44.

170. S. Óskarsdóttir, ed., *Egil's Saga* (trans. B. Scudder; New York: Penguin, 2002), 3.

(*Beowulf* ll. 105–120), or Yahweh's thunder in battle (1 Sam. 7:10) reveal that the ancient writers of these accounts were operating with ontological presuppositions about past reality that modern historians simply do not hold. But what is significant about these ancient texts for this chapter's investigation are those moments when literary references to a more remote past resonate with the time in which these stories are set and, against expectations, do not simply mirror the later cultural concerns and historical contexts in which they were written down. Such references, even if infrequent, indicate that in spite of the great pressures to revise and update past stories so that they would speak more clearly to a present audience, references to a past world could nonetheless persist and enter into later literary texts—even if such references may have struck later audiences as unfamiliar or unknown.

How and why certain past referents were retained when others were not is a question whose varied and complex historical contingencies elude a straightforward answer. But in the case of Philistine Gath and those other literary references examined here, one prominent clue does come to the surface: a remembered past endures more readily when it is tethered to the physical environs of a place. Unable to access representations of a past world through texts or images that made reference to it, ancient writers could however visit and experience meaningful sites in which past incidents were said to have once occurred. In this sense, we can theorize that a past connected to such sites was more resilient to the effects of revision and forgetting since, on this view, the memories affixed to such locations persisted with the persistence of the locations remembered.

Perhaps the best indication, then, as to why Gath features so prominently in what are mostly Judahite stories of an early Iron Age past is the evidence that the site of Gath came into Judahite control for a brief moment in the late Iron Age period. Thus, at the moment when the technology of prose writing was being harnessed to narrate stories about the past, situated among the ruins of Gath in its Upper City was a community who now held ties to Judah, the capital in Jerusalem, and its scribal apparatus. Surrounding by the visible remains of Gath's prior prominence, old memories of the Philistine center may have found their way into Hebrew texts because traces of this remembered past were still preserved in the ruins familiar to those who began to write these stories down.

Conclusion

Drawing on the work of E. Casey, P. Ricoeur observes that the link between place and memory is a tie essential to the possibility of remembering. Ricoeur comments:[171]

---

171. P. Ricoeur, *La Mémoire, L'Histoire, L'Oubli* (Paris: Éditions du Seuil, 2000), 49.

. . . it is not by chance that we say of what has happened that it took place. It is indeed at this primordial level that the phenomenon of "lieux de mémoire" [places of memory] are constituted before they become a reference for historical knowledge. These places of memory function principally in the way of reminders, of indices of recall, offering in turn a support for failing memory, a struggle in the struggle against forgetting, indeed a silent proxy for dead memory. These places "remain" as inscriptions, monuments, potentially as documents, whereas memories transmitted only by way of oral means fly away with the words themselves.

The argument of this chapter is that Philistine Gath functioned as a particular "place of memory" with regard to an early Iron Age past for the biblical writers. Even more, this place of memory was one that evinced a particular resiliency to the pressures of revision and erasure so common to the transmission of communal recollections over time in antiquity. The resilience of memories pertaining to Gath likely had something to do with the place of Gath itself and its history in the Iron Age period. Situated on Judah's western border, the sheer size of Gath's confines and its impressively built environment would have left a deep impression on local populations in the southern Levant even in those later periods when much of Gath lay in ruins. The very materiality of the location, on this view, called to mind and reinforced older memories about its former prominence.

From a more theoretical vantage point, this premise would receive support from H. Bergson's great work, *Matter and Memory*, in which the contention is made that past moments continually coexist with the present but in latent form, always available to be actualized in our memories if our experience of the world occasion them. A significant catalyst for the virtual to become actual, Bergson argued further, was our encounter with material phenomena that bore the traces of former eras. What this response of memory suggested, Bergson concluded, is that our sense of time is, in each and every moment, multi-temporal and discontinuous, with many and varied past memories braced to erupt once more into the present.[172] "Time is unhinged," Al-Saji comments in her insightful reading of Bergson, "by contact with other pasts. . . ."[173]

This unhinging of linear time through the encounter with the materiality of past places returns us to where this chapter first began. *The Epic of Gilgamesh*,

---

172. So Bergson's famous image of the inverted cone of past time placed on the plane of present experience. H. Bergson, *Matter and Memory* (trans. N. Paul and W. Palmer; New York: Zone Books, 1991), 161–63.

173. A. Al-Saji, "The Memory of Another Past: Bergson, Deleuze and a New Theory of Time," *Continental Philosophy Review* 37. 2 (2004): 230.

it was argued earlier, offers an ancient awareness that the things embedded in place—landscapes and walls and city precincts—attest to a particular depth of time that would have been unknown in antiquity without the presence of these physical remains. And, with Gilgamesh, one finds an acute recognition of the possibility that the endurance of the physical features of a location could also sustain the memory of individuals and events once connected to it.

In the case of Philistine Gath, this relationship between place and memory bears with it distinct and important epistemological implications for the type of knowledge conveyed to later Hebrew scribes through their sources. The resonance between biblical references to Gath and the archaeological evidence recovered from the early Iron Age strata of Tell es-Safi indicates that these scribes had access to information about Gath that could have only descended from the early Iron Age period. Consequently, it appears that in a time when a Hebrew prose tradition matured in the southern Levant, those who wrote out narrative accounts about the past had access to some source material that preserved information that arose within an early Iron Age world. The knowledge that informed the stories the biblical writers told was, at least in certain instances, those of memories framed by the possibilities of preservation. The full significance of this insight will only become apparent in the studies that follow, in which it will be shown that other scribal sources did not exhibit this manner of resilience. It is to these stories that we turn next.

3

David on the Desert Fringe

THE ENTANGLEMENTS OF MEMORY

*And thus the question must be raised for each substance and
each concept: From where does it come, and what development has it undergone?*[1]

NEAR THE MIDPOINT of Book II of the *Histories* (2.99), Herodotus turns
from his investigation into the Egyptian landscape and toward what he has
learned from others of the great deeds performed by past pharaohs.[2] One ruler,
named Sesostris, is given particular prominence with this section of Herodotus's
work and stands out among the various pharaohs described (Hdt. 2.102–110). In
a distant past, Herodotus reports, this ancient ruler completed a naval campaign
along the Arabian Gulf and then set out with a great army northward. The forces
under Sesostris's command subdued various peoples of the Levant until they ultimately "entered Europe and defeated the Scythians and Thracians" (Hdt. 2.102)
in what is today the Balkan region and south Russia. Herodotus remarks that
the pharaoh then returned to Egypt after his conquests in the far north, but not
before a segment of his army established the kingdom of Colchis on the eastern
banks of the Black Sea.

The evidence Herodotus cites for Sesostris's campaign are stories
recounted to him by Egyptian informants, most frequently identified as
local priests who, in this instance, appear to have resided in Memphis.[3] The

---

1. H. Greßmann, *Albert Eichhorn und die Religionsgeschichtliche Schule* (Göttingen Vandenhoeck
& Ruprecht, 1914), 35.

2. Herodotus writes: "Up to this point I have limited what I have written to what I myself
saw (ὄψις), my judgment (γνώμη), and inquiry (ἱστορίη). But now I will record Egyptian *logoi*,
according to what I have heard" (*Hdt.* 2.99).

3. A. Lloyd, "Book II," in *A Commentary on Herodotus: Books I–IV* (eds. O. Murray and A.
Moreno; Oxford: Oxford University Press, 2007), 228–39.

potential problems involved with this dependence on stories told by others is recognized by Herodotus himself, who assures his audience that the Egyptian accounts are to be "supplemented" by information gathered from elsewhere, which, in the case of Sesostris, consisted of a series of royal steles that Sesostris allegedly left behind within the regions he subjugated. What is fascinating about these particular monuments, however, is that Herodotus claims to have direct knowledge of them since a number are said to have been located in his native Ionia along the western reaches of Anatolia. So Herodotus comments (Hdt. 2.106):

> In Ionia also there are two images of Sesostris cut on rock, on the road from Ephesus to Phocaea, the other on the road between Sardis and Smyrna; in each case the carved figure is nearly seven feet high and represents a man with a spear in his right hand and a bow in his left, and the rest of his equipment to match. . . . Across the breast from shoulder to shoulder runs an inscription, cut in the Egyptian sacred script: *By the strength of my shoulders I won this land.* The name and country of the conqueror are not here recorded, and some who have seen this image suppose it to represent Memnon; however, they are wide of the mark, for Sesostris has made the truth plain enough elsewhere.

We now know that Sesostris (or, better, a likely conflation of several pharaohs centered on Senwosret III) never led a large expedition across the Levant and into Europe.[4] Nor have any Egyptian monuments been found in those places that Herodotus locates them. While the former misunderstanding can be attributed to legendary tales told about a remote, near-mythic pharaoh, the testimony Herodotus offers with regard to the Egyptian steles he claims to have seen is more difficult to explain. Why did Herodotus attest to the authenticity of Sesostris's campaign and the presence of the pharaoh's monuments when we now know that none existed in the places Herodotus identifies?

One can answer this question, as some do, by labeling Herodotus a fraud bent on deceiving his audience.[5] But in light of the fact that Herodotus is able to record relatively accurate information with regard to other monuments and

---

4. W. Hayes, "The Middle Kingdom in Egypt," in *Cambridge Ancient History* vol. 1, part 2 (eds. I. Edwards et al.; Cambridge: Cambridge University Press, 1971), 499–508.

5. D. Fehling, *Herodotus and His "Sources": Citation, Invention, and Narrative Art* (trans. J. Howie; Liverpool: Cairns, 1989), 12–17, 105–13; O. Armayor, "Sesostris and Herodotus' Autopsy of Thrace, Colchis, Inland Asia Minor, and the Levant," *Harvard Studies in Classical Philology* 84 (1980): 51–74.

remains at various moments in his work, such a response raises more problems than it solves.[6] A better approach to this question is that of S. Dalley, who suggests that Herodotus was recounting genuine information related to him by Egyptian priests who revered the memory of a distant, deified pharaoh.[7] The reason Herodotus took this information as credible, Dalley contends further, is because he connected the stories of Sesostris to a number of monuments that were known to exist in Ionia during Herodotus's time: namely, Late Bronze Age Hittite rock-cut reliefs inscribed with sayings in the Hieroglyphic Luwian script.[8]

On this view, Herodotus's statements about Sesostris's campaign arose because memories of the Hittite Empire and knowledge of Hieroglyphic Luwian had died out by the fifth century BCE when Herodotus was active. Confronted by already ancient monuments such as the one carved above the Karabel Pass, fashioned hundreds of years before by the thirteenth century BCE ruler of Mira, Tarkasnawa,[9] one means by which to make sense of these enigmatic royal reliefs carved in a forgotten hieroglyphic script was to connect them to a powerful Egyptian pharaoh of long ago. (See Figure 3.1.) Such an affiliation was only abetted by the fact that Late Bronze Age Hittite royal iconography could employ forms that found some semblance to Egyptian motifs still visible in the fifth century BCE, including the stance of the ruler and the crown worn.[10] Thus, in light of the knowledge available to Herodotus about a Late Bronze Age world, his discussion of ancient Egyptian activity in the region at this time was cogent and reasonable—even if his statements about Sesostris were wholly mistaken.[11]

---

6. On Herodotus's complicated relationship to epigraphic sources, see the penetrating study of S. West, "Herodotus' Epigraphic Interests," *Classical Quarterly* 35.2 (1985): 278–305. Cf. R. Osborne, "Archaic Greek History," in *Brill's Companion to Herodotus* (eds. E. Bakker et al.; Leiden: Brill, 2002): 510–13.

7. S. Dalley, "Why Did Herodotus Not Mention the Hanging Gardens of Babylon?" in *Herodotus and His World* (eds. P. Derow and R. Parker; Oxford: Oxford University Press, 2003): 171–89. On Herodotus's relationship to Egyptian informants, see also N. Luraghi, "Local Knowledge in Herodotus' *Histories*," in *The Historian's Craft in the Age of Herodotus* (ed. N. Luraghi; Oxford: Oxford University Press, 2001), 138–61.

8. Dalley, "Hanging Gardens," 176–77. For a similar assessment, see S. West, "Sesostris Stelae (Herodotus 2.102–106)," *Historia: Zeitschrift für Alte Geschichte* 41.1 (1992): 117–20.

9. For a reading and discussion of this inscription, see J. D. Hawkins, "Tarkasnawa King of Mira 'Tarkondemos', Boğazköy Sealings and Karabel," *Anatolian Studies* 48 (1998): 1–31.

10. Dalley, "Hanging Gardens," 175–77.

11. West comments: "Given Herodotus' premises it was eminently reasonable to take hieroglyphic inscriptions as evidence for Sesostris' presence." West, "Sesostris," 119.

FIGURE 3.1 Drawing of the Relief of Tarkasnawa of Mira, Karabel Pass (Picture: Public Domain).

Equipped with archaeological and historical insights unavailable to Herodotus and his contemporaries, what our modern vantage point affords is the possibility of discerning within Herodotus's account a past fraught with a number of entanglements. Not only do we encounter the intertwining of distinct cultural perspectives within the stories surrounding this pharaoh (an Egyptian past reframed through Hittite monuments and recast once more through the perspective of an Ionian author), but also geographical (Egypt, Asia Minor, Europe) and chronological (a fifth century BCE writer composing a text about a putative nineteenth century BCE pharaoh in light of thirteenth century BCE monuments) threads of different pasts woven together within a single narrative account. Reading Herodotus's statements with an eye toward the historical evidence we now possess, however, helps us to unravel the varied material that contributed to this narrative and the information contained in it, offering a more nuanced historical appreciation of what knowledge Herodotus drew on in order to create the narratives that he did.

Herodotus finds importance for our investigation, then, because of what these writings reveal about how predominantly oral traditions, memorized and passed on for generations, took on prose form within texts composed by an ancient writer with genuine antiquarian preoccupations. In light of this study's epistemological interests, what the various entanglements present in Herodotus's account encourages is attentiveness toward how a similar phenomenon may have circumscribed and shaped the body of knowledge drawn on by biblical scribes to compose narratives about times previous to their own. For what Herodotus reveals is that the information he used to construct his account of Sesostris was quite malleable, adaptive to both new cultural contexts and more recent geopolitical configurations.[12]

Entanglements of the sort present in Herodotus have increasingly drawn the attention of theorists who have inquired into how stories about a past are remembered within a society over time. Over against studies that would bound the memories of a particular past to a specific geography and chronology, isolating who and how this past is remembered by adopting a more synchronic, insular lens (i.e., *the* French memories of *the* French Revolution), more recent approaches have drawn attention to the transcultural, at times contradictory and conflicting, recollections of a past elicited by different populations at different moments in light of new experiences and historical catalysts.[13] Included within an assemblage of memories kept alive within a society across generations, on this view, are often distinct, even discordant perspectives that resist an easy harmonization of their claims. "[I]t is actually since ancient times," A. Erll comments in her important study, "that memory lives in and through its movements, and

---

12. That is, stories of Sesostris not only served the later interests of the Egyptian priests who commemorated him in the time of Herodotus, but were also reframed through the perspective of Herodotus who, in naming the Thracians and Scythians, was referring to his own geopolitical context and not to an ancient Egyptian past.

13. For a discussion, see A. Erll, "Traveling Memory," *Parallax* 17.4 (2011): 4–18; N. Fischer et al., "Introduction: 'Entangled Pasts,'" *Crossings: A Journal of Migration and Culture* 4.1 (2013): 3–11; G. Feindt et al., "Entangled Memory: Toward a Third Wave in Memory Studies," *History and Theory* 53 (2014): 24–44; L. Bond et al., "Introduction: Memory on the Move," in *Memory Unbound: Tracing the Dynamics of Memory Studies* (New York: Bergham, 2016), 1–26.

that mnemonic forms and contents are filled with new life and new meaning in changing social, temporal and local contexts."[14] What results from the transmission of a memory across such contexts, on this view, is the sedimentation of varied past viewpoints and interests that accrued as these remembrances were imparted to new, future audiences.[15]

With such theoretical issues in view, Herodotus's description of Sesostris also finds importance for this chapter's study because it demonstrates how such entanglements could be occasioned and abetted through the experience of older material remains. A key factor that led Herodotus to affirm the authenticity of the tales surrounding Sesostris, it seems, was that the Egyptian memories attached to this pharaoh were supported through the strange monuments that dotted the Ionian landscape of Herodotus's time. Herodotus was, in fact, quick to point out when he found certain sources suspect—so his famous reflection on the origin of the Nile River earlier in Book II (Hdt. 2.19–35)—but in this collection of oral traditions Herodotus found something credible because he believed he had experienced the monuments of this Pharaoh himself, or at least was convinced of their existence.[16] The material remains of a more ancient past, in this sense, both altered and reinforced Herodotus's understanding of the stories transmitted to him.[17]

---

14. Erll, "Travelling Memory," 11.

15. Feindt et al., "Entangled Memory," 33–35. On this point, see also Schwartz's remarks on the dynamic interplay of the "keying" and "framing" of new experiences onto older memories in B. Schwartz, "Where There's Smoke, There's Fire: Memory and History," in *Memory and Identity in Ancient Judaism and Early Christianity: A Conversation with Barry Schwartz* (ed. T. Thatcher; Atlanta: SBL, 2014), 7–40; and A. Rigney's observations on "convergence" in A. Rigeny, "Plenitude, Scarcity, and the Circulation of Cultural Memory," *Journal of European Studies* 35.1 (2005): 11–28.

16. Given the fact that the monuments Herodotus identifies were not written in Egyptian Hieroglyph, the quotation Herodotus cites is a mystery. He most likely fabricated it, or, perhaps, adopted it from elsewhere. In either case, as West remarks, "the easy confidence with which a translation of the inscription is offered is disturbing" [West, "Herodotus' Epigraphic Interests," 302]. As West concludes, such a cavalier approach to this inscription (and others) was likely due to the fact that Herodotus worked in an oral culture that did not accord ancient writings great value for information about the past and therefore did not attend to their claims with great philological interest.

17. Such a relationship between memory and material remains was theorized already by M. Halbwachs in his study of early Christian pilgrimage sites, where he writes that it was due to the stability of the material remains of a Christian past that "memories endured. But that stability is at the mercy of all the material accidents that slowly transform or even destroy" these material frameworks. M. Halbwachs, *On Collective Memory* (ed. L. Coser; Chicago: University of Chicago Press, 1992), 204–205.

It is with these twin themes of entangled memory and material remains in view that this chapter's investigation into stories surrounding David's outlaw days in the Book of Samuel unfolds. To be sure, the example of Herodotus can only be pressed so far in a consideration of a Hebrew scribal culture working in a much different time and place than that of fifth century BCE Ionia. In contrast to Herodotus, we know very little about the historical circumstances that gave rise to the material appropriated by Hebrew scribes within their story of David's rise to the throne in 1 Samuel 16–2 Samuel 5[18] or, even more, the timeframe and settings in which these stories were written down.[19] But with regard to the epistemological underpinnings of the knowledge conveyed to these scribes about an early Iron Age past, Herodotus's account of Sesostris and his reference to a familiar landscape to substantiate his claims offers a constructive point of departure by which to consider the development of stories told about David's early career in the Book of Samuel.

---

18. Within these chapters there is one explicit reference to a written source, that of the "Scroll of Yashar," on which, according to 2 Samuel 1:18, David's lament over Saul and Jonathan was inscribed. Other source material cited in these stories is dominated by references to orality—so the sayings attached to Saul's prophetic capabilities (1 Sam. 10:11, 19:24), for example, or David's military prowess (1 Sam. 18:7, 1 Sam. 29:5). For studies on the broader oral features of the storytelling present in the Book of Samuel, see already H. Greßmann, "The Oldest History Writing in Israel," in *Narrative and Novella in Samuel: Studies by Hugo Gressmann and Other Scholars 1906–1923* (trans. D. Orton; ed. D. Gunn; Sheffield: JSOT Press, 1991), 13–16; but also R. Rendtorff, "Beobachtungen zur altisraelitischen Geschichtsschreibung anhand der Geschichte vom Aufstieg Davids," in *Probleme biblischer Theologie* (ed. H. Wolff; München: Chr. Kaiser, 1971), 435–36; D. M. Gunn, *The Story of King David: Genre and Interpretation* (Sheffield: JSOT Press, 1978), 49–62; F. Polak, "The Oral and the Written: Syntax, Stylistics and the Development of Biblical Prose Narrative," *JNES* 26 (1998): 78–105; idem, "The Book of Samuel and the Deuteronomist: A Syntactic-Stylistic Analysis," in *Die Samuelbücher und die Deuteronomisten* (ed. C. Schäfer-Lichtenberger; Stuttgart: Kohlhammer, 2010), 34–73; W. Dietrich, *The Early Monarchy in Israel: The Tenth Century B.C.E.* (trans. J. Vette; Atlanta: SBL, 2007), 264–68, J. Hutzli, "The Distinctness of the Samuel Narrative Tradition," in *Is Samuel Among the Deuteronomists? Current Views on the Place of Samuel in a Deuteronomistic History* (eds. C. Edenburg and J. Pakkala; Atlanta: SBL Press, 2013), 171–205; D. Pioske, "Prose Writing in an Age of Orality: A Study of 2 Sam 5:6–9," *VT* 66.2 (2016): 261–79. So Polak's succinct conclusion: "the Samuel-Saul-David tales clearly reflect an orate culture." Polak, "The Book of Samuel," 66.

19. For more recent overviews of these debates, see W. Dietrich and T. Naumann, *Die Samuelbücher* (Darmstadt: Wissenschaftliche Buchgesellschaft, 1995), 68–86; the essays in G. Knoppers and J. G. McConville, eds., *Reconsidering Israel and Judah: Recent Studies on the Deuteronomistic History* (Winona Lake: Eisenbrauns, 2000), 260–358; C. Schäfer-Lichtenberger, ed., *Die Samuelbücher und die Deuteronomisten* (Stuttgart: Kohlhammer, 2010); and C. Edenburg, and J. Pakkala, eds., *Is Samuel Among the Deuteronomists? Current Views on the Place of Samuel in a Deuteronomistic History* (Atlanta: SBL Press, 2013).

In what follows, this study examines two accounts in the Book of Samuel that pertain to David's activities in the desert south. The first concerns David's leadership over the Philistine outpost of Ziklag (1 Sam. 27:1–28:2); the second, of David's distribution of gifts to the elders of Judah stationed at different Judahite sites in Hebron and to Hebron's south (1 Sam. 30:26–31). The particular geographic focus of these accounts once again provides the opportunity, as pursued in the previous chapter, to map the narrative world represented within these texts alongside what is known about the locations named within them through recent archaeological excavations. What results from this approach, I argue, are insights into a past alloyed with references to different eras and geographies, entanglements that arose because the sources on which the biblical scribes relied were shaped by memories reflective of a changing landscape and varied political interests during the Iron Age period.

Ziklag (1 Sam. 27:2–3, 5–6a, 7–11)

The story of David's acquisition of Ziklag in 1 Samuel 27:1–28:2[20] is built around essentially one primary source that tells of how David and his fighters came to Achish, king of Gath (1 Sam. 27: 2–3), were given possession of the southern Philistine site of Ziklag (vv. 5–6a),[21] and used this location as their base of operations to make raids in the region (vv. 7–11). This account is preceded by the addition of an introductory gloss by the narrator (v. 1) and the further observation that Saul suspended his pursuit of David (v. 4), and then is interrupted again

---

20. For other insightful approaches to the composition history of this account, see J. Grønbaek, *Die Geschichte vom Aufstieg Davids (1. Sam. 15–2. Sam. 5): Tradition und Komposition* (Copenhagen: Munksgaard, 1971), 183–94; H. Stoebe, *Das Erste Buch Samuelis* (Gütersloh: Verlagshaus Gerd Mohn, 1973), 472–82; J. Klein, "Davids Flucht zu den Philistern (1 Sam XXI 11ff.; XXVII–XXIX)," *VT* 55.2 (2005): 176–84; R. Kratz, *The Composition of the Narrative Works of the Old Testament* (trans. J. Bowden; London: T&T Clark, 2005), 177–86; Dietrich, *Early Monarchy*, 264–91; J. Hutton, *The Transjordanian Palimpsest: The Overwritten Texts of Personal Exile and Transformation in the Deuteronomistic History* (Berlin: Walter de Gruyter, 2009), 271–73, 364–71.

21. Wright's proposal that 1 Samuel 27:5–6 was an early addition to 1 Samuel 27:2–3, 7–11 (J. Wright, *David, King of Israel, and Caleb in Biblical Memory* [Cambridge: Cambridge University Press, 2013] 235 fn. 8) carries merit in light of the literary connection that obtains between 1 Samuel 27:3a and 1 Samuel 27:7–11. But if early traditions connected to Ziklag stated that the location, like Keilah, was originally a semi-independent settlement simply rescued by David from marauders, as Wright contends, it is difficult to understand why the biblical scribes would ever concoct the story that Ziklag was originally Gittite crown property given as a royal grant to David (a claim not made about Keilah, for example, or other locations that witness David's activity). The distinctiveness of Ziklag and its Philistine associations, in this sense, stands out.

with the observation that the city of Ziklag continued to belong "to the kings of Judah to this day" (v. 6b).[22] First Samuel 27:7–11 then continues the story of David's stay at Ziklag by describing the length of time spent in Philistine territory (v. 7) and the various incursions carried out from the location. First Samuel 27:12–28:2 concludes this narrative block by noting the trust Achish placed in David, thus setting up events later reported in 1 Samuel 29–30.

The account included within 1 Samuel 27 finds particular significance within the overarching story of David's life by detailing the first location over which David was given charge. What is remarkable about this site is that it is described as neither Israelite nor Judahite, but Philistine. The fact that this was a discomfiting feature of David's life for those behind these stories can be sensed in the reason given by the storyteller for why David retreated to the confines of the foreign city of Gath (1 Sam. 27:1):

> Now David said to himself, "I will perish one day by the hand of Saul. There is nothing better for me than to escape to the land of the Philistines. Then Saul will despair from seeking after me any longer within the borders of Israel, and I will have escaped from his hand."

Forced to flee into the hands of Israel's rivals by Saul's designs on David's life, David subsequently comes before Achish with six hundred of his men for safe haven. Soon, David requests that he be given jurisdiction over a Philistine settlement where David and his fighters could reside. Achish agrees: "On that day, Achish gave him Ziklag" (1 Sam. 27:6a). Later, it becomes clear that what Achish grants David is a military fief for services to be rendered, with David put in place to guard the southern borders of Gath's kingdom (1 Sam 27:10).

From the perspective of the biblical scribes who brought together this account, the difficulty with the story of Ziklag was the credence it lent to the charge that David was a Philistine agent, disloyal toward Israelite interests and a traitor.[23] Not only had David fled to Philistine territory, but he is so valued by the ruler of Gath that David is granted control of crown property in the Gittite realm. That this story was something of a problem for the storyteller is again found in the justification offered for David's withdrawal to this location: namely, that Saul had given David no choice but to defect to the Philistines. Even more,

---

22. On the phrasing of this gloss, see Brevard Childs, "A Study of the Formula 'Until This Day,'" *JBL* 82 (1963): 279–92; Jeffrey C. Geoghegan, "'Until This Day' and the Preexilic Redaction of the Deuteronomistic History," *JBL* 122.2 (2003): 201–27.

23. P. K. McCarter, "The Apology of David," *JBL* 99.4 (1980): 500–501; B. Halpern, *David's Secret Demons: Messiah, Murderer, Traitor, King* (Grand Rapids: Eerdmans, 2001), 78–80.

the narrator take pains to assert that David had, in fact, been a double agent all along, protecting Judahite territory while keeping Achish in the dark about his motives (1 Sam. 27:8–10).

The best historical explanation for why the biblical scribes included a potentially damaging anecdote about David's service to a Philistine ruler is that the source material attached to this moment in David's life claimed that this was so. Given the anti-Philistine sentiment found, at moments, within these narratives, it is unlikely that later biblical scribes contrived a tale in which David first came to rule over a Philistine site granted to him by Achish when such an account only complicates the story they are trying to tell. Instead, being constricted in their storytelling by what was likely a well-known memory of David's past, the biblical scribes were compelled to include this episode in their story of how David came to be king.[24]

This story was nevertheless made to serve a purpose. Placing David at Ziklag at this moment in their narrative allowed the biblical scribes to protect David from a far more harmful charge than being an agent for the Philistine cause: namely, that David was complicit in Saul and Jonathan's deaths at the battle of Mt. Gilboa (1 Sam. 29:31).[25] Situated far away from the Jezreel Valley and Mt. Gilboa, Ziklag offered a sizable distance from the site where Israel's king and crown prince would meet their demise. Achish's decision to send David back to Philistine lands on the eve of battle (1 Sam. 29:6–11) did nothing to take away from the accusation that David was once a Philistine vassal, but this story did absolve David from being responsible for the death of Israel's first ruler.

Within the story of Ziklag in 1 Samuel 27 little explicit information is offered about the Philistine outpost. A few features can be teased out from the narrative, the most important of which is that the settlement was situated within the realm of the kingdom of Gath and ostensibly had connections, culturally and politically, with Philistine populations. By virtue of the peoples and regions named in the dialogue between David and Achish in 1 Samuel 27:8–10 (the Amalekites and Geshurites, and the Negev of Judah, the Negev of Jerahmeel, and the Negev of the Kenizzites), it can also be surmised that Ziklag was positioned somewhere in the far south of Gath's domain since the populations attacked by David and targeted by Achish resided in the desert regions of the northern Negev. Ziklag is depicted as being large enough to accommodate David's family and the families

---

24. On this feature of cultural memory, broadly speaking, see again Schwartz, "Where There's Smoke, There's Fire: Memory and History," 7–40.

25. McCarter, "The Apology of David," 500; Halpern, *David's Secret Demons*, 80.

of his fighters, and it is of enough strategic significance that David is able to use it as a base of operations to carry out attacks in the surrounding countryside.

A few more details emerge about the site from the handful of references to it outside of 1 Samuel 27. Joshua 15:31 further attests to Ziklag's location near the Negev region by placing it alongside Hormah in the "far south" of Judah; Joshua 19:5 also positions Ziklag next to Hormah in Simeonite territory, within Judah's southwestern most district. In addition, the Book of Samuel reports that Ziklag was set aflame by an Amalekite attack and burned down (1 Sam. 30:14). But later David will use Ziklag as a staging ground for a magnanimous display of generosity to the elders of Judah, sending gifts from Ziklag to various southern Judahite settlements (1 Sam. 30:26–31), suggesting that the site had either been rebuilt or had not suffered the sweeping destruction alluded to during the Amalekite raid. And, further, it is to Ziklag that an Amalekite messenger will depart to disclose the news to David that Saul and Jonathan had died (2 Sam. 1:1). In spite of the site's earlier conflagration, Ziklag thus endures within the story of David's rise as a base of operations before David's eventual coronation at Hebron (2 Sam. 2:4).

The Identification of Ziklag

Site identifications in southwestern Judah have long been some of the most difficult to ascertain, having been complicated throughout the twentieth century by the various locations proposed for the cities of Gath and Lachish.[26] In the case of Ziklag, problems with identification were further compounded by the absence of a close Arabic toponym in the region that might preserve where the settlement was once situated and, perhaps most of all, by the fact that a number of important excavations in the northwestern Negev have only been partially published or, in certain cases, have not been published at all.

For such reasons suggestions for Ziklag's whereabouts have varied considerably. Early proposals included Alt's recommendation of Tel Halif [27] and Albright's appeal to the site of Khirbet Zuheilikah, both located near the Wadi Gerar in the Gerar Basin.[28] Recent studies of medieval pilgrim accounts and the

---

26. On the history and identification of Gath, see comments in Chapter 2. The renewed excavations of Tell ed-Duweir by Tel Aviv University under the direction of David Ussishkin (1973–1994) has offered conclusive evidence that this location was Lachish.

27. A. Alt, "Beiträge zur Historischen Geographie und Topographie des Negeb: III. Saruhen, Ziklag, Horma, Gerar," *Journal of the Palestine Oriental Society* 15 (1935): 318.

28. W. F. Albright, "Researches of the School in Western Judea," *BASOR* 15 (1924): 157. This identification was given up, however, after the realization that no ancient ruins from the Bronze or Iron Age were located at this settlement.

work of early modern geographers have invited other possibilities,[29] including suggestions connected to the more northern locations of Tel el-Hesi, Tel Erani, and Tel Nagila, and more southern locales that, in addition to Alt and Albright's proposals, include Tel Sera',[30] Tel Masos,[31] and Tel Beersheba.[32]

In the century that has passed since the work of Alt and Albright, a more refined investigation into Ziklag's location has nevertheless been made possible through the evidence obtained from a few excavations carried out in the southern coastal plain. Biblically speaking, expectations connected to Ziklag's location would consist of a site that was inhabited during the late Iron I/early Iron IIA periods (ca. eleventh and tenth centuries BCE) and which enclosed material culture indicative of some connections (whether through trade or its inhabitants) to Philistine populations (i.e., ceramics, foodways, architecture, cultic items, etc.).

With these criteria in mind a number of sites proposed for Ziklag can be discounted. Albright's suggestion of Khirbet Zuheilikah, for example, can be safely dismissed since the site was not inhabited during the Iron I–IIA periods, making it an unlikely candidate for the location described in the Hebrew Bible. H. Harris's tentative identification of Ziklag with either Tel el-Hesi or Tel Nagila is also problematic in light of the remains recovered from these settlements. In terms of geography and the biblical references to Ziklag, Tel Nagila and Tel el-Hesi are certainly within the bounds of where the settlement could be situated. But the overall paucity of Iron I and early IIA Philistine material culture at these sites makes it unlikely that either were once Ziklag's location. For this reason, attempts to link Ziklag with Tel Nagila or Tel el-Hesi have been rejected by the excavators of these settlements.[33]

---

29. J. Blakely, "The location of medieval/pre-modern and biblical Ziklag," *PEQ* 139.1 (2007): 21–26; H. Harris, "The Location of Ziklag: Its Identification by Felix Fabri," *PEQ* 143.1 (2011): 19–30; idem, "The Location of Ziklag: A Review of the Candidate Sites, Based on Biblical, Topographical and Archaeological Evidence," *PEQ* 143.2 (2011): 119–33.

30. E. Oren, "Ziglag: A Biblical City on the Edge of the Negeb," *BA* 45.3 (1982): 161–63; idem, "Sera', Tel," *NEAEHL*, IV, 1332–33.

31. F. Crüsemann, "Überlegungen zur Identifikation der Hirbet el-Msas (Tel Masos)," *ZDPV* 8 (1973): 211–24.

32. V. Fritz, "Der Beitrag der Archäologie zur historischen Topographie Palästinas am Beispiel von Ziklag," *ZDPV* 106 (1990): 78–85; idem, "Where is David's Ziklag?" *BAR* 19.3 (1993): 58–61, 76.

33. On the rejection of Tell el-Hesi as Ziklag on archaeological grounds, for example, see J. Blakely and F. Horton, "On Site Identifications Old and New: The Example of Tell el-Hesi," *NEA* 64.1–2 (2001): 31. On the paucity of Iron I/early IIA remains at Tel Nagila and the likelihood that it is not mentioned in any biblical text, see I. Shai et al., "The Iron Age Remains at Tel Nagila," *BASOR* 363 (2011): 25–43.

The more southern locales suggested for Ziklag's whereabouts have therefore proven to be better candidates for the biblical site. Both Tel Masos and Tel Beersheba, for example, were large and important towns in the Iron I/IIA period, and both exhibit evidence of interactions with Philistine culture at this time. The difficulty with these locations in the Beersheba Valley, however, is that they lay well south of where the biblical references to Ziklag situate the settlement (i.e., Josh. 15 and 19, 1 Sam. 27 and 30), and hence the connection between Ziklag and these early Iron Age sites have garnered little support since the time when they were first proposed.[34]

Such considerations, then, return us to the region of the Gerar Basin and settlements situated along the Wadi Besor and Wadi Gerar of the northwestern Negev, including the sites of Tell Jemmeh, Tel Haror, Tel Sera', and Tel Halif that lay along these ancient waterways. These locations receive support, on the one hand, from the geographical perspective of the Hebrew Bible and its town lists that include references to Ziklag's position alongside of Hormah, Madmannah, and Sansannah in the region of Simeon (so again Josh. 15: 20–32; cf. Josh. 19:4–5; 1 Chron. 4:28–32). (See Figure 3.2.) These sites also find significance, archaeologically speaking, because they were settled and inhabited in the Iron I–IIA periods.[35] Tell Jemmeh, however, has long been identified with the city of Yurza, cited in both Egyptian and Assyrian records as a key outpost for their imperial ambitions,[36] and Tel Haror has consistently been linked to the biblical city of Gerar,[37] especially in conjunction with traditions of Abraham in the book of Genesis. Both sites, furthermore, would likely reside too far west for the geographical perspective put forward in the biblical traditions.

---

34. More recently, it has been argued that Tel Masos and Tel Beersheba may have formed their own independent desert polity centered at Tel Masos Stratum II, outside direct control of Philistine Gath, which would again lessen the probability that these locations be identified with Ziklag. See, for example, A. Fantalkin and I. Finkelstein, "The Sheshonq I Campaign and the 8th-century BCE Earthquake: More on the Archaeology and History of the South in the Iron I–IIA," *TA* 33 (2006): 18–42.

35. On Tel Jemmeh, see G. van Beek, "Jemmeh, Tel" in *NEAEHL*, II, 669–72; for Tel Haror, E. Oren, "Haror, Tel" in *NEAEHL*, II, 582–83; on Tel Sera', see again Oren, "Ziglag: A Biblical City," 161–63; idem, "Sera', Tel" 1332–33; on Tel Halif, see J. Seger, "Halif, Tel," *NEAEHL*, II, 557–58.

36. Van Beek, "Jemmeh," 667–68. Though see the more recent discussion by Koch who argues against this identification on archaeological grounds and situates Yurza further east at Tel Haror (I. Koch, "Notes on Three South Canaanite Sites in the el-Amarna Correspondence," *TA* 43 [2016]: 91–93).

37. Oren, "Haror," 580; H. Niemann and G. Lehmann, "Zwischen Wüste und Mittelmeer: Qubur al-Walaydah und seine Umgebung in Südwest-Palästina," *Die Welt des Orients* 40.2 (2010): 225–32.

Nablus

Tel Aviv-Yafo

Rishon
LeTsiyon

Ramallah

Jericho

Ashdod

Jerusalem

● **Gath**

Ashkelon

Kiryat Gat

Hebron

Sderot

Gaza

Ein Gedi

Netivot **Tel Sera**

Tell Jemmeh ●   ● Rahat   ● **Tel Halif**

Khan Yunis   **Tel Haror**

Rafah

Be'er Sheva   Arad

Ein Bokek

Google My Maps   Neve Zohar

FIGURE 3.2 Map of Sites in Gerar Basin (Map: Author).

Through a long process of elimination, then, the most likely candidates for Ziklag are Tel Sera' and Alt's original suggestion of Tel Halif.[38] Geographically, these locations comport to expectations of Ziklag's whereabouts by being situated on the edge of the coastal plain in territory that was within the orbit of Gath's authority in the early Iron Age period.[39] Tel Sera' and Tel Halif's positions are also well suited to the description of the site offered in the town lists of Joshua 15 and 19, which place Ziklag in the far southwestern region of Judah, and to the

---

38. For scholars who support this identification, see A. Rainey, "Ziklag," in *Interpreters Dictionary of the Bible Supplement* (ed. K. Crim; Nashville: Abingdon, 1976): 984–85; A. Rainey and S. Notley, *The Sacred Bridge* (Jerusalem: Carta, 2006), 148–49; Y. Aharoni, *The Land of the Bible* (3rd ed.; Philadelphia: Westminster, 1979), 260, 353; N. Na'aman, "The Inheritance of the Sons of Simeon," *ZDPV* 96.2 (1980): 142–45; Blakely, "Biblical Ziklag," 21–26.

39. On this point, see again the discussion of Gath in Chapter 2.

portrayal of the settlement in 1 Samuel 27 and 30 that locates Ziklag along the northern border of the Negev where raids are made on Negevite tribal groups.[40]

From an archaeological perspective, Tel Sera's material culture is perhaps better suited to the biblical descriptions of Ziklag. First, Tel Sera' produced substantial archaeological evidence from the late Iron I/early IIA periods,[41] including abundant material culture connected to the region of Philistia.[42] Furthermore, the location also yielded impressive seventh century BCE remains (so the likely time frame of the composition of the town list in Josh. 15 and the "to this day" reference in 1 Sam. 27:6b)[43] and was a site of some status in the Persian period (so the reference to Ziklag in Neh. 11:28).[44] The connection of Tel Halif with Ziklag has been contested on precisely these archaeological grounds: namely, Tel Halif's rather muted status during the eleventh and tenth centuries BCE and more meager presence of Philistine cultural wares.[45] Nevertheless, due caution must be exercised before equating pots with peoples, and Tel Halif's strategic value overlooking the Gerar Basin, its imposing fortifications in the Iron II period, and its close proximity to the settlements of Sansannah (Kh. Samsniyat) and Madmannah (Kh. Umm Demme) are factors that cannot be discounted within this discussion.[46] (See Figure 3.3.)

If Tel Sera' and Tel Halif emerge as the best candidates for Ziklag's location, then, we can nevertheless only push these connections so far. But the importance of directing our attention to these two neighboring sites and the region in which

---

40. Rainey and Notley, *Sacred Bridge*, 149 and the discussion of Gath in Chapter 2.

41. Oren, "Ziglag," 161–63; idem, "Sera', Tel" *NEAEHL*, IV, 1332–33.

42. Oren, "Ziglag," 163.

43. See A. Alt, "Judas Gaue unter Josia," *Palästina-Jahrbuch* 21 (1925): 100–116; Nadav Na'aman, "The Kingdom of Judah under Josiah," *TA* 18.1 (1991): 1–71; Geoghegan, "Until This Day," 201–27; Ron Tappy, "Historical and Geographical Notes on the 'Lowland Districts' of Judah in Joshua xv 33–47," *VT* 58 (2008): 381–403.

44. Oren, "Ziglag," 158–61; idem, "Sera', Tel" 1333–34.

45. Seger, for example, acknowledges the paucity of Iron I remains at Tel Halif and the general absence of Philistine material culture from the site (J. Seger, "The Location of Biblical Ziklag," *BA* 47.1 [1984]: 49). For a more recent, nuanced assessment of Tel Halif's material culture during this time, see P. Jacobs and J. Seger, "Glimpses of the Iron Age I at Tel Halif," in *"Up to the Gates of Ekron": Essays on the Archaeology and History of the Eastern Mediterranean in Honor of Seymour Gitin* (ed. S. Crawford; Jerusalem: Israel Exploration Society, 2007), 146–65. In terms of geography, it has also been argued that Tel Halif is too far east, well within Judahite territory, to fit the description of Ziklag in the Hebrew Bible (A. Rainey and S. Notley, *Sacred Bridge*, 148–49)—though as Koch points out, the Philistines are reported as having outposts well within later Judahite territory throughout the Book of Samuel.

46. Seger, "Halif, Tel," 557–58. My thanks to I. Koch for emphasizing these important points.

FIGURE 3.3 View of the Gerar Basin from atop Tel Halif, looking west toward Tel Sera' (Picture: Author).

they are located is the specific geographical perspective this overview affords. For what is crucial about Ziklag's position within this particular area of the northwestern Negev is the biblical claims that this territory was under some manner of Gittite jurisdiction in the early Iron Age period. And this claim finds historical significance precisely because an association between Gath and locations in the northwestern Negev could only be rooted in an early Iron Age context. After the ninth century BCE, in the late Iron Age or in the subsequent centuries, no Philistine center, Gath or otherwise, would ever extend their authority into this area of the Negev.

The Northwestern Negev in the Iron Age

As with much of the Levant, the northwestern Negev underwent a number of significant political and demographic changes during the centuries that transpired during the Iron Age period.[47] In a recent study, A. Faust calls attention to the nature of Philistine influence, more specifically, in the region at this time.[48] First, Faust observes that during the Iron I era Philistine populations appear to have expanded their influence from the coastal plain eastward, including into the northern reaches of the Negev and sites located along the Wadi Besor and

47. On this point, see the overview of I. Finkelstein, "The Southern Steppe of the Levant ca. 1050–750 BCE: A Framework for a Territorial History," *PEQ* 146.2 (2014): 89–104.

48. A. Faust, "From Regional Power to Peaceful Neighbor: Philistia in the Iron I–II Transition," *IEJ* 63 (2013): 174–204.

Wadi Gerar, where ample evidence of Philistine material culture has been recovered. Nevertheless, with the advent of the tenth century BCE there was almost a complete withdrawal of Philistine settlements from these same areas. The large Philistine settlements at Tell Jemmeh and Tel Haror, for example, were mostly abandoned in the late Iron I/early Iron IIA period,[49] as were the nearby locations of Tel Ma'arvim, Nahal Patish, Qubur al-Walaydah, and a number of small, rural settlements in their vicinity.[50] Furthermore, a collection of sites that had been within the orbit of Philistine influence elsewhere in the southern Levant during the Iron I period were no longer so in the Iron IIA era, including locations such as Tel Mor near Ashdod and the site of Tell Qasile located further north along the Yarkon River.[51] Similarly, locations that once evinced pronounced connections with Philistine material culture, such as Tel Batash and Tel Halif, now exhibited a much stronger orientation toward highland communities in the east during the late tenth and ninth centuries BCE.[52]

What is significant about the withdrawal of Philistine influence from the northwestern Negev is that the Philistines would never return. Certain locations once under Philistine control are no longer inhabited after Philistine disengagement, and other sites, such as Tel el-Hesi, were resettled by populations who descended principally from highland communities to the east.[53] By the eighth century BCE, another, more consequential change occurred within the region. At this time a new power entered the southern Levant and enacted a series of measures that altered the entire landscape of the Negev: namely, the Assyrian Empire. Using sites situated along the northwestern Negev to create a buffer zone between Assyrian holdings in the region and the Egyptian kingdom to the south, the Wadi Gerar became a key border area for Assyrian control as it expanded its empire in the late Iron Age. Tell Jemmeh,[54] Tel Haror,[55] and Tel Sera',[56] for example, were all rebuilt in the eighth century BCE as impressive Assyrian garrison

---

49. Oren, "Haror," 583.

50. Faust, "Peaceful Neighbor," 181–82.

51. Ibid., 182–86.

52. Jacobs and Seger, "Tel Halif," 154–55.

53. Blakely and Horton, "Site Identifications," 29–31; Seger, "Halif," 557–58.

54. D. Ben-Shlomo, "Tell Jemmeh, Philistia and the Neo-Assyrian Empire during the Late Iron Age," *Levant* 40.1 (2014): 58–88.

55. Oren, "Haror," 583–84.

56. Oren, "Sera', Tel" 1333; idem, "Ethnicity and Regional Archaeology: The Western Negev Under Assyrian Rule," in *Biblical Archaeology Today, 1990* (eds. A. Biran and J. Naveh; Jerusalem: Israel Exploration Society, 1993), 102–105.

fortresses that were either controlled by Assyrian personnel or administered by local vassals loyal to the Assyrian cause.

From this perspective, Tel Sera' finds importance once again because its remains are representative of this transition from Canaanite to Philistine to Assyrian control in the Iron Age. Excavated over six seasons (1972–79) by Ben-Gurion University under the direction of E. Oren, the material culture unearthed at the location indicates that it grew into an imposing Canaanite city during the very end of the Middle Bronze Age II period and, in the Late Bronze Age, developed into an important Egyptian administrative center used to gather and store taxes for the Nineteenth and early Twentieth Dynasties (ca. thirteenth and twelfth centuries BCE).[57] Sometime in the mid-twelfth century BCE Tel Sera' was destroyed (Stratum IX) in a violent conflagration attributed to either Philistine peoples or semi-nomadic populations from the Negev desert to the south.[58] Built on the ruins of the former LBA Canaanite city were three phases of late Iron I settlements (eleventh century BCE, Stratum VIII) that contained a notable assemblage of ceramics associated with Philistine material culture, suggesting that the site had come into contact with Philistine populations at this moment in time.

What distinguishes Tel Sera' from many other sites in its vicinity, however, is that it continued to exist, and even thrive, in the time after Philistine withdrawal from the region. During the tenth century BCE (Stratum VII), for example, Tel Sera' continued as an inhabited location that retained connections to Philistine culture while also exhibiting new architectural forms (four room homes, ashlar masonry) typically affiliated with Phoenician and highland populations. Yet in spite of the novel architectural traditions that appeared at this time, the transition from Stratum VIII to VII did not appear to include a destruction layer or a period of abandonment. Oren comments:[59]

> It also became clear that the transition from stratum VIII to stratum VII showed no signs of destruction and no gap in occupation. Consequently, because the Israelite settlement of the tenth century BCE must have developed organically from the Philistine habitation, it would seem that the ethnic nucleus of Tel Sera' in the Iron Age I–II was Philistine.

---

57. Oren, "Sera', Tel" 1330–31; idem, "Ziglag," 165–66. On the ostraca detailing Egyptian economic transactions, see O. Goldwasser, "Hieratic Inscriptions from Tel Sera' in Southern Canaan," *TA* 11 (1984): 77–93.

58. Oren, "Sera', Tel," 1331; idem, "Ziglag," 166.

59. Oren, "Sera', Tel," 1331.

Whether Stratum VII at Tel Sera' should be considered Israelite is questionable in light of the varied traditions present in the settlement's architecture and material culture at this time.[60] More important about this location for our purposes here, however, is that this site continued to feature Philistine associations into the Iron IIA period (tenth and ninth centuries BCE) at a moment when few other sites in northwestern Negev would exhibit a similar cultural connection.

To those living in a time after the Iron IIA period, however, references to Philistine associations along this area of the Wadi Gerar would have made little sense. Instead, during the eighth century BCE, Tel Sera', Tel Haror, and Tell Jemmeh were rebuilt, as noted above, as large Assyrian fortresses positioned along the southern border of what was then the Assyrian Empire. At Tel Sera' specifically, a large citadel was unearthed with walls running 5m thick and fine Assyrian palace wares housed within it, attesting to the importance of the settlement for the Assyrian Empire in the region.[61] Indeed, late Iron Age Tel Sera' and the nearby location of Tel Jemmeh produced a greater quantity and quality of Assyrian remains than all of the settlements located in seventh century BCE Philistia combined.[62] With the collapse of the Assyrian Empire in the late seventh century, however, the Assyrian fortresses were destroyed, perhaps by Egyptian forces pushing northward or, later, by Nebuchadnezzar during his march toward Egypt.

What is significant about the settlement history of a location such as Tel Sera' for our investigation here is that it shines a spotlight on important regional changes that came to pass at a site that, at the very least, was quite proximate to where Ziklag would have been situated. Though once located well within the orbit of Philistine influence throughout the twelfth and tenth centuries BCE, the settlements located along the Wadi Besor and Wadi Gerar experienced the retreat of Philistine interest after this time and, in the eighth and seventh centuries BCE came under Assyrian jurisdiction. Since this territory in the northwestern Negev experienced the retreat of Philistine influence by the end of the ninth century (if not earlier), it is unlikely, then, that references to this area's Philistine affiliation in the Hebrew Bible would have originated in a period after this time. Those scribes at work after the ninth century BCE, in other words, would have

---

60. The absence of a final excavation report also complicates this assessment. So Faust remarks, "Of the larger mounds in the region during the Iron Age I, two—Tel Jemmeh... and Tel Sera'... exhibit continuity into the Iron Age II, although the nature of settlement in the latter is complex and unclear." Faust, "Peaceful Neighbor," 182.

61. Ibid., 1333.

62. D. Master, "Trade and Politics: Ashkelon's Balancing Act in the Seventh Century B. C. E.," *BASOR* 330 (2003): 51.

never known a world in which the northwestern Negev was associated with Philistine polities and culture.

Rather, much like the references to Gath explored in the previous chapter, it is more plausible that stories about David's control of a Philistine settlement in the northwestern Negev were rooted in source material that arose in an early Iron Age context when sites in this region were still within the sphere of Philistine economic and political interests. The substantial Iron I Philistine material culture unearthed at these sites offers important points of convergence, from this perspective, with memories of a Philistine enclave in this area of Negev that, according to stories recalled about David, was placed under the authority of a highland warrior from the east.

Though Egyptian, Aramaic, and Hebrew inscriptions have been recovered from the area,[63] none of these short texts offer information about the region's early Iron Age past or the events that once transpired within it during this time. The only possible textual references from antiquity that attest to the northwestern Negev's early Iron Age affiliation with Philistine groups, rather, are those embedded in the stories surrounding David's command of Ziklag in the Book of Samuel.

Consequently, alongside I. Finkelstein,[64] M. Liverani,[65] W. Dietrich,[66] and J. Wright,[67] among others, it is reasonable to conclude that accounts of David's time at Ziklag were located in some of the oldest source material available to the biblical scribes about David's rise to the throne. The perseverance of those memories connecting David to Ziklag were likely predicated, in part, on the peculiar claim that Jerusalem's first Hebrew king was formerly a Philistine vassal who controlled a Philistine outpost to the far southwest of Jerusalem. But much like Gath, such memories would also have been supported by the continued physical existence of older locations in the northwestern Negev, such as Tell Jemmeh, Tel Haror, Tel Sera', and Tel Halif, that endured into a late Iron Age context when

---

63. Goldwasser, "Hieratic Inscriptions," 77–93; F. Cross, "Inscriptions from Tel Sera' " in *Leaves from an Epigrapher's Notebook: Collected Papers in Hebrew and West Semitic Paleography and Epigraphy* (Winona Lake: Eisenbrauns, 2003), 155–63.

64. I. Finkelstein, "Geographical and Historical Realities Behind the Earliest Layer in the David Story," *SJOT* 27.2 (2013): 134–39.

65. M. Liverani, *Israel's History and the History of Israel* (trans. C. Peri and P. Davies; London: Equinox, 2005), 93.

66. W. Dietrich, "David and the Philistines: Literature and History," in *The Ancient Near East in the 12th–10th Centuries BCE: Culture and History* (eds. G. Galil et al.; Münster: Ugarit Verlag, 2012), 85–89.

67. Wright, *David*, 35–37.

stories about David's outlaw days were first being gathered together and woven into a larger narrative about David's rise to the throne. What makes sites from this region significant, from this perspective, is that they endured into a late Iron Age context, as did memories, it seems, that connected David to this region's Philistine past.

David's Gifts to Judah's Elders (1 Sam. 30:26–31)

If memories of David's command of Ziklag resonate best with a late Iron I/early IIA historical context, other textual references within the stories of David's rise to the throne nevertheless suggest a somewhat later compositional setting.[68] Already, traces of scribal hands working in a period postdating the early Iron Age have been detected in the gloss that Ziklag belonged "to the kings of Judah to this day" (1 Sam 27:6), in addition to other information and observations woven into this account by its writers. In turning to our second narrative, however, particular geographical allusions embedded in this story also indicate that source material pertaining to David's activities in the desert south were also connected to later chronological horizons. (See Figure 3.4.)

The passage under consideration here is that of David's distribution of gifts to the elders of Judah in 1 Samuel 30:26–31. This account is preceded by the story recorded in 1 Samuel 30:1–25 of how David and his fighters, after returning to Ziklag from Aphek, found their homes destroyed and families taken. David and his men track the Amalekite bandits by way of divine command (1 Sam. 30:7–8) and with the aid of an Egyptian captive (1 Sam. 30:11–16). The Amalekites are surprised, mostly slaughtered, and the families and plunder returned to Ziklag (1 Sam. 30: 17–25). The tale of David's assault on the Amalekites then concludes with a list of locations in Judah that receive spoil from David's victory (1 Sam. 30:26–31). The purpose of David's offerings, it appears, is that of winning over tribal leaders in regions around Hebron and to Hebron's south, thus further strengthening David's base of support in the territory of the northern Negev. But David's gifts also serve as a reminder of the one responsible for driving out the Amalekites from the "Negev of Caleb" and the "Negev of Judah" (1 Sam. 30:14), or those areas in which the towns of 1 Samuel 30:27–31 are located. In this sense, David's actions in 1 Samuel 30:26–31 prepare the reader for David's later

---

68. On the compositional history of this text and its setting in 1 Samuel 30, see Grønbaek, *Die Geschichte vom Aufstieg Davids*, 203–11; H. Stoebe, *Das Erste Buch Samuelis*, 517–19; McCarter, *1 Samuel*, 435–38; A. Fischer, "Beutezug und Segensgabe: Zur Redaktionsgeschichte der Liste in 1 Sam. XXX 26–31," *VT* 53.1 (2003): 48–64; Dietrich, *Early Monarchy*, 265–67.

FIGURE 3.4 Iron Age Remains, Field II, from Tel Halif (Picture: Author).

coronation by the elders of Judah at Hebron in 2 Samuel 2:1–4a. The list of towns that receive gifts from David makes clear to the audience once again that David is not only the defender of Philistine Ziklag, but also the villages and towns of southern Judah.

How the town list in 1 Samuel 30:26–31 came to be included within the story of David's Amalekite raid is a matter of debate. On the one hand, 1 Samuel 30:25 and its concluding etymology behind the practice of dividing plunder suggests that the account of David's assault on the Amalekites may have originally ended at this juncture in the narrative. A stronger literary connection, then, is perhaps discerned between 1 Samuel 30:26–31 and the earlier stories surrounding David's raids in the northern Negeb found in 1 Samuel 27:7–11 due to the reference to the Jerahmeelites and the Kenites in both accounts (1 Sam. 27:10; 1 Sam. 30:29). On this view, the town-list recorded in 1 Samuel 30:26–31 was written in connection with the report of David's raids in nearby Negev regions as described in 1 Samuel 27.[69] That the town list in 1 Samuel 30:26–31 appears to have been an independent tradition later attached to the story of David's Amalekite raid has been further argued by A. Fischer,[70] who retraces a number of editorial decisions used to bind

69. See, for example, Wright, *David*, 43–45.

70. On the originally independent character of the town-list, see already A. Alt, "Geographie und Topographie des Negeb, III. Saruhen, Ziklag, Horma, Gerar," 418.

the entire chapter of 1 Samuel 30 together and marry it with incidents related earlier in 1 Samuel 27.[71]

More important than the precise redactional history of 1 Samuel 30:26–31 for the study at hand however are the locations named within this literary unit. These include:

> those in Bethel, in Ramoth of the Negeb, in Yattir, in Aroer, in Siphmoth, in Eshtemoa, in Carmel,[72] in the towns of the Jerahmeelites, in the towns of the Kenites, in Hormah, in Bor-ashan, in Athach, in Hebron, all the places where David and his men had roamed. (1 Sam. 30:27–31)

The geographical dispersion of the places named in this town list lay within a region running south of Hebron to the vicinity of the Beersheba Valley. (See Figure 3.5.) Of the locations cited, a number can be identified with some confidence:[73] Ramoth-negeb (Tel 'Ira); Yattir (Kh. 'Attir); Aroer (Tel 'Aroer); Eshtemoa (es-Samu'); Carmel (Kh. Kirmil); and Hebron (Tell er-Rumeideh).[74] Though the location of the Jerahmeelites is uncertain,[75] Judges 1:6 places the Kenites in the area around Arad (Tel Arad) in the eastern Beersheba Valley.

Important about the sites mentioned above is that they all have witnessed some archaeological activity with varying degrees of intensity. Consequently, the remains from these sites allow us to explore their Iron Age occupational history

---

71. In short, Fischer argues that 1 Samuel 30:26 and 30:31 were redactional elements used to frame the town list and tie it into the story of David. The reference to the towns of the Jerahmeelites and Kenites in 1 Samuel 30:29, as well as the references to Judah and the Negev of Caleb in 1 Samuel 30:14 and 30:16, are also identified as later editorial insertions use to bring coherence to 1 Samuel 27 and 30 as a whole. A. Fischer, "Beutezug und Segensgabe," 48–64.

72. The LXX[B] has the name Carmel, a site named previously in David's sojourn (1 Sam. 25:2) in place of the unknown MT location of Racal, unattested elsewhere in the Hebrew Bible and not preserved within any known toponym in the southern Levant.

73. The LXX[B] includes an additional five locations, none of which are, however, known from antiquity (nor 4QSam[a]) and may have been duplicate renderings of the Hebrew names. For discussion, see McCarter, I Samuel, 434.

74. Na'aman identifies Tel Beersheba with Bethel, but this connection rests on shaky ground, as do the identifications of Bor-ashan with Tell Beit Mirsim and Athach with Tell Aitun. Because of the substantial uncertainty surrounding these identifications, they will not be addressed here. N. Na'aman, "The Date of the List of Towns that Received the Spoil of Amalek (1 Sam 30:26–31)," TA 37 (2010): 179–81. For doubts about these identifications, see especially Finkelstein, "Geographical and Historical Realities," 143.

75. Rainey and Notley, on the basis of toponym 110 on Sheshonq's Bubastite Portal, suggest that the Jerahmeelites were also located in the Beersheba Valley adjacent to the Kenites. Rainey and Notley, Sacred Bridge, 149–50.

FIGURE 3.5 Map of Site Mentioned in 1 Samuel 30:26–31 (Map: Author).

in an effort to discern when, more precisely, these locations were once inhabited. And what comes to light is of particular interest.

A number of sites mentioned in the town list of 1 Samuel 30 produced some late Iron I/early IIA remains (eleventh and tenth centuries BCE) that overlap with the time of David. At Hebron, for example, domestic architectural features from the Iron I era were recovered in Area I.3 and I.6 of Hammond's excavations, along with a thick layer of Iron I pottery near the entrance to the settlement.[76] Iron I material culture also emerged in Eisenberg's more limited excavations at the site, and Iron I–IIA remains were recovered from Ofer's brief expedition to Hebron from 1984–1986.[77] Consequently, though Hebron had likely declined considerably since

76. A. Ofer, "Hebron," in *NEAEHL* II (1993), 608–609; J. Chadwick, "Discovering Hebron," *BAR* 31.5 (2005): 24–33, 70–71.

77. E. Eisenberg and A. Nagorski, "Tel Hevron (Er-Rumeidi)," *Hadashot Arkheologiyot* 114 (2002): 91–92; Ofer, "Hebron," 608.

the Middle Bronze Age when it was a substantial fortified city, evidence from the location indicates that it was nevertheless occupied during the Iron I era and into the Iron IIA period.[78]

Other locations also evince early Iron Age remains. At es-Samu' (Esthemoa), Iron I and IIA pottery were recovered in excavations carried out at the site and in a survey of the area, suggesting some settlement activity at the location during this time.[79] Moving further south and east, Arad (Tel Arad) produced more substantial remains connected to the establishment of a new settlement that was founded during the early Iron IIA period (Stratum XII), including a cluster of around twenty homes built atop the ruins of an Early Bronze Age city that had been abandoned for some fifteen hundred years.[80] Alongside of these settlements it should also be noted that the Beersheba Valley as a whole, which contained a number of other Iron I sites (e.g., Tel Masos III, Tel Beersheba IX–VIII), experienced a wave of new settlements and an increase in population at the beginning of the Iron IIA period.[81]

The settlement history of these sites finds some resonance, then, with the Davidic past recalled in 1 Samuel 30:26–31. Within this account, the image of an outcast and his band of fighters roaming amid the desert lands south of Hebron coheres well with an Iron I/IIA landscape when this area still retained its own regional autonomy, unaffected by Philistine, Egyptian, or Judahite efforts to control it.[82] The attempt to garner loyalty from tribal populations around Hebron and within the Beersheba Valley by defending their interests, furthermore, would have been a deft political maneuver by anyone seeking to consolidate power in the southern reaches of Judah during this early period in time.

Yet in tension with these observations are those sites included within the town list that were settled only after the time of David. These include, for

---

78. Ofer, "Hebron," 608.

79. Finkelstein, "Geographical and Historical Realities," 142.

80. Z. Herzog, "The Fortress Mound at Tel Arad: An Interim Report," *TA* 29.1 (2002): 14–20; Z. Herzog and L. Singer-Avitz, "Redefining the Centre: The Emergence of State in Judah," *TA* 31.2 (2004): 209–18, 224.

81. Herzog and Singer-Avitz, "Redefining the Centre," 222–26; I. Finkelstein, "Khirbet en-Nahas, Edom and Biblical History," *TA* 32 (2005): 121–22; idem, "The Southern Steppe of the Levant ca. 1050–750 BCE," 95–98.

82. It appears that only in the ninth century BCE were the Negev highlands incorporated into Judah, sealed with the marriage alliance of Ahaziah of Judah to Zibia of Beersheba (2 Kings 12:2) and the establishment of Judahite fortresses at Arad (Stratum XI) and Beersheba (Stratum V) during this time. On this point, see N. Na'aman, "The Kingdom of Judah in the 9th Century BCE: Text Analysis Versus Archaeological Research," *TA* 40 (2013): 247–76.

example, the site of Ramoth Negeb (Tel 'Ira), which was established as an impressive fortress in the late eighth century BCE (Stratum VII). After the destruction of Tel Beersheba by the Assyrians, Tel 'Ira became, in fact, the largest fortified location in the Beersheba Valley during the course of the seventh century BCE (Stratum VI) at a period in time in which the kingdom of Judah invested heavily in its southern domain.[83] Tel 'Ira did exist as a small, inhabited location before this era (Stratum VIII), but this very modest settlement most likely arose only in the late tenth century BCE after a long period of abandonment.[84] Just to the south of Tel 'Ira lay the site of Aroer (Tel 'Aroer) which again is marked by significant fortifications and construction activity in the eighth and seventh centuries BCE, but was not occupied before this period in time.[85] And, lastly, the large mound at Yattir (Khirbet 'Attir) conforms to this general pattern by thus far yielding only Iron IIC ceramic evidence.[86]

Even more, of those sites referred to above that did produce Iron I–IIA remains, many of these locations became much larger and more consequential with the advent of the eighth century BCE. Eshtemoa, to cite one example, produced one of the largest Iron Age silver hoards ever recovered from the southern Levant. Yet in spite of numerous attempts to link this cache with David's gifts to the elders of Eshtemoa in 1 Samuel 30, it is now clear that the silver hoard belongs to a later period, most likely to that of the eighth century BCE, when Esthtemoa prospered and had taken on new significance in the region.[87] During this era Hebron also experienced some growth,[88] and Arad existed on a much larger scale as an imposing fortified settlement both before and after the Assyrians destroyed the site (ca. 701 BCE).[89] Given the likelihood that a number of the unidentified

---

83. I. Beit-Arieh, "Stratigraphy and Historical Background," in *Tel 'Ira: A Stronghold in the Biblical Negev* (ed. I. Beit-Arieh; Tel Aviv: Emery and Claire Yass, 1999), 170–71; Y. Thareani-Sussely, "The 'Archaeology of the Days of Manasseh' Reconsidered in Light of Evidence from the Beersheba Valley," *PEQ* 139.2 (2007): 72.

84. Beit-Arieh, "Stratigraphy," 170–77.

85. A. Biran, "And David Sent Spoils . . . to the Elders in Aroer (1 Sam 30:26–28)," *BARev* 9.2 (1983): 28–37; idem, "Aroer (in Judea)," *NEAEHL*, I, 89–92; Y. Thareani, ed., *Tel 'Aroer. The Iron Age II Caravan Town and the Hellenistic-Early Roman Settlement* (Jerusalem: Hebrew Union College—Jewish Institute of Religion, 2011).

86. H. Eshel, J. Magness, and E. Shenhav, "Khirbet Yattir, 1995–1999: Preliminary Report," *IEJ* 50 (2000):167. This site, however, has witnessed only limited excavations.

87. R. Kletter and E. Brand, "A New Look at the Iron Age Silver Hoard from Eshtemoa," *ZDPV* 114.2 (1998): 139–54.

88. Eisenberg and Nagorski, "Tel Hevron," 92; Chadwick, "Hebron," 70–71.

89. Herzog, "Tel Arad," 96–102.

locations on the town list were situated in the more western zones of Judah near the Shephelah (so Bor-Ashan, Athach, and Hormah [cf. Joshua 15]) it is also significant that this region experienced a burst of settlement activity and population growth in the ninth and eighth centuries BCE,[90] with fewer and smaller settlements in the centuries before.

What the archaeological remains from Ramoth-negev (Tel 'Ira), Aroer (Tel 'Aroer), Yattir (Kh. Yattir), Eshtemoa (es-Samu'), Hebron (er-Rumeideh), and the Shephelah region indicate, consequently, is that the town list of 1 Samuel 30:26–31 as we have it now was revised, if not composed entirely, after the tenth century BCE.[91] By how long is uncertain. The citation of places that existed only in the late Iron Age within this story and the rising importance of the Beersheba Valley for Judah in the eighth and seventh centuries BCE suggests that the compositional setting of the town-list occurred in a period that postdated the early Iron Age by a generation or more. I. Finkelstein, in his own study of 1 Samuel 30:26–31, suggests that this account was written down sometime in the ninth century BCE before Hazael of Damascus's incursion into Philistia and Judah (ca. 830 BCE),[92] whereas N. Na'aman prefers a late eighth century date just prior to Sennacherib's devastation of the Shephelah and numerous other southern Judahite holdings (ca. 701 BCE.)[93] Given the allusions to Tel 'Ira and Tel 'Aroer within this account, however, a seventh century BCE context cannot be ruled out.[94]

The Entanglements of a Davidic Past

Our study of 1 Samuel 27 and 30 indicates that the information drawn on to construct these stories descended from varied periods in time and were shaped by a changing landscape in the southern Levant. For those narratives connected to Ziklag, allusions to David's control of a Philistine outpost on the southern border of Gath's domain find resonance with a late Iron I/early Iron IIA context when Gath existed as a formidable Philistine city and when settlements in the northwestern Negev possessed a cultural assemblage with strong ties to Philistia.

---

90. See, more recently, A. Faust, "The Shephelah in the Iron Age: A New Look on the Settlement of Judah," *PEQ* 145.3 (2013): 203–19.

91. So the conclusion reached, in different ways, by Na'aman, "Date of the List," 181–83; and Fischer, "Beutezug und Segensgabe," 61–63.

92. Finkelstein, "Geographical and Historical Realities," 148.

93. Na'aman, "Date of the List," 182–83.

94. So Fischer, "Beutezug und Segensgabe," 63.

In light of the fact that the remains from these sites would never again exhibit this type of Philistine orientation, later in the late Iron Age or in the centuries after, it can be ascertained that the references to Ziklag and David's activity at this location were drawn from source material of a more antiquated variety.

Nevertheless, when one turns to the town list of 1 Samuel 30:26–31 a different understanding of the source material used to compose these stories comes to the fore. To be sure, a number of references within this short account find points of contact with historical conditions in the Iron I–IIA period and may have originated during this era, perhaps most strikingly in the depiction of David and his small band of discontents making raids into an area south of Hebron that appears to be outside the authority of any centralized polity or local kingdom in the region. But the predominant impression one receives from the settlement history of the locations referred to in this text is that of a late Iron Age context (Iron IIB–IIC) when the Beersheba Valley became an important component of the Judahite realm, including the founding of new locations and a string of fortresses in the eighth and seventh centuries BCE. A Davidic past, in this instance, appears to have been negotiated and recast in light of later realities within this region of the southern Levant.

Consequently, what results from this study of 1 Samuel 27 and 30 is a central historical insight into the referential claims expressed within these narratives: namely, that the body of knowledge drawn on to compose these passages was rather heterogeneous and fluid, restricted neither to a specific era or particular geography even if the events that transpire within these stories seem short-lived and closely connected. In light of the settlement history behind the places that are referred to in these texts, it is possible that some of the information that led to the composition of these narratives was quite old, connected to a period proximate, or even contemporaneous with, the eleventh and tenth centuries BCE. But other material used to recount these moments in David's life seems less antiquated, connected, it appears, to the emergence of a more developed Judahite kingdom whose borders began to stretch to new territories that also claimed an affiliation with a Davidic past.

That the story of David's rise to power in the Book of Samuel was composed of a number of distinct sources, eventually gathered together and woven into a larger narrative complex, is not a novel insight. Nor is the claim that these stories may retain, as a consequence, diachronic features reflective of the scribal revisions that contributed to the shaping of these narrative traditions.[95] Suggesting

---

95. For discussion on both these points, see especially Hutton, *Transjordanian Palimpsest*, 228–88. Cf. P. K. McCarter, *I Samuel*, 12–30; R. Kratz, *Composition*, 153–58; Dietrich, *Early Monarchy*, 262–67; K. Schmid, *The Old Testament: A Literary History* (trans. L. Maloney; Minneapolis: Fortress, 2012), 66–69.

that the episodes of David's outlaw days in 1 Samuel were written from different perspectives and arose at different times would conform, then, to what has been discerned by redaction-critical approaches toward the formation of the Book of Samuel as a whole.

But what our turn to the archaeological record affords is a much richer understanding of the source material behind these accounts. In contrast to those scholars who recognize the importance of the sources that contributed to Samuel but who contend that nothing can be discerned, historically, about their character and when they emerged,[96] what this chapter's investigation offers is a constructive method of using archaeological evidence in order to gain insights into precisely such concerns. For whatever form its sources took and whatever the historicity of their claims, the information drawn on for stories about David's control of Ziklag, this study has demonstrated, retained some associations with an early Iron Age context; alternatively, the knowledge that undergirded the narrative of David's gifts to Judah's elders was shaped, at least in part, by the experience of a late Iron Age world.

Questions initially posed by Gunkel and Greßmann[97] about the preliterary background of the biblical narrative would thus be upheld and considered anew in the case of these stories surrounding David, but now analyzed with access to archaeological evidence that these scholars simply did not have available. This approach has the advantage, then, of responding to a fundamental historical concern surrounding these accounts: the question of why references that stem from what appear to be different centuries in time are included within a story that details but a few years of David's life. Why, in other words, were these diachronic elements not simply removed or flattened out into a single chronological horizon that corresponded either to the time of David or to that era in which these texts came together into their principal narrative form?

The most frequent reply to this question is one that privileges the written word. On this view, allusions to different temporal horizons within these Davidic stories were the result of centuries of textual production. As later

---

96. Paradigmatic is Kratz, who contends that in the case of "reminiscences" about David's flight from Saul in 1 Samuel "it is impossible to locate the reminiscences historically in any way, unless one thinks that they are all made up." Kratz, *Composition*, 182.

97. See again comments in the introductory chapter to this work and the comments about method expressed by Gunkel and Greßmann in H. Gunkel, "Aus Wellhausen's neuesten apokalyptischen Forschungen. Einige principielle Eröterungen" *ZWT* 42 (1899) 581–611; idem, "Ziele und Methoden der Erklärung des Alten Testamentes" in *Reden und Aufsätze* (Göttingen: Vandenhoeck & Ruprecht, 1913), 11–29; H. Greßmann, "Die Aufgaben der alttestamentlichen Forschung" *ZAW* 24 (1924) 1–33.

writers copied and reshaped older documents handed down to them, new references were introduced into these writings, sometimes consciously and other times unconsciously so, during the course of many generations of scribal activity.[98] The long, protracted development of these writings, in which earlier documents about David were added onto and rewritten by later scribal hands, thus left behind an ensemble of allusions to different eras that built up within these accounts over the centuries. According to this perspective, the composition of these writings was primarily a cumulative process rather than a reductive one, with early texts about David accruing other texts that also came to be associated with him.

An accent on the lengthy process by which stories about David in the Book of Samuel came to be written down and revised cannot be lost from view. But what is often overlooked with this acute concentration on textual production and redaction for theories of diachronicity within these narratives is the larger, extra-textual world in which these writings took form. Historicizing the mechanisms by which stories about the past were transmitted to Hebrew scribes in the Iron Age, as detailed in Chapter 1, urges caution, for example, when attributing heavy text production already to the early tenth century BCE.[99] In addition to brief written sources from the early Iron Age, much of the source material about David's rise would have been transmitted primarily through an oral storytelling tradition and the memories contained therein.

But what is also lost with this focus on the self-enclosed processes of textual production and revision for understandings of the diachronic features present in Samuel is the specificity of the locations named in texts such as 1 Samuel 27 and 1 Samuel 30. What a purely literary approach to these texts fails to address,

---

98. So a broad spectrum of scholarship, including, for example, H. Ewald, *History of Israel*, I (trans. R. Martineau; London: Longmans, Green, 1883), 133–59; J. Wellhausen, *Prolegomena to the History of Israel* (3rd ed. New York: Meridian, 1961 [1882]), 228, 263–65; S. R. Driver, *An Introduction to the Literature of the Old Testament* (9th ed.; New York: Meridian, 1957), 5; H. Hertzberg, *I & II Samuel* (trans. J. Bowden; Philadelphia: Westminster, 1964 [1960]), 19; W. L. Humphreys, "The Rise and Fall of King Saul: A Study of an Ancient Narrative Stratum in 1 Samuel," *JSOT* 22 (1980): 74–90; O. Kaiser, "David und Jonathan: Tradition, Redaktion und Geschichte in 1 Sam 16–20—Ein Versuch," *ETL* 66 (1990): 281–96; and J. Vermeylen, "La maison de Saül et la maison de David: Un écrit de propagande théologic-politique de 1 Sm 11 à 2 Sm 7," in *Figures de David à travers la Bible* (eds. L. Dorousseaux and J. Vermeylen; Paris: Cerf, 1999), 35–74.

99. On the modest character of early Iron Age text production in ancient Israel, see again W. Schniedewind, *How the Bible Became a Book* (Cambridge: Cambridge University Press, 2004), 48–90; S. Sanders, *The Invention of Hebrew* (Champaign: University of Illinois Press, 2009), 103–22; D. Carr, *The Formation of the Hebrew Bible: A New Reconstruction* (Oxford: Oxford University Press, 2011), 375–85.

in other words, is a crucial historical question pertaining to these writings: why do our narratives refer to these particular locations in the story of David's life, and not others? Why this past among alternative imaginings? An answer to this question cannot be found in the texts of Samuel themselves, regardless of how well-trained is the historian's eye for literary seams or layers.

Reading these texts alongside the archaeological remains of the locations named within them, however, offers another vantage point by which to take up these concerns. Distinct about this approach is the evidence it provides of the strong influence exerted on these Davidic stories by the physical terrain of the northern Negev region. Outside the domain of any kingdom or empire during early Iron Age, new growth and political alliances emerged in and around this area after the tenth century BCE, including the withdrawal of more concentrated Philistine activity and a substantial increase in population, settlements, and fortifications in the eighth to early sixth centuries BCE when this area became a significant component of the Judahite realm.[100] Certain memories of David's past activity in Judah's south were adapted, it seems, to this changing landscape over time, giving these stories a tangibility and concreteness that otherwise may have been lacking for later audiences who would have been unfamiliar with the sparsely settled, unruly lands depicted in stories told about David's former activity in the desert south.[101]

Conversely, the continued existence of older settlements, such as Tel Sera' and Tel Halif to Judah's southwest, did not attract older memories to it so much as bolster and sustain what was recalled about it. Though a number of locations in this region passed out of Canaanite and Philistine hands and into the control of new powers that came to dominate the Levant, certain sites were able to endure as locations of some significance for much of the Iron Age period. The ability to withstand the changes that occurred about them offers an important historical clue as to why memories about a location such as Ziklag and its Philistine past endured in the sources available to later scribes: namely, the survival and continued significance of such locations over time. If the town list of 1 Samuel 30:26–31 made older Davidic memories more concrete to later audiences

---

100. I. Finkelstein, "The Archaeology of the Days of Manasseh," in *Scripture and Other Artifacts: Essays on Archaeology and the Bible in Honor of Philip J. King* (eds. M. Cogan, C. Exum, and L. Stager; Louisville: Westminster, 1994), 176–77; Thareani-Sussely, "'Archaeology of the Days of Manasseh' Reconsidered," 69–77.

101. For a similar approach toward references to Moab in the Book of Judges, see E. Bloch-Smith, "A Stratified Account of Jephthah's Negotiations and Battle: Judges 11:12–33 from an Archaeological Perspective," *JBL* 134.2 (2015): 309–11; for the exodus narratives, see I. Finkelstein and N. Silberman, *The Bible Unearthed: Archaeology's New Vision of Ancient Israel and the Origin of Its Sacred Texts* (New York: Free Press, 2001), 65–71.

by adapting them to a more familiar landscape in the centuries after a Davidic era, the perseverance of other sites in the northwestern Negev, on this view, led to the perseverance of older memories connected to this territory.

Another way to account for the diachronic elements discerned within these Davidic stories, then, is to draw attention to the diachronic features embedded in the ancient landscape in which these stories were formed. Such an approach would seek to balance out theories for why the biblical writings preserve references to varied time periods by connecting these entanglements not simply to the lengthy processes of textual transmission, but also to how the built and natural environments that ancient Hebrew scribes experienced shaped the writings they produced.

If we pursue this angle for our Davidic narratives and the Iron Age landscape of Judah's southern domain, what we find is a territory dotted by the remains of multiple time periods scattered throughout region. In an era after Sennacherib's devastation of Judah at the end of the eighth century BCE, for example, an inhabitant of the Judahite kingdom would have encountered the ruins of the Assyrian campaign everywhere in Judah's south, from the wreckage present at the more western sites of Tell Beit Mirsim,[102] Tel 'Eton,[103] and Tel Halif,[104] to the central and eastern locations of Tel Beer-Sheba,[105] Tel Malhata,[106] and Tel Arad.[107] But even in a time previous to this an individual traveling through the region would have experienced older remains among locations in Judah's south, such as the abandoned Iron I–IIA ruins at Tel Masos situated, centuries later, alongside a very modest Iron IIC fortress,[108] or the numerous small Ḥaṣerim settlements of the western Beersheba Valley that had been uninhabited since the end of the tenth century BCE.[109] And, even at those sites that continued to be occupied over

---

102. I. Finkelstein and N. Na'aman, "The Judahite Shephelah in the Late 8th and early 7th Centuries BCE," *TA* 31 (2004): 61–64.

103. H. Katz and A. Faust, "The Assyrian Destruction Layer at Tel 'Eton," *IEJ* 62 (2012): 22–53.

104. O. Borowski, "Tell Halif: in the Path of Sennacherib," *BAR* 31.3 (2005): 24–35.

105. Y. Aharoni, *Beer-Sheba I: Excavations at Tel Beersheba 1969–1971* (Tel Aviv: Tel Aviv University Press, 1973), 5–7.

106. I. Beit-Arieh, "Excavations at Tel Malhata: An Interim Report," in *The Fire Signals of Lachish: Studies in the Archaeology and History of Israel in the Late Bronze Age, Iron Age, and Persian Period in Honor of David Ussishkin* (eds. I. Finkelstein and N. Na'aman; Winona Lake: Eisenbrauns, 2006), 21.

107. Herzog, "Tel Arad," 14, 98.

108. A. Kempinski, "Masos, Tel," in *NEAEHL* III, 986–89.

109. Herzog and Singer-Avitz, "Redefining the Centre," 222–25.

FIGURE 3.6 Ruins of Roman City of Scythopolis (foreground), with Ruins of pre-Roman Tel Beth-Shean (background) (Picture: Author).

the centuries, the traces of much more ancient periods, such as the large Middle Bronze Age wall that had once encircled Hebron,[110] would have been readily visible to those who came across such locations in subsequent eras.

For a scribal culture whose sense of the past depended, at least in part, on the places and things they encountered in their surroundings,[111] there is little doubt that these material frameworks would have left an imprint on how they conceived of the past transmitted to them through older sources. Foregrounding the influence of landscape on the stories they developed is not then to diminish the importance of the scribal practices that constituted these texts, but is put forward in order to situate this scribal activity within a world of lived, embodied experience. An accent on this physical environment serves as a reminder that the texts written by these scribes were the product of a particular constellation of contexts,[112] social, linguistic, cultural—but also material—with the topography and geography of the southern Levant exerting their own influence on how the past was portrayed within these scribes' writings. (See Figure 3.6.) Herodotus, on this view, was not the only ancient writer to step out from home and be affected by the terrain and ruins that were then encountered.

This argument finds support on the one hand through the writings of a Herodotus who demonstrates his dependence on various landscapes for his understanding of the past, including monuments he believed were fashioned by rulers of a much more distant age. But this perspective is also buttressed by

---

110. Ofer, "Hebron," 608.

111. For recent discussions of how material realia actively influenced human behavior and cognition in antiquity, see for example and their effect on cultural transmission over time, see I. Hodder, "Human-Thing Entanglement: Towards an Integrated Archaeological Perspective," *Journal of the Royal Anthropological Institute* 17.1 (2011): 154–77; L. Malafouris, *How Things Shape the Mind: A Theory of Material Engagement* (Cambridge: MIT Press, 2013), esp. 35–56.

112. Gabrielle Spiegel, "History, Historicism, and the Social Logic of the Text in the Middle Ages," *Speculum* 65.1 (1990): 59–86.

more recent theoretical studies that have highlighted the entanglements that develop when a remembered past is transmitted over time through the stories told within a community. "Diachronically evolving interpretations of one mnemonic signifier," in such instances, have been found to arise and coalesce around others "without necessarily substituting for the previous ones,"[113] resulting in an amalgamation of multiple pasts preserved within stories recounted about a particular event or figure. Rather than consistency and uniformity with regard to what is remembered, the past recalled by different generations in different historical contexts has instead been found to reflect "multiple perspectives, asymmetries, and cross-referential mnemonic practices"[114] that retain their vitality precisely because of their elasticity.[115]

What archaeological research contributes to this perspective is evidence that the entanglements of memory theorized here find a counterpart in the entangled pasts preserved in the material remains of particular landscapes. If, as a number of studies have maintained,[116] memories of both individuals and communities are shaped in response to the visible, material frameworks that surround them (i.e., monuments, public buildings, natural landscapes), then it becomes necessary for the historian to consider how an ancient terrain, so often a repository of the physical ruins of previous eras, influenced the knowledge transmitted through memories recalled in response to this familiar environment.

A striking instance from antiquity of the phenomenon described here is that of the oft-studied "Catalogue of Ships" found in Book II of the *Iliad* (Hom. *Il.* 2.484–93). How this section of the *Iliad* formed and when it was incorporated into the rest of the epic is a matter of long-standing debate.[117] But from a historical perspective this passage has frequently garnered interest because of the great number of locations named within it from across the Aegean world. After many decades of archaeological research, it now is clear that some

113. Feindt et al., "Entangled Memory," 34.

114. Ibid., 35. On the diachronic features of memories recalled over time, see also S. Conrad, "Entangled Memories: Versions of the Past in Germany and Japan, 1945–2001," *Journal of Contemporary History* 38.1 (2003): 85–99.

115. Conrad, "Entangled Memories," 86–87.

116. See again M. Halbwachs, *La Mémoire Collective* (2nd ed.; Paris: Presses Universitaires de France, 1968), 130–67; G. Bachelard, *The Poetics of Space* (trans. by M. Jolas. Boston: Beacon, 1994): 3–37; and E. Casey, *Remembering: A Phenomenological Study* (Bloomington: Indiana University Press, 1987), 181–215.

117. For an overview of these debates, see the summary in B. Sammons, *The Art and Rhetoric of the Homeric Catalogue* (Oxford: Oxford University Press, 2010), 4–8.

of the sites mentioned in the Catalogue refer to Late Bronze Age settlements that no longer existed when the Homeric poems were first set down in writing centuries later.[118] Such references to a Late Bronze Age past thus would have endured over many centuries in oral tradition, sustained through the oral storyteller's craft and the cultural memories embedded in the epic traditions recalled. Yet the Catalogue also alludes to much later, late Iron Age sites that were contemporaneous, or nearly contemporaneous, to the era in which these oral epics first began to be textualized (ca. the late eighth/seventh centuries BCE).[119] Consequently, though the events surrounding the Catalogue are said to have taken place during a specific time period in the Late Bronze Age, the participants named in the list nevertheless reflect many centuries of Aegean settlement history.

The pronounced diachronic features of the Catalogue have been explained in different ways, but a number of studies have recently drawn attention to the changing landscape of the Aegean world in order to do so. On this view, older, oral traditions were appropriated and updated over time by later bards in reference to the world in which they lived, thus explaining why, for example, the region of Boeotia finds such a place of prominence in the Catalogue but not in the epic as a whole, or why important Late Bronze Age centers such as Thebes or Tanagra do not appear within the Catalogue when one would expect their inclusion in light of the impressive LBA archaeological remains recovered from these locations.[120]

In an attempt to explain these chronological features of the Catalogue, G. Kirk suggests two important factors that contributed to this development. First, Kirk argues that certain sites came to be included in the textualized form of the Catalogue because these places had remained inhabited over the centuries, thereby reinforcing the memories attached to them for later Homeric poets.

---

118. R. H. Simpson and J. F. Lazenby, *The Catalogue of the Ships in Homer's Iliad* (Oxford: Oxford University Press, 1970); E. Visser, *Homers Katalog der Schiffe: Die epische Beschreibung Griechenlands in der Ilias* (Teubner: Stuttgart and Leipzig: 1997), 741–50.

119. J. K. Anderson, "The Geometric Catalogue of Ships," in *The Ages of Homer: A Tribute to Emily Townsend Vermeule* (eds. J. Carter and S. Morris; Austin: University of Texas Press, 1995): 181–92; M. Finkelberg, "Homer as a Foundation Text," in *Homer, the Bible, and Beyond: Literary and Religious Canons in the Ancient World* (eds. M. Finkelberg and G. Stroumsa; Leiden: Brill, 2003): 75–96.

120. G. S. Kirk, *The Iliad: A Commentary*, I (Cambridge: Cambridge University Press, 1985), 237–40; For other diachronic features within the Homeric poems as a whole, see especially Susan Sherratt, "Archaeological Contexts," in *A Companion to Ancient Epic* (ed. J. Foley; Malden: Blackwell, 2005): 119–40; and M. Wiener, "Homer and History: Old Questions, New Evidence," in *Epos: Reconsidering Greek Epic and Aegean Bronze Age Archaeology* (eds. S. Morris and R. Laffineur; Liège: Université de Liège, 2007), 3–33.

Second, older settlements were named in the text of the Catalogue because of the continued visibility of their material remains, attesting to their former existence in a more distant past for the later Homeric scribes who inscribed the epic.[121] In a separate study, J. Anderson goes so far as to argue that Iron Age Homeric poets constructed the Catalogue anew by reconfiguring their poems in light of the experience of Late Bronze Age ruins that existed when they set their poems down in writing.[122]

The relationship between place and memory underscored in these studies of Homer offers a significant, extra-biblical example from the ancient world of how the textualization of a remembered past was susceptible to the vicissitudes of a changing landscape over time. Such views find a number of points of convergence with this chapter's analysis of stories surrounding David's rise, in which it has been suggested that tales of a Davidic past were shaped by the experience of southern Judah's changing terrain during the Iron Age period. In both instances, the relationship between archaeological evidence and textual references encourages an approach that gives proper historical weight to the landscapes in which older source material was transmitted to later writers.

The importance of these changing material frameworks for perceptions of the past in antiquity, so often overlooked in theories surrounding the text-building of the Hebrew Bible, are increasingly coming to our attention from other historical fields and disciplines. In her incisive study of Greek memory under Roman imperial control, S. Alcock, for example, draws attention to the Agora in Athens and the profound transformations that occurred within it during the first and second centuries CE when it came under increased Roman attention. (See Figure 3.7.) Some of the most drastic modifications were found in the relocation of older buildings from elsewhere in Attica to the Agora (including a complete fifth century BCE temple [the Temple of Ares]), that were situated in and around newly constructed Roman monuments during this time.[123]

---

121. Kirk writes in regard to references to Late Bronze Age sites, "but many Mycenaean elements derive from places like Argos, Mukenai or Tiruns whose connexion with the tale of the Trojan War was maintained by monuments like the Lion Gate or Cyclopean walls as well as by continuity of habitation." Kirk, *The Iliad*, I, 238–39.

122. Anderson remarks, "Wherever our poet went, ruins which had once been assigned to the Cyclopes or Pelasgians . . . were now being pointed out as the homes of the heroes of the Trojan War." Anderson, "Catalogue of Ships," 191.

123. S. Alcock, "The Reconfiguration of Memory in the Eastern Roman Empire," in *Empires: Perspectives from Archaeology and History* (eds. S. Alcock et al.; Cambridge: Cambridge University Press, 2001), 323–50.

FIGURE 3.7 Statue of Emperor Hadrian in the Agora, Athens (Wikicommons).

In light of the patchwork of old and new structures now visible at the location, Alcock writes:[124]

> Presentation of the Hellenic past did not seek to escape the imperial present, but was continually and deliberately admixed with it, fitting Roman elements into a Greek matrix, establishing a new amalgam of what was memorable in Greek eyes. Recollection of the past involved the synthesis and recreation, not the isolation and protection, of memories.

The effect of these material entanglements of past and present was felt not only among the Greeks. Citing passages from Cicero (*de Finibus Bonorum et Malorum* 5.2–5), Alcock observes how Roman aristocracy frequently visited ancient Greek ruins and imagined themselves participating in what they considered to be an illustrious Greek past.[125] Thus, when Roman accounts of hostilities with eastern

---

124. Alcock, "The Reconfiguration of Memory," 338.

125. Ibid., 346–48.

Parthian forces were couched in imagery adopted from Greek victories over Persians from many centuries before, here, too, literature reflected landscape.[126]

In fact, whether one turns to the Old Babylonian period in Mesopotamia,[127] the emerging Syro-Hittite kingdoms of the early Iron Age,[128] or Berossos's reflections on a distant Babylonian past,[129] material evidence continues to mount with regard to how landscapes populated with the ruins and physical traces of multiple time periods introduced certain entanglements into how a past was represented within written texts composed after the events remembered. The biblical stories that bring together David's time at Ziklag and his gifts to Judah's elders would conform to this general pattern of "synthesis and recreation"[130] of a past recalled and reshaped in response to a terrain familiar to those scribes who wrote these stories down. At work in a world already ancient, scribes from across the ancient Near East wrote down numerous stories that had been formed in response to landscapes that reflected many centuries of previous human activity.

Such findings suggest that other entanglements, in addition to those traced out above, may have also been preserved in the source material appropriated by the biblical scribes about David's life in the Book of Samuel. Indeed, certain references from these stories, alongside those of Gath already examined in the previous chapter, suggest a more antiquated, early Iron Age context. These would include those referred to in the previous chapter, including the stunted account of Jerusalem's capture in 2 Samuel 5:6–9, in which David's future ruling center is adorned with few buildings or royal prestige, much in keeping with the location's status in the early Iron Age period but quite different from how the location appeared in the eighth to early sixth centuries BCE.[131] References to David's stronghold at Adullam (1 Sam. 22:1) or his activities at Keilah (1 Sam 23:1–13) also

---

126. A. Spawforth, "Symbol of Unity? The Persian-Wars Tradition in the Roman Empire," in *Greek Historiography* (ed. S. Hornblower; Oxford: Oxford University Press, 1994), 233–47.

127. G. Jonker, *The Topography of Remembrance: The Dead, Tradition, and Collective Memory in Mesopotamia* (Leiden: Brill, 1995), 129–32.

128. Ö. Harmansah, *Cities and the Shaping of Memory in the Ancient Near East* (Cambridge: Cambridge University Press, 2013), 40–45; cf. D. Bonatz, "Mnemohistory in Syro-Hittite Iconography," in *Proceedings of the XLVe Rencontre Assyriologique Internationale: Part I* (eds. T. Abusch et al.; Bethesda: CDL Press, 2001), 65–77.

129. R. Bollinger, "Berossus and the Monuments: City Walls, Sanctuaries, Palaces and the Hanging Garden," in *The World of Berossos* (eds. J. Haubold et al.; Wiesbaden: Harrassowitz Verlag, 2013), 137–64.

130. Alcock, "The Reconfiguration of Memory," 338.

131. Y. Shiloh, *Excavations at the City of David, I* (Jerusalem: Hebrew University, 1984), 26–27; A. De Groot and H. Bernick-Greenberg, *Excavations at the City of David 1978–1985 Directed by Yigal Shiloh, Vol. VIIA* (Jerusalem: Hebrew University, 2012), 150–53; and M.

provide scenes reminiscent of these locations' independent status in a more distant past before local kingdoms arose in the southern Levant and included them within their territory.[132] And the fact that David's warriors (2 Sam. 23:8–39) are said to have descended from a limited geographical region located primarily in small towns of the central hill country, some even from nameless locations identified by mountains and streams, is also more redolent of an early Iron Age context than a later one in terms of the Iron Age settlement history of the region.[133]

Yet at the same time, references to later eras that postdate the early Iron Age also seem to have been introduced into accounts devoted to David's life from centuries before. The most glaring anachronism is perhaps found in the reference to David worshipping in the "Temple of Yahweh" in Jerusalem after the death of his first-born child with Bathsheba (2 Sam. 12:20), a temple that, according to 1 Kings 6–8, was first built by David's son, Solomon. But other, more subtle examples can be cited. In a manner not far removed from this chapter's study of 1 Samuel 30:26–31, David's flight from Saul to the southern Judean Hills (1 Sam. 23:14–29) alludes to a sparsely settled, restive region that retains some semblance to an early Iron Age context. Yet certain allusions embedded in the story, such as David holing up at the strongholds of En-Gedi (1 Sam. 23:29), fit better with a later period when En-Gedi became a significant Judahite settlement for the first time (seventh and sixth centuries BCE).[134] A similar picture may be present in David's decision to station disgraced emissaries at Jericho (2 Sam. 10:5), which was, at most, a very modest and sparsely settled village in the early tenth century BCE, but a large town three centuries later.[135] When David's forces deal Edom a devastating defeat (2 Sam. 8:13), it is noteworthy, in this vein, that the victory occurs in precisely the same location as Amaziah's eighth century BCE triumph over Edom recounted in 2 Kings 14:7.[136] And though one could imagine

---

Steiner, *Excavations by Kathleen Kenyon in Jerusalem, 1961–1967: Vol. III* (London: Sheffield, 2001), 41–53.

132. N. Na'aman, "David's Sojourn in Keilah in Light of the Amarna Letters," *VT* 60 (2010): 87–97.

133. McCarter, *II Samuel*, 501; Finkelstein and Silberman, *David and Solomon*, 53–56.

134. B. Mazar, "En Gedi," in *NEAEHL* II, 401–403.

135. K. Kenyon, "Jericho," *NEAEHL* II, 680–81; idem, *Excavations at Jericho*. Vol. 3, *The Architecture and Stratigraphy of the Tell* (ed. T. A. Holland; London, 1981). Cf. 1 Kings 16:34 and the claim that the site was first settled by Ahab. Earlier, Saul and Samuel use the nearby site of Gilgal as an important center of operations (1 Sam. 7:16; 1 Sam. 13:4), but nowhere is mention made in the texts of Jericho.

136. N. Na'aman, "In Search of the Reality Behind the Account of David's Wars with Israel's Neighbors," *IEJ* 52.2 (2002): 214–15.

a highland warrior's forces attacking a number of small sites across the Jordan River in the general vicinity of Ammon in the late Iron I/Iron IIA period,[137] the description of the Ammonite capital as a large, fortified "royal city" (2 Sam 11–12) pertains much better to the Iron IIC period when the location flourished than its muted status during the early tenth century BCE.[138]

The diachronic entanglements discerned in 1 Samuel 27 and 1 Samuel 30 were thus likely not restricted to these texts alone within the Book of Samuel. Historical explanations for the varied temporalities potentially preserved in these very different traditions about David cannot, of course, be reduced to a single factor. But the archaeological and textual evidence pertaining to our analysis of David's time at Ziklag and his gifts to Judah's elders suggest that an important, often overlooked influence bearing on the diachronic features of Davidic storytelling was the landscape that helped to shape the memories recalled about a Davidic past. Setting their stories amid a topography and geography that was familiar to them, the scribes who drew on source material about David and worked to fashion these sources into prose form would have been surrounded by an already ancient terrain defined by the ruins of many centuries in time. The argument here is that this terrain would have impressed itself, at moments, onto the memories recalled within the sources the biblical scribes consulted about a Davidic past.

Conclusion

The compositional history behind the stories of David's rise to the throne in 1 Samuel 16–2 Samuel 5 has long been a source of debate among scholars who have investigated these narratives. If a majority opinion can be gleaned from these studies, it is that the narrative of David's Rise evinces only modest Deuteronomistic reworkings in comparison to other biblical books often identified with the Deuteronomistic History, such as Joshua or Kings.[139] Accordingly, it is likely that many of the stories included in Samuel preceded the work of a putative Deuteronomistic scribal circle by some time. Yet when this pre-Dtr Samuel

---

137. C. Ji, "Iron Age I in Central and Northern Transjordan: An Interim Summary of Archaeological Data," *PEQ* 127 (1995): 122–40.

138. E. Stern, *Archaeology of the Land of the Bible: The Assyrian, Babylonian, and Persian Periods, 732–332 BCE*, vol. 2 of *Archaeology of the Land of the Bible* (New York: Doubleday, 2001), 245–46.

139. So Noth's observation in his classic work. M. Noth, *The Deuteronomistic History* (2nd ed.; JSOTSup 15; Sheffield: JSOT Press, 1991), 86. More recently, see again the essays in C. Schäfer-Lichtenberger, *Die Samuelbücher und die Deuteronomisten*; C. Edenburg, and J. Pakkala, eds., *Is Samuel Among the Deuteronomists?*.

narrative took shape, where it was written, or the identity of the individuals behind it remains contentious.

The intent of this chapter has not been to resolve these enigmas but to ask a
different set of questions about how these stories took form: namely, what knowledge contributed to the development of these writings? In reading 1 Samuel 27
and 1 Samuel 30:26–31 alongside the archaeological remains of the settlements
named in these texts, the answer is not as straightforward as one might assume.
In part, it appears that the biblical scribes had access to sources that evince connections to the early Iron Age period (Iron I–IIA), regardless of the precise historicity of the claims made about David within them. This conclusion would then
support the observations made in the previous chapter surrounding the description of Philistine Gath, in which knowledge that arose in an early Iron Age past
endured into the time in which the biblical writings were first crystallizing into
narrative prose.

Yet it is also appears that the information drawn on by these scribes included
late Iron Age (Iron IIB–IIC) references. Here, a different landscape and new
geopolitical configurations shaped how a Davidic past came to be remembered
within these scribes' texts. In a matter not far removed from Herodotus and one
frequently theorized within studies devoted to transgenerational memory, the
sources used to construct these stories appear to have been adapted to new contexts by referring to phenomena more familiar to these writers and their audiences.[140] The result of this process, this study has argued, was the rendering of
narratives that evinced particular chronological and geographical layers that
came to be entangled within the stories told of David's outlaw days.

One can, of course, account for the varied temporalities expressed in these
narratives by other means. But in doing so the question that must be addressed
is why the biblical scribes decided to represent the past in the way that they did
with the locations they described. The contention put forward in this chapter's investigation is that the influence of a changing landscape of the southern
Levant on memories recalled about David offers another, distinct and compelling approach to this question of "why." Inhabiting a world populated by older
and newer settlements within the region of Judah, the biblical scribes, I contend,
appropriated sources into their narratives that had been shaped by a terrain filled
with the remains of multiple periods in time. Unable to excavate these sites and

---

140. For other early Iron Age instances of this phenomenon, among others, see Sherratt,
"Archaeological Contexts," 119–40; idem, "Homeric Epic and Contexts of Bardic Creation,"
in *Archaeology and Homeric Epic* (eds. S. Sherratt and J. Bennet; Oxford: Oxbow, 2017),
35–52; Na'aman "David's Wars," 200–24; and A. Gilboa, I. Sharon, and E. Bloch-Smith,
"Capital of Solomon's Fourth District? Israelite Dor," *Levant* 47.1 (2015): 51–74.

unravel the varied chronological references in the sources, these scribes produced a work that preserved diachronic elements within its storytelling because these varied temporalities were also present and substantiated in the environment that surrounded them. In addition, then, to the dynamics of resilience outlined in the previous chapter's study of Philistine Gath, this chapter's investigation concludes by putting forward another modality of remembering that would have shaped what knowledge about the past was conveyed to later biblical writers: the entanglements of time and place.

4

A Past No Longer Remembered

THE HEBREW BIBLE AND THE QUESTION OF ABSENCE

*Take care to watch yourselves closely, lest you forget the things
which your eyes have seen. (Deut. 4:9)*

*. . . for the people shape their memory according to what they
have experienced. (Thuc. 2.54.3)*

AROUND 160 CE the Greek author Pausanias began writing what would later
be entitled the Ἑλλάδος Περιήγεσις, or the "Tour of Greece." Over the course
of two decades Pausanias frequented the Greek mainland from his home in
Asia Minor in order to chronicle the local histories of places situated within the
Roman provinces of Achaea and Macedonia, giving special attention to those
material remains that called to mind how these regions appeared before they
came under Roman control.[1] The work itself is difficult to define.[2] Equal parts
travel literature, historical geography, political history, art criticism, and the
study of religious customs and beliefs, Pausanias's text offers detailed accounts
about a landscape that still bore the traces of an earlier Greek world at its height.
Meticulous observations on the topographical features of the ancient Agora in
Athens (Paus. 1.3–17), for example, or reports of the small temples and monuments strewn along the road from Sparta to Arcadia (Paus. 3.20.8–21.1) have,

---

1. K. W. Arafat, *Pausanias' Greece: Ancient Artists and Roman Rulers* (Cambridge: Cambridge
University Press, 1996), 8; C. Habicht, *Pausanias' Guide to Ancient Greece* (Berkeley: University
of California Press, 1998 [1985]), 3–13, 102–103; W. Hutton, *Describing Greece: Landscape
and Literature in the "Periegesis" of Pausanias* (Cambridge: Cambridge University Press,
2005), 9–10; M. Pretzler, *Pausanias: Travel Writing in Ancient Greece* (London: Duckworth,
2007), 16–31.

2. E. Bowie, "Inspiration and Aspiration: Date, Genre, and Readership," in *Pausanias: Travel
and Memory in Roman Greece* (eds. S. Alcock et al.; Oxford: Oxford University Press, 2001),
21–32; Hutton, *Describing Greece*, 241–72; Pretzler, *Pausanias*, 1–15.

among many other instances, proved crucial to archaeologists and modern historians alike in their reconstructions of this ancient Greek landscape.³

The principal of selection that governs Pausanias's work, as he puts it in Book III, are those affairs "most worthy of remembrance" ([ἄξια μνήμης] Paus. 3.11.1). The locations in Greece that correspond to this standard number in the several hundred, some given relatively short shrift of a sentence or two while other phenomena, such as the numerous victor statues standing in Olympia, are given lengthy descriptions over the course of eighteen full chapters, including the readings of inscriptions on the bases of which statues were no longer present (Paus. 6.1–18). What was most worth remembering for Pausanias was often a time quite distant from his own, particularly events and topographic features from the Classical and Hellenistic eras (fifth to early second centuries BCE) and those traces of a past that recalled, or suggested, Greek resistance to foreign influence and power.⁴ A few indications of more recent Roman dominance in the region are alluded to within the *Periegesis*, such as the statue of Zeus dedicated by Hadrian in Athens (Paus. 1.18.6), but overall the work is devoted chiefly to a time before 146 BCE.⁵

After his work was rediscovered during the Renaissance, the descriptions enclosed in Pausanias's writings functioned as an instrumental guide to early antiquarians of ancient Greece who sought to explore its remains and, later, to those interested in a more systematic study of its material culture.⁶ What Pausanias deemed worthy of remembrance during his time thus came to be what, over a millennium later, archaeologists deemed worthy of excavation, thereby bringing to light a world Pausanias wanted his readers to know but often leaving

---

3. On this point, see especially Habicht, *Pausanias*, 28–63. For the use of Pausanias's text within historical and archaeological research, see also M. Jost, "Pausanias en Mégalopolitide," *Revue des études anciennes* 75.3 (1973): 241–67; R. Wycherley, "Pausanias and Praxiteles," *Hesperia Supplements* 20 (1982): 182–91; W. K. Pritchett, *Pausanias Periegetes*, vol. II (Amsterdam: J. C. Gieben, 1999), 39–167. For a nuanced perspective on the complications of this pursuit, see the more recent study of D. Stewart, "'Most Worth Remembering': Pausanias, Analogy, and Classical Archaeology," *Hesperia* 82.2 (2013): 231–61.

4. Habicht, *Pausanias*, 102; Arafat, *Pausanias*, 43–57; Pretzler, *Pausanias*, 100–104; W. Hutton, "Pausanias and the Mysteries of Hellas," *Transactions of the American Philological Association* 140 (2010): 423–59; Stewart, "Most Worth Remembering," 238–40.

5. E. L. Bowie, "Greeks and Their Past in the Second Sophistic," *Past & Present* 46 (1970): 22–24; Habicht, *Pausanias*, 102–105, 134–35.

6. J. Elsner, "Picturesque and Sublime: Impacts of Pausanias in Late-Eighteenth-and Early-Nineteenth-Century Britain," *Classical Receptions Journal* 2 (2010): 219–53; S. Alcock, "The Peculiar Book IV and the Problem of the Messenian Past," in *Pausanias: Travel and Memory in Roman Greece* (eds. S. Alcock et al.; Oxford: Oxford University Press, 2001), 142–53.

unexplored a past Pausanias did not disclose. The relationship between archaeology and Pausanias's text was only strengthened by the fact that Pausanias was commonly found to be a sober and reliable guide for those places depicted in his work, with the portrayal of various sanctuaries, public structures, and epigraphs often squaring well with what was later recovered and identified through archaeological research.[7]

Yet it is precisely against this background that omissions or errors within Pausanias's account are of particular interest. In a study of Pausanias's muted discussion of the sights in Messenia (Book IV), S. Alcock, for example, observes how recent archaeological excavations have complicated Pausanias's claims about the region within the *Periegesis*.[8] Rather than a district whose past had little worth recording for the early Classical period, as the *Periegesis* makes it out to be, it is now apparent that Messenia was a region populated with a number of helot and *periokoi* settlements during this time, dominated by Sparta but also deeply connected to a wider Lakedaimonian cultural and political sphere. There was a story to tell here, in other words, but Pausanias did not tell it, an absence that was likely precipitated in part by later Messenian informants who were not eager to recall their region's period of Spartan enslavement.[9]

But the history of Messenia also provided Pausanias the opportunity to pursue themes that mattered to his work, foremost among them the topic of Greek political autonomy and freedom from foreign rule.[10] The decision to overlook the era of Messenian servitude and to focus instead on the region's liberation (ca. 370 BCE; Paus. 4.26.3–4.27.11) allowed Pausanias, however subtly, to represent what he believed his Greece should be. So it is the sights of this later, autonomous Messenia, such as the remains of the refounded capital of Messene (Paus 4.27.1–11, 4.31.5–4.32.6), that are recalled in Pausanias's narrative in ways

---

7. On the important moments of semblance between material remains and Pausanias's account, see again Habicht, *Pausanias*, 28–63, 71–77; on the epigraphic evidence, see idem, "Pausanias and the Evidence of Inscriptions," *Classical Antiquity* 3 (1984): 40–56. Cf. A. R. Meadows, "Pausanias and the Historiography of Classical Sparta," *The Classical Quarterly* 45.1 (1995): 92–113. On the problems nevertheless found within this relationship, see the important comments in Alcock, "The Peculiar Book IV," 146–49; Pretzler, "Pausanias and Oral Tradition," *Classical Quarterly* 55 (2005): 243–49; and the more recent study of Stewart, "Most Worth Remembering," 231–61.

8. Alcock, "The Peculiar Book IV," 142–53.

9. So the politics of memory underscored by N. Luraghi, *The Ancient Messenians: Constructions of Ethnicity and Memory* (Cambridge: Cambridge University Press, 2008), 323–29.

10. Alcock, "The Peculiar Book IV," 152. Cf. Habicht, *Pausanias*, 102–16; J. Elsner, "Pausanias: A Greek Pilgrim in a Roman World," *Past & Present* 135 (1992): 3–29; N. Luraghi, "Becoming Messenian," *Journal of Hellenic Studies* 122 (2002): 45–69.

not true of phenomena from the era before. D. Stewart finds a similar fraught relationship between material culture and the claims of Pausanias's text with regard to the city of Sicyon where, as was so often the case, Pausanias's account bypasses a number of Roman structures present during his day in order to call attention to the location's more remote Greek past. So pronounced is Pausanias's preference for something beyond his own Roman context, Stewart notes, that "in some cases he must have been clambering over or standing on later monuments in order to record those of earlier periods."[11] Indeed, most dismaying to Pausanias are the inhabitants of Sicyon who have lost their connection with the city's more ancient past and its more venerable Greek traditions, a community now surrounded, in Pausanias's estimation, by the ruins of temples in which no one worshipped.[12]

Other omissions or errors within the *Periegesis* however appear to be less deliberate. In Book VIII, Pausanias remarks that near the sanctuary of Poseidon outside of the city of Mantinea he had come across a trophy of a battle that the Mantineans erected in the mid-third century BCE (Paus. 8.10.5–10).[13] Connected to this trophy, Pausanias comments, was the story of how the Spartan king Agis was defeated in battle and died at the hands of the coalition that the Mantineans had led. No Spartan king by this name however lived during this time, and in fact other features of Pausanias's account of Mantinea appears garbled, including the report of how Mantinea had fought bravely on behalf of the Achaean League in the Cleomenean War against Sparta (8.8.11). The actual history of Mantinea appears to be the opposite. According to both Polybius and Plutarch (Plb. II.57; Plut. Arat. 45), Mantinea was conquered by Aratus during the war, its leading citizens executed and others sold into slavery for their treachery toward the Achaean League, and the city itself forcibly renamed after a leading figure of its opposition, Antigonus Doson (Antigonea).

Pausanias, in these instances, seems dependent on artifacts and traditions that had been manipulated by others.[14] Pausanias was quite aware that the *logoi* told to him were not always to be trusted. As M. Pretzler observes, Pausanias remarks in Book II that only seven principal heroes were remembered in the Argive campaign against Thebes because this story had come under the later influence of

---

11. Stewart, "Most Worth Remembering," 244.

12. Ibid., 255. For Pausanias's conflicted account of Corinth and a similar disjunction between text and archaeology—what Hutton terms an intentional "rhetoric of smallness" with regard to the Roman era city—see the detailed account in Hutton, *Describing Greece*, 145–74.

13. Habicht, *Pausanias*, 101–102.

14. Habicht, *Pausanias*, 101; Pretzler, "Pausanias and Oral Tradition," 247–48.

Aeschylus's famous work about the event; originally, Pausanias notes in an aside, there were "more chiefs than this in the expedition" (Paus. 2.20.5).[15] Yet despite Pausanias's caution he was nevertheless vulnerable to such transgressions. It is a striking feature of Pausanias's work as a whole that when errors appear in his text in relationship to historical and archaeological evidence now available, they are often the result of Pausanias's reliance on local tradition rather than his own "autopsy" of the ruins he comes across.[16] Some of the most baffling mistakes within the *Periegesis*—the strange descriptions of western Sicily (Paus. 5.25.5), the city of Sybaris (Paus. 6.19.9)—are often the outcome of stories told about locations or monuments Pausanias never saw, informed instead by traditions others communicated to him.

What Pausanias provides us, then, is an example of an ancient writer whose portrayal of a past was vulnerable to what A. Assmann has termed "active" and "passive" forms of forgetting,[17] instances of which are apparent to us now in light of the archaeological evidence we possess of the topography that Pausanias once described. By "active forgetting" Assmann alludes to moments of willful erasure or disregard, those conscious attempts aimed at destroying, censoring, or negating a past.[18] To this could be joined P. Ricoeur's notions of "blocked" and "manipulated" memory, where a past is purposefully repressed or transformed so as to reshape how this past is later remembered.[19] In the context of Pausanias's writings, this mode of forgetting can be linked to the discussion of Messenia that omitted its period of enslavement or Pausanias' frequent refusal to record the appearances of memorials and structures connected to his own Roman landscape. But Pausanias's account was subject to more passive forms of forgetting as well, which Assmann defines as "non-intentional acts such as losing, hiding, dispersing, neglecting, abandoning, or leaving something behind," in which "objects are not materially destroyed; they fall out of the frames of attention, valuation, and use."[20] Such instances in the *Periegesis* are most apparent in those

---

15. Pretzler, "Pausasnias and Oral Tradition," 242.

16. Pritchett, *Pausanias Periegetes*, vol. II, 161–67; Habicht, *Pausanias*, 63.

17. A. Assmann, "Canon and Archive," in *A Companion to Cultural Memory Studies* (eds. A. Erll et al.; Berlin: De Gruyter, 2010), 97–108.

18. Assmann, "Canon and Archive," 98–99.

19. P. Ricoeur, *Memory, History, Forgetting* (trans. K. Blamey and D. Pellauer; Chicago: University of Chicago Press, 2004), 80–86, 443–52. Cf. P. Connerton, "Cultural Memory," in *Handbook of Material Culture* (eds. C. Tilley et al.; London: Sage, 2006), 319–24.

20. Assmann, "Canon and Archive," 98.

cases where Pausanias errs because the informants on which he relied did not provide accurate information or because the stories he mistakenly reports were those of a past reality that was no longer in view during his travels. Such a past had been lost to Pausanias, so to speak, or hidden from him.[21]

The problem of forgetting in fact runs throughout Pausanias's work, beset, as Pausanias was, by the overwhelming presence of Roman imperial power transposed onto the vestiges of a more vaunted Greek past that Pausanias believed were rapidly slipping away. So potent was the impulse to preserve in the *Periegesis* that J. Porter views the entire work as a project that strives to make "memory into an antidote to decline," a project undertaken in order to document and discuss what its author thought was soon to be lost.[22] Some features of this past had already disappeared. In the final Book X of the *Periegesis* we stand alongside Pausanias near the River Cephisus in Phocis, vaguely aware of a city once called Parapotamii but whose remains are no longer visible. So Pausanias comments: "I found no ruins of Parapotamii left, nor is the site of the city remembered" (Paus. 10.33.8).

The argument of the following is that Pausanias was not the only ancient writer confronted by the problems and possibilities of forgetting when writing down stories of a more ancient past. Within the corpus of stories told about the early Iron Age period in the Hebrew Bible, I contend, are numerous instances in which key places and phenomena, often of substantial tactical, political, or economic significance for the period in which they existed, are never alluded to or described in these writings even when stories told about this era are often situated in the very areas these places and phenomena were once located. Whether such absences were intentional or accidental—the work of "active" or "passive" forms of forgetting within Assmann's terminology—is a question that will be bracketed at the outset and returned to at this chapter's end after other absences from ancient literary works are explored. To begin, however, this chapter proceeds in a descriptive vein, charting the historical character of various sites and regions from the early Iron Age period that are of interest to this investigation. To conclude, this study then considers what the absence of these places from the biblical narrative might mean for our understanding of the knowledge available to Hebrew scribes about this period in time.

---

21. Though, as Ricoeur contends, such "passive" forms of forgetting can carry with them a certain ambiguity, stemming, in part—and certainly at moments in the case of Pausanias—of a complicit "wanting-not-to-know." Ricoeur, *Memory, History, Forgetting*, 449.

22. J. Porter, "Ideals and Ruins: Pausanias, Longinus, and the Second Sophistic," in *Pausanias: Travel and Memory in Roman Greece* (eds. S. Alcock et al.; Oxford: Oxford University Press, 2001), 76.

Sites

The starting point for this chapter's discussion are particular archaeological sites from the southern Levant that descend from the early Iron Age period but which, to the best of our knowledge, do not receive mention in biblical stories devoted to this era. After more than a century of intense archaeological activity in the region, it is now apparent that numerous instances of this phenomenon are available to us, revealing a landscape that had been lost before the advent of modern archaeological research. Those places investigated here will move in a particular geographical pattern, commencing with the site of Khirbet Qeiyafa in the Upper Shephelah region, traveling further south and then east to the sites of Tel Masos and Khirbat en-Nahas, and then moving northward to the locations of Khirbet ed-Dawwara, Tel Rehov and, lastly, the site of Tell Qasile near the Mediterranean coast. (See Figure 4.1.)

What the archaeological evidence of these places provides, I argue, is the opportunity to hold in view a landscape attested by these remains and to compare this perspective to how the biblical narrative represents this terrain in order to trace out the relationship between them. In what follows we thus proceed along a path also established by scholars of the *Periegesis*, adopting once more a methodology in which ancient textual references are mapped against the results of archaeological research.

Khirbet Qeiyafa

The first site to be examined here is that of Khirbet Qeiyafa, excavated for seven seasons by a team from Hebrew University and the Israel Antiquities Authority under the direction of Y. Garfinkel and S. Ganor from 2007 to 2013.[23] Kh. Qeiyafa is situated approximately thirty kilometers to Jerusalem's southwest and some eleven kilometers to the east of Gath (Tell es-Safi) in the Upper Shephelah at a midway point between the locations of Azekah and Socoh. The settlement itself occupied an elevated, strategic position above the Elah Valley where the ravine broadens momentarily in its westward course through the highlands and toward the coastal plain. (See Figure 4.2.)

During the early Iron Age period Kh. Qeiyafa was ca. 2.3 hectares in size and encircled by a casemate city wall roughly 700m in length, with two four-chamber gates leading into the settlement from the south and from the west and a tower

---

23. Y. Garfinkel and S. Ganor, *Khirbet Qeiyafa Volume I: Excavation Report 2007–2008* (Jerusalem: Israel Exploration Society, 2009); Y. Garfinkel, S. Ganor, and M. Hasel, *Khirbet Qeiyafa Volume II: Excavation Report 2009–2013* (Jerusalem: Israel Exploration Society, 2014).

FIGURE 4.1 Map of Locations Discussed in Chapter 4 (Map: Author).

guarding the southern approach to the site.[24] In addition to the numerous private and public structures and two piazzas excavated along the casemate wall enclosure, a large storage building in Area F and an administrative building, perhaps three floors in height and located at the center of the settlement near its summit in Area A, were unearthed.[25] With walls constructed from megalithic stones that could reach eight

24. Garfinkel and Ganor, *Khirbet Qeiyafa Volume I*, 78–109; Garfinkel, Ganor, and Hasel, *Khirbet Qeiyafa Volume II*, 3–20.

25. Garfinkel, Ganor, and Hasel, *Khirbet Qeiyafa II*, 14; Yosef Garfinkel, "The Iron Age City of Khirbet Qeiyafa," in *The Shephelah During the Iron Age: Recent Archaeological Studies* (eds. O. Lipschits and A. Maeir; Winona Lake: Eisenbrauns, 2017), 116–22; idem, "Khirbet Qeiyafa in the Shephelah: Data and Interpretations," in *Khirbet Qeiyafa in the Shephelah* (eds. S. Schroer and S. Münger; Fribourg: Academic Press Fribourg, 2017), 17–25.

FIGURE 4.2 Southern Gate Complex of Khirbet Qeiyafa, Looking South Over Elah Valley (Picture: Author).

tons in weight and which still stand upwards of three meters in height,[26] the ruins of Kh. Qeiyafa are some of the finest recovered from any location in the southern Levant that descend from the eleventh and tenth centuries BCE outside of the major Philistine centers. (See Figure 4.3.)

In their interpretation of the remains unearthed at Kh. Qeiyafa, the excavators of the site make three arguments that would hold substantial historical implications if sustained. First, it is argued that the material culture of Kh. Qeiyafa should be considered Judahite, making this settlement, according to the excavators, the third principal city of a Judahite kingdom (after Jerusalem and Hebron) during the early tenth century BCE.[27] Second, the existence of an

26. Y. Garfinkel, S. Ganor, and M. Hasel, "The Iron Age City of Khirbet Qeiyafa after Four Seasons of Excavations," in G. Galil et al. (eds.), *The Ancient Near East in the 12th–10th Centuries BCE Culture and History. Proceedings of the International Conference held at the University of Haifa, 2–5 May 2010* (Leiden: Brill, 2012), 164–65.

27. Garfinkel and Ganor, *Khirbet Qeiyafa I*, 12–14; Y. Garfinkel, S. Ganor, and M. Hasel, "The Contribution of Khirbet Qeiyafa to our Understanding of the Iron Age Period," *Strata* 28 (2010): 49–50; Y. Garfinkel et al., "State Formation in Judah: Biblical Tradition, Modern Historical Theories, and Radiometric Dates at Khirbet Qeiyafa," *Radiocarbon* 54 (2012): 359; Garfinkel, "Khirbet Qeiyafa in the Shephelah," 44–47.

FIGURE 4.3 Pillared Room G from Structure C2, Khirbet Qeiyafa (Picture: Author).

impressive Judahite stronghold this far west in the Shephelah region provides definitive evidence of an extensive Davidic kingdom that finally puts to rest previous efforts to minimize the scope of David's realm or to deny it altogether.[28] Third, this reconstruction of the extent of David's kingdom on the basis of finds from Kh. Qeiyafa, in turn, accords the biblical references to David considerable historical value since the archaeological evidence from this site demonstrates that the biblical writings were formed from material contemporaneous with the era in which David would have ruled[29]

Such bold interpretations of Kh. Qeiyafa's remains have not gone unchallenged. The positing of a late eleventh/tenth century BCE Judahite kingdom with borders that encompassed the Shephelah region and which included Kh. Qeiyafa, for example, has met with criticism, and the site's connection with the reign of the biblical David has been impugned from different angles as both premature and, in terms of the chronology of David's presumptive reign, perhaps

28. Garfinkel and Ganor, *Khirbet Qeiyafa I*, 3–16; Garfinkel et al., "The Contribution of Khirbet Qeiyafa," 49–50; Garfinkel et al., "State Formation," 367–68.

29. Garfinkel, "Khirbet Qeiyafa in the Shephelah," 47–48.

mistaken.[30] In addition, the proposal of the location's stature vis-à-vis Jerusalem and Hebron also encounters certain difficulties, as Kh. Qeiyafa's consignment beneath the two in status appears to be influenced more by the depiction of an early Iron Age past within the Hebrew Bible than by straightforward considerations of the site's material culture.

For if one were to dissolve the biblical references to an early Iron Age past and the allusions to Jerusalem and Hebron within these stories, considerations drawn from the archaeological evidence alone would offer little warrant for positing that Kh. Qeiyafa was an ancillary site to either of the biblical David's presumptive royal centers. Indeed, at a time when the eastern Shephelah and highland regions consisted of mostly small, unwalled villages and a limited population,[31] the fortifications of Kh. Qeiyafa offer an unanticipated testament to political will and human capital at this point along the Elah Valley. The sophisticated casemate wall construction of the settlement and its two monumental gates would have been tremendous undertakings for this period in time,[32] and the battlements recovered from Kh. Qeiyafa easily surpass the architectural features unearthed from contemporaneous periods at Hebron, Jerusalem, or any other highland site to the east. With its position along the strategic corridor of the Elah Valley, Kh. Qeiyafa was also an important regional center of trade and commerce, including material culture whose origins can be traced to areas of the Transjordan, the Arabah, Egypt, and Philistine settlements along the coastal plain, among other locations.[33] From a defensive and economic point of view, Kh. Qeiyafa was at least equal to either Jerusalem or Hebron in

---

30. Nadav Na'aman, "Khirbet Qeiyafa in Context," *UF* 42 (2010): 508–10; idem, "Was Khirbet Qeiyafa a Judahite City? The Case Against it," *JHS* 17.7 (2017): 1–40; I. Finkelstein and A. Fantalkin, "Khirbet Qeiyafa: An Unsensational Archaeological and Historical Interpretation," *TA* 39 (2012): 51–55; A. Fantalkin and I. Finkelstein, "The Date of Abandonment and Territorial Affiliation of Khirbet Qeiyafa: An Update," *TA* 44.1 (2017): 53–60.

31. A. Ofer, "'All the Hill Country of Judah': From a Settlement Fringe to a Prosperous Monarchy," in I. Finkelstein and N. Na'aman (eds.), *From Nomadism to Monarchy: Archaeological and Historical Aspects of Early Israel,* (Jerusalem: Israel Exploration Society, 1994), 92–121; G. Lehmann, "The United Monarchy in the Countryside: Jerusalem, Judah, and the Shephelah during the Tenth Century B. C. E.," in A. Vaughn and A. Killebrew (eds.), *Jerusalem in Bible and Archaeology: The First Temple Period* (Atlanta: SBL, 2003), 117–63; A. Faust, "The Shephelah in the Iron Age: A New Look on the Settlement of Judah," *PEQ* 145.3 (2013), 203–19.

32. Garfinkel and Ganor, *Khirbet Qeiyafa I,* 4; Garfinkel, Ganor, and Hasel, *Khirbet Qeiyafa II,* 80, 128–35.

33. On the evidence of Kh. Qeiyafa's extensive trade connections, see Garfinkel, "Iron Age City," 122–26; idem, "Khirbet Qeiyafa in the Shephelah," 28; cf. Na'aman, "Was Khirbet Qeiyafa a Judahite City?" 18.

terms of tactical significance during the late Iron I/early Iron IIA period in light of what is currently known about these locations from the archaeological record.

The cultural and political affiliations of the early Iron Age population that once resided at Kh. Qeiyafa are also a matter of debate. Affinities between Kh. Qeiyafa and highland sites are present in the material record, including certain ceramic forms, cultic paraphernalia, and food preferences that often exhibit associations with highland communities (i.e., Iron I/IIA Jerusalem).[34] The fortification system surrounding Kh. Qeiyafa also finds significance because of the manner in which these architectural features are connected to wider Iron Age regional trends. Whereas some Iron I Transjordanian sites (Tall al-'Umayri, Khirbet el-Mudayna el-Aliya, Khirbet Lehun)[35] and Iron I (Khirbet ed-Dawwara) and Iron IIA (Tell en-Nasbeh) highland locations also retain casemate wall construction, it is a significant feature of Philistine settlements to the west of Kh. Qeiyafa that they do not.[36] For such reasons, among others,[37] Kh. Qeiyafa would not have been a satellite settlement of the city of Gath, but was culturally and politically distinct from this nearby Philistine center. (See Figure 4.4.)

A better counterpart to the material culture recovered at Kh. Qeiyafa, rather, is the nearly contemporaneous remains from the site of Beth-Shemesh (Stratum 4), located 6 km to Kh. Qeiyafa's north.[38] The relationship between these two

---

34. Y. Garfinkel and M. Mumcuoglu, "Triglyphs and Recessed Doorframes on a Building Model from Khirbet Qeiyafa: New Light on Two Technical Terms in the Biblical Descriptions of Solomon's Palace and Temple," *IEJ* 63.2 (2013): 135–63; Garfinkel, "The Iron Age City of Khirbet Qeiyafa," 115–31; Aren Maeir, "Khirbet Qeiyafa in its Regional Context: A View from Philistine Gath," in *Khirbet Qeiyafa in the Shephelah* (eds. S. Schroer and S. Münger; Fribourg: Academic Press Fribourg, 2017), 61–72.

35. On these sites, see I. Finkelstein, "Tall al-Umayri in the Iron Age I: Facts and Fiction with an Appendix on the History of the Collared Rim Pithoi," in I. Finkelstein and N. Na'aman, eds., *The Fire Signals of Lachish: Studies in the Archaeology and History of Israel in the Late Bronze Age, Iron Age, and Persian Period in Honor of David Ussishkin* (Winona Lake: Eisenbrauns, 2011), 118–21.

36. Finkelstein and Fantalkin, "Khirbet Qeiyafa," 51–55; Na'aman, "Khirbet Qeiyafa in Context," 509–11. Gunnar Lehmann and Hermann Michael Niemann, "When Did the Shephelah Become Judahite?" *TA* 41 (2014): 78; Maeir, "Khirbet Qeiyafa," 61–72.

37. Na'aman, "Khirbet Qeiyafa," 507–508; Faust, "The Shephelah in the Iron Age," 212–14; Maeir, "Khirbet Qeiyafa," 66–67.

38. Garfinkel and Ganor, *Khirbet Qeiyafa I*, 119–50; Lily Singer-Avitz, "The Relative Chronology of Khirbet Qeiyafa," *TA* 27 (2010): 81; idem, "Khirbet Qeiyafa: Late Iron Age I in Spite of It All," *IEJ* 62.2 (2012): 181; idem, "Khirbet Qeiyafa: Late Iron Age I in Spite of it All—Once Again," *IEJ* 66.2 (2016): 237; S. Bunimovitz and Z. Lederman, "A Peasant Community on the Philistine Border Levels 6–4: Iron I ca. 1150–950 BCE," in *Tel Beth-Shemesh: A Border Community in Judah. Renewed Excavations 1990–2000: The Iron Age* (eds. S. Bunimovitz and Z. Lederman; Tel Aviv: Emery and Claire Yass, 2016), 213–15.

FIGURE 4.4 Casemate Wall Construction, Khirbet Qeiyafa (Picture: Author).

settlements however underscores how difficult it is to connect Kh. Qeiyafa within any specific regional polity or culture at this time, as Beth-Shemesh, too, was positioned within the liminal spaces of the Shephelah region between Philistine and highland societies and, much like Kh. Qeiyafa, evinced a distinct local assemblage of finds that differed from sites situated further west and east.[39] For such reasons, the excavators of Beth-Shemesh argue that the late Iron I settlement was neither Philistine nor Judahite but, instead, Canaanite, and continued to be so until the location was eventually subsumed into an emerging Judahite kingdom toward the end of the tenth century BCE.[40] An assessment of Kh. Qeiyafa's status could, then, be made along similar lines, with its famous shrine model, for example, suggesting a continuity of Canaanite cultural traditions at the site,[41] and its domestic architecture and certain ceramic forms being

39. Bunimovitz and Lederman, "Peasant Community," 213–33. Cf. Finkelstein and Fantalkin, "Khirbet Qeiyafa," 49–50.

40. S. Bunimovitz and Z. Lederman, "Canaanite Resistance: The Philistines and Beth-Shemesh—A Case Study from the Iron I," *BASOR* 364 (2011): 37–51; idem, "Peasant Community," 224–33.

41. A. Mazar, "Religious Practices and Cult Objects during the Iron Age IIA at Tel Rehov and Their Implications Regarding Religion in Northern Israel," *Hebrew Bible and Ancient Israel* 4 (2015): 37.

typical of the Shephelah region but distinct from settlements located further in-land among the highlands.[42] Other putative Judahite characteristics of the material culture of the location advanced by the excavators are also more ambiguous than presented in their studies, where the scarcity of pig bones or the inscriptions recovered, for example, are not necessary indicators of Judahite cultural affiliation in the Iron I/early IIA period.[43]

From this perspective, one may advance a somewhat different historical understanding of Kh. Qeiyafa that resists strong assertions surrounding a singular cultural identity for its populace or which positions the site within fixed political boundaries maintained by centralized polities.[44] Instead, what would be accented is the highly fluid character of both borders and ethnicity at this moment in the Iron Age history of the Shephelah region,[45] particularly within the area that Kh. Qeiyafa occupied between the developing kingdoms of Gath, Israel, and Judah. Disagreements surrounding the interpretation of Kh. Qeiyafa's remains would thus be an effect of the material culture of the location itself, where the ancient inhabitants of the site, much like Beth-Shemesh, negotiated their status and relationships to neighboring communities through distinct local cultural preferences and displays, a collection of material markers that had affiliations with highland features but also exhibited local traits that persisted at the settlement in

---

42. Finkelstein and Fantalkin, "Khirbet Qeiyafa," 49–50; Lily Singer-Avitz, "Khirbet Qeiyafa: Late Iron I in Spite of it All," 178–81; idem, "Khirbet Qeiyafa: Late Iron Age I in Spite of It All — Once Again," 232–44; Na'aman, "Khirbet Qeiyafa," 511–14. So Singer-Avitz's succinct observation: "The Khirbet Qeiyafa pottery assemblage differs from those of Philistine sites in the Shephelah (Tel Batash, Tell es-Safi and Tel Miqne) and Coastal Plain sites (Ashdod and Tell Qasile), as well as from the highland sites." Singer-Avitz, "Khirbet Qeiyafa: Late Iron Age I in Spite of It All — Once Again," 236.

43. Finkelstein and Fantalkin, "Khirbet Qeiyafa," 49; C. Rollston, "The Khirbet Qeiyafa Ostracon: Methodological Musings and Caveats," *TA* 38 (2011): 67–82; L. Sapir-Hen et al., "Pig Husbandry in Iron Age Israel and Judah: New Insights Regarding the Origin of the 'Taboo,'" *ZDPV* 129 (2013): 1–20.

44. Na'aman asserts that this author, in an earlier piece (Pioske, "Memory and its Materiality") interpreted Kh. Qeiyafa as a Judahite city connected with a Judahite kingdom (Na'aman, "Was Khirbet Qeiyafa a Judahite City? The Case Against it," 1 fn. 2). Throughout that piece, however, I remained intentionally agnostic about the political affiliation of this settlement, a misreading of my study somewhat surprising since I drew on Na'aman's fine work for this nuance.

45. S. Weitzman, "Samson Story as Border Fiction," *BibInt* 10.2 (2002): 158–74; idem, "Crossing the Border with Samson: Beth-Shemesh and the Bible's Geographical Imagination," in *Tel Beth-Shemesh: A Border Community in Judah. Renewed Excavations 1990–2000: The Iron Age*, vol. I (ed. S. Bunimovitz and Z. Lederman; Tel Aviv: Emery and Claire Yass, 2016), 266–80; Maeir, "Khirbet Qeiyafa," 65.

a manner similar to other nearby locations.[46] This process of cultural negotiation was likely mirrored in the political sphere, in which populations in the eastern Shephelah both withstood and acquiesced to the interests of the emerging kingdoms adjacent to them, and only gradually became integrated into the polities administered from the highlands later in the Iron II period.[47]

Sometime in the course of the tenth century BCE the settlement at Kh. Qeiyafa came to an end. Regardless of the disagreements concerning the precise reading of carbon[14] dates from the site,[48] all indications suggest that the settlement was abandoned before the tenth century came to a close, and that the location was not rebuilt and occupied again until the late Persian/early Hellenistic period some seven hundred years later. Theories surrounding the cause of Kh. Qeiyafa's sudden destruction range from Gittite hostilities to Pharaoh Sheshonq I's raid through the region in the late tenth century BCE,[49] but more definitive evidence pertaining to the cause of its ruin has not been recovered. However Kh. Qeiyafa came to its end, the time in which settlement functioned as an inhabited site was short-lived, perhaps limited to only a few decades in time.[50]

---

46. I. Finkelstein, "New Canaan," *Er-Isr* 27 (2003): 189–95 (Hebrew); idem, "From City-States to States: Polity Dynamics in the 10th-9th Centuries B.C.E.," in W. Dever and S. Gitin (eds.), *Symbiosis, Symbolism, and the Power of the Past: Canaan, Ancient Israel, and Their Neighbors from the Late Bronze Age through Roman Palaestina* (Winona Lake: Eisenbrauns: 2003), 75–83. I. Koch, 'The geopolitical organization of the Judean Shephelah during Iron Age I-IIA', *Cathedra* 143 (2012): 45–64 (Hebrew); Na'aman, "Khirbet Qeiyafa in Context," 513.

47. So Mazar prefers characterizing Kh. Qeiyafa as "Proto-Judean" rather than "Judahite," where he, too, recognizes the importance of the continuity of Canaanite material culture at the site. A. Mazar, "Archaeology and the Bible: Reflections on Historical Memory in the Deuteronomistic History," in *Congress Volume Munich 2014* (ed. C. Maier; Leiden: Brill, 2014), 361–64. On Judah's slow and belated expansion into the Shephelah region, see N. Na'aman, "The Kingdom of Judah in the 9th Century BCE: Text Analysis versus Archaeological Research," *TA* 40 (2013): 252–55; Lehmann and Niemann, "When Did the Shephelah Become Judahite?" 88–90.

48. Garfinkel and Ganor, *Khirbet Qeiyafa I*, 35–38; Finkelstein and Fantalkin, "Khirbet Qeiyafa," 41; Garfinkel, Ganor, and Hasel, *Khirbet Qeiyafa II*, 367–74; Y. Garfinkel, K. Streit, S. Ganor, and P. Reimer, "King David's City at Khirbet Qeiyafa: Results of the Second Radiocarbon Dating Project," *Radiocarbon* 57.5 (2015): 881–90; I. Finkelstein and E. Piasetzky, "Radiocarbon Dating Khirbet Qeiyafa and the Iron I-IIA Phases in the Shephelah: Methodological Comments and a Bayesian Model," *Radiocarbon* 57.5 (2015): 891–907.

49. Na'aman, "Khirbet Qeiyafa in Context," 514–15; Finkelstein and Fantalkin, "Khirbet Qeiyafa," 54–55; Maier, "Khirbet Qeiyafa," 66–67.

50. Garfinkel and Ganor, *Khirbet Qeiyafa I*, 75; Garfinkel and Ganor, *Khirbet Qeiyafa II*, 367–74; A. Fantalkin and I. Finkelstein, "The Date of Abandonment," 53–60.

What makes Kh. Qeiyafa of particular interest for this chapter's investigation is the dearth of biblical allusions to it in spite of its regional import and monumental remains.[51] The lack of references to this location is all the more mystifying considering that a number of events within Kh. Qeiyafa's vicinity are recounted in the biblical narrative and are said to have occurred at that moment in the early Iron Age when Kh. Qeiyafa was most likely populated and functioning, and whose fortifications and commercial contacts would have made the location both highly visible and of substantial tactical import during the development and consolidation of local polities in the southern Levant at this time. Foremost among these tales is that devoted to the battle between Saul's forces and the Philistines "in the valley of Elah" somewhere to the east of Gath (1 Sam. 17:19), or quite close to where Kh. Qeiyafa stood. During this conflict, narrated at length and in multiple versions within the biblical manuscript, David famously slays Goliath and the Philistines are driven back westward to "Gath and the gates of Ekron." A number of other biblical stories and anecdotes are also placed within Kh. Qeiyafa's surroundings, including accounts about the ark's travels in and out of Philistine territory (1 Sam. 5–7:17), David's flight from Saul (1 Sam. 21, 27), and Shimei's fateful departure to Gath early in Solomon's reign (1 Kings 2:39–41). In addition, allusions to Azekah, Socoh, Ekron, and Beth-Shemesh are scattered throughout these narratives (Josh. 10:10–11; Judg. 1:33; 1 Sam. 6:9–20; 1 Sam 17:1; 1 Kings 4:10). There is, in short, an explicit awareness within the biblical writings of the importance of the region of the Elah Valley where Kh. Qeiyafa once stood. Nevertheless, no clear allusions to the imposing fortress and economic hub are found within these texts.

---

51. For an overview of proposed identifications of Kh. Qeiyafa, see Y. Levin, "The Identification of Khirbet Qeiyafa: A New Suggestion," *BASOR* 367 (2012), 73–86. Levin himself argues that Khirbet Qeiyafa should not be linked to any toponym in the Hebrew Bible, but rather to an encampment (מעגל) used by Saul's army that is mentioned briefly in 1 Samuel 17:20. The association of the term מעגל with a well-fortified stronghold however does not accord with any usage of the expression in Biblical Hebrew. The most compelling conclusion for the site's identification is that of Adams, who writes: "Given the relatively short history of the settlement at Khirbet Qeiyafa, the most probable conclusion seems to be that *it is not mentioned by name in any biblical text*." (my italics). See D. Adams, "Between Socoh and Azekah: The Role of the Elah Valley in Biblical History and the Identification of Khirbet Qeiyafa," in Y Garfinkel and S. Ganor (eds.), *Khirbet Qeiyafa Volume I: Excavation Report 2007–2008* (Jerusalem: Israel Exploration Society, 2009), 47–68. On the absence of Kh. Qeiyafa from ancient writings, see also the more recent comments of Na'aman, "Khirbet Qeiyafa in Context," 514.

Tel Masos and Khirbat en-Nahas

Our next locations bring us south to the Beer-Sheba valley and then east to the Arabah region south of the Dead Sea (see figure 4.1 above). The first of these sites is that of Tel Masos, excavated by Y. Aharoni, V. Fritz, and A. Kempinski on behalf of Tel Aviv University and the University of Mainz over the course of three seasons from 1972 to 1975, followed by one season of salvage excavations in 1979.[52] The site of Tel Masos is situated on the northern bank of the Wadi es-Seba' about 12 km to the east of the modern city of Beer-Sheba among a bevy of nearby ancient settlements that include Tel 'Ira to its immediate north and Tel Aro'er and Tel Malhata to its south and east, respectively. Tel Masos itself consists of three distinct single-period settlements located near wells at different areas of the site, but which are nevertheless known by the collective name of "Tel Masos."

Though located within the arid conditions of the northern Negev desert, the ground water readily available at a number of wells within Tel Masos's vicinity made the site desirable for settlement already in the Late Chalcolithic period.[53] After a gap in settlement activity, the area of Tel Masos was once again inhabited during the Middle Bronze Age II period when an initial fortress and, later, a fortified enclosure were erected, the latter of which was surrounded by an extensive rampart and moat. Both structures, it seems, were most likely built in an effort to control the trade networks that were developing through this area of the Beer-Sheba valley at the time.[54] Later in the MBII period a fortress was constructed nearby at Tel Malhata and Tel Masos was consequently abandoned, and it would remain uninhabited throughout the centuries of the Late Bronze Age period.

The most important moment of Tel Masos's history occurred however during the early Iron Age (Iron I–IIA). After an initial Iron I settlement made up of semi-nomadic populations took hold at the site (Stratum III), a larger and more densely settled town of ca. 6 ha arose later in the late Iron I/early IIA period (Stratum II),[55] making the site larger than the contemporaneous settlement at

---

52. V. Fritz and A. Kempinski, eds., *Ergebnisse der Ausgrabungen auf der Ḥirbet el-Mšāš (Tēl Māsōs) 1972–1975*, 3 vols. (Wiesbaden: Harrassowitz, 1983); V. Fritz, "Tel Masos: A Biblical Site in the Negev," *Archaeology* 36.5 (1983): 30–37; A. Kempinski, "Masos, Tel" in *NEAEHL*, III, 986–89.

53. Fritz and Kempinski, *Ergebnisse der Ausgrabungen*, I, 114–22; Kempinski, "Masos, Tel" 986; Fritz, "Tel Masos," 32.

54. Fritz, "Tel Masos," 32–33; Kempinski, "Masos, Tel," 986.

55. The excavators dated this settlement to the twelfth and eleventh centuries BCE, but more recent studies of the material culture situate it in the late Iron I/early Iron IIA period, i.e., late eleventh and tenth centuries BCE, the ceramic assemblage appearing to be somewhat earlier than Arad XII. Ze'ev Herzog and Lily Singer-Avitz, "Redefining the Centre: The Emergence

Jerusalem, for example (at ca. 4 ha), and double the size of Kh. Qeiyafa. Within its precincts numerous clusters of homes appear throughout, as do public and administrative buildings of some stature,[56] and, within certain structures (such as House 96), evidence of extensive copper smelting activity was unearthed.[57] The material culture recovered from the early Iron Age settlement also reveals trade connections with a number of regions throughout the Levant, including a pottery assemblage that includes instances of Phoenician, Philistine, "Midianite," and Canaanite ceramic traditions.[58] A residence modeled on Egyptian architectural features[59] and a finely carved ivory lion's head, most likely from Phoenicia and found in a cultic room in Area H, further attests to the exchange networks and diverse influences that shaped the community at Tel Masos during this time.[60]

The reason for Tel Masos's expansion in the early Iron Age can now be linked to its participation in the lucrative copper ore trade that was established through the Beer-Sheba valley during the Iron I–IIA periods once the former source of copper ore production in the eastern Mediterranean, located in Cyprus, no longer ferried the metal eastward to the Levant after the twelfth century BCE.[61] Recent remains unearthed at Khirbat en-Nahas (below) and Timna of a large-scale copper industry that was operative during the twelfth through ninth centuries BCE offer evidence that Tel Masos prospered in conjunction with the production of copper ore to its east.[62] The leftover debris of copper smelting activities at various

---

of State in Judah," *TA* 31 (2004): 222–23; E. van der Steen, "Judha, Masos, and Hayil: The Importance of Ethnohistory and Oral Tradition," in *Historical Biblical Archaeology and the Future: The New Pragmatism* (ed. T. Levy; London: Equinox, 2010), 175–76.

56. Kempinski, "Masos, Tel," 987; Fritz, "Tel Masos," 33.

57. Fritz and Kempinski, *Ergebnisse der Ausgrabungen*, 21; Fritz, "Tel Masos," 33.

58. Fritz and Kempinski, *Ergebnisse der Ausgrabungen*, 91–102; Fritz, "Tel Masos," 33; Kempinski, "Masos, Tel," 988–89.

59. C. Higginbotham, "Elite Emulation and Egyptian Governance in Ramesside Canaan," *TA* 23 (1996): 154–69

60. F. Crüsemann, "Der Löwenkopf von Ḥirbet el-Mšāš—ein Elfenbeinfund aus der frühen Eisenzeit," in *Sefer Rendtorff: Festschrift zum 50 Geburtstag von Rolf Rendtorff* (ed. K. Rupprecht; Dielheim: Selbstverlag der Autoren, 1975), 9–23; Fritz, "Tel Masos," 35.

61. T. Levy and M. Najjar, "Some Thoughts on Khirbet En-Nahas, Edom, Biblical History and Anthropology: A Response to Israel Finkelstein." *TA* 33.1 (2006): 13; T. Levy, M. Najjar, and E. Ben-Josef, "Conclusion," in T. Levy, M. Najjar, and E. Ben-Yosef, eds., *New Insights into the Iron Age Archaeology of Edom, Southern Jordan* (Los Angeles: Cotsen Institute of Archaeology, 2014), 982–83.

62. Fritz, "Tel Masos," 35; I. Finkelstein, "Khirbet en-Nahas, Edom, and Biblical History," *TA* 32 (2005): 119–25; T. Levy et al., "High-Precision Radiocarbon Dating and Historical Biblical Archaeology in Southern Jordan," *Proceedings of the National Academy of Sciences*

structures in Tel Masos, in addition to the large quantity of copper and bronze items recovered at the site, such as knives, sickles, and even a lugged axe,[63] can thus be interpreted as remnants of Tel Masos's participation in the copper industry and its status as a production center that helped process the large quantity of copper ore that emanated out of the Arabah on its way to the Mediterranean coast and more northern polities during the early Iron Age period.

In light of Tel Masos's substantial size and economic activity relative to other settlements of its time, a number of studies have been put forward that characterize the location as either part of an emerging Edomite polity[64] or as the center of its own independent "chiefdom" that exercised authority over smaller sites along the trade corridor that Tel Masos oversaw.[65] Regardless of how we characterize its specific social and political affiliations, more important for our purposes here, however, is the sheer size and significance of this site during the Iron I–IIA period, especially during the late eleventh and tenth centuries BCE when copper production in the Arabah began to expand and Tel Masos grew to its largest extent.[66] During this era, Tel Masos was the largest settlement in the Beer-Sheba valley, replete with public structures and impressive administrative buildings at a moment when few contemporary sites in the region boasted of such elite infrastructure.[67]

---

105 (2008): 16460–65; E. Ben-Josef et al., "The Beginning of Iron Age Copper Production in the Southern Levant: New Evidence from Khirbat al-Jariya, Faynan, Jordan," *Antiquity* 84 (2010): 724–46; E. Ben-Josef et al, "A New Chronological Framework for Iron Age Copper Production at Timna (Israel)," *BASOR* 367 (2012): 63–65; E. Ben-Josef, "Back to Solomon's Era: Results of the First Excavations at 'Slaves' Hill' (Site 34, Timna, Israel)," *BASOR* 376 (2016): 169–98.

63. Fritz and Kempinski, *Ergebnisse der Ausgrabungen*, 91–102; Fritz, "Tel Masos," 35.

64. Levy and Najjar, "Some Thoughts," 3–17; E. Ben-Yosef et al., "A New Chronological framework," 31–71; Ben-Yosef, "Back to Solomon's Era," 194–95.

65. E. Knauf, "Edom: The Social and Economic History," in *You Shall Not Abhor an Edomite for He Is Your Brother: Edom and Seir in History and Tradition* (ed. D. Edelman; Atlanta: Scholars Press, 1995), 93–117; I. Finkelstein, *Living on the Fringe: The Archaeology and History of the Negev, Sinai and Neighbouring Regions in the Bronze and Iron Ages* (Sheffield: Sheffield Academic Press, 1995), 103–26. A. Fantalkin and I. Finkelstein, "The Sheshonq I Campaign and the 8th century BCE Earthquake: More on the Archaeology and History of the South in the Iron I-IIA," *TA* 33 (2006): 18–42; I. Finkelstein, "The Southern Steppe of the Levant ca. 1050–750 BCE: A Framework for a Territorial History," *PEQ* 146.2 (2014): 89–104.

66. T. Levy et al., "Reassessing the Chronology of Biblical Edom: New Excavations and C[14] Dates from Khirbat en-Nahas (Jordan)," *Antiquity* 78 (2004): 865–79; T. Levy and M. Najjar, "Some Thoughts," 3–17; Ben-Josef, "Back to Solomon's Era," 191–95.

67. Fritz, "Tel Masos," 33; Herzog and Singer-Avitz, "Redefining the Centre," 222; Fantalkin and Finkelstein, "The Sheshonq I Campaign," 19; van der Steen, "Judha, Masos, and Hayil," 175–78.

Whoever traveled through the Beer-Sheba valley during this period, then, would have encountered the residences and the diverse population that were active in the exchange network Tel Masos controlled, with the site's wealth and industry likely contributing to Pharaoh Sheshonq I's decision in the late tenth century BCE to focus on this settlement and the northern Negev more broadly in order to bring its resources under Egyptian control.[68] The final fate of the early Iron Age settlement at Tel Masos remains uncertain, but it appears to have been abandoned sometime in the late tenth or early ninth century BCE, perhaps after Egyptian withdrawal from the site or due to increasing pressure on the region from a Judahite polity to its north.[69] A small fortress, destroyed after a brief duration, was erected in the seventh century BCE,[70] but Tel Masos would never again reach the size and prosperity it enjoyed in the late Iron I/early IIA period.

In spite of its stature during the twelfth to ninth centuries BCE, the identity of Tel Masos remains uncertain. Y. Aharoni offered the early argument that Tel Masos should be equated with the biblical site of Hormah,[71] and others have since linked the location to Baalath-beer (Josh. 19:8)[72] and "a city of Amalek" mentioned in 1 Samuel 15:5.[73] No identification has, however, won consensus in light of the discrepancies between the impressive early Iron Age archaeological remains of Tel Masos and the limited descriptions provided in the biblical

---

68. Fantalkin and Finkelstein, "The Sheshonq I Campaign," 19–28; T. Levy, "Ethnic identity in Biblical Edom, Israel and Midian: Some Insights from Mortuary Contexts in the Lowlands of Edom," in *Exploring the Longue Durée: Essays in Honor of Lawrence E. Stager* (ed. D. Schloen; Winona Lake: Eisenbrauns, 2008), 251–61; Stefan Münger and Thomas E. Levy, "The Iron Age Egyptian Amulet Assemblage," in *New Insights into the Iron Age Archaeology of Edom, Southern Jordan* (eds. T. Levy, M. Najjar and E. Ben-Yosef, Los Angeles: Cotsen Institute of Archaeology, 2014), 740–765.

69. Herzog and Singer-Avitz, "Redefining the Centre," 222–23; Fantalkin and Finkelstein, "The Sheshonq I Campaign," 28–29; T. Levy, E. Ben-Yosef and M. Najjar, "New perspectives on Iron Age copper production and society in the Faynan Region, Jordan," in *Eastern Mediterranean Metallurgy and Metalwork in the Second Millennium BC* (eds. V. Kassianidou and G. Papasavvas; Oxford: Oxbow, 2012), 210; Finkelstein, "Southern Steppe," 98; Na'aman, "The Kingdom of Judah in the 9th Century BCE," 257–69.

70. Kempinski, "Masos, Tel" 989; Fritz, "Tel Masos," 36.

71. Y. Aharoni, *The Land of the Bible: A Historical Geography* (ed. A. Rainey; 2nd ed.; Philadelphia: Westminster, 1979), 215–16. Another early (though unlikely) proposal by Crüsemann of connecting the site to Ziklag was discussed in the previous chapter. F. Crüsemann, "Überlegungen zur Identifikation der Hirbet el-Msas (Tel Masos)," *ZDPV* 8 (1973): 211–24.

72. A. Rainey and S. Notley, *The Sacred Bridge* (Jerusalem: Carta, 2006), 147.

73. Z. Herzog, "Enclosed Settlements in the Negeb and the Wilderness of Beer-sheba," *BASOR* 250 (1983): 41–49.

narrative of the various locations put forward by scholars. And, even if one of the proposed locations were to gain acceptance, what is surprising about Tel Masos is how infrequent and insignificant are the proposed identifications to it within the Hebrew Bible—a point all the more so if one follows V. Fritz's contention that Tel Masos is not mentioned within these writings.[74] The absence of more detailed allusions to Tel Masos is also enigmatic considering that a number of biblical texts refer to locations within Tel Masos's vicinity during the era in which it thrived, including stories related to David's rise to the throne (1 Sam. 27, 30) and, later, within those narratives that equate David and Solomon's kingdoms with the land the stretches from Beer-Sheba to Dan (2 Sam. 3:10; 24:2, 7, 15; 1 Kings 4:15)—or a territory that would have included sites in the Beer-Sheba valley such as Tel Masos. Nevertheless, much like the absence of Kh. Qeiyafa from the biblical stories that are recounted about events that take place quite near to it, allusions to Tel Masos's stature or its crucial economic role in the region are lacking within the biblical narrative.

The importance of the copper ore trade that passed through the Beer-Sheba valley in the early Iron Age period brings us next to the origins of the copper ore itself, namely, the Arabah region located south of the Dead Sea and, more specifically, to the site of Khirbat en-Nahas (KEN) situated along the Wadi Faynan. (See Figure 4.5.)

Excavated by a team from the University of California at San Diego and the Department of Antiquities of Jordan from 1997 to 2009,[75] the site has garnered increased scholarly interest—and debate—in light of the impressive early Iron Age finds that have been unearthed from this rather desolate region. What these recent excavations have made clear is that the Arabah, and especially the Faynan district in its north, became the primary source of copper ore for the Levant during the early Iron Age, superseding and replacing the former copper ore production centers in Cyprus.[76] The importance of KEN for this chapter's investigation is thus the era in which it oversaw and administered the mining industry that took shape in the Faynan during the early Iron Age. In contrast to earlier studies that had argued that the Arabah valley was only sparsely settled

---

74. Fritz, "Tel Masos," 32. cf. Fritz and Kempinski, *Ergebnisse der Ausgrabungen*, 238.

75. T. Levy, M. Najjar, and E. Ben-Yosef, "The Iron Age Edom Lowlands Regional Archaeology Project," in Levy, Najjar, and Ben-Yosef, eds., *New Insights into the Iron Age Archaeology of Edom, Southern Jordan* (Los Angeles: Cotsen Institute of Archaeology, 2014), 1–88.

76. Levy et al., "Chronology of Biblical Edom," 866–67; Levy, Ben-Yosef, and Najjar, "New perspectives," 199–212; T. Levy, E. Ben-Yosef, and M. Najar, "The Iron Age Edom Lowlands," 15–21.

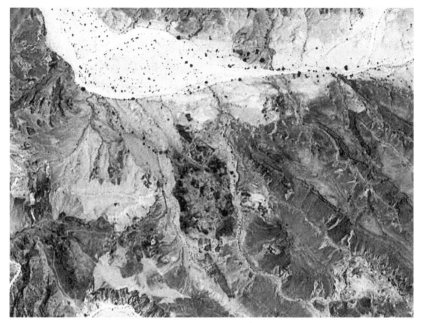

FIGURE 4.5 Satellite Image of Khirbat en-Nahas (Picture: Google Maps).

and experienced very minimal copper ore extraction during this era,[77] the material culture unearthed at KEN, and especially the new carbon[14] dates attached to these remains, have provided decisive evidence that the copper industry in the Faynan district was revitalized already in the twelfth century BCE and reached its height of production two centuries later (tenth and ninth centuries BCE).[78]

The mining of copper ore carried out in the Faynan was controlled and defended by an early Iron Age settlement that developed at KEN. With only

77. Much of the reason for this perspective, as Levy et al. note (Levy et al., "Lowland Edom and the High and Low Chronologies," in *The Bible and Radiocarbon Dating: Archaeology, Text and Science* [eds. T. Levy and T. Higham; London: Equinox, 2005] 131–32), was the previous emphasis on highland settlements in south Jordan and the lack of excavations in the lowland regions of the Arabah. For earlier arguments on the late Iron Age settlement of Edom, see P. Bienkowski, "The Beginning of the Iron Age in Edom: A Reply to Finkelstein," *Levant* 24 (1992): 167–69; idem, "Iron Age Settlement in Edom: A Revised Framework," in *The World of the Aramaeans* (eds. Daviau et al., Sheffield: Sheffield Academic Press, 2001), 257–69; P. Bienkowski and E. van der Steen, "Tribes, Trade, and Towns: A New Framework for the Late Iron Age in Southern Jordan and the Negev," *BASOR* 323 (2001): 21–47.

78. Levy et al., "Lowland Edom and the High and Low Chronologies, "134–56; Levy et al., "High-Precision Radiocarbon Dating," 16460–65; T. Levy, M. Najjar, and E. Ben-Josef, "Conclusion," 982–85.

minimal activity taking place at the site in the Late Bronze Age, KEN expanded with the expansion of the copper ore industry. By the tenth and ninth centuries BCE, the settlement had grown to ca. 10 ha in size and was composed of over one hundred distinct structures.[79] Thus, much as with the appearance and growth of Tel Masos, KEN appears to have also flourished during that moment in the late Iron I/early Iron IIA period when the copper ore industry reached its peak in the Arabah region.

The consequences of this new, earlier dating of the copper ore industry in Faynan district are far reaching. Against earlier studies that associated increased settlement activity and social complexity in southern Jordan (biblical Edom) only with the Assyrian empire's involvement in the region during the late Iron Age (eighth to sixth centuries BCE), the evidence unearthed at KEN pushes back this settlement history by nearly five hundred years to a time when local tribal populations began developing the copper ore trade at that moment when the economic incentive to do so emerged in the twelfth century BCE.[80] And, in a manner similar to Tel Masos, it was during the late Iron I/Iron IIA period that KEN experienced a burst of development when a number of new, monumental structures were built throughout the site. Included among these was a substantial fortress in Area A—"one of the largest fortifications from this period in the southern Levant"[81]—that was connected to a four-chamber gate that faced the Arabah trade corridor and guarded access to the mining and smelting operations of the settlement. Additionally, two monumental buildings of multiple stories, most likely erected as elite residences, were constructed at this time in Areas R and T, and elsewhere at the site clusters of more modest domestic buildings from this era were found.[82] The slag mound excavated in Area M of the settlement revealed a tenth to ninth century BCE layer 3 meters thick of metallurgical debris, further attesting to the intensified production of copper ore at the site during this time.[83]

---

79. Levy et al., "Reassessing the Chronology of Biblical Edom," 868; T. Levy et al., "Excavations at Khirbet en-Nahas 2002–2009," in Levy, Najjar, and Ben-Yosef, eds., *New Insights into the Iron Age Archaeology of Edom, Southern Jordan* (Los Angeles: Cotsen Institute of Archaeology, 2014), 89–246; T. Levy, M. Najjar, and E. Ben-Josef, "Conclusion," 985–86.

80. Levy et al., "Reassessing the Chronology of Biblical Edom," 867–77; T. Levy, M. Najjar, and E. Ben-Josef, "Conclusion," 982–85; Ben-Yosef, "Back to Solomon's Era," 191–95.

81. Levy et al., "Lowland Edom," 139.

82. T. Levy et al., "New Perspectives on Iron Age Copper Production," 200–204; T. Levy et al., "Excavations at Khirbet en-Nahas 2002–2009," 89–246; T. Levy, M. Najjar, and E. Ben-Josef, "Conclusion," 982–83.

83. T. Levy, M. Najjar, and E. Ben-Josef, "Conclusion," 982.

Sometime in the late tenth century BCE, the copper industry in the Faynan district was disrupted. The second largest mining center in the region, located nearby at Khirbat al-Jariya, was abandoned, and at KEN the fortress was decommissioned and new, improved smelting technologies were introduced.[84] In light of Egyptian remains recovered from this period at KEN and the claims of Sheshonq I himself located on the Bubastite Portal at Karnak,[85] it is likely that this turn in affairs was initiated by agents from the Egyptian empire.[86] On this view, Sheshonq I sought to commandeer the copper industry of the Arabah valley from local authorities in order to introduce greater efficiency and redirect the flow of its copper trade toward Egyptian markets and interests. Though highly fragmented, the toponyms that are decipherable on the Bubastite Portal suggest that Sheshonq I drove his army through the Beer-Sheba valley and conquered Arad, and, therefore, likely also took control of the nearby site of Tel Masos and other settlements along this trade route.[87] The Egyptians then would have continued eastward to the copper production centers in the Arabah that, many centuries before, the Egyptian empire had formerly controlled, displacing local authorities and setting up their own administrators in the region.[88] Whatever the profit of this expedition for the Egyptians, however, it was brief. With renewed trade contacts opening up once more with Cyprus in the ninth century BCE, the copper industry in the Arabah began to falter. By century's end, KEN was abandoned and the populations once present in the region moved north and eastward where they founded settlements on the Edomite plateau.[89]

In contrast to Khirbet Qeiyafa and Tel Masos, more direct biblical associations with KEN and the copper ore industry in the northern Arabah have been put forward. The primary link between the early Iron Age archaeological remains from the region and the biblical writings center on references to "Edom"

---

84. Levy et al., "Lowland Edom," 210; Ben-Yosef et al, "A New Chronological Framework," 47-48, 63-65; T. Levy, M. Najjar, and E. Ben-Josef, "Conclusion," 984-85.

85. K. Kitchen, *The Third Intermediate Period in Egypt (1100—600 B.C.)* (2nd ed.; Warminster: Aris & Philips, 1986), 432–47.

86. T. Levy, M. Najjar, and E. Ben-Josef, "Conclusion," 984–85; Fantalkin and Finkelstein, "The Sheshonq I Campaign," 19–28; Ben-Yosef, "Back to Solomon's Era," 193.

87. Fantalkin and Finkelstein, "The Sheshonq I Campaign," 26–28; Finkelstein, "Southern Steppe," 96–97.

88. Levy et al., "Reassessing the Chronology of Biblical Edom," 874-75; Levy et al., "High Precision Radiocarbon Dating," 16464; Levy et al., "New Perspectives on Iron Age Copper Production," 210; Levy et al., "Conclusion," 983-85.

89. Levy et al., "New Perspectives on Iron Age Copper Production," 210; Levy et al., "Conclusion," 985.

scattered among a large collection of biblical texts, including two explicit references to the Faynan district—biblical Punon—preserved in the wilderness itinerary of Numbers 33:42–43. More specific biblical connections to the region however have also been proposed, including activities carried out during the reigns of David and Solomon and, later, to the ninth century BCE Judahite kings Jehoshaphat and Jehoram. Early in their archaeological fieldwork the excavators of KEN, for example, proffered the possibility of affiliating the large Iron IIA fortifications of the site with the garrisons David was said to have constructed in Edom (2 Sam. 8:13–14), or linking this building activity to David's son, Solomon, among other potential agents.[90] An allusion to Edom's rebellion during the reign of Jehoshaphat's son, Jehoram, in the mid-ninth century BCE (2 Kings 8:20–22) was also cited as a conceivable explanation for the disruption and enhancement in copper production at KEN during this period in time.[91]

The extensive early Iron Age remains of the copper industry in the Arabah region makes the biblical references to tenth and ninth century BCE Edom, long thought to be anachronistic and mistaken, now worthy of historical consideration once more. And, as Na'aman observes, it is a significant feature of the biblical references to early Iron Age Edom that they always locate this polity in the lowland regions in and adjacent to the Arabah, a geographical perspective that is accurate for the early Iron Age period but which was not true for the late Iron Age when the area was mostly abandoned and an Edomite kingdom had developed further east on the Edomite plateau.[92] Descriptions of Judah's commercial and economic interests in Edom, especially during the ninth century BCE (1 Kings 22:48–50), would also comport to the value of the copper trade and its heightened production during this time.

Yet given the economic and tactical import of the copper ore that flowed out of the Arabah from the twelfth through ninth centuries BCE, what is conspicuous about the biblical references to Edom is the absence of any mention of this copper industry or the monumental construction measures carried out at KEN to administer and defend it. To be sure, the allusions to garrisons built by David in Edom (2 Sam. 8:13–14) and Solomon's apparent authority over the region (1 Kings 9:26) are suggestive, though there is no material evidence that connects the fortress and monumental buildings erected at KEN with Cisjordanian highland polities or peoples, and both the ceramic and mortuary evidence from the

90. Levy et al, "Some Thoughts," 11, 13; Levy et al., "Lowland Edom," 159.

91. Levy et al., "Lowland Edom," 159; cf. Nadav Na'aman, "Kingdom of Judah in the 9th Century BCE," 255–58; Chris McKinny, *My People as Your People: A Textual and Archaeological Analysis of the Reign of Jehoshaphat* (New York: Peter Lang, 2016), 140–47.

92. Na'aman, "Kingdom of Judah," 257.

site indicates that the population present at KEN consisted of local tribal groups throughout this period.[93] And with Solomon, the only biblical references to his dealings with Edom are in fact to the Red Sea port of Ezion-geber (1 Kings 9:16), located far away from the copper mines of the Arabah, and to an adversary from the royal house of Edom named Hadad the Edomite (1 Kings 11:14) whose residence is not named. Some resonance between KEN's high economic production in the ninth century BCE and the biblical allusions to Jehoshaphat's interest in the region may certainly be present within the biblical narrative, though it is striking that despite the fact that these texts make explicit mention of economic pursuits undertaken by this Judahite king, they never allude to the copper ore industry of the Arabah or the large settlement located at KEN. When Jehoshaphat's fleet, also said to have been stationed at Ezion-geber, is mentioned in 1 Kings 22:48, it is built for the purpose of transporting the famed gold of Ophir and not the copper ore of the Faynan district.

Little of KEN's early Iron Age past, then, appears to be present in biblical narratives about this period in time outside of the important, but very broad, recognition of the Arabah region being settled in the early Iron Age by a population labeled "Edom" by the biblical writers. What is absent from these writings, however, is significant: no mention of the copper ore trade that emanated out of the Arabah and which passed through the Beer-Sheba valley, no reference to Sheshonq I's disruption and possible appropriation of this industry in the late tenth century BCE, and no notion of the considerable fortifications and monumental architecture at KEN, though such structures were equal, if not superior, to anything constructed in Jerusalem or other highland sites of the Cisjordan in the late Iron I/early Iron IIA era.

Khirbet ed-Dawwara

With the site of Khirbet ed-Dawwara we make our first entrance into the Cisjordanian highlands and the region that would be home to the Iron Age kingdoms of Israel and Judah. Kh. ed-Dawwara was situated ca. 10 km to the northeast of Jerusalem on the eastern desert fringe of the Benjamin Hill Country. Located on a hilltop that overlooked an important road that led from Bethel east to Michmash and which eventually descended into Jericho and the Jordan Valley, the settlement at Kh. ed-Dawwara would have commanded a strategic post on a

93. The ceramic assemblage of the tenth century BCE, as the excavators point out, is "dominated by local traditions." Levy et al., "Conclusion," 983. On the mortuary evidence from the Wadi Fidan 40 cemetery, see T. Levy, "Ethnic Identity in Biblical Edom, Israel, and Midian," 251–61.

corridor that ran through the steep valleys and hills north of Jerusalem.[94] First discovered in a survey of the Benjamin and Ephraim regions[95] in 1967 and later excavated by I. Finkelstein during two brief seasons in 1985 and 1986,[96] Kh. ed-Dawwara finds importance for this chapter's investigation because of the era in which it was occupied and the substantial fortifications that surrounded it.

Much like Khirbet Qeiyafa, Kh. ed-Dawwara is a single-period site that was inhabited for short time, perhaps only a few decades,[97] during the late Iron I/ early IIA period. The site itself was small (0.5 ha), housing perhaps a little over one hundred residents, but similar in size to many of the local villages that were founded in this area of the Benjamin Hills during the beginning of the Iron Age.[98] I. Finkelstein initially dated the founding of the settlement to the late eleventh century and its abandonment sometime toward the end of the tenth century BCE,[99] though more recently he has shifted these dates and placed them within the confines of the tenth century alone.[100] The identity of those who constructed the site and the reason for its desertion are debated, but it appears that the settlement was abandoned in an orderly fashion and not destroyed by conflagration or force, with the result that few remains were left behind beyond a pottery assemblage of incomplete vessels and some architectural features preserved at the periphery of the site.[101]

Of these remains, the most impressive feature of Kh. ed-Dawwara is the massive casemate wall that encircled it. Unique for its time and setting—it is the earliest known instance of casemate wall construction in the highlands and, overall,

---

94. D. Dorsey, *The Roads and Highways of Ancient Israel* (Baltimore: Johns Hopkins Press, 1991), 204. Cf. N. Na'aman, "Ḥirbet ed-Dāwwara—A Philistine Stronghold on the Benjamin Desert Fringe," *ZDPV* 128 (2012): 3.

95. Z. Kallai, "The Land of Benjamin and Mt. Ephraim," in M. Kochavi, ed., *Judaea, Samaria and the Golan. Archaeological Survey 1967–1968* (Jerusalem: Publications of the Archaeological Survey of Israel 1), 182 [Hebrew].

96. I. Finkelstein, "Excavations at Khirbet ed-Dawwara. An Iron Age Site Northeast of Jerusalem," *TA* 17 (1990): 163–208.

97. Na'aman, "Ḥirbet ed-Dāwwara," 2.

98. I. Finkelstein, *The Archaeology of the Israelite Settlement* (Jerusalem: Israel Exploration Society, 1988), 295–314; E. Bloch-Smith and B. Nakhai, "A Landscape Comes to Life: The Iron I Period," *NEA* 62.2 (1999): 70–73.

99. Finkelstein, "Khirbet ed-Dawwara," 195. Cf. I. Finkelstein, "Dawwara, Khirbet-ed," in *NEAEHL*, vol. I, 333.

100. I. Finkelstein and E. Piasetzky, "The Iron I-IIA in the Highlands and Beyond: ¹⁴C Anchors, Pottery Phases and The Shoshenq I Campaign," *Levant* 38 (2006): 53–58.

101. Finkelstein, "Khirbet ed-Dawwara," 166; Na'aman, "Ḥirbet ed-Dāwwara," 1.

"the earliest example of a developed Iron Age defence [*sic*] system in the hill country"[102]—the outer wall of the massive casemate enclosure reached upwards of 3m in width and was adjoined to the pillared houses that were built into it. In addition to its unusual fortifications for such a diminutive site, what is also peculiar about the location is the lack of evidence related to agrarian activities carried out in or near the settlement. In contrast to other late Iron I/early IIA sites excavated in its near vicinity (Khirbet Raddana, et-Tell) in which agricultural remains were evident throughout (e.g., silos for grain storage, sickle blades for harvest), no such finds were present at Kh. ed-Dawwara, a phenomenon that is also in keeping with its more eastward position near the arid regions of the Jordan Valley where farming would have been more difficult.[103]

For such reasons, the function of Kh. ed-Dawwara has been at the center of scholarly discussions. Because it was built during a time when the highland regions were marked by modest farmsteads and villages without protective walls, the motivations and agents behind the sudden construction of the fortress at Kh. ed-Dawwara remain enigmatic. In his excavation report, I. Finkelstein offered three possible historical scenarios behind the emergence of this stronghold:[104] 1) the settlement was constructed as an Israelite fortress during the conflict with Philistine forces; 2) the site was constructed after the defeat of the Philistines and later abandoned once it had lost its tactical importance; or 3) the site was built by the Philistines as an eastern outpost used to exert jurisdiction over nearby Israelite villages during their push into the highlands. Whereas Finkelstein initially favored the first of these possibilities,[105] the third scenario, with some modifications, also has its supporters.[106]

---

102. Finkelstein, "Khirbet ed-Dawwara," 197.

103. Finkelstein, "Khirbet ed-Dawwara," 201–202; A. Faust, "Settlement Patterns and State Formation in Southern Samaria and the archaeology of (a) Saul," in *Saul in Story and Tradition* (ed. C. Ehrlich; Tübingen: Mohr Siebeck, 2006), 26–27; Na'aman, "Hirbet ed-Dāwwara," 3.

104. Finkelstein, "Khirbet ed-Dawwara," 202.

105. In more recent publications, Finkelstein now links the end of Kh. ed-Dawwara to the campaign of Pharaoh Shoshenq I in the region (see, for example, the discussion in I. Finkelstein, *The Forgotten Kingdom: The Archaeology and History of Northern Israel* [Atlanta: SBL, 2013], 41–61) though this reconstruction would be somewhat at odds with Finkelstein's earlier observations on the absence of evidence of destruction at the site.

106. Faust, too, argues that the outpost was an Israelite fortress built to counter Philistine aggression (Faust, "Settlement Patterns," 32–34); Na'aman contends, however, that the location was a Philistine stronghold erected after the King of Gath conquered the Shephelah and pushed into the highlands (Na'aman, "Hirbet ed-Dāwwara" 5–7).

Common among studies of Kh. ed-Dawwara is the recourse made to various biblical references in the Books of Samuel and Kings to better understand the circumstances behind the construction of its fortifications. Much of this discussion has centered on the clashes described in the biblical narrative between Philistines and Israelites in the tribal area of Benjamin. Finkelstein, for example, situates the appearance of the site against the background of the biblical stories of Samuel's leadership and Saul's reign over a "Gibeon/Gibeah" polity that Finkelstein asserts Saul once controlled.[107] Na'aman, too, contends that the allusions in 1 Samuel (1 Sam. 9:16, 10:5, 13:2–14:46) offer some background to the site's history, though he argues that references to Philistine control of the Benjamin highlands hint at the strong possibility that Kh. ed-Dawwara was constructed by the Philistines as an eastern outpost used to subjugate the neighboring villages and to guard the road that passed by the site.[108] The dearth of Philistine finds at the location is explained by Na'aman as the outcome of the fort being stationed by *apiru* outlaws who had been hired to enforce Philistine rule in a manner parallel to David's control of the southern Philistine outpost at Ziklag.[109]

What is of interest about these particular historical reconstructions, however, is that the biblical sources used to cast light on the Kh. ed-Dawwara's history never make mention of the site itself.[110] In contrast to the references to a number of well-known locations surrounding the stronghold, such as Bethel (Beitin [1 Sam. 13:2, 5; 14:23]), Mizpah (Tell en-Nasbeh [1 Sam. 10:17]), Michmash (Muhkmas [1 Sam. 13:2–23]), Gibeah (Tell el-Ful? [1 Sam. 13:2, 15; 14:2, 16]), or Geba (Jab'a [1 Sam. 13:3, 16; 14:5]), the fortress at Kh. ed-Dawwara does not appear to play a role within the biblical accounts of Philistine-Israelite animosities, even though the crucial victory of Saulide forces over the Philistines and the daring maneuvers of Jonathan occur precisely in the area in which Kh. ed-Dawwara was located. The one fortress that would have existed when these events were said to have taken place according to the biblical narrative is nevertheless the one location not referred to within these stories of conflict and war. So Na'aman concludes that "the author of the Saul story-cycle was not privy to a story/tradition" about the site of Kh. ed-Dawwara, and that these scribes were thus unaware of the extent and

---

107. Finkelstein, "Khirbet ed-Dawwara," 201–203; idem, *The Forgotten Kingdom*, 37–61.

108. Na'aman, "Ḥirbet ed-Dāwwara," 5–6.

109. Ibid.

110. Finkelstein initially suggested that Kh. ed-Dawwara be identified with Gilgal ("Khirbet ed-Dawwara," 203–205), but this has won few supporters and Finkelstein himself no longer appears to hold this view.

FIGURE 4.6 Tel Rehov Upper Mound (Picture: Author).

range of Philistine excursions in this area of the highland region—leaving "the background of the conquest in the dark."[111]

Tel Rehov

From the highland fortress of Khirbet ed-Dawwara we move northward along the Jordan River to the Beth-Shean valley and the site of Tel Rehov. Located 6 km west of the Jordan and ca. 30 km south of the Sea of Galilee, Tel Rehov occupied a central position atop a modest hill within the broad alluvial plain of the valley floor and the prominent transit routes that passed through it. (See Figure 4.6.)

The excavations at Tel Rehov were directed by A. Mazar on behalf of Hebrew University for eleven season between 1997 and 2012, resulting in the exposure of four areas on the upper mound of the site and five areas in the lower mound.[112]

---

111. Na'aman, "Ḥirbet ed-Dāwwara," 5.

112. A. Mazar, "Reḥov, Tel," in *NEAEHL*, vol. 5, 2013–18; idem, "Rehob," in *The Oxford Encyclopedia of Bible and Archaeology*, vol. 1 (ed. D. Master et al., New York: Oxford University Press, 2013), 221–30.

These excavations revealed that Tel Rehov was a major, multi-period settlement that supported a massive fortification system already in the Early Bronze Age (late third millennium BCE). After a gap in occupation, Tel Rehov was resettled in the Late Bronze I period (sixteenth and fifteenth centuries BCE) and became one of the most prominent cities in the region.[113] The location was then continuously inhabited until its destruction six centuries later in the mid-ninth century BCE (Stratum IV), most likely by Aramean forces.[114] A more modest settlement was rebuilt on the upper mound of the site afterward, yet this town, too, was destroyed, but this time at the hands of the Assyrians in 732 BCE.[115]

During the Late Bronze and early Iron Age periods (sixteenth to ninth centuries BCE) Tel Rehov was one of the largest cities in the southern Levant (at ca. 10 ha) and, alongside Beth-Shean to its north, a principal city of the Beth-Shean valley.[116] As it was somehow able to avoid the destructions that befell so many of the prominent Late Bronze cities in the region, including the Egyptian garrison at Beth-Shean, what is significant about Tel Rehov's early Iron Age history is its stability and the fact that it continued to be a relatively large, prosperous settlement during the volatile transition from the Late Bronze to Iron Age periods. The one change that did occur during this transitional moment is the retreat of Egyptian presence in the Beth-Shean valley and Tel Rehov's newfound status as an autonomous Canaanite city state at the beginning of the Iron Age. This independent Iron I city (twelfth to early tenth centuries BCE) witnessed a number of renovations and architectural transformations during this time, including evidence of massive building projects and new administrative structures in Area D and, elsewhere in Area C, indications of recently established trade relations with both Phoenician and Philistine populations.[117] (See Figure 4.7.) The site would have continued to be an autonomous Canaanite city until it was eventually subsumed

---

113. Mazar, "Reḥov," 2014; idem, "Rehob," 222.

114. Mazar, "Reḥov," 2018; idem, "Rehob," 228; idem, "Religious Practices and Cult Objects During the Iron Age IIA at Tel Reḥov," 27. More recently, Finkelstein has argued, on the basis of radiocarbon dates that place Tel Rehov's destruction just prior to Hazael's reign, that the site was destroyed by the Omrides of the Kingdom of Israel. I. Finkelstein, "Does Rehob of the Beth-Shean Valley Appear in the Bible?" *BN* 169 (2016): 4.

115. A. Mazar, "Tel Rehov in the Assyrian Period: Squatters, Burials, and a Hebrew Seal," in *The Fire Signals of Lachish: Studies in the Archaeology and History of Israel in the Late Bronze Age, Iron Age, and Persian Period in Honor of David Ussishkin* (eds. N. Naʾaman and I. Finkelstein; Winona Lake: Eisenbrauns, 2011), 265–80.

116. Mazar, "Rehob," 222.

117. Mazar, "Reḥov," 2014; idem, "Rehob," 223.

FIGURE 4.7   View of Areas C and D and Beth Shean Valley, Tel Rehov (Picture: Author).

into the kingdom of Israel sometime during the Iron IIA period (ca. 980—830 BCE).[118]

It is the Iron IIA city at Tel Rehov (Strata VI-IV) that has been most heavily excavated. Unearthed from these layers of the city are fifteen homes that attest to both the daily rhythms of domestic activities and their foodways, the latter of which offered strong evidence that "Iron Age Reḥov harbored an elite stratum of society"[119] due to the choice portions of meat consumed within these houses. In addition to these affluent homes the most complete open-air sanctuary in north Israel was exposed in Area E, revealing sacred standing stones (*maṣṣeboth*), an altar, and a room with unique plaster decoration depicting volutes, lotus flowers, and buds in Phoenician style.[120] The prosperous character of the site was further

---

118. H. Bruins, A. Mazar, and J. van der Plicht, "The End of the 2nd Millennium BCE and the Transition from Iron I to Iron IIA: Radiocarbon Dates of Tel Rehov, Israel," in *The Synchronisation of Civilisations in the Eastern Mediterranean in the Second Millennium B.C. III* (eds. M. Bietak and E. Czerny; Vienna: Österreichische Akademie der Wissenschaften, 2007), 79–99.

119. N. Marom et al., "Backbone of Society: Evidence for Social and Economic Status of the Iron Age Population of Tel Reḥov, Beth Shean Valley, Israel," *BASOR* 354 (2009): 72.

120. Mazar, "Rehob," 226–28; idem, "Religious Practices," 27–28.

indicated by the large olive groves that once surrounded the settlement and the presence of an industrial apiary, consisting of one hundred to two hundred hives (Area C), that once housed Anatolian bees known for their high productivity.[121] Ten Iron IIA inscriptions have been recovered from location, including two names—*Nimshi* and *Elisha*—that are also attested in the Hebrew Bible.[122]

In stepping back from the early Iron Age remains of the location, what we find at Tel Rehov is a wealthy, flourishing city of around two thousand residents, surrounded by fertile agricultural land and situated at an important juncture near the Jordan River where numerous fords were once present for trade and transportation between the eastern Mediterranean coast and the Transjordan. Since Tel Rehov served as a hub of economic activity, wide-ranging cultural influences were present at the site, including Egyptian, Phoenician, north Syrian, and Transjordanian traditions,[123] though its Iron Age population, much as with settlements to its west in the Jezreel Valley, would have likely consisted primarily of local Canaanite inhabitants who over the course of the Iron IIA period were "slowly integrating into the emerging Israelite political and cultural entity."[124] In contrast to the previous locations examined above, and in keeping with Tel Rehov's notable economic and strategic importance within the southern Levant, a number of ancient texts do in fact make mention of the location (*rḥb*), particularly in Egyptian sources (the Stele of Set I; Papyrus Anastasi I; Bubasite Portal of Sheshonq I) because of Tel Rehov's close proximity to the Egyptian garrison once stationed at Beth-Shean.[125]

Nevertheless, "Rehọv in the Beth-Shean Valley is never mentioned in the Hebrew Bible."[126] The absence is glaring. In terms of stories set in the early Iron Age period, a number of biblical texts allude to the Beth-Shean valley, perhaps most famously in the account of Saul and his sons' deaths at Mt. Gilboa and the decision of the Philistines to fasten their bodies to the walls of Beth-Shean (1 Sam. 31:10–12; 1 Chron. 10:8–12). Curious about this episode is that Beth-Shean

121. A. Mazar and N. Panitz-Cohen, "It is the Land of Honey: Beekeeping at Tel Rehọv," *NEA* 70.4 (2007): 202–19.

122. A. Mazar and S. Aḥituv, "Inscriptions from Tel Rehob and Their Contribution to the Study of Writing and Literacy During the Iron Age IIA," *Er-Isr* 30 (2011): 300–16; Mazar, "Religious Practices," 41–44.

123. Mazar, "Rehob," 227; idem, "Religious Practices," 32–41.

124. Mazar, "Rehob," 227; idem, "Religious Practices," 45–47.

125. Mazar, "Rehọv," 2013; idem, "Rehob," 221.

126. Mazar, "Rehọv," 2013. Cf. idem, "Rehob," 221; idem, "Religious Practices," 25.

was much diminished after being destroyed in the twelfth century BCE and, "if there is any historical truth" to the biblical account about the fate of the House of Saul, "it cannot be corroborated by archaeology."[127] Meanwhile, at Tel Rehov, located only a few kilometers south of Beth-Shean, one would have found a thriving settlement at this time where, in contrast to Beth-Shean, some traces of Philistine material culture were present.[128] Tel Rehov is, however, never mentioned in connection with Saul's final days, nor is it present in other biblical tales that allude to locations in its vicinity, such as texts that describe the House of David's contacts with the kingdom of Geshur (2 Sam. 3:3; 13:37–38; 14:23, 32) just to Tel Rehov's north along the Sea of Galilee or within Solomon's district lists in 1 Kings 4 that mention a number of locations in the Beth-Shean valley but fail to mention Tel Rehov. Finkelstein's efforts to overcome this biblical absence of "one of the largest and culturally most important Iron IIA cities in the region" by positing that Tel Rehov is indeed mentioned once in the biblical narrative as "Beth-Rehob" in David's war with the Ammonites (2 Sam. 10:6–8) only works if, as Finkelstein himself admits, the "fading memory of Beth-Rehob in the Beth-Shean valley" became "confused" with the Beth-Rehob that, everywhere else in the biblical writings, is identified with an Aramean polity much further north in the Beqa'a valley of Lebanon.[129] Though quite unlikely, such confusion would only underscore the processes of forgetting surrounding the early Iron Age city of Tel Rehov, where the one clear textual reference to the location is found not within stories written by Hebrew scribes, but in a list of sites composed by the distant Egyptian pharaoh, Sheshonq I.[130]

Tell Qasile

The final location of interest for this chapter's study brings us west toward the Mediterranean coast and to the site of Tell Qasile. Tell Qasile is situated on a sandstone ridge just north of the Yarkon River around two miles east of the river's estuary, now positioned within the boundaries of the modern city of Tel Aviv. The site was originally excavated for four seasons by B. Mazar on behalf of the Israel Exploration Society from 1949 through 1951 and in 1955; and excavations

---

127. A. Mazar, "Tel Beth-Shean: History and Archaeology," in *One God—One Cult—One Nation: Archaeological and Biblical Perspectives* (eds. R. Kratz and H. Spieckermann; Berlin: de Gruyter, 2010), 262.

128. Mazar, "Rehov," 2014; idem, "Rehob," 223.

129. Finkelstein, "Rehob of the Beth-Shean Valley?" 6–7.

130. That is, toponym 17, following Beth-Shean on the Bubasite Portal of Sheshonq I.

were continued from 1971 to 1974 and 1982 to 1989 under the direction of A. Mazar of Hebrew University.[131] Most consequential for this chapter's investigation was the discovery at Tell Qasile of a prominent, early Iron Age settlement of ca. 1.3 ha that was constructed and administered by inhabitants connected to the Philistines from the mid-twelfth to early tenth centuries BCE.

Tell Qasile's history in the early Iron Age was intimately bound up with that of the Yarkon River. Irrigation channels from the river fed the area around Tell Qasile and made it a zone of rich agricultural resources, and the Yarkon itself was likely of a depth and breadth at this juncture in its course that Tell Qasile also functioned as an anchorage for the small vessels that transported goods along the eastern Mediterranean coast at this time.[132] Given the decline in other ports on the central Levantine coast in the early Iron Age, Tell Qasile appears to have been the most important maritime settlement between Ashdod and Dor during the twelfth to tenth centuries BCE and a central hub of economic activity at a moment when other prominent sites within the Yarkon basin, such as Joppa and Aphek, were only sparsely inhabited.[133] Evidence of renewed Iron Age trade contacts, in fact, were recovered from the remains at Tell Qasile, especially from the final phase of Philistine occupation (Stratum X), including goods that were affiliated with peoples from Egypt, Phoenicia, Cyprus, and the Cisjordanian highlands.[134]

Due to its natural resources and mercantile potential, groups associated with the Philistines established the city of Tell Qasile on a previously unsettled hill sometime in the mid-to-late twelfth century BCE (Stratum XII). The founding of Tell Qasile was thus likely part of an expansion of Philistine territory in the region after the organization of initial Philistine settlements in the southern Levant a generation earlier, with Tell Qasile being built somewhat later than those Philistine locations established further south at Ashdod or Ekron, for example.[135] This initial Philistine settlement endured for around a half-century until it gave

---

131. A. Mazar, *Excavations at Tell Qasile, Part One* (Jerusalem: Hebrew University, 1980); idem, *Excavations at Tell Qasile, Part Two* (Jerusalem: Hebrew University, 1985); idem, "Qasile, Tell," in *NEAEHL*, vol. IV, 1207–212.

132. Mazar, *Tell Qasile*, I, 4; idem, *Tell Qasile*, II, 120–21; idem, "Iron Age Dwellings at Tell Qasile," in *Exploring the Longue Durée: Essays in Honor of Lawrence E. Stager* (ed. D. Schloen; Winona Lake: Eisenbrauns, 2009), 331–34.

133. Mazar, *Tell Qasile*, I, 10; idem, *Tell Qasile*, II, 121. Cf. Y. Gadot, "Aphek in the Sharon and the Philistine Northern Frontier," *BASOR* 341 (2006): 21–36; A. Fantalkin and O. Tal, "Navigating Between the Powers: Joppa and its Vicinity in the 1st Millennium B.C.E.," *UF* 40 (2008): 236.

134. Mazar, *Tell Qasile*, II, 124–27; idem, "Iron Age Dwellings," 331.

135. Mazar, *Tell Qasile*, II, 119–22.

FIGURE 4.8 Tell Qasile, Public Structures and Domestic Homes, Looking South (Picture: Author).

way to a new, larger, and more affluent town that was built above it (Stratum XI). The settlement of Stratum XI, however, would also come to be replaced, perhaps after an earthquake, and the final Philistine city of Stratum X was constructed sometime in the eleventh century BCE. This, the largest and most densely populated phase at the site, then suffered a violent destruction and conflagration in the early tenth century BCE.[136] Tell Qasile would later be rebuilt by residents whose cultural background was likely not Philistine, but the site would not reach the size and prosperity it had attained during its Stratum X phase, and eventually this town was destroyed in the late eighth century BCE. (See Figure 4.8.)

Tell Qasile was consequently a Philistine-dominated center for around two hundred years. The towns of Strata XII and XI were more modest centers, perhaps functioning as trading outposts, that were situated primarily at the center of the site. Recovered from this area of the settlement was the large "hearth residence," probably an assembly hall or palace of some type,[137] and a series of temples

---

136. Mazar, *Tell Qasile*, I, 10; idem, "Iron Age Dwellings," 331–34.

137. A. Mazar, "Excavations at Tell Qasile, 1982–1984: Preliminary Report," *IEJ* 36 (1986): 3–6.

that were constructed nearby this large enclosure.[138] During the transition to Stratum X, however, the settlement at Tell Qasile expanded outward to include a new, well-planned quarter of homes and commercial buildings at the periphery of the site (Area A). The absence of Philistine pottery from buildings erected in Area A and the appearance of "pillared" homes within this quarter, a type of domicile found nowhere else in Iron I Philistia, immediately raised the question of the cultural affiliations of this new influx of people at Tell Qasile, with its early excavator, B. Mazar, suggesting that this was a "post-Philistine" city.[139] The demographic situation appears, however, to have been more complex. The continued presence of Philistine material culture in Area C of the site and the continuity in architectural traditions from this central area of the settlement into Stratum X would indicate that the community at Tell Qasile instead consisted of a heterogeneous population of Philistines and non-Philistines, with groups having a closer association with the Philistines residing in the larger and more affluent precinct (Area C) of the city at its summit.[140] Indeed, this "eclectic," "Philisto-Canaanite"[141] population at Tell Qasile was probably present already during its founding, with Stratum XII evincing a cultural assemblage that is both Philistine and Canaanite in origin.[142]

Unearthed at Tell Qasile, then, was an initial early Iron Age Philistine outpost on the Yarkon river, constructed along a northern frontier zone of small villages that arose during a new wave of settlements that took hold of the Yarkon basin in the twelfth century BCE. With little competition from other nearby ports and few towns of any size in its vicinity, the Iron I community at Tell Qasile thrived and grew to be the only urban site of its time in the central coastal plain.[143] The remains of elite residences, an impressive central temple, (see Figure 4.9.) public storehouses, and imports from various eastern Mediterranean locales attest to the importance of the site in the early Iron Age period when it functioned as a key inland anchorage along a river that connected the Cisjordanian highlands with the Mediterranean Sea. Tell Qasile was densely settled by the eleventh century BCE and housed a population of Philistine and non-Philistine residents, with those who lived there making their livelihood principally from

---

138. Mazar, *Tell Qasile*, I, 13–30.

139. B. Mazar, "The Excavations at Tell Qasile," *IEJ* 1 (1950–1951): 128.

140. Mazar, *Tell Qasile*, II, 123; idem, "Iron Age Dwellings," 333–34.

141. Mazar, *Tell Qasile*, II, 120.

142. Ibid., 120–22.

143. Gadot, "Aphek in the Sharon," 31.

FIGURE 4.9 Tell Qasile, Early Iron Age Temple Complex (Picture: Author).

the fertile agricultural land that surrounded the settlement and the trade that passed through it.

Nevertheless, as with the other locations surveyed here, the "ancient name of the site is unknown."[144] Biblical connections to the site have nonetheless been put forward. The early excavators of Tell Qasile suggested, for example, that the demise of the large town of Stratum X could be attributed to the activities of David,[145] a conquest that would make some sense if leaders of a highland polity sought to control the exchange networks running from local highland sites and along the Yarkon to ports on the Mediterranean in the early tenth century BCE. What is difficult about this attribution, however, is that the biblical narrative makes no claim of David's conquering Tell Qasile or any site within the region around it, a rather surprising omission when other victories abroad and against the Philistines specifically are recorded in these stories (e.g., 2 Sam. 5:17–25; 8:1–15, 10:6–19). This absence is all the more enigmatic given that the site of Aphek, located 15 km to the east of Tell Qasile along the Yarkon, is mentioned

---

144. Mazar, "Iron Age Dwellings," 319.

145. B. Maisler (Mazar), "The Stratification of Tell Abu Hawam on the Bay of Acre," *BASOR* 124 (1951): 23; cf. Mazar, *Tell Qasile,* II, 127.

repeatedly in the Book of Samuel as a crucial site of Philistine activity and encampment during conflicts with the Israelites (1 Sam. 4:1; 1 Sam. 29:1). What is
strange about these references is that the primary Philistine center in the area
would not have been Aphek during the time in which these biblical stories are
set, but Tell Qasile. Aphek in the Iron I period was, rather, a "village inhabited
by a small number of families," perhaps best understood as a "farmstead."[146] It
was the fate of the vital port at Tell Qasile, however, that it would be forgotten
while other, more minor locations would find their way into tales told within the
Hebrew Bible.

The Evidence of Absence

There is an important maxim among archaeologists that the "absence of evidence
is not evidence of absence." Some finds simply await further discovery through
future excavations and the prudent therefore resist conclusions drawn in haste.
The absences examined in this chapter however are of a different sort. These are
not voids within the archaeological record that may be overcome in the years
ahead with more research and a lucky spade, but are rather textual absences from
a closed, ancient corpus of writings whose stories have been known for millennia.
What this means is that the absences surveyed here will not be supplemented
in the years ahead through the recovery of new evidence heretofore unknown
and buried away. We already know of these settlements and their history. What
requires explanation is why they are not referred to within the Hebrew Bible.

In order to address this question, perhaps the first inclination would be to
posit these locations' insignificance and, consequently, an indifference to them
by the biblical writers. From this perspective, the paucity of allusions to these
sites would explained by way of disinterest, with the settlements examined above
grouped among the host of small villages, towns, and rural landscapes of the
southern Levant that never receive mention in the biblical writings but which
were no doubt integral to the social fabric of the Iron Age kingdoms the Hebrew
Bible has in view. But what is immediately apparent about the places at the center
of this chapter's study is that each held special significance for the period in which
they were inhabited in the early Iron Age, often housing elite or monumental infrastructure at a time when such material expressions of power were rare and
which wielded substantial influence, whether of the economic, cultural, or tactical kind, over the lands and populations that surrounded them. The reason for
the dearth of biblical references to these sites cannot be resolved, then, along lines
related to unimportance. The utility and value of these places in the early Iron

---

146. Gadot, "Aphek in the Sharon," 25–27.

Age period is without question, as these sites functioned as key fortifications or economic hubs or even as ruling centers in their own right. In the case of Tel Rehov we know this to be true since a Pharaoh names it as a target of conquest.

Conceding that the dearth of references to these places cannot be attributed to inconsequence only makes the question of their absence from the biblical corpus more acute. So also does the recognition that the biblical scribes often embed their stories in terrain that adjoined or which was quite proximate to these locations during the period in which they were inhabited, meaning that the biblical scribes were well aware of the regions in which these sites were situated. The places examined here were not, in short, positioned within undesirable or underpopulated landscapes outside the purview of the biblical lens. For such reasons, a response to the question of the lack of references to these sites requires us to return to their archaeological remains. And when examining this evidence once more, certain patterns materialize in a manner that offers important historical insights into the question of their absence from the biblical narrative.

The first is that of duration. What is striking about the places investigated here is that so many were short-lived. Kh. Qeiyafa and Kh. ed-Dawwara may have subsisted for a few generations, but there is a distinct possibility that these locations survived for a shorter period in time, perhaps less than fifty years.[147] And even in the case of Tel Masos, KEN, and Tell Qasile, the length of time in which these sites thrived as large settlements was only around a century (e.g., Tel Masos Stratum II, Tell Qasile Stratum X). These brief spans of occupation or prominence are in contrast to many of the early Iron Age places that are mentioned within the Hebrew Bible, whether that of Jerusalem, Mizpah, or Bethel in the central highlands,[148] Beth-Shemesh in the Shephelah,[149] or the Philistine cities of Ashkelon, Ashdod, or Ekron,[150] all of which evince evidence of nearly continual

---

147. Garfinkel and Ganor, *Khirbet Qeiyafa* I, 75; Na'aman, "Ḥirbet ed-Dāwwara," 2.

148. See, for example, I. Finkelstein and L. Singer-Avitz, "Reevaluating Bethel," *ZDPV* 125 (2009): 33–48; Y. Shiloh, *Excavations at the City of David*, I (Jerusalem: Hebrew University, 1984), 26–29; A. De Groot and H. Bernick-Greenberg, *Excavations at the City of David 1978–1985 Directed by Yigal Shiloh. Vol. VIIA. Area E: Stratigraphy and Architecture* (Jerusalem: Hebrew University, 2012), 141–74; Jeffrey Zorn, *Tell en-Nasbeh: A Re-Evaluation of the Architecture and Stratigraphy of the Early Bronze Age, Iron Age and Later Periods* (Ph.D. diss., University of California, Berkeley, 1993), 46–69.

149. Bunimovitz and Lederman, "Border Communities," 114–42.

150. D. Ben-Shlomo, "The Iron Age Sequence of Tel Ashdod: A Rejoinder to 'Ashdod Revisited' by I. Finkelstein and L. Singer-Avitz," *TA* 30 (2003): 83–107; L. Stager, J. D. Schloen, and D. Master, eds., *Ashkelon 1: Introduction and Overview (1985–2006)* (Winona Lake: Eisenbrauns, 2008), 3–10; T. Dothan, S. Gitin, and Y. Garfinkel, *Tel Miqne-Ekron Field IV Lower—The Elite Zone, The Iron Age I and IIC, The Early and Late Philistine Cities* (Winona Lake: Eisenbrauns, 2016).

occupation from the early Iron Age into the late Iron Age period, with a number of these locations expanding in size and population over time. The one exception to this pattern would be the site of Tel Rehov, yet this location is the only site of those investigated above that is named within an Iron Age text—even if that text is not found in the Hebrew Bible.

The second factor is that of geography. Though the locations examined above were situated within prominent regions and along key trade routes, most were positioned some distance away from Jerusalem. Such an observation matters if we posit that many of our biblical writings were either produced in or around Jerusalem, were revised and rewritten at this location, or, at the very least, hold a geographical perspective in which Jerusalem frequently sits at the center.[151] Of course, the grand vision of a Solomonic realm inclusive of all the settlements examined above is present within the biblical narrative (1 Kings 4:21–24; 2 Chron. 9:26), as are lists of cities and regions that permeate the entirety of the southern Levant, including the repeated claim that those who ruled in Jerusalem governed a realm from "Dan to Beersheba" (e.g., 2 Sam. 3:10; 1 Kings 4:25; 1 Chron. 21:2)—or a kingdom that again would have encompassed all the sites discussed above save KEN.

Yet when reading stories about the early Iron Age period we find that it is events and figures associated with the central hill country, from Shechem in the north to Hebron in the south, that are most often within the purview of the biblical writers. When we move outside of these bounds the picture presented becomes somewhat more murky. Cities along the Jezreel and Beth-Shean valleys to the north are referred to from time to time within stories set in this era (e.g., Josh. 17:11; Judg. 5:19; 1 Kings 4:12) but, outside the early admission that within these valleys "the Canaanites continued to live" (Judg. 1:27), there are few details that are provided about these populations or their relationship to the emerging highland polities to their south. Any sense of an early conquest of these areas or their inclusion within highland territories, such as may be assumed by references in the Book of Joshua or to stories of David and Solomon's reigns in Samuel–Kings, is tempered by the lack of archaeological evidence that suggests their incorporation into a nascent highland kingdom during this period in time.[152] Instead, Finkelstein, for example, calls attention to how the Jezreel

---

151. On this point, see W. Schniedewind, *How the Bible Became a Book* (Cambridge: Cambridge University Press, 2004), 64–90; K. van der Toorn, *Scribal Culture and the Making of the Hebrew Bible* (Cambridge: Harvard University Press, 2007), 1–8.

152. Finkelstein, "City-States to States," 75–83; idem., *The Forgotten Kingdom*, 28–32. Cf. Nadav Na'aman, "The Northern Kingdom in the Late Tenth-Ninth Centuries BCE," in *Understanding the History of Ancient Israel* (ed. H. Williamson; London: British Academy, 2007), 401–403.

and Beth-Shean valleys exhibit strong continuity in their political organization and cultural features from the Late Bronze Age and into the centuries that followed, a continuity, Finkelstein argues, that progresses well into the tenth century BCE.[153] When, more precisely, these early Iron Age Canaanite centers (i.e., Megiddo, Yoqne'am, Taanach, Tel Rehov) were subsumed into a northern Israelite kingdom and how this process ensued (war, diplomacy, etc.), is not disclosed within the biblical writings.

Within Philistia the situation is similar. To be sure, the region of Philistia and its five principal cities appear often within biblical stories set in the early Iron Age period (i.e., Judg. 13–16; 1 Sam. 4–7, 9–31). But as P. Machinist notes in his careful study, much of this early Philistine history is treated "unevenly, sketchily, or not at all" by the biblical writers.[154] Neglected within these tales are not only more specific details pertaining to Philistine culture (i.e., the lack of descriptions pertaining to the Philistine language, religion, architecture, or family organization) but also information regarding a number of prominent Philistine settlements, such as Tel Mor, Tell Jemmeh, or, as described above, Tell Qasile. Perhaps most conspicuously, it is striking that the biblical scribes seem unaware that "the Philistines were not a society acting alone," as Machinist puts it, but were rather part of broader collection of "Sea Peoples" who journeyed to various locations along the eastern Mediterranean coast during the onset of the Iron Age.[155] The fact that the biblical writers never allude to the many other groups that made up the Sea Peoples beyond the Philistines is "all the more puzzling in view of the presence of two of them... in the Palestine of the Iron I [period]" near the sites of Dor (the Sikil) and Acco (the Sherdani) along the coastal plain.[156]

Why these groups "are not noticed in the Bible can only be guessed at,"[157] but, in light of our discussion here, such absences may have something to do with geography and a general lack of knowledge of events and peoples populating areas more distant from the central hill country, such as the Mediterranean

---

153. Finkelstein, "City-States to States," 78–81; idem., *The Forgotten Kingdom*, 28–32.

154. Peter Machinist, "Biblical Traditions: The Philistines and Israelite History," in *The Sea Peoples and Their World: A Reassessment* (ed. E. Oren; Philadelphia: University of Pennsylvania Press, 2000), 65.

155. Machinist, "Biblical Traditions," 65.

156. Machinist, "Biblical Traditions," 65. Cf. Ayelet Gilboa, "Fragmenting the Sea Peoples, with an Emphasis on Cyprus, Syria and Egypt: A Tel Dor Perspective," *Scripta Mediteranea* 27–28 (2006–2007): 209–44.

157. Machinist, "Biblical Traditions," 65.

coastline, during the early Iron Age period. The influence of geography may also help to explain why so little information appears in the biblical narrative about the Beer-sheba valley and the relatively large settlement of Tel Masos or the copper industry at KEN in the Arabah. The vague memories surrounding David's forays into Edom—a region some distance away from where the biblical scribes most likely resided—would only support the view that information connected to these excursions became more nebulous and opaque over time.

The third and most consequential evidence related to the absence of the sites surveyed above, however, is that time period in which these places met their end. For if there is one single factor that unites the material remains of the six locations that have sat at the center of this chapter's study, it is the fact that each suffers a major destruction or is abandoned before the ninth century comes to a close: Kh. Qeiyafa is destroyed sometime in the early to mid-tenth century BCE,[158] as is Tell Qasile,[159] and Kh. ed-Dawwara is abandoned by that century's end;[160] Tel Masos declines sometime in the late tenth or early ninth century;[161] Tel Rehov is destroyed around the mid-ninth century;[162] and KEN is abandoned not long thereafter.[163] Though a few of these locations are resettled in the late Iron Age period or after, they are rebuilt on a much reduced scale and none of these sites reach the size and prosperity they enjoyed previously in the centuries before. The residents of Tel Rehov, for example, abandon the site's large lower town after its destruction and eventually inhabit an area on the summit about half the size the location was before.[164] At Tell Qasile, a smaller town is built atop the Philistine city, though this town, too, is eventually destroyed.[165] At Tel Masos a

---

158. Y. Garfinkel et al., "King David's City at Khirbet Qeiyafa: Results of the Second Radiocarbon Dating Project," *Radiocarbon* 57.5 (2015): 881–90.

159. A. Mazar, "The Debate Over the Chronology of the Iron Age in the Southern Levant: Its History, Current Situation, and a Suggested Resolution," in *The Bible and Radiocarbon Dating* (ed. T. Levy; London: Equinox, 2005), 13–28.

160. Finkelstein and Piasetzky, "The Iron I-IIA in the Highlands and Beyond," 53–58.

161. Herzog and Singer-Avitz, "Redefining the Centre," 222–23; Finkelstein, "Southern Steppe," 98; Na'aman, "The Kingdom of Judah," 257–69.

162. A. Mazar, "The Ladder of Time at Tel Rehov: Stratigraphy, Archaeological Context, Pottery and Radiocarbon dates," in *The Bible and Radiocarbon Dating* (ed. T. Levy; London: Equinox, 2005), 193–255.

163. Levy et al., "New Perspectives on Iron Age Copper Production," 210; Levy et al., "Conclusion," 985.

164. Mazar, "Reḥov," 2018; idem, "Rehob," 228.

165. Mazar, *Tell Qasile,* II, 127–28.

single building, perhaps a fortress, is constructed in the seventh century BCE, but this solitary structure was destroyed after a brief period of use.[166]

The era in which these sites were razed or deserted matters when we return to the scribes behind the stories of the early Iron Age period in the Hebrew Bible. For if, as argued in Chapter 1, we can trace the emergence of Hebrew prose writing to the dawn of the late Iron Age (ninth century BCE), then the world in which these biblical texts would have been possible was one in which the locations investigated above no longer existed, or which existed in much diminished forms. A scribe familiar with the settlements along the Elah valley in the late Iron Age would have encountered the Judahite sites of Azekah and Socoh,[167] but no occupants amid the ruins at Kh. Qeiyafa; further south, a number of towns and strongholds were established in Beersheba valley during the eighth and seventh centuries BCE,[168] but Tel Masos was not among them; north of Jerusalem, the sites of Mizpah and Bethel were still inhabited in the late Iron Age, but the fortress at Kh. ed-Dawwara had long fallen out of use. Khirbat en-Nahas, Tel Rehov, and Tell Qasile, too, paled at this time in comparison to their early Iron Age predecessors. Having few written sources to consult about this early Iron Age past, our putative Hebrew scribes would have been dependent primarily on oral traditions for information about this period and on their own experience of the landscape with which they were familiar. With regard to this landscape, it no longer featured the prominent locations at the center of this chapter's discussion. In terms of the source material available to these scribes, it appears that few memories were connected to the places investigated above. There was, it seems, a particular materiality to the remembrance of early Iron Age places, wherein the loss of a location's physical, tangible features—either through destruction or decay—resulted in the loss of memories about it.[169]

---

166. Kempinski, "Tel Masos," 989.

167. O. Lipschits, Y. Gadot, and M. Oeming, "Tel Azekah 113 Years After: Preliminary Evaluation of the Renewed Excavations at the Site," *NEA* 75.4 (2012): 200–205.

168. Itzhaq Beit-Arieh, "Settlement in the Eastern Negev," in *Tel 'Ira: A Stronghold in the Biblical Negev* (ed. I. Beit-Arieh; Tel Aviv: Emery and Claire Yass, 1999), 9–16; Herzog and Singer-Avitz, "Redefining the Centre," 222–26; Yifat Thareani-Sussely, "The 'Archaeology of the Days of Manasseh' Reconsidered in the Light of Evidence from the Beersheba Valley," *PEQ* 139.2 (2007): 69–77.

169. On this point, see again M. Halbwachs, *La Topographie légendaire des Évangiles en Terre sainte* (2nd ed.; Quadrige; Paris: PUF, 2008), 117–57; Y. Hamilakis and J. Labanyi, "Introduction: Time, Materiality, and the Work of Memory," *History and Memory* 20.2 (2008): 5–17; J. Winter, "Sites of Memory," in: *Memory: Histories, Theories, Debates* (eds. S. Radstone and B. Schwartz; New York: Fordham Press, 2010) 312–24; Daniel Pioske, "Memory and its Materiality: The Case of Early Iron Age Khirbet Qeiyafa and Jerusalem," *ZAW* 127.1 (2015): 78–95.

On Forgetting

"Write this as a reminder (זכרון) on a scroll," Moses is commanded after the battle of Rephidim (Exod. 17:14), and elsewhere, too, in the ancient world we find explicit connections between remembering and writing down (i.e., Enmerkar and the Lord of Aratta [COS 1.170]; KAI 222 C:1–6; *Phaedrus* 274).[170] What these claims also indicate, accordingly, is an awareness that when a past did not persist within written texts, when a past was erased, overlooked, or was simply unknown to later writers, then this past was vulnerable to being surrendered by those who might otherwise wish it retain it—a point recognized by both Herodotus ("an inquiry... so that human achievements may not be lost to time" [Hdt. 1.1]) and the biblical writers (Exod. 32:32: "... if not, blot me out of the book you have written"). And in the case of the six locations at the center of this chapter's study, the result of their absence from the biblical narrative was that they were, in fact, effectively forgotten, and with them the events and figures from the early Iron Age period that may have been affiliated with their precincts.

What remains to be addressed is whether the lack of references to these locations, to return to A. Assmann's discussion at the outset of this chapter, was an intentional act by the biblical scribes or an accidental one. If the former, then the omission of these sites from the biblical narrative would be understood as a deliberate move, a result of particular motivations such as those found, for example, in Pausanias's writings and his clear distaste for the presence of Roman imperial power in former Greek lands. If accidental, such absences would be a result of the source material conveyed to the biblical writers wherein little information about these settlements was retained and transmitted.

On this point, the archaeological evidence pertaining to the duration, geography, and chronology of the six locations examined above is of crucial importance, with each suggesting, in turn, that the absence of these places from the biblical narrative was much more likely the outcome of Hebrew scribes not having access to information about these settlements than an intentional act of suppressing what knowledge they had. Undoubtedly, more intentional forms of forgetting can be discerned within the biblical writings, including those instances when the "selective function of the narrative" enabled scribes to omit a particular past in order to focus their efforts on another,[171] such as is apparent in the very few biblical references to the founder of the powerful Omride dynasty in Israel[172] or in the case of the meager

---

170. For a larger discussion of this point, see Daniel Pioske, *David's Jerusalem: Between Memory and History* (New York: Routledge, 2015), 35–37.

171. Ricoeur, *Memory, History, Forgetting*, 85.

172. Na'aman, "Northern Kingdom," 401–13; Finkelstein, *Forgotten Kingdom*, 83–118.

details provided about the post-586 BCE communities in Judah who survived the destruction of Jerusalem.[173] More explicit forms of erasure and emendation are also evident within the Hebrew Bible, the renaming of Saul's sons Ishba'al and Meribba'al (2 Sam. 2–4) to Ishbosheth and Mephibosheth being among them, or the famous editing of the allusion to the "number of gods" in Deuteronomy 32:8 to the "number of the children of Israel" so as to recast this text's polytheistic worldview. In such instances, ideological discomfort with earlier claims compelled later scribes to revise the traditions handed down to them so that they would conform better to the beliefs present in their own time. Such acts were purposeful, considered methods of revision that sought to remove particular claims from cultural memory.

Attempts at forgetting a past by intentionally bypassing or expunging certain facets of it are, in fact, widespread in antiquity. A famous example stems from Egypt and Pharaoh Amenophis IV, also known as Akhenaten, whose widespread religious reforms, deemed heretical and even catastrophic at his death, led to his name being removed entirely from Egyptian record.[174] Akhenaten no longer appeared in Egyptian king-lists, the monuments he created were tore down, his capital city abandoned, and any inscriptions or representations of him were effaced from public buildings. No trace of his existence being in view, the memory of Akhenaten was essentially lost in Egypt within a few generations, only to be recovered with the advent of archaeology and the unearthing of his royal center, Akhetaten, some three thousand years later. The technique of erasing references to particular figures also found prominence later in the Roman Empire where the practice of *damnatio memoriae*, or official memory sanctions, was frequent for those deemed enemies (*hostes*) to the imperial order.[175] Rogue members of the imperial family, individual usurpers, and even emperors themselves were singled out for this legal mandate, confirmed by vote in the Senate, whereby the condemned had their names and titles removed from all written

173. Hans Barstad, *The Myth of the Empty Land: A Study in the History and Archaeology of Judah During the "Exilic" Period* (Oslo: Scandinavian University Press, 1996); Oded Lipschits, *The Fall and Rise of Jerusalem* (Winona Lake: Eisenbrauns, 2005), 272–378; David Carr, *Holy Resilience: The Bible's Traumatic Origins* (New Haven: Yale University Press, 2014), 67–109; Daniel Pioske, "Mizpah and the Possibilities of Forgetting," in *Memory and the City in Ancient Israel* (eds. D. Edelman and E. Ben Zvi; Winona Lake: Eisenbrauns, 2014), 245–57.

174. Donald Redford, *Akhenaten: The Heretic King* (Princeton: Princeton University Press, 1984), 222–35; Jan Assmann, *Moses the Egyptian: The Memory of Egypt in Western Monotheism* (Cambridge: Harvard University Press, 1997), 23, 215–18.

175. Eric Varner, *Mutilation and Transformation: Damnatio Memoriae and Roman Imperial Portraiture* (Leiden: Brill, 2004), 1–20; Harriet Flower, *The Art of Forgetting: Disgrace and Oblivion in Roman Political Culture* (Chapel Hill: University of North Carolina Press, 2011) 1–16.

FIGURE 4.10 Triumph Relief Panel of Marcus Aurelius, with Commodus' Image Removed (Picture: Wikicommons).

records, in addition to references within books, citations of property held, and deeds created. Images of the condemned, too, were destroyed, such as when Commodus's likeness was chiseled out from the famed panel reliefs of his father, Marcus Aurelius, a practice the Romans appear to have adapted from Greek precedent.[176] (See Figure 4.10.)

Yet in other instances, the elision of a past was directed at broader phenomena than the reigns of certain rulers and through less explicit means than

---

176. Flower, *Disgrace and Oblivion*, 17–40.

that of erasure. S. Richardson points up the strange dearth of accounts pertaining to the city of Babylon's downfall in 1595 BCE among later Babylonian writers, though indirect allusions to this moment are scattered within a wide collection of cuneiform documents and indicate that knowledge surrounding this event had clearly persisted over time.[177] But so difficult was this moment to explain in light of beliefs about Babylon's cosmological and cultural primacy, Richardson contends, that the city's downfall was suppressed and sublimated over the centuries "in order to assuage cultural anxieties and traumas" surrounding the event.[178] Nevertheless, such silence on the topic only reinforced the unease that accompanied it, its conspicuous avoidance among later scribes being indicative, in Richardson's assessment, of their preoccupation with this event, or what he terms a form of "failed forgetting."[179] A difficult forgetting is also found within the amnesty enacted in Athens after the brutal civil war between the Thirty Tyrants and the supporters of democracy in 403 BCE. To promote reconciliation, the victorious democrats, according to a speech given by Andocides (Andoc. 1.81), put forward an oath that no Athenian, victor or vanquished, was allowed to publicly recall the misfortunes that had ensued during the conflict: "You considered the safety of Athens of more importance than the settlement of private scores," Andocides recounts, "so both sides, you decided, were to forget the past" (μὴ μνησικακεῖν). N. Loraux, in her seminal study of this political decision, nevertheless observes how this forced forgetting led to a particular fixation on the civil war within speeches and legal arguments of the next half-century among leading Athenians, not unlike the outcome of the Babylonians refusal to deliberate on the meaning of their city's downfall. By virtue of the law preventing open discussions of past grievances, the ban on memory, Loraux asserts, "had no other consequence than to accentuate a hyperbolized, though fixed, memory"[180]of the civil war among Athens' later citizenry.

Examples such as these reinforce the argument that the absence of our six locations from the stories of an early Iron Age past in the Hebrew Bible is not within this domain of active or coerced forgetting. Rather, the archaeological evidence indicates that such omissions are better understood as the result of the biblical

---

177. Seth Richardson, "The Many Falls of Babylon and the Shape of Forgetting," in *Envisioning the Past Through Memories: How Memory Shaped Ancient Near Eastern Societies* (ed. D. Nadali; London: Bloomsbury, 2016), 101–42.

178. Richardson, "The Many Falls," 123.

179. Ibid., 123, 126.

180. Nicole Loraux, *The Divided City: On Memory and Forgetting in Ancient Athens* (New York: Zone, 1995), 261–62.

scribes not being contemporaries of the period in which these locations were most prominent and, though having source material about particular moments in the early Iron Age conveyed to them, they did not have sources that contained information about these locations. In addition to what was remembered about this era, then, were those places that had fallen out of memory, a forgetting occasioned, I have argued here, because these locations had lost their significance by the time in which past memories were being textualized by Hebrew scribes into stories of narrative prose.

In an era when older texts were rare and political turmoil familiar, the loss of past knowledge through such passive, incidental means, especially of the early Iron Age period, was no doubt quite common across the eastern Mediterranean world. N. Na'aman, for example, calls attention to the "remarkable case of historical amnesia" with regard to the strange lack of references to the Egyptian empire's control of Canaan among biblical writings that nevertheless recount many stories set during the Late Bronze/Early Iron Age transition when Egyptian holdings in Canaan were still present.[181] M. Bachvarova, too, notes the elisions present in Homer, including the absence of any reference to Ephesus within the epics in spite of its import throughout the era in which the Homeric poems are set.[182] Outside of the biblical and Homeric corpus one finds other instances, including the few textual allusions to the fine Neo-Hittite cities of the early Iron Age that populated north Syria,[183] writings that describe the early Iron Age Greek societies that endured the collapse of the Late Bronze Age and prepared the way for the flourishing of the Archaic period that followed,[184] or texts that cast light on the background of the Sea Peoples and the reasons for their movements.[185]

---

181. Nadav Na'aman, "Memories of Canaan in the Old Testament," *UF* 47 (2016): 131.

182. Mary Bachvarova, *From Hittite to Homer: The Anatolian Background of Ancient Greek Epic* (Cambridge: Cambridge University Press, 2016), 352–54.

183. Stefania Mazzoni, "Crisis and Change: The Beginning of the Iron Age in Syria," in *Proceedings of the First International Congress on the Archaeology of the Ancient Near East* (eds. P. Matthiae et al.; Rome: Universita degli Studi di Roma, 2000), 1043–60; Trevor Bryce, *The World of the Neo-Hittite Kingdoms: A Political and Military History* (Oxford: Oxford University Press, 2012), 9–46.

184. Anthony Snodgrass, *The Dark Age of Greece: an Archaeological Survey of the Eleventh to the Eighth Centuries BC* (Edinburgh: Edinburgh University Press, 1971), 360–442; Robin Osborne, *Greece in the Making: 1200–479 BC* (2nd ed.; London: Routledge, 2009), 35–65; Susan Langdon, *Art and Identity in Dark Age Greece: 1100–700 BC* (Cambridge: Cambridge University Press, 2008), 56–125.

185. Lawrence Stager, "Forging an Identity: The Emergence of Ancient Israel," in *The Oxford History of the Biblical World* (ed. M. Cogan; New York: Oxford, 1998), 152–71; Assaf Yasur-Landau, *The Philistines and Aegean Migration at the End of the Late Bronze Age* (Cambridge: Cambridge University Press, 2012), 335–46; Susan Sherratt, "The Ceramic

Knowledge about such phenomena from an early Iron Age past was, by and large, lost in antiquity since local forms of writing were quite limited during this time and because the putative texts that may have been composed did not survive. And though modern excavations have brought to light elements of this forgotten past, we can be certain that considerably more has been lost of this period than what archaeology is able to reclaim, with countless individuals, events, beliefs, and practices leaving behind neither text nor artifact in the ruins that can be unearthed. Viewed in this light, the Hebrew Bible is remarkable in its attempt to remember the centuries of the early Iron Age period with the tenacity that it does.

Even so, this chapter concludes with a more somber assessment of the dynamics of remembrance that conditioned the biblical stories written down of this time. Alongside those resilient memories connected to particular early Iron Age locations such as Gath, as examined in Chapter 2, and among the particular entanglements of memory that could surround the life of David that were explored in Chapter 3, we end here on the note of forgetting. In terms of our study of epistemology and the knowledge conveyed about an early Iron Age past, what is gained from this chapter's analysis is the recognition that this body of information was limited, punctuated with gaps and breaks and forms of misremembering and forgetting that are characteristic of so many other written works from antiquity steeped in the memories of others. For every Gath or Ziklag that have stories that appear to hearken back to a past no longer present when the biblical scribes were writing, there were also locations such as Khirbet Qeiyafa, Tel Masos, or Tel Rehov that had fallen out of memory before these scribes were active. But it is perhaps the forgetting of this past, as many have observed, that permitted, in the end, the remembering of others: *"remembering* is possible only on the basis of forgetting, *and not the other way around...."*[186]

Phenomenon of the 'Sea Peoples': An Overview," in *The Philistines and Other "Sea Peoples" in Text and Archaeology* (eds. A. Killebrew and G. Lehmann; Atlanta: SBL Press, 2013), 619–44.

186. Martin Heidegger, *Sein und Zeit* (8th ed.; Tübingen: Max Niemeyer Verlag, 2001), 339 [italics original]. Cf. Søren Kierkegaard, *Either/Or*, I (eds. H. Hong and E. Hong; Princeton: Princeton University Press, 1987), 292–95; Friedrich Nietzsche, "On the Uses and Disadvantages of a History for Life," in *Untimely Meditations* (ed. D. Breazeale; Cambridge: Cambridge University Press, 1997), 60–65; and the remarkable passages in Ricoeur, *Memory, History, Forgetting*, 427–43.

Conclusion

Since it is the mode of being of all that is given us in expe-
rience, History has become the unavoidable element in our
thought . . . This event, probably because we are still caught
inside it, is largely beyond our comprehension.[1]

For those reared and educated in the modern West it is
often hard to grasp that a concern with history, let alone the
writing of history, is not an innate endowment of human
civilization.[2]

THE FOREGOING CHAPTERS have attempted to cast some light on how
biblical claims about an early Iron Age world came to be. Inhibited at the
outset of our investigation by Hebrew scribes who took no credit for the texts
they wrote and who did not disclose how, when, or even where they produced
their writings, this study pursued a more oblique historical approach to the
stories they told by attending to what knowledge informed the referential
claims made within them. Situating their portrayal of an early Iron Age past
alongside of what we now know about this era through the archaeological
evidence available, the intent of this investigation has been to historicize
the past knowledge that shaped the tales the biblical writers decided to tell.
Throughout the various studies of this book, the aim, then, has been to answer
a deceptively simple question: what did Hebrew scribes know about times previous to their own?

What has come into view through the preceding chapters are moments
of both affinity and disconnect between the biblical past and the early Iron
Age world known to us today. Plying their craft in an ancient society that

---

1. M. Foucault, *The Order of Things* (London: Routledge, 2002), 238–39.

2. Y. Yerushalmi, *Zakhor: Jewish History and Jewish Memory* (Seattle: University of
Washington Press, 1996), 6.

communicated cultural knowledge predominantly through the spoken word, the distinct portrait of the past rendered by the biblical scribes was one often formed, I have argued, on the basis of the memories conveyed to them by way of an oral storytelling tradition. The peculiar relationship that emerged between the biblical past and our understanding of a historical one, marked by moments of both close affiliations and notable discrepancies, was one, I contend, that was effected through a distinct sense of the past separate from our own, what E. Blum terms a "different rationality"[3] and what G. von Rad before him had described as Israel's "own intellectual schema" that abided by a "different frame of reference."[4] Following Foucault,[5] I have connected these epistemological insights to what is described as an "episteme," or the normative assumptions particular to an era by which knowledge is constituted and sustained. In short, the means for knowing an early Iron Age past and the significance attached to it by the biblical writers were wed foremost to the faculty of remembrance.

The three case studies of this book illustrate how this episteme of memory would have contributed to the past knowledge made available to later Hebrew scribes, knowledge that was then textualized by these individuals through their remarkable decision to do so in vernacular prose writing. Marshaling recent archaeological evidence by which to view and compare certain biblical references connected to the early Iron Age period, what has been made apparent through these chapters is the dynamic character of the information conveyed to the biblical writers through memory, a dynamism that resists efforts to flatten processes of remembering into something one dimensional, whether in works that accent only memory's revisionary or, conversely, preservative features. Instead, the stories told by the biblical scribes were found to be rooted in not one type of memory but multiple instantiations of it that would have often worked simultaneously to shape the source material transmitted to them over time. At moments, certain memories were found to evince a particular resiliency toward potential transformations that could occur during generations of transmission, where tales told of Gath or Ziklag, for example, find moments of coherence with what we know of the early Iron Age world in which they likely arose. In other instances, the mechanisms of remembering, affected by a transforming landscape to which certain memories were attached, introduced entanglements into the past recalled about

---

3. E. Blum, "Historiography or Poetry? The Nature of the Hebrew Bible Prose Tradition," in *Memory in the Bible and Antiquity* (eds. S. Barton et al.; Tübingen: Mohr Siebeck, 2007), 28.

4. G. von Rad, *Old Testament Theology*, Vol. 2 (trans. D. M. G. Stalker; Louisville: Westminster John Knox, 1965), 427, 417.

5. Foucault, *Order of Things*, xxiii–xxvi.

Davidic activities, including those that were said to have taken place in locations that came to prominence only many years after a David would have ruled. And, finally, others acts of remembering were contravened by the familiar constraints of forgetting, where the destruction or abandonment of a site left it vulnerable to the loss of its significance within the memories of those who would later come to live in these regions of the southern Levant.

In stepping back from the results of this investigation, certain implications emerge for how we might approach these referential claims. In part, the conclusions reached through this study would urge caution when likening the biblical past to our understanding of a historical one.[6] To be sure, the Hebrew Bible's manifest interest in the tangible affairs of a particular people and its development of narrative prose to recount events connected to them are preconditions for those histories still written today.[7] But what is lost through such equivalencies is precisely the crucial epistemological differences highlighted throughout this investigation, where the modes of retrospection that guided ancient Hebrew scribes and those that shape modern, critical history are conceptualized and substantiated through distinct epistemological frameworks.[8] Knowledge about the

---

6. So the ideas expressed, for example, in the titles of B. Halpern and M. Brettler's important works. See B. Halpern, *The First Historians: The Hebrew Bible and History* (San Francisco: Harper & Row, 1988); M. Brettler, *The Creation of History in Ancient Israel* (London: Routledge, 1995). On the rise of historicism specifically within biblical studies, see especially Magne Saebø, "Fascination with 'History'—Biblical Interpretation in a Century of Modernism and Historicism," in *Hebrew Bible / Old Testament: The History of Its Interpretation. Volume III/1: From Modernism to Post-Modernism (The Nineteenth and Twentieth Centuries)* (ed. M. Saebø; Göttingen: Vandenhoeck & Ruprecht, 2013), 17–30.

7. On this topic, see also A. Heinrich, *David und Klio: Historiographische Elemente in der Aufstiegsgeschichte Davids und im Alten Testament* (Berlin: De Gruyter, 2009), esp. 1–49, 372–76. In addition to the points raised in this book, Heinrich argues for a certain critical spirit that appears among the biblical writings through the phenomenon of *Fortschreibung*, or the rewriting and revisions over time of past stories performed by later scribes, in which older assertions are emended or reworked to conform to new perspectives. Nevertheless, as Heinrich admits throughout his fine discussion, the divergences between biblical storytelling and modern historiography are substantial, hanging together in only "very limited" (*nur bedingt*) instances such as in their narrative form and their interest in past human affairs. For such reasons, Heinrich, in a manner similar to the conclusions reached here but from a different direction, opts to see biblical prose as "precursor" (*Vorform*) to modern historiography, or as the "first steps" in the direction toward (*erste Schritte in Richtung*) the historiography that would later be developed in the modern era (p. 376).

8. A. Momigliano, "Ancient History and the Antiquarian," *Journal of the Warburg and Courtauld Institutes* 13 (1950): 285–315. In addition, Schiffman, for example, points toward the crucial awareness of anachronism that arises during the Renaissance [Z. Schiffman, *The Birth of the Past* (Baltimore: Johns Hopkins, 2011)]; Grafton notes the flood of printed information that appeared with the printing press and a newfound interest in ancient works through the notion of *ad fontes* [A. Grafton, *What was History? The Art of History in Early Modern Europe* (Cambridge: Cambridge University Press, 2007), 1–61]; Saebø underscores

past has a history, in other words, and to collapse how the biblical writers conceived of the past with how we think about the past today has the effect of eliding the important epistemological developments that have arisen over the course of that history.[9]

What these considerations also indicate is that drawing on the referential claims of biblical narrative for historical reconstructive pursuits requires some sensitivity toward these narratives' specific epistemic underpinnings. When certain biblical references cannot be supported or refuted on the basis of extra-biblical evidence, when there are few avenues open to ascertain their historical worth outside of the naked references themselves, the historian is confronted by the dissatisfying possibility that ancient texts rooted in the types of memory investigated in this study could retain what we deem as historically credible information but also could not. The decision to make recourse to the claims of these texts will thus often fall on the judgment of the historian and the sense she or he has of the historical character of this literature. The reason for this ambivalence, borne out through the case studies of this work, is that the shared horizon of a past reality beyond memory and history prevents the referential claims of remembrance from ever being fully decoupled from the realm of the historian's potential sources. But neither does this shared horizon guarantee these sources' historical value.[10]

Finally, this study has also revealed both subtle and more consequential divisions between the biblical past and our own understanding of the ancient world. In part, this manner of inquiry has the benefit of dislodging us from our own epistemological assumptions, inviting us to be mindful that other possibilities for knowing a past are viable, and that these other forms of cultural knowledge are as distinct and meaningful as our own historical configurations. But what

---

humanistic individualism and empiricism [Saebø, "Fascination with 'History,'" 21–22]. All observe a rupture in historical thinking birthed in the modern period.

9. J. Huizinga's oft-quoted definition of history—"the intellectual *form* in which a civilization renders account to itself of a past" [J. Huizinga, "A Definition of the Concept of History," in *Philosophy and History: Essays Presented to Ernst Cassirer* (eds. R. Klibansky and H. J. Paton; New York: Harper & Row, 1963), 9 (my italics)]—cited at the outset to J. Van Seters' influential work [J. Van Seters, *In Search of History: Historiography in the Ancient World and the Origins of Biblical History* (New Haven: Yale University Press, 1983), 1], among others in the field of biblical studies, is problematic insofar as it focuses on form and bypasses crucial epistemic questions surrounding content.

10. On this point, see P. Ricoeur, *Memory, History, Forgetting* (trans. K. Blamey and D. Pellauer; Chicago: University of Chicago Press, 2004), 497–500; A. Megill, *Historical Knowledge, Historical Error: A Contemporary Guide to Practice* (Chicago: University of Chicago Press), 1–62; D. Pioske, "Retracing a Remembered Past: Methodological Remarks on Memory, History, and the Hebrew Bible," *Bib Int* 23 (2015): 301–10.

also becomes apparent through this research is the gulf that separates us from the Hebrew scribes behind the biblical writings, a gulf deepened not only by great divergences in culture and temporal distance but also by epistemology. Caught within the event of History, we swim, as Veyne might put it, in the fishbowl that our time dictates just as ancient writers swam in theirs. The sense of melancholy among those who have confronted this divide is palpable, from the *Unheimlichkeit* underscored by Ricoeur,[11] the feeling of loss that Fritzsche observes,[12] the searing discontentedness expressed by Yerushalmi,[13] the burden felt by von Rad.[14] But perhaps by perceiving the faint contours of their fishbowl and ours we will swim better, or may even find a way into more favorable waters.

11. Ricoeur, *Memory, History, Forgetting*, 393–411.

12. P. Fritzsche, *Stranded in the Present: Modern Time and the Melancholy of History* (Cambridge: Harvard University Press, 2004), 201–20.

13. Yerushalmi, *Zakhor*, 77–104.

14. G. von Rad, *Old Testament Theology*, Vol. 1 (trans. D.M.G. Stalker; Louisville: Westminster John Knox, 1962), 108.

Bibliography

Adams, David. "Between Socoh and Azekah: The Role of the Elah Valley in Biblical History and the Identification of Khirbet Qeiyafa." Pp. 47–68 in *Khirbet Qeiyafa Volume I: Excavation Report 2007–2008*. Edited by Y. Garfinkel and S. Ganor. Jerusalem: Israel Exploration Society, 2009.

Aharoni, Yohanon. *Beer-Sheba I: Excavations at Tel Beersheba 1969–1971*. Tel Aviv: Tel Aviv University Press, 1973.

———. *The Land of the Bible*. 3rd edition. Philadelphia: Westminster, 1979.

Aḥituv, Shmuel, and Amihai Mazar. "The Inscriptions from Tel Rehov and Their Contribution to the Study of Script and Writing during the Iron Age IIA." Pp. 39–68 in *"See, I will bring a scroll recounting what befell me" (Ps 40:8): Epigraphy and Daily Life from the Bible to the Talmud Dedicated to the Memory of Professor Hanan Eshel*. Edited by E. Eshel and Y. Levin. Göttingen: Vandenhoeck & Ruprecht, 2014.

Ahlström, Gösta. "Oral and Written Transmission: Some Considerations." *HTR* 59.1 (1966): 69–81.

Albright, William F. "Contributions to the Historical Geography of 1922 Palestine." *Annual of the American School of Oriental Research in Jerusalem* 2–3 (1921–1922): 10–12.

———. *From Stone Age to Christianity*. Baltimore: Johns Hopkins University Press, 1957.

———. "Researches of the School in Western Judea." *BASOR* 15 (1924): 3–11.

Alcock, Susan. "The Peculiar Book IV and the Problem of the Messenian Past." Pp. 142–53 in *Pausanias: Travel and Memory in Roman Greece*. Edited by S. Alcock, J. Cherry, and J. Elsner. Oxford: Oxford University Press, 2001.

———. "The Reconfiguration of Memory in the Eastern Roman Empire." Pp. 323–50 in *Empires: Perspectives from Archaeology and History*. Edited by S. Alcock, T. D'Altroy, K. Morrison, and C. Sinopoli. Cambridge: Cambridge University Press, 2001.

Alcoff, Linda Martin. "Foucault's Normative Epistemology." Pp. 207–25 in *A Companion to Foucault*. Edited by C. Falzon. New York: Wiley, 2013.

Alexandre, Yardenna. "A Canaanite-Early Phoenician Inscribed Bronze Bowl in an Iron Age IIA–B Burial Cave at Kefar Veradim, Northern Israel." *Maarav* 13 (2006): 7–41.

Al-Saji, Alia. "The Memory of Another Past: Bergson, Deleuze and a New Theory of Time." *Continental Philosophy Review* 37. 2 (2004): 203–39.

Alt, Albrecht. "Beiträge zur Historischen Geographie und Topographie des Negeb: III. Saruhen, Ziklag, Horma, Gerar." *Journal of the Palestine Oriental Society* 15 (1935): 294–324.

———. "Erwägungen Über die Landnahme der Israeliten in Palästina." Pp. 168–72 in *Kleine Schriften zur Geschichte des Volkes Israel*. Volume I. Munich: C. H. Beck, 1953.

———. "Josua." Pp.176–93 in *Kleine Schriften zur Geschichte des Volkes Israel*. Volume I. Munich: C. H. Beck, 1953.

———. "Judas Gaue unter Josia." *Palästina-Jahrbuch* 21 (1925): 100–116.

———. "Die Staatenbildung der Israeliten in Palästina." Pp. 1–65 in *Kleine Schriften zur Geschichte des Volkes Israel*. Volume II. München: Beck, 1964.

Alter, Robert. *The Art of Biblical Narrative*. 2nd edition. New York: Basic Books, 2011.

———. *The David Story*. New York: W. W. Norton & Company, 1999.

Amodio, Mark. *Writing the Oral Tradition: Oral Poetics and Literate Culture in Medieval England*. South Bend: University of Notre Dame Press, 2004.

Anderson, J. K. "The Geometric Catalogue of Ships." Pp. 181–92 in *The Ages of Homer: A Tribute to Emily Townsend Vermeule*. Edited by J. Carter and S. Morris. Austin: University of Texas Press, 1995.

Arafat, K. W. *Pausanias' Greece: Ancient Artists and Roman Rulers*. Cambridge: Cambridge University Press, 1996.

Armayor, O. Kimball. "Sesostris and Herodotus' Autopsy of Thrace, Colchis, Inland Asia Minor, and the Levant." *Harvard Studies in Classical Philology* 84 (1980): 51–74.

Asscher, Yotam, Dan Cabanes, Louise Hitchcock, Aren Maeir, Steve Weiner, and Elisabetta Boaretto. "Radiocarbon Dating Shows an Early Appearance of Philistine Material Culture in Tell es Safi/Gath, Philistia." *Radiocarbon* 57.5 (2015): 1–26.

Asscher, Yotam, Gunnar Lehmann, Steven A. Rosen, Steve Weiner, and Elisabetta Boaretto. "Absolute Dating of the Late Bronze to Iron Age Transition and the Appearance of Philistine Culture in Qubur el-Walaydah, Southern Levant." *Radiocarbon* 57.1 (2015): 77–97.

Assmann, Aleida. "Canon and Archive." Pp. 97–108 in *A Companion to Cultural Memory Studies*. Edited by A. Erll, A. Nunnung, and S. Giessen. Berlin: De Gruyter, 2010.

Assmann, Jan. "Communicative and Cultural Memory." Pp. 109–18 in *Cultural Memory Studies: An International and Interdisciplinary Handbook*. Edited by A. Erll and A. Nünning. Berlin, New York, 2008.

———. *Moses the Egyptian: The Memory of Egypt in Western Monotheism.* Cambridge: Harvard University Press, 1997.

———. *Religion and Cultural Memory: Ten Studies.* Translated by R. Livingstone. Stanford: Stanford University Press, 2011.

Auerbach, Erich. *Mimesis: The Representation of Reality in Western Literature.* Princeton: Princeton University Press, 1953.

Bachelard, Gaston. *La formation de l'esprit scientifique: contribution à une psychanalyse de la connaissance objective.* Paris: J. Vrin, 2004.

———. *The Poetics of Space.* Translated by M. Jolas. Boston: Beacon Press, 1994.

Bachvarova, Mary. *From Hittite to Homer: The Anatolian Background of Ancient Greek Epic.* Cambridge: Cambridge University Press, 2016.

Bakhtin, Mikhail. *Speech Genres and Other Late Essays.* Translated by V. McGee. Edited by C. Emerson and M. Holquist. Austin: University of Texas Press, 1986.

Bakker, Egbert. "Activation and Preservation: The Interdependence of Text and Performance in an Oral Tradition." *Oral Tradition* 8.1 (1993): 5–20.

———. "The Making of History: Herodotus' Histories Apodexis." Pp. 3–32 in *Brill's Companion to Herodotus.* Edited by E. Bakker et al. Leiden: Brill, 2002.

Barstad, Hans. *The Myth of the Empty Land: A Study in the History and Archaeology of Judah During the "Exilic" Period.* Oslo: Scandinavian University Press, 1996.

Baumgartner, Walter. "Zum 100. Geburtstag von Hermann Gunkel. Vortrag auf dem Alttestamentlerkongreß Bonn 1962." Pp. 1–18 in *Congress Volume: Bonn 1962.* Leiden: Brill, 1963.

Beaulieu, Paul-Alain. "Official and Vernacular Languages: The Shifting Sands of Imperial and Cultural Identities in First Millennium B.C. Mesopotamia." Pp. 187–216 in *Margins of Writing, Origins of Culture.* Edited by S. Sanders. Chicago: Oriental Institute of the University of Chicago, 2006.

Beit-Arieh, Itzhaq. "Excavations at Tel Malhata: An Interim Report." Pp. 17–32 in *The Fire Signals of Lachish: Studies in the Archaeology and History of Israel in the Late Bronze Age, Iron Age, and Persian Period in Honor of David Ussishkin.* Edited by I. Finkelstein and N. Na'aman. Winona Lake: Eisenbrauns, 2006.

———. "Settlement in the Eastern Negev." Pp. 9–16 in *Tel 'Ira: A Stronghold in the Biblical Negev.* Edited by I. Beit-Arieh. Tel Aviv: Emery and Claire Yass, 1999.

———. "Stratigraphy and Historical Background." Pp. 170–80 in *Tel 'Ira: A Stronghold in the Biblical Negev.* Edited by I. Beit-Arieh. Tel Aviv: Emery and Claire Yass, 1999.

Ben-Ami, Doron. *Jerusalem: Excavations in the Tyropoeon Valley (Giv'ati Parking Lot).* Jerusalem: Israel Antiquities Authority, 2013.

Ben-Dov, Moshe. "A Fragmentary First Temple Period Hebrew Inscription from the Ophel." Pp. 73–75 in *Ancient Jerusalem Revealed.* Edited by H. Geva. Jerusalem: Israel Exploration Society, 1994.

Ben-Josef, Erez. "Back to Solomon's Era: Results of the First Excavations at 'Slaves' Hill' (Site 34, Timna, Israel)." *BASOR* 376 (2016): 169–98.

Ben-Josef, Erez, Thomas Levy, Thomas Higham, Mohammad Najjar, and Lisa Tauxe. "The Beginning of Iron Age Copper Production in the Southern Levant: New Evidence from Khirbat al-Jariya, Faynan, Jordan." *Antiquity* 84 (2010): 724–46.

Ben-Josef, Erez, Ron Shaar, Lisa Tauxe, and Hagai Ron. "A New Chronological Framework for Iron Age Copper Production at Timna (Israel)." *BASOR* 367 (2012): 31–71.

Ben-Shlomo, David. "Food Preparation Habits and Cultural Interaction During the Late Bronze and Iron Age in Southern Israel." Pp. 273–86 in *On Cooking Pots, Drinking Cups, Loomweights and Ethnicity in Bronze Age Cyprus and Neighbouring Regions*. Edited by V. Karageorghis and O. Kouka. Nikosia: A. G. Leventis Foundation, 2011.

———. "Introduction." Pp. 1–10 in *Ashdod VI. The Excavations at Areas H and K (1968–1969)*. Jerusalem: Israel Antiquities Authority, 2005.

———. "The Iron Age Sequence of Tel Ashdod: A Rejoinder to 'Ashdod Revisited' by I. Finkelstein and L. Singer-Avitz." *TA* 30 (2003): 83–107.

———. "Petrographic Analysis of Iron Age IIA Figurines from the Ophel." Pp. 563–68 in *The Ophel Excavations to the South of the Temple Mount, 2009–2013: Final Reports*. Volume 1. Edited by E. Mazar. Jerusalem: Shoham, 2015.

———. "Tell Jemmeh, Philistia and the Neo-Assyrian Empire during the Late Iron Age." *Levant* 40.1 (2014): 58–88.

Ben-Shlomo, David, Itzhak Shai, Alexander Zukerman, and Aren Maeir. "Cooking Identities: Aegean-Style Cooking Jugs and Cultural Interaction in Iron Age Philistia and Neighboring Regions." *AJA* 112.2 (2008): 225–46.

Ben Zvi, Ehud. "On Social Memory and Identity Formation in Late Persian Yehud: A Historian's Viewpoint with a Focus on Prophetic Literature, Chronicles and the Dtr. Historical Collection." Pp. 95–148 in *Texts, Contexts and Readings in Postexilic Literature Explorations into Historiography and Identity Negotiation in Hebrew Bible and Related Texts*. Edited by L. Jonker. Tübingen: Mohr-Siebeck, 2011.

Benz, Brendon. *The Land Before the Kingdom of Israel: A History of the Southern Levant and the People Who Populated It*. Winona Lake: Eisenbrauns, 2016.

Bergson, Henri. *Matter and Memory*. Translated by N. Paul and W. Palmer. New York: Zone Books, 1991.

Bienkowski, Piotr. "The Beginning of the Iron Age in Edom: A Reply to Finkelstein." *Levant* 24 (1992): 167–69.

———. "Iron Age Settlement in Edom: A Revised Framework." Pp. 257–69 in *The World of the Aramaeans*. Edited by P. Daviau, J. Weevers, and M. Weigl. Sheffield: Sheffield Academic Press, 2001.

Bienkowski, Piotr, and Eveline van der Steen. "Tribes, Trade, and Towns: A New Framework for the Late Iron Age in Southern Jordan and the Negev." *BASOR* 323 (2001): 21–47.

Biran, Avraham. "And David Sent Spoils...to the Elders in Aroer (1 Sam 30:26–28)." *BARev* 9.2 (1983): 28–37.

———. "Aroer (in Judea)." Pp. 89–92 in *NEAEHL*. Volume 1. Edited by E. Stern. Jerusalem: Israel Exploration Society, 1993.

Birnbaum, S. A. "The Inscriptions." Pp. 33–34 in *Samaria-Sebaste III: The Objects from Samaria*. Edited by J. W. Crowfoot, G. M. Crowfoot, Kathleen M. Kenyon. London: Palestine Exploration Fund, 1957.

Blakely, Jeffrey. "The location of medieval/pre-modern and biblical Ziklag." *PEQ* 139.1 (2007): 21–26.

Blakely, Jeffrey, and Fred Horton. "On Site Identifications Old and New: The Example of Tell el-Hesi." *NEA* 64.1–2 (2001): 24–36.

Bloch-Smith, Elizabeth. "Israelite Ethnicity in Iron I: Archaeology Preserves What Is Remembered and What Is Forgotten in Israel's History." *JBL* 122.3 (2003): 401–25.

———. "A Stratified Account of Jephthah's Negotiations and Battle: Judges 11:12–33 from an Archaeological Perspective." *JBL* 134.2 (2015): 291–311.

Bloch-Smith, Elizabeth, and Beth Alpert Nakhai. "A Landscape Comes to Life: The Iron I Period." *NEA* 62.2 (1999): 62–127.

Blum, Erhard. "Historiographie oder Dichtung? Zur Eigenart alttestamentlicher Geschichtsüberlieferung." P. 67 in *Das Alte Testament—Ein Geschichtsbuch?*. Edited by E. Blum, W. Johnstone, and C. Markschies. Munich: Lit, 2005.

———. "Historiography or Poetry? The Nature of the Hebrew Bible Prose Tradition." Pp. 25–46 in *Memory in the Bible and Antiquity*. Edited by S. Barton, L. Stuckenbruck, and B. Wold. Tübingen: Mohr Siebeck, 2007.

Boehmer, Rainer Michael. "Uruk-Warka." Pp. 294–98 in *The Oxford Encyclopedia of Archaeology in the Near East*, Volume 5. Edited by Eric Meyers. New York: Oxford University Press, 1997.

Bollinger, Robert. "Berossos and the Monuments: City Walls, Sanctuaries, Palaces and the Hanging Garden." Pp. 137–62 in *The World of Berossos*. Edited by Johannes Haubold, Giovanni Lanfranchi, Robert Rollinger, and John Steele. Wiesbaden: Harossowitz, 2013.

Bonatz, Dominik. "Mnemohistory in Syro-Hittite Iconography." Pp. 65–77 in *Proceedings of the XLVe Rencontre Assyriologique Internationale: Part I*. Edited by T. Abusch. Bethesda: CDL Press, 2001.

Bond, Lucy, Stef Craps, and Pieter Vermeulen. "Introduction: Memory on the Move." Pp. 1–26 in *Memory Unbound: Tracing the Dynamics of Memory Studies*. Edited by L. Bond, S. Craps, and P. Vermeulen. New York: Bergham, 2016.

Bowie, E. L. "Greeks and Their Past in the Second Sophistic." *Past & Present* 46 (1970): 3–41.

Borowski, Oded. "Tell Halif: in the Path of Sennacherib." *BAR* 31.3 (2005): 24–35.

Bowie, Ewen. "Inspiration and Aspiration: Date, Genre, and Readership." Pp. 21–32 in *Pausanias: Travel and Memory in Roman Greece*. Edited by Susan Alcock, John Cherry, and Jas Elsner. Oxford: Oxford University Press, 2001.

Boyer, Pascal. "Cognitive Predispositions and Cultural Transmission." Pp. 288–320 in *Memory in Mind and Culture*. Edited by P. Boyer and J. Wertsch. Cambridge: Cambridge University Press, 2009.

Brettler, Marc. *The Creation of History in Ancient Israel*. London: Routledge, 1995.

Bruins, Hendrik, Amihai Mazar, and Johannes van der Plicht. "The End of the 2nd Millennium BCE and the Transition from Iron I to Iron IIA: Radiocarbon Dates of Tel Rehov, Israel." Pp. 79–99 in *The Synchronisation of Civilisations in the Eastern Mediterranean in the Second Millennium B.C. III*. Edited by M. Bietak and E. Czerny. Vienna: Österreichische Akademie der Wissenschaften, 2007.

Bryce, Trevor. *The World of the Neo-Hittite Kingdoms: A Political and Military History*. Oxford: Oxford University Press, 2012.

Bunimovitz, Shlomo. "Sea Peoples in Cyprus and Israel: A Comparative Study of Immigration Processes." Pp. 103–13 in *Mediterranean Peoples in Transition: Thirteenth to Early Tenth Centuries BCE: In Honor of Trude Dothan*. Edited by S. Gitin, A. Mazar, and E. Stern. Jerusalem: Israel Exploration Society, 1998.

Bunimovitz, Shlomo, and Zvi Lederman. "The Archaeology of Border Communities: The Renewed Excavations at Beth Shemesh, Part I." *NEA* 72.3 (2009): 114–42.

———. "Canaanite Resistance: The Philistines and Beth-Shemesh—A Case Study from Iron Age I." *BASOR* 364 (2011): 37–51.

———. "Close Yet Apart: Diverse Cultural Dynamics at Iron Age Beth-Shemesh and Lachish." Pp. 33–53 in *The Fire Signals of Lachish: Studies in the Archaeology and History of Israel in the Late Bronze Age, Iron Age, and Persian Period in Honor of David Ussishkin*. Edited by I. Finkelstein and N. Na'aman. Winona Lake: Eisenbrauns, 2011.

———. "A Peasant Community on the Philistine Border Levels 6–4: Iron I ca. 1150—950 BCE." Pp. 159–245 in *Tel Beth-Shemesh: A Border Community in Judah. Renewed Excavations 1990–2000: The Iron Age*. Edited by S. Bunimovitz and Z. Lederman. Tel Aviv: Emery and Claire Yass, 2016.

Bunimovitz, Shlomo, and Zvi Lederman (eds.) *Tel Beth-Shemesh: A Border Community in Judah. Renewed Excavations 1990–2000*. 2 vols. Winona Lake: Eisenbrauns, 2016.

Byock, Jesse. *Viking Age Iceland*. New York: Penguin, 2001.

Byock, Jesse, and Davide Zori. "Viking Archaeology, Sagas, and Interdisciplinary Research in Iceland's Mosfell Valley." *Backdirt: Annual Review of the Cotsen Institute of Archaeology at UCLA* (2013): 124–41.

Byock, Jesse. Phillip Walker, Jon Erlandson, Per Hock, Davide Zori, Magnus Gudmundsson, and Mark Tveskov. "A Viking-Age Valley in Iceland. The Mosfell Archaeological Project." *Medieval Archaeology* 49 (2005): 195–218.

Byrne, Ryan. "The Refuge of Scribalism in Iron I Palestine." *BASOR* 345 (2007): 1–31.

Callaway, Joseph, and Robert Cooley. "Salvage Excavation at Raddana, in Bireh." *BASOR* 201 (1971): 9–19.

Campbell, Antony. "The Emergence of the Form-critical and Traditio-historical Approaches." Pp. 125–47 in *Hebrew Bible/Old Testament: The History of Its Reception*. Volume III/1. Edited by M. Saebø. Göttingen: Vandenhoeck & Ruprecht, 2015.

Carr, David. *The Formation of the Hebrew Bible: A New Reconstruction*. Oxford: Oxford University Press, 2011.

———."Orality, Textuality *and* Memory: The State of Biblical Studies." Pp. 161–74 in *Contextualizing Israel's Sacred Writings: Ancient Literacy, Orality, and Literary Production*. Edited by B. Schmidt. Atlanta: SBL, 2015.

———. *Writing on the Tablet of the Heart: Origins of Scripture and Literature*. New York: Oxford, 2005.

Carroll, David. "The Subject of Archaeology or the Sovereignty of the Episteme." *Modern Language Notes* 93 (1978): 695–722.

Casey, Edward. *The Fate of Place: A Philosophical History*. Berkeley: University of California Press, 1997.

———. *Remembering: A Phenomenological Study*. 2nd edition. Bloomington: Indiana University Press, 2000.

Cassuto, Umberto. "Israelite Epic." Pp. 69–109 in *Biblical and Oriental Studies*. Volume II. Jerusalem Magnes Press, 1973.

Chadwick, Jeffrey. "Discovering Hebron." *BAR* 31.5 (2005): 24–33, 70–71.

Chafe, Wallace. *Discourse, Consciousness and Time: The Flow and Displacement of Conscious Experience in Speaking and Writing*. Chicago: University of Chicago Press, 1994.

Chambon, Alain. "Far'ah, Tell el- (North)." Pp. 433–40 in *NEAEHL*. Volume II. Edited by E. Stern. Jerusalem: Israel Exploration Society, 1993.

Chavel, Simeon. *Oracular Law and Priestly Historiography in the Torah*. Tübingen: Mohr Siebeck, 2014.

———. "*Oracular Novellae*' and Biblical Historiography: Through the Lens of Law and Narrative." *Clio* 39 (2009): 1–27.

Childs, Brevard. *Memory and Tradition in Ancient Israel*. London: SCM Press, 1962.

———. "A Study of the Formula 'Until This Day,'" *JBL* 82 (1963): 279–92.

Cohen, Yoram. *The Scribes and Scholars of the City of Emar in the Late Bronze Age*. Winona Lake: Eisenbrauns, 2009.

Cohen-Weinberger, Anat, Nahshon Szanton, and Joe Uziel. "Ethnofabrics: Petrographic Analysis as a Tool for Illuminating Cultural Interactions and Trade Relations between Judah and Philistia during the Iron Age II." *BASOR* 377 (2017): 1–20.

Coman, Alin, Ida Momennejada, Rae Drachc, and Andra Geanaa. "Mnemonic convergence in social networks: The emergent properties of cognition at a collective level." *PNAS* 113.29 (2016): 8171–76.

Connerton, Paul. "Cultural Memory." Pp. 315–24 in *Handbook of Material Culture*. Edited by C. Tilley, W. Keane, S. Küchler, M. Rowlands, and P. Spyer. London: Sage, 2006.

Conrad, Sebastian. "Entangled Memories: Versions of the Past in Germany and Japan, 1945–2001." *Journal of Contemporary History* 38.1 (2003): 85–99.

Cook, R. M. "Thucydides as Archaeologist." *The Annual of the British School at Athens* 50 (1955): 266–70.

Cormack, Margaret. "Fact and Fiction in the Icelandic Sagas." *History Compass* 5.1 (2007): 201–17.

Cross, Frank Moore. "The Arrow of Suwar, Retainer of 'Abday." Pp. 195–202 in *Leaves from an Epigrapher's Notebook: Collected Papers in Hebrew and West Semitic Paleography and Epigraphy*. Winona Lake: Eisenbrauns, 2003.

———. Canaanite Myth and Hebrew Epic: Essays in the History of the Religion of Israel. Cambridge: Harvard University Press, 1973.

———. "A Fragment of a Monumental Inscription from the City of David." *IEJ* 51 (2001): 44–47.

———. *From Epic to Canon: History and Literature in Ancient Israel*. Baltimore: Johns Hopkins University Press, 1998.

———. *Leaves from an Epigrapher's Notebook: Collected Papers in Hebrew and West Semitic Paleography and Epigraphy*. Winona Lake: Eisenbrauns, 2003.

———. "Inscriptions from Tel Sera'" Pp. 155–63 in *Leaves from an Epigrapher's Notebook: Collected Papers in Hebrew and West Semitic Paleography and Epigraphy*. Winona Lake: Eisenbrauns, 2003.

———. "Palaeography and the Dead Sea Scrolls." Pp. 379–402 in *The Dead Sea Scrolls After Fifty Years: A Comprehensive Assessment*. Volume 1. Edited by P. Flint and J. VanderKam. Leiden: Brill, 1998.

Crüsemann, Frank. "Der Löwenkopf von Ḥirbet el-Mšāš—ein Elfenbeinfund aus der frühen Eisenzeit." Pp. 9–23 in *Sefer Rendtorff: Festschrift zum 50 Geburtstag von Rolf Rendtorff*. Edited by K. Rupprecht. Dielheim: Selbstverlag der Autoren, 1975.

———. "Überlegungen zur Identifikation der Hirbet el-Msas (Tel Masos)." *ZDPV* 8 (1973): 211–24.

Culley, Robert. "Oral Tradition and Biblical Studies." *Oral Tradition* 1.1 (1986): 30–65.

Dalley, Stephanie. "Sennacherib and Tarsus." *Anatolian Studies* 49 (1999): 73–80.

———. "Why did Herodotus not Mention the Hanging Gardens of Babylon?" Pp. 171–89 in *Herodotus and His World*. Edited by P. Derow and R. Parker. Oxford: Oxford University Press, 2003.

Damrosch, David. *The Narrative Covenant: Transformations of Genre in the Growth of Biblical Literature*. San Francisco: Harper & Row, 1987.

Darbo-Peschanski, Catherine. "The Origin of Greek Historiography." Pp. 27–38 in *A Companion to Greek and Roman Historiography*. Volume 1. Edited by J. Marincola. Malden: Blackwell, 2007.

David, Brent, Aren Maeir, and Louise Hitchcock. "Disentangling Entangled Objects: Iron Age Inscriptions from Philistia as a Reflection of Cultural Processes." *IEJ* 65 (2015): 140–66.

Davies, Philip. *Scribes and Schools: The Canonization of the Hebrew Scriptures*. Louisville: Westminster John Knox, 1998.

Davies, Philip, and Thomas Römer. (eds.) *Writing the Bible: Scribes, Scribalism, and Script*. Durham: Acumen, 2013.

de Certeau, Michel. *The Writing of History*. Translated by T. Conley. New York: Columbia University Press, 1988.

De Groot, Alon, and Hannah Bernick-Greenberg. *Excavations at the City of David 1978–1985 Directed by Yigal Shiloh*. Volume VIIA. Jerusalem: Hebrew University, 2012.

Dever, William. *What Did the Biblical Writers Know and When Did They Know It?* Grand Rapids: Eerdmans, 2001.

Dickinson, O. T. P. K. "Homer, the Poet of the Dark Age." *Greece & Rome* 33.1 (1986): 20–37.

Dickson, Keith. "The Walls of Uruk: Iconicities in *Gilgamesh*." *JANER* 9.1 (2009): 25–50.

Dietrich, Manfried, Oswald Loretz, and Joaquín Sanmartín. *The Cuneiform Alphabetic Texts: From Ugarit, Ras Ibn Hani, and Other Places*. 2nd edition. Münster: Ugarit-Verlag, 1995.

Dietrich, Walter. "David and the Philistines: Literature and History." Pp. 79–98 in *The Ancient Near East in the 12th–10th Centuries BCE: Culture and History*. Edited by G. Galil et al. Münster: Ugarit Verlag, 2012.

———. *The Early Monarchy in Israel: The Tenth Century B.C.E.* Translated by J. Vette. Atlanta: Society of Biblical Literature, 2007.

Dietrich, Walter, and Thomas Naumann. *Die Samuelbücher*. Darmstadt: Wissenschaftliche Buchgesellschaft, 1995.

Dionysius of Halicarnassus. *Critical Essays*, I. Translated by S. Usher; Cambridge: Harvard University Press, 1974.

Doak, Brian. *The Last of the Rephaim: Conquest and Cataclysm in the Heroic Ages of Ancient Israel*. Washington: Center for Hellenic Studies, 2012.

Doane, A. N. "The Ethnography of Scribal Writing and Anglo-Saxon Poetry: Scribe as Performer." *Oral Tradition* 9.2 (1994): 420–39.

Dobbs-Allsopp, F. W. *On Biblical Poetry.* Oxford: Oxford University Press, 2015.

Dobbs-Allsopp, F. W., J. J. M. Roberts, Choon-Leong Seow, and Robin Whitaker. *Hebrew Inscriptions: Texts from the Biblical Period of the Monarchy with Concordance.* New Haven: Yale University Press, 2005.

Dorsey, David. *The Roads and Highways of Ancient Israel.* Baltimore: Johns Hopkins, 1991.

Dothan, Moshe, and David Ben-Shlomo. *Ashdod VI: Excavations of Areas H–K* Jerusalem: Israel Antiquities Authority, 2005.

Dothan, Trude, Seymour Gitin, and Yosef Garfinkel. *Tel Miqne-Ekron Field IV Lower—The Elite Zone, The Iron Age I and IIC, The Early and Late Philistine Cities.* Winona Lake: Eisenbrauns, 2016.

Driver, Samuel R. *An Introduction to the Literature of the Old Testament.* 9th edition. New York, Meridian: 1957.

———. *Notes on the Hebrew Text of the Books of Samuel.* Oxford: Clarendon, 1890.

Edenburg, Cynthia. "Notes on the Origin of the Biblical Tradition Regarding Achish King of Gath." *VT* 61 (2011): 34–38.

Edenburg, Cynthia, and Juha Pakkala, eds. *Is Samuel Among the Deuteronomists? Current Views on the Place of Samuel in a Deuteronomistic History.* Atlanta: SBL Press, 2013.

Eichenbaum, Howard. *The Cognitive Neuroscience of Memory: An Introduction.* 2nd edition. Oxford: Oxford University Press, 2012.

Eisenberg, Emmanuel, and Alla Nagorski. "Tel Hevron (Er-Rumeidi)." *Hadashot Arkheologiyot* 114 (2002): 91–92.

Eißfeld, Otto. *The Old Testament: An Introduction.* Translated by P. R. Ackroyd. Oxford: Blackwell, 1965

Elsner, Jás. "Pausanias: A Greek Pilgrim in a Roman World." *Past & Present* 135 (1992): 3–29.

———. "Picturesque and Sublime: Impacts of Pausanias in Late-Eighteenth-and Early-Nineteenth-Century Britain." *Classical Receptions Journal* 2 (2010): 219–53.

Emanuel, Jeffrey. "Cretan Lie and Historical Truth: Examining Odysseus' Raid on Egypt in its Late Bronze Age Context." Pp. 1–41 in *Donum Natalicium Digitaliter Confectum Gregorio Nagy Septuagenario a Discipulis Collegis Familiaribus Oblatum.* Edited by V. Bers. Washington, D.C.: Center for Hellenic Studies, 2012.

Erll, Astrid. "Traveling Memory." *Parallax* 17.4 (2011): 4–18.

Erll, Astrid, and Ann Rigney. "Introduction: Cultural Memory and its Dynamics." Pp. 1–14 in *Mediation, Remediation, and the Dynamics of Cultural Memory.* Edited by A. Erll and A. Rigney. Berlin: De Gruyter, 2009.

Eshel, Hanan, Jodi Magness, and Eli Shenhav. "Khirbet Yattir, 1995–1999: Preliminary Report." *IEJ* 50 (2000): 153–68.

Ewald, Heinrich. *History of Israel.* Volume I. Translated by R. Martineau. London: Longmans Green, 1883.

Fantalkin, Alexander, and Israel Finkelstein. "The Date of Abandonment and Territorial Affiliation of Khirbet Qeiyafa: An Update." *TA* 44.1 (2017): 53–60.

———. "The Sheshonq I Campaign and the 8th-Century BCE Earthquake: More on the Archaeology and History of the South in the Iron I-IIa." *TA* 33 (2006): 18–42.

Fantalkin, Alexander, and Oren Tal. "Navigating Between the Powers: Joppa and its Vicinity in the 1st Millennium B.C.E." *UF* 40 (2008): 225–76.

Foucault, Michel. *Order of Things*. London: Routledge, 2002.

Faust, Avraham. "The Chronology of Iron Age IIA in Judah in Light of the Tel 'Eton Tomb C3 and Other Assemblages." *BASOR* 371 (2014): 103–27.

———. "From Regional Power to Peaceful Neighbor: Philistia in the Iron I–II Transition." *IEJ* 63.2 (2013): 174–204.

———. "The 'Philistine Tomb' at Tel 'Eton: Cultural Contact, Colonialism, and Local Responses in Iron Age Shephelah, Israel." *Journal of Anthropological Research* 71.2 (2015): 195–230.

———. "Settlement Patterns and State Formation in Southern Samaria and the archaeology of (a) Saul." Pp. 14–38 in *Saul in Story and Tradition*. Edited by C. Ehrlich. Tübingen: Mohr Siebeck, 2006.

———. "The Shephelah in the Iron Age: A New Look on the Settlement of Judah." *PEQ* 145.3 (2013): 203–19.

———. "Trade, Ideology, and Boundary Maintenance in Iron Age Israelite Society." Pp. 17–35 in *A Holy Community*. Edited by M. Parthuis and J. Schwartz. Leiden: Brill, 2006.

Faust, Avraham, and Hayak Katz. "Philistines, Israelites and Canaanites in the Southern Trough Valley during the Iron Age I." *Egypt and the Levant* 21 (2011): 231–47.

Faust, Avraham, and Justin Lev-Tov. "The Constitution of Philistine Identity: Ethnic Dynamics in Twelfth to Tenth Century Philistia." *OJA* 30.1 (2011): 13–31.

Faust, Avraham, and Ehud Weiss. "Judah, Philistia, and the Mediterranean World: Reconstructing the Economic System of the Seventh Century B.C.E." *BASOR* 338 (2005): 71–92.

Fehling, Detlev. *Herodotus and His 'Sources': Citation, Invention, and Narrative Art.* Translated by J. Howie. Liverpool: Cairns, 1989.

Feindt, Gregor, Félix Krawatzek, Daniela Mehler, Friedemann Pestel, and Rieke Trimçev. "Entangled Memory: Toward a Third Wave in Memory Studies." *History and Theory* 53 (2014): 24–44.

Finkelberg, Margalit. "Homer as a Foundation Text." Pp. 75–96 in *Homer, the Bible, and Beyond: Literary and Religious Canons in the Ancient World*. Edited by M. Finkelberg and G. Stroumsa. Leiden: Brill, 2003.

Finkelstein, Israel. "The Archaeology of the Days of Manasseh." Pp. 169–87 in *Scripture and Other Artifacts: Essays on the Bible and Archaeology in Honor of Philip J. King*. Edited by M. Coogan. Louisville: Westminster, 1994.

———. *The Archaeology of the Israelite Settlement.* Translated by D. Saltz. Jerusalem: Israel Exploration Society, 1988.

———. "Dawwara, Khirbet-ed." Pp. 332–34 in *NEAEHL*, Volume I. Edited by E. Stern. Jerusalem: Israel Exploration Society, 1993.

———. "Does Rehob of the Beth-Shean Valley Appear in the Bible?" *BN* 169 (2016): 3–10.

———. "Excavations at Khirbet ed-Dawwara. An Iron Age Site Northeast of Jerusalem." *TA* 17 (1990): 163–208.

———. *The Forgotten Kingdom: The Archaeology and History of the Northern Kingdom.* Atlanta: SBL Press, 2013.

———. "From City-States to States: Polity Dynamics in the 10th–9th Centuries BCE." Pp. 75–83 in *Symbiosis, Symbolism, and the Power of the Past: Canaan, Ancient Israel, and Their Neighbors from the Late Bronze Age through Roman Palestine.* Edited by W. Dever and S. Gitin. Winona Lake: Eisenbrauns, 2003.

———. "Geographical and Historical Realities Behind the Earliest Layer of the David Story." *SJOT* 27.2 (2013): 131–50.

———. "Khirbet en-Nahas, Edom, and Biblical History." *TA* 32 (2005): 119–25.

———. *Living on the Fringe: The Archaeology and History of the Negev, Sinai and Neighbouring Regions in the Bronze and Iron Ages.* Sheffield: Sheffield Academic Press, 1995.

———. "New Canaan." *Er-Isr* 27 (2003): 189–95. (Hebrew).

———. "The Philistine Countryside." *IEJ* 46 (1996): 225–42.

———. "The Philistine Settlements: When, Where and How Many." Pp. 159–80 in *The Sea Peoples and Their World. A Reassessment.* Edited by E. Oren. Philadelphia: University of Pennsylvania, 2000.

———. "The Philistines in the Bible: A Late-Monarchic Perspective." *JSOT* 27.2 (2002): 131–67.

———. "The Shephelah and Jerusalem's Western Border in the Amarna Period." *Ägypten und Levante* 24 (2014): 267–76.

———. "The Southern Steppe of the Levant ca. 1050–750 BCE: A Framework for a Territorial History." *PEQ* 146.2 (2014): 89–104.

———. "Tall al-Umayri in the Iron Age I: Facts and Fiction with an Appendix on the History of the Collared Rim Pithoi." Pp. 113–28 in *The Fire Signals of Lachish: Studies in the Archaeology and History of Israel in the Late Bronze Age, Iron Age, and Persian Period in Honor of David Ussishkin.* Edited by I. Finkelstein and N. Na'aman. Winona Lake: Eisenbrauns, 2011.

Finkelstein, Israel, and Alexander Fantalkin. "Khirbet Qeiyafa: An Unsensational Archaeological and Historical Interpretation." *TA* 39 (2012): 38–63.

Finkelstein, Israel, and Lily Singer-Avitz. "Ashdod Revisited." *TA* 28 (2001): 231–59.

———. "Reevaluating Bethel." *ZDPV* 125 (2009): 33–48.

Finkelstein, Israel, and Nadav Na'aman. "The Judahite Shephelah in the Late 8th and early 7th Centuries BCE." *TA* 31 (2004): 60–79.

Finkelstein, Israel, and Neil Silberman. *The Bible Unearthed: Archaeology's New Vision of Ancient Israel and the Origin of its Sacred Texts.* New York: Free Press, 2001.

Finkelstein, Israel, and Eli Piasetzky. "The Iron I-IIA in the Highlands and Beyond: ¹⁴C Anchors, Pottery Phases and The Shoshenq I Campaign." *Levant* 38 (2006): 45–61.

———."The Iron Age Chronology Debate: Is the Gap Narrowing?" *NEA* 74.1 (2011): 50–54.

———. "Radiocarbon Dating Khirbet Qeiyafa and the Iron I-IIA Phases in the Shephelah: Methodological Comments and a Bayesian Model." *Radiocarbon* 57.5 (2015): 891–906.

Finkelstein, Israel, and Benjamin Sass. "West Semitic Alphabetic Inscriptions, Late Bronze II to Iron IIA: Archeological Context, Distribution and Chronology." *HeBAI* 2 (2013): 149–220.

Finkelstein, Israel, Shlomo Bumimovitz, and Zvi Lederman. *Shiloh: The Archaeology of a Biblical Site.* Tel Aviv: Tel Aviv University, 1993.

Finkelstein, Israel, Benjamin Sass, and Lily-Singer-Avitz. "Writing in Iron IIA Philistia in the Light of Tel Zayit/Zeta Abecedary." *ZDPV* 124 (2008): 1–14.

Finkelstein, Israel, David Ussishkin, and Eric Cline. *Megiddo V: The 2004–2008 Seasons.* Volumes I–III. Winona Lake: Eisenbrauns, 2013.

Finley, Moses. "Myth, Memory, and History." *History and Theory* 4.3 (1965): 281–302.

Finnegan, Ruth. "A Note on Oral Tradition and Historical Evidence." *History and Theory* 9.2 (1970): 195–201.

———. *Oral Literature in Africa.* London: Clarendon, 1970.

———. *Oral Traditions and the Verbal Arts: A Guide to Research Practices.* London: Routledge, 1992.

Fischer, Alexander. "Beutezug und Segensgabe: Zur Redaktionsgeschichte der Liste in 1 Sam. XXX 26–31." *VT* 53.1 (2003): 48–64.

Fischer, Nina, Jacqueline Lo, and Kate Mitchell. "Introduction: 'Entangled Pasts.'" *Crossings: A Journal of Migration and Culture* 4.1 (2013): 3–11.

Flower, Harriet. *The Art of Forgetting: Disgrace and Oblivion in Roman Political Culture.* Chapel Hill: University of North Carolina Press, 2011.

Flynn, Thomas. "Foucault's Mapping of History." Pp. 28–46 in *A Cambridge Companion to Foucault.* Edited by G. Gutting. Cambridge: Cambridge University Press, 1994.

Foley, John Miles. *Immanent Art: From Structure to Meaning in Traditional Oral Epic.* Bloomington, Ind.: Indiana University Press, 1991.

———. "Memory in Oral Tradition." Pp. 83–96 in *Performing the Gospel: Orality, Memory, and Mark.* Edited by R. Horsely, J. Draper, J. Foley, and W. Kelber. Minneapolis: Fortress, 2011.

———. "Signs, Texts, and Oral Tradition." *Journal of Folklore Research* 33.1 (1996): 21–29.

———. "Towards an Oral Aesthetic: A Response to Jesse Gellrich." *Philological Quarterly* 67 (1988): 475–80.

———. *Traditional Oral Epic: The Odyssey, Beowulf, and the Serbo-Croatian Return Song*. Berkeley: University of California Press, 1990.

Foucault, Michel. *The Order of Things*. London. Routledge, 2002.

Fowler, Robert. "Early *Historie* and Literacy." Pp. 95–115 in *The Historian's Craft in the Age of Herodotus*. Edited by N. Luraghi. Oxford: Oxford University Press, 2007.

Fox, Adam. *Oral and Literature Culture in England 1500–1700*. Oxford: Oxford University Press, 2000.

Frame, Grant. *Rulers of Babylonia: From the Second Dynasty of Isin to the End of Assyrian Domination (1157–612 BC)*. Toronto: University of Toronto Press, 1995.

Frese, Daniel, and Thomas Levy. "The Four Pillars of the Iron Age Low Chronology." Pp. 187–202 in *Historical Biblical Archaeology and the Future: The New Pragmatism*. Edited by T. Levy. London: Equinox, 2010.

Frey, Northrup. *Anatomy of Criticism: Four Essays*. Princeton: Princeton University Press, 1957.

Fritzsche, Peter. *Stranded in the Present: Modern Time and the Melancholy of History*. Cambridge: Harvard University Press, 2004.

Fritz, Volkmar. "Der Beitrag der Archäologie zur historischen Topographie Palästinas am Beispiel von Ziklag." *ZDPV* 106 (1990): 78–85.

———. "Tel Masos: A Biblical Site in the Negev." *Archaeology* 36.5 (1983): 30–37.

———. "Where is David's Ziklag?" *BAR* 19.3 (1993): 58–61, 76.

Fritz, Volkmar, and Aharon Kempinski (eds). *Ergebnisse der Ausgrabungen auf der Ḥirbet el- Mšāš (Tēl Māsōś) 1972–1975*. 3 Volumes. Wiesbaden: Harrassowitz, 1983.

Fugman, Einar. *Hama. Fouilles et recherches de la Fondation Carlsberg 1931–38 II: architecture des périodes pré-hellénistique*. Copenhagen: National Museum, 1958.

Gadot, Yuval. "Aphek in the Sharon and the Philistine Northern Frontier." *BASOR* 341 (2006): 21–36.

Gafijczuk, Dariusz. "Dwelling Within: The Inhabited Ruins of History." *History and Theory* 52 (2013): 149–70.

Garfinkel, Yosef. "The Iron Age City of Khirbet Qeiyafa." Pp. 115–32 in *The Shephelah During the Iron Age: Recent Archaeological Studies*. Edited by O. Lipschits and A. Maeir. Winona Lake: Eisenbrauns, 2017.

———. "Khirbet Qeiyafa in the Shephelah: Data and Interpretations." Pp. 5–60 in *Khirbet Qeiyafa in the Shephelah*. Edited by S. Schroer and S. Münger. Fribourg: Academic Press Fribourg, 2017.

Garfinkel, Yosef, and Saar Ganor. *Khirbet Qeiyafa Vol. I: Excavation Report 2007–2008*. Jerusalem: Israel Exploration Society, 2009.

Garfinkel, Yosef, and M. Mumcuoglu. "Triglyphs and Recessed Doorframes on a Building Model from Khirbet Qeiyafa: New Light on Two Technical Terms in the Biblical Descriptions of Solomon's Palace and Temple." *IEJ* 63.2 (2013): 135–63.

Garfinkel, Yosef, Katharina Streit, Saar Ganor, and Paula Reimer. "King David's City at Khirbet Qeiyafa: Results of the Second Radiocarbon Dating Project." *Radiocarbon* 57.5 (2015): 881–90.

Garfinkel, Yosef, Saar Ganor, and Michael Hasel. *Khirbet Qeiyafa Volume II: Excavation Report 2009–2013*. Jerusalem: Israel Exploration Society, 2014.

———. "The Iron Age City of Khirbet Qeiyafa after Four Seasons of Excavations." Pp. 149–74 in G. Galil et al. (eds.), *The Ancient Near East in the 12th–10th Centuries BCE Culture and History. Proceedings of the International Conference held at the University of Haifa, 2–5 May 2010*. Leiden: Brill, 2012.

———. "The Contribution of Khirbet Qeiyafa to our Understanding of the Iron Age Period." *Strata* 28 (2010): 39–54.

Garfinkel, Yosef, Katharina Streit, Saar Ganor, and Michael Hasel. "State Formation in Judah: Biblical Tradition, Modern Historical Theories, and Radiometric Dates at Khirbet Qeiyafa." *Radiocarbon* 54 (2012): 359–69.

Garfinkel, Yosef, Mitka Golub, Haggai Misgav, and Saar Ganor. "The 'Išba'al Inscription from Khirbet Qeiyafa." *BASOR* 373 (2015): 217–33.

Gaß, Erasmus. *Die Ortsnamen des Richterbuchs in historischer und redaktioneller Perspektive*. Wiesbaden: Harrassowitz, 2005.

Geoghegan, Jeffrey. "'Until This Day' and the Preexilic Redaction of the Deuteronomistic History." *JBL* 122.2 (2003): 201–27.

George, Andrew. *The Babylonian Gilgamesh Epic: Introduction, Critical Edition, and Cuneiform Texts*. Volume I. Oxford: Oxford University Press, 2003.

———. *The Epic of Gilgamesh: A New Translation*. New York: Penguin, 1999.

Gertz, Jan. "Konstruierte Erinnerung: Alttestamentlich Historiographie im Spiegel von Archäologie und literarhistorischer Kritik am Fallbeispiel des salomonischen Königtums." *BthZ* 21 (2004): 3–29.

Gilboa, Ayelet. "Fragmenting the Sea Peoples, with an Emphasis on Cyprus, Syria and Egypt: A Tel Dor Perspective." *Scripta Mediteranea* 27–28 (2006–2007): 209–44.

Gilboa, Ayelet, Ilan Sharon, and Elizabeth Bloch-Smith. "Capital of Solomon's Fourth District? Israelite Dor." *Levant* 47.1 (2015): 51–74.

Gitin, Seymour. "Philistia in Transition: The Tenth Century BCE and Beyond." Pp. 162–83 in *Mediterranean Peoples in Transition: Thirteenth to Early Tenth Centuries BCE*. Edited by S. Gitin, A. Mazar, and E. Stern. Jerusalem: Israel Exploration Society, 1998.

Ghountas, Hadi. *The Elisha-Hazael Paradigm and the Kingdom of Israel: The Politics of God in Ancient Syria-Palestine*. Routledge: New York, 2013.

Glassner, Jean-Jacques. *Mesopotamian Chronicles*. Atlanta: SBL Press, 2004.

Goldhill, Simon. *The Invention of Prose*. Oxford: Oxford University Press, 2002.

Goldwasser, Orly. "From the Iconic to the Linear—The Egyptian Scribes of Lachish and the Modification of the Early Alphabet in the Late Bronze Age." Pp. 118–60 in *Alphabets, Texts and Artifacts in the Ancient Near East: Studies Presented to Benjamin Sass*. Edited by I. Finkelstein et al. Paris: Van Dieren, 2017.

———. "Hieratic Inscriptions from Tel Seraʿ in Southern Canaan." *TA* 11 (1984): 77–93.

Goody, Jack. *The Interface Between the Written and the Oral*. Cambridge: Cambridge University Press, 1987.

———. "Memory in Oral Tradition." Pp. 73–94 in *Memory*. Edited by P. Fara and K. Patterson. Cambridge: Cambridge University Press, 1998.

Goren, Yuval, Israel Finkelstein, and Nadav Naʾaman. *Inscribed in Clay: Provenance Study of the Amarna Letters and other Ancient Near Eastern Texts*. Tel Aviv: Tel Aviv University Press, 2004.

Grafton, Anthony. *The Footnote: A Curious History*. Cambridge: Harvard University Press, 1997.

———. *What was History? The Art of History in Early Modern Europe*. Cambridge: Cambridge University Press, 2007.

Gramsci, Antonio. *Selections from Cultural Writings*. Edited by D. Forgacs and G. Nowell-Smith. Cambridge: Harvard University Press, 1991.

Grant, Elihu. "Découverte épigraphique à Beth šémèš." *RB* 39 (1930): 401–02.

Grayson, A. K. "Assyria and Babylonia." *Or* 49.2 (1980): 140–94.

Green, Douglas. *"I Undertook Great Works": The Ideology of Domestic Achievements in West Semitic Royal Inscriptions*. Tübingen: Mohr Siebeck, 2010.

Greenfield, Jonas. "The Hebrew Bible and Canaanite Literature." Pp. 545–60 in *The Literary Guide to the Bible*. Edited by R. Alter and F. Kermode. Cambridge: Harvard University Press, 1987.

Greenstein, Edward. "The Formation of the Biblical Narrative Corpus." *AJS Review* 15.2 (1990): 165–78.

———. "On the Genesis of Biblical Prose Narrative." *Prooftexts* 8.3 (1988): 347–54.

———. "What was the Book of Yashar?" *Maarav* 21.1–2 (2014): 25–35.

Greenstein, Edward, and David Marcus. "The Akkadian Inscription of Idrimi." *JANES* 8 (1976): 59–96.

Greßmann, Hugo. *Albert Eichhorn und die Religionsgeschichtliche Schule*. Göttingen: Vandenhoeck & Ruprecht, 1914.

———. "Die Aufgaben der alttestamentlichen Forschung." *ZAW* 42 (1924): 1–33.

———. "The Oldest History Writing in Israel." Pp. 9–22 in *Narrative and Novella in Samuel: Studies by Hugo Gressmann and Other Scholars 1906–1923*. Translated by D. Orton. Edited by D. Gunn. Sheffield: Sheffield Academic Press, 1991.

Grethlein, Jonas. "The Many Faces of the Past in Archaic and Classical Greece." Pp. 234–55 in *Thinking, Recording, and Writing History in the Ancient World*. Edited by K. Raaflaub. Malden: Wiley-Blackwell, 2014.

———. "The Rise of Greek Historiography and the Invention of Prose." Pp. 148–70 in *The Oxford History of Historical Writing: Volume I, Beginnings to AD 600*. Edited by A. Feldherr and G. Hardy. Oxford: Oxford University Press, 2011.

Grønbaek, Jacob. *Die Geschichte vom Aufstieg Davids (1. Sam. 15–2. Sam. 5): Tradition und Komposition*. Copenhagen: Prostant Apud Munksgaard, 1971.

Gunkel, Hermann. "Aus Wellhausen's neuesten apokalyptischen Forschungen. Einige principielle Eröterungen." *Zeitschrift für wissenschaftliche Theologie* 42 (1899): 581–611.

———. *Genesis*. 3rd edition. Göttingen: Vandenhoeck & Ruprecht, 1910.

———. "Geschichtsschreibung im A.T." Pp. 1248–54 in *Religion in Geschichte und Gegenwart*. 1st edition. Edited by H. Gunkel. Tübingen: Mohr, 1919–23.

———. "Geschichtsschreibung im A.T." Pp. 1112–15 in *Religion in Geschichte und Gegenwart*. 2nd edition. Tübingen: Mohr, 1927.

———. *Schöpfung und Chaos in Urzeit und Endzeit*. Göttingen: Vandenhoeck & Ruprecht, 1895.

———. "Ziele und Methoden der Erklärung des Alten Testamentes." Pp. 11–29 in *Reden und Aufsätze*. Göttingen: Vandenhoeck & Ruprecht, 1913.

Gunn, David. "Narrative Patterns and Oral Tradition in Judges and Samuel." *VT* 24 (1974): 286–317.

———. *The Story of King David: Genre and Interpretation*. Sheffield: JSOT Press, 1978.

Gunneweg, J., F. Asaro, H. Michel, and I. Perlman. "Interregional Contacts Between Tell en-Nasbeh and Littorial Philistine Centres in Canaan During the Early Iron Age I." *Archaeometry* 36.2 (1994): 227–39.

Gutting, Gary. *Michel Foucault's Archaeology of Scientific Reason*. Cambridge: Cambridge University Press, 1989.

Habicht, Christian. "Pausanias and the Evidence of Inscriptions." *Classical Antiquity* 3 (1984): 40–56.

———. *Pausanias' Guide to Ancient Greece*. Berkeley: University of California Press, 1998.

Hackett, Jo Ann, P. Kyle McCarter, Ada Yardeni, Andre Lemaire, Esther Eshel, and Avi Hurvitz. "Defusing Pseudo-Scholarship: The Siloam Inscription Ain't Hasmonean." *BAR* 23 (1997): 41–50, 68.

Halbwachs, Maurice. *Les cadres sociaux de la mémoire*. 2nd edition. Paris: Presses Universitaires de France, 1952.

———. *La Mémoire Collective*. 2nd edition. Paris: Presses Universitaires de France, 1968.

———. *On Collective Memory*. Edited by L. Coser. Chicago: University of Chicago Press, 1992.

———. *La Topographie légendaire des Évangiles en Terre sainte: Étude de Mémoire Collective*. 2nd edition. Paris: Presses Universitaires de France, 2008.

Halpern, Baruch. *The Constitution of the Monarchy in Israel*. Chico: Scholars Press, 1981.

———. "David Did It, Others Did Not: The Creation of Ancient Israel." Pp. 424–37 in *The Bible and Radiocarbon Dating: Archaeology, Text, and Science*. Edited by T. Levy and T. Higham. London: Routledge, 2005.

———. *David's Secret Demons: Messiah, Murderer, Traitor, King*. Grand Rapids: Eerdmans, 2001.

———. *The First Historians: The Hebrew Bible and History*. San Francisco: Harper & Row, 1988.

Hamilakis, Yannis, and Jo Labanyi. "Introduction: Time, Materiality, and the Work of Memory." *History & Memory* 20.2 (2008): 5–17.

Hamilton, Gordon. "Reconceptualizing the Periods of Early Alphabetic Scripts." Pp. 39–49 in *An Eye for Form: Epigraphic Essays in Honor of Frank Moore Cross*. Edited by J. Hackett and W. Aufrecht. Winona Lake: Eisenbrauns, 2014.

———. "Two Methodological Issues Concerning the Expanded Collection of Early Alphabetic Texts." Pp. 127–56 in *Epigraphy, Philology, and the Hebrew Bible: Methodological Perspectives on Philological & Comparative Study of the Hebrew Bible in Honor of Jo Ann Hackett*. Edited by J. Hutton and A. Rubin. Atlanta: SBL, 2015.

Harmansah, Ömür. *Cities and the Shaping of Memory in the Ancient Near East*. Cambridge: Cambridge University Press, 2013.

Harris, Horton. "The Location of Ziklag: Its Identification by Felix Fabri." *PEQ* 143.1 (2011): 19–30.

———. "The Location of Ziklag: A Review of the Candidate Sites, Based on Biblical, Topographical and Archaeological Evidence." *PEQ* 143.2 (2011): 119–33.

Harris, William V. *Ancient Literacy*. Cambridge: Harvard University Press, 1991.

Harrison, Timothy. "Neo-Hittites in the 'Land of Palistin,': Renewed Excavations at Tell Ta'yinat on the Plain of Antioch." *NEA* 72.4 (2009): 174–89.

———. "Recent Discoveries at Tayinat (Ancient Kunulua/Calno) and their Biblical Implications." Pp. 396–425 in *Congress Volume Munich 2003*. Edited by C. Maier. Leiden: Brill, 2014.

Haubold, Johanes, Giovanni Lanfranchi, Robert Rollinger, and John Steele. (eds.) *The World of Berossus*. Wiesbaden: Harassowitz Verlag, 2013.

Havelock, Eric. *The Muse Learns to Write: Reflections on Orality and Literacy from Antiquity to the Present*. New Haven: Yale University Press, 1986.

———. *Preface to Plato*. Cambridge: Belknap Press, 1963.

———. *Prologue to Greek Literacy*. Cincinnati: University of Cincinnati Press, 1971.

Hawkins, J. D. "Tarkasnawa King of Mira 'Tarkondemos', Boğazkäy Sealings and Karabel." *Anatolian Studies* 48 (1998): 1–31.

Hawley, Robert, Dennis Pardee, and Carole Roche-Hawley. "The Scribal Culture of Ugarit." *JANEH* 2.2 (2016): 229–67.

Hayes, William. "The Middle Kingdom in Egypt." Pp. 461–534 in *Cambridge Ancient History*. Volume 1, Part 2. Edited by I. Edwards, J. Gadd, and N. G. L. Hammond. Cambridge: Cambridge University Press, 1971.

Heidegger, Martin. *Sein und Zeit.* 8th edition. Tübingen: Max Niemeyer Verlag, 2001.

Heinrich, André. *David und Klio: Historiographische Elemente in der Aufstiegsgeschichte Davids und im Alten Testament.* Berlin: De Gruyter, 2009.

Hendel, Ronald. "Cultural Memory." Pp. 28–46 in *Reading Genesis: Ten Methods.* Edited by R. Hendel. Cambridge: Cambridge University Press, 2010.

———. "The Date of the Siloam Inscription: A Rejoinder to Rogerson and Davies." *BA* 59 (1996): 233–37.

———. *Remembering Abraham: Culture, Memory, and History in the Hebrew Bible.* Oxford: Oxford University Press, 2005

Hertzberg, Hans Wilhelm. *I & II Samuel.* Translated by J. Bowden. Philadelphia: W estminster, 1964.

Herzog, Ze'ev. "Enclosed Settlements in the Negeb and the Wilderness of Beer-sheba." *BASOR* 250 (1983): 41–49.

———. "The Fortress Mound at Tel Arad: An Interim Report." *TA* 29.1 (2002): 3- 109.

Herzog, Ze'ev, and Lily Singer-Avitz. "Redefining the Centre: The Emergence of State in Judah." *TA* 31.2 (2004): 209–44.

Higginbotham, Carolyn. "Elite Emulation and Egyptian Governance in Ramesside Canaan." *TA* 23 (1996): 154–69.

Hitchcock, Louise, and Aren Maeir. "Beyond Creolization and Hybridity: Entangled and Transcultural Identities in Philistia." *ARC* 28.1 (2013): 43–65.

Hodder, Ian. "Human-Thing Entanglement: Towards an Integrated Archaeological Perspective." *Journal of the Royal Anthropological Institute* 17.1 (2011): 154–77.

Hoffner, Harry. "Propaganda and Political Justification in Hittite Historiography." Pp. 49–62 in *Unity and Diversity: Essays in the History, Literature, and Religion of the Ancient Near East.* Edited by H. Goedicke and J. J. M. Roberts. Baltimore: The Johns Hopkins University Press, 1975.

Holtorf, Cornelius, and Howard Williams. "Landscapes and Memories." Pp. 235–54 in *The Cambridge Companion to Historical Archaeology.* Edited by D. Hicks. Cambridge: Cambridge University Press, 2006.

Hornblower, Simon. *A Commentary on Thucydides.* Volume I. Oxford: Clarendon, 1991.

———. *Thucydides.* Baltimore: Johns Hopkins, 1987.

Horowitz, Wayne, Takayoshi Oshima, and Seth Sanders. *Cuneiform in Canaan: Cuneiform Sources from the Land of Israel in Ancient Times.* Jerusalem: Israel Exploration Society, 2006.

Horowitz, Wayne, Takayoshi Oshima, and Filip Vukosavovic. "Hazor 18: Fragments of a Cuneiform Law Collection from Hazor." *IEJ* 62.2 (2012): 158–76.

Huehnegard, John, and Jo Ann Hackett. "The Hebrew and Aramaic Languages." Pp. 3–24 in *The Biblical World.* Volume II. Edited by J. Barton. London: Routledge, 2002.

Huizinga, Johann. "A Definition of the Concept of History." Pp. 1–10 in *Philosophy and History: Essays Presented to Ernst Cassirer.* Edited by R. Klibansky and H. J. Paton. New York: Harper & Row, 1963.

Humphreys, W. Lee. "The Rise and Fall of King Saul: A Study of an Ancient Narrative Stratum in 1 Samuel." *JSOT* 22 (1980): 74–90.

Hutton, Jeremy. *The Transjordanian Palimpsest: The Overwritten Texts of Personal Exile and Transformation in the Deuteronomistic History*. Berlin: Walter de Gruyter, 2009.

Hutton, William. *Describing Greece: Landscape and Literature in the "Periegesis" of Pausanias*. Cambridge: Cambridge University Press, 2005.

———. "Pausanias and the Mysteries of Hellas." *Transactions of the American Philological Association* 140 (2010): 423–59.

Hutzli, Jürg. "The Distinctness of the Samuel Narrative Tradition." Pp. 171–205 in *Is Samuel Among the Deuteronomists? Current Views on the Place of Samuel in a Deuteronomistic History*. Edited by C. Edenburg and J. Pakkala. Atlanta: SBL Press, 2013.

Hyder, Syed Akbar. *Reliving Karbala: Martyrdom in South Asian Memory*. Oxford: Oxford University Press, 2006.

Inglmundarson, Valur. "The Politics of Memory and the Reconstruction of Albanian National Identity in Postwar Kosovo." *History and Memory* 19.1 (2007): 95–123.

Innes, Matthew. "Orality, Memory, and Literacy in Early Medieval Society." *Past & Present* 158 (1998): 3–36.

Jacobs, Paul, and Joe Seger. "Glimpses of the Iron Age I at Tel Halif." Pp. 146–65 in *"Up to the Gates of Ekron": Essays on the archaeology and history of the Eastern Mediterranean in honor of Seymour Gitin*. Edited by S. Crawford. Jerusalem: Israel Exploration Society, 2007.

Jacobsen, Thorkild. "The Gilgamesh Epic: Romantic and Tragic Visions." Pp. 231–49 in *Lingering Over Words: Studies in Ancient Near Eastern Literature in Honor of William L. Moran*. Edited by T. Abusch et al. Atlanta: Scholars Press, 1990.

———. *The Harps that Once....: Sumerian Poetry in Translation*. New Haven: Yale University Press, 1987.

Jamieson-Drake, David. *Scribes and Schools in Monarchic Judah: A Socio-Archaeological Approach*. Sheffield: Almond Press, 1991.

Japhet, Sara. *I & II Chronicles: A Commentary*. Louisville: Westminster John Knox, 1993.

Ji, Chang-Ho. "Iron Age I in Central and Northern Transjordan: An Interim Summary of Archaeological Data." *PEQ* 127 (1995): 122–40.

Jobling, David. *1 Samuel*. Collegeville: Liturgical Press, 1998.

Johnson, William. "Oral Performance and the Composition of Herodotus' *Histories*." *Greek, Roman and Byzantine Studies* 35.3 (1994): 229–54.

Jones, Andrew. *Memory and Material Culture*. Cambridge: Cambridge University Press, 2007.

Jonker, Gerdien. *The Topography of Remembrance: The Dead, Tradition, and Collective Memory in Mesopotamia*. Leiden: Brill, 1995.

Jost, Madeleine. "Pausanias en Mégalopolitide." *Revue des études anciennes* 75.3 (1973): 241–67.

Kahn, Charles. "Writing Philosophy: Prose and Poetry from Thales to Plato." Pp. 139–61 in *Written Texts and the Rise of Literate Culture in Ancient Greece*. Edited by H. Yunis. Cambridge: Cambridge University Press, 2003.

Kahn, Dan'el. "The Kingdom of Arpad (Bit Agusi) and 'all Aram': International Relations in Northern Syria in the Ninth and Eighth Centuries BCE." *ANES* 44 (2007): 66–89.

Kaiser, Otto. "David und Jonathan: Tradition, Redaktion und Geschichte in 1 Sam 16–20—Ein Versuch." *ETL* 66 (1990): 281–96.

Kallai, Zeharia. "The Land of Benjamin and Mt. Ephraim." Pp. 153–93 in *Judaea, Samaria and the Golan. Archaeological Survey 1967–1968*. Edited by M. Kochavi. Jerusalem: Publications of the Archaeological Survey of Israel 1. (Hebrew).

Katz, Hayak, and Avraham Faust. "The Assyrian Destruction Layer at Tel 'Eton." *IEJ* 62 (2012): 22–53.

———. "The Chronology of the Iron IIA in Judah in Light of the Tel 'Eton Tomb C3 and Other Assemblages." *BASOR* 371 (2014): 103–27.

Kawashima, Robert. *Biblical Narrative and the Death of the Rhapsode*. Bloomington: Indiana University Press, 2004.

Kempinski, Aharon. "Masos, Tel." Pp. 986–89 in *NEAEHL*. Volume 3. Edited by E. Stern. Jerusalem: Israel Exploration Society, 1993.

Kenyon, Kathleen. *Excavations at Jericho: The Architecture and Stratigraphy of the Tell*. Volume III. Edited by T. A. Holland. London, 1981.

———. "Jericho." Pp. 674–81 in *NEAEHL*. Volume 2. Edited by E. Stern. Jerusalem: Israel Exploration Society, 1993.

Kierkegaard, Søren. *Either/Or*, I. Edited by H. Hong and E. Hong. Princeton: Princeton University Press, 1987.

Kirk, G. S. *The Iliad: A Commentary*. Volume I. Cambridge: Cambridge University Press, 1985.

Kisilevitz, Shua. "The Iron IIA Judahite Temple at Tel Moza." *TA* 42.2 (2015): 147–64.

———. "Ritual Finds from the Iron Age at Tel Motza." Pp. 38–46 in *New Studies in the Archaeology of Jerusalem and its Region VII*. Edited by G. Stiebel. Jerusalem, 2013. (Hebrew).

Kitchen, Kenneth. *The Third Intermediate Period in Egypt (1100—600 B.C.)*. 2nd edition. Warminster: Aris & Philips, 1986.

Kittay, Jeffrey and Wlad Godzich. *The Emergence of Prose: An Essay in Prosaics*. Minneapolis: University of Minnesota Press, 1987.

Klatt, Werner. *Hermann Gunkel: Zu seiner Theologie der Religionsgeschichte und der Entstehung der formgeschichtlichen Methode*. Göttingen: Vandenhoeck & Ruprecht, 1969.

Klein, Johannes. "Davids Flucht zu den Philistern (1 Sam XXI 11ff.; XXVII-XXIX)." *VT* 55.2 (2005): 176–84.

Klein, Ralph. *1 Chronicles: A Commentary*. Minneapolis: Fortress, 2006.

Kletter, Raz, and Etty Brand. "A New Look at the Iron Age Silver Hoard from Eshtemoa." *ZDPV* 114.2 (1998): 139–54.

Knapp, Andrew. *Royal Apologetic in the Ancient Near East*. Atlanta: SBL Press, 2015.

Knauf, Axel. "Edom: The Social and Economic History." Pp. 93–117 in *You Shall Not Abhor an Edomite for He Is Your Brother: Edom and Seir in History and Tradition*. Edited by D. Edelman. Atlanta: Scholars Press, 1995.

Knight, Douglas. *Rediscovering the Traditions of Ancient Israel*. 3rd edition. Atlanta: SBL, 2006.

Knoppers, Gary. *1 Chronicles 10–29*. AB 12. New York: Doubleday, 2004.

Knoppers, Gary, and J. Gordon McConville, eds. *Reconsidering Israel and Judah: Recent Studies on the Deuteronomistic History*. Winona Lake: Eisenbrauns, 2000.

Koch, Ido. "The geopolitical organization of the Judean Shephelah during Iron Age I-IIA." *Cathedra* 143 (2012): 45–64. (Hebrew).

———. "Notes on Three South Canaanite Sites in the el-Amarna Correspondence." *TA* 43 (2016): 91–98.

Koselleck, Koselleck. *Futures Past: On the Semantics of Historical Time*. Translated by K. Tribe. New York: Columbia University Press, 2004.

Kratz, Reinhard. *The Composition of the Narrative Works of the Old Testament*. Translated by J. Bowden. London: T&T Clark, 2005.

———. *Historical and Biblical Israel: The History, Tradition, and Archives of Israel and Judah*. Translated by P. Kurtz. Oxford: Oxford University Press, 2016.

Kurke, Leslie. "Plato, Aesop, and the Beginnings of Mimetic Prose." *Representations* 94 (2006): 6–52.

Kurtz, Paul. "Axes of Inquiry: The Problem of Form and Time in Wellhausen and Gunkel." *SJOT* 29.2 (2015): 247–95.

———. "Waiting at Nemi: Wellhausen, Gunkel, and the World behind their Work." *HTR* 109.4 (2016): 567–85.

L'Heureux, Conrad. "The *yᵉlîdê hārāpā*—a Cultic Association of Warriors." *BASOR* 221 (1976): 83–85.

Langdon, Susan. *Art and Identity in Dark Age Greece: 1100–700 BC*. Cambridge: Cambridge University Press, 2008.

Lehmann, Gunnar. "The United Monarchy in the Countryside: Jerusalem, Judah, and the Shephelah during the Tenth Century B. C. E." Pp. 117–63 in *Jerusalem in Bible and Archaeology: The First Temple Period*. Edited by A. Vaughn and A. Killebrew. Atlanta: SBL, 2003.

Lehmann, Gunnar, and Hermann Michael Niemann. "When Did the Shephelah Become Judahite?" *TA* 41 (2014): 77–94.

Lemaire, André. *Les Écoles et la formation de la Bible dans l'ancien Israël*. Fribourg: Éditions Universitaires, 1981.

———. "Hazaël de Damas, roi d'Aram." Pp. 91–108 in *Marchands, Diplomates et Empereurs: Études sur la Civilisation Mésopotamienne Offertes à Paul Garelli.* Edited by D. Charpand and F. Joannès. Paris: Éditions Recherche sure les Civilisations, 1991.

———. "Levantine Literacy ca. 1000–750 BCE." Pp. 11–46 in *Contextualizing Israel's Sacred Writings: Ancient Literacy, Orality, and Literary Production.* Edited by B. Schmidt. Atlanta: SBL Press, 2015.

———. "La stèle de Mésha et l'histoire de l'ancien Israël." Pp. 143–69 in *Storia e tradizioni di Israele: scritti in anore di J. Alberto Soggin.* Edited by D. Garrone and F. Israel. Brescia: Paidcill, 1991.

Lemche, Nils Peter. "The Origin of the Israelite State: A Copenhagen Perspective on the Emergence of Critical Historical Studies of Ancient Israel in Recent Times." *SJOT* 12 (1998): 44–63.

Leuchter, Mark. "The Rhetoric of Convention: The Foundational Saul Narratives (1 Sam 9-11) Reconsidered." *Journal of Religious History* 40.1 (2016): 3–19.

———. "The Sociolinguistic and Rhetorical Implications of the Source Citations in Kings." Pp. 119–34 in *Soundings in Kings: Perspectives and Methods in Contemporary Scholarship.* Edited by M. Leuchter and K. P. Adam. Minneapolis: Fortress, 2010.

Leveen, Adriane. *Memory and Tradition in the Book of Numbers.* Cambridge: Cambridge University Press, 2008.

Levin, Yigal. "The Identification of Khirbet Qeiyafa: A New Suggestion." *BASOR* 367 (2012): 73–86.

———. "Philistine Gath in the Biblical Record." Pp. 141–52 in *Tell es Safi/Gath I: The 1996–2005 Seasons, Part I: Texts.* Edited by A. Maeir. Wiesbaden: Harrassowitz Verlag, 2012.

Levy, Thomas. "Ethnic identity in Biblical Edom, Israel and Midian: Some Insights from Mortuary Contexts in the Lowlands of Edom." Pp. 251–61 in *Exploring the Longue Durée: Essays in Honor of Lawrence E. Stager.* Edited by D. Schloen. Winona Lake: Eisenbrauns, 2008.

Levy, Thomas, and Mohammed Najjar. "Some Thoughts on Khirbet En-Nahas, Edom, Biblical History and Anthropology: A Response to Israel Finkelstein." *TA* 33.1 (2006): 3–17.

Levy, Thomas, Thomas Higham, Christopher Bronk Ramsey, Neil Smith, Erez Ben-Yosef, Mark Robinson, Stefan Münger, Kyle Knabb, Jürgen Schulze, Mohammad Najjar and Lisa Tauxe. "High-Precision Radiocarbon Dating and Historical Biblical Archaeology in Southern Jordan." *Proceedings of the National Academy of Sciences* 105 (2008): 16460–65.

Levy, Thomas, Russell Adams, Mohammad Najjar, Andreas Hauptmann, James. Anderson, Baruch Brandl, Mark Robinson, and Thomas Higham. "Reassessing the Chronology of Biblical Edom: New Excavations and C^{14} Dates from Khirbat en-Nahas (Jordan)." *Antiquity* 78 (2004): 865–79.

Levy, Thomas, Mohammed Najjar, and Erez Ben-Josef. "Conclusion." Pp. 977–1001 in *New Insights into the Iron Age Archaeology of Edom, Southern Jordan*. Edited by T. Levy, M. Najjar and E. Ben-Yosef. Los Angeles: Cotsen Institute of Archaeology, 2014.

Levy, Thomas, Mohammad Najjar, Thomas Higham, Yoav Arbel, Adolfo Muniz, Erez Ben-Yosef, Neil Smith, Marc Beherec, Aaron Gidding, Ian Jones, Daniel Frese, Craig Smitheram, and Mark Robinson. "Excavations at Khirbet en-Nahas 2002–2009." Pp. 89–246 in *New Insights into the Iron Age Archaeology of Edom, Southern Jordan*. Edited by Levy, Najjar, and Ben-Yosef. Los Angeles: Cotsen Institute of Archaeology, 2014.

Levy, Thomas, Mohammed Najjar, and Erez Ben-Josef. "The Iron Age Edom Lowlands Regional Archaeology Project." Pp. 1–88 in *New Insights into the Iron Age Archaeology of Edom, Southern Jordan*. Edited by T. Levy, M. Najjar, and E. Ben-Yosef. Los Angeles: Cotsen Institute of Archaeology, 2014.

Levy, Thomas, Erez Ben-Josef, and Mohammed Najjar. "New perspectives on Iron Age copper production and society in the Faynan Region, Jordan." Pp. 197–214 in *Eastern Mediterranean Metallurgy and Metalwork in the Second Millennium BC*. Edited by V. Kassianidou and G. Papasavvas. Oxford: Oxbow, 2012.

Levy, Thomas, Mohammed Najjar, Johannes van der Plicht, Hendrik Bruins, and Thomas Higham. "Lowland Edom and the High and Low Chronologies." Pp. 129– 63 in *The Bible and Radiocarbon Dating: Archaeology, Text and Science*. Edited by T. Levy and T. Higham. London: Equinox, 2005.

Linafelt, Tod. *The Hebrew Bible as Literature: A Very Short Introduction*. Oxford: Oxford University Press, 2016.

Lipschits, Oded, Yuval Gadot, and Manfred Oeming. "Tel Azekah 113 Years After: Preliminary Evaluation of the Renewed Excavations at the Site." *NEA* 75.4 (2012): 196–207.

Liverani, Mario. *Israel's History and the History of Israel*. Translated by C. Peri and P. Davies. London: Equinox, 2005.

Lloyd, Alan. "Book II." Pp. 219–378 in *A Commentary on Herodotus: Books I-IV*. Edited by O. Murray and A. Moreno. Oxford: Oxford University Press, 2007.

Loraux, Nicole. *The Divided City: On Memory and Forgetting in Ancient Athens*. New York: Zone, 1995.

Lord, Albert. *Singer of Tales*. Cambridge: Harvard University Press, 1960.

Luraghi, Nino. *The Ancient Messenians: Constructions of Ethnicity and Memory*. Cambridge: Cambridge University Press, 2008.

———. "Becoming Messenian." *Journal of Hellenic Studies* 122 (2002): 45–69.

———. "Local Knowledge in Herodotus' *Histories*." Pp. 138–61 in *The Historian's Craft in the Age of Herodotus*. Edited by N. Luraghi; Oxford: Oxford University Press, 2001.

———. "The Stories before the *Histories:* Folktale and Traditional Narrative in Herodotus." Pp. 87–112 in *Herodotus: Volume I.* Edited by R. Munson. Oxford: Oxford University Press, 2013.

Machinist, Peter. "Assyria and Its Image in the First Isaiah." *JAOS* 103.4 (1983): 719–37.

———. "Biblical Traditions: The Philistines and Israelite History." Pp. 53–84 in *The Sea Peoples and Their World: A Reassessment.* Edited by E. Oren. Philadelphia: University of Pennsylvania Press, 2000.

———. "The Voice of the Historian in the Ancient Near Eastern and Mediterranean World." *Interpretation* 57.2 (2003): 117–37.

Maeir, Aren. "The Historical Background and Dating of Amos VI 2: An Archaeological from Tell eṣ-Ṣâfi/Gath." *VT* 54.3 (2004): 319–34.

———. "History of Research: 1838–1996." Pp. 89–108 in *Tell es Safi/Gath I: The 1996–2005 Seasons, Part I: Texts.* Edited by A. Maeir. Wiesbaden: Harrassowitz Verlag, 2012.

———. "Insights on the Philistine Culture and Related Issues: An Overview of 15 years of Work at Tell eṣ-Ṣafi/Gath." Pp. 345–404 in *The Ancient Near East in the 12th–10th Centuries BCE: Culture and History.* Edited by G. Galil, A. Gilboa, A. Maeir, and D. Kahn. Münster: Ugarit Verlag, 2012.

———. "Khirbet Qeiyafa in Its Regional Context: A View from Philistine Gath." Pp. 61–71 in *Khirbet Qeiyafa in the Shephelah.* Edited by S. Schroer and S. Münger. Fribourg: Academic Press, 2017.

———. "Philistia and the Judean Shephelah After Hazael: The Power Play Between the Philistines, Judeans and Assyrians in the 8th Century BCE in Light of the Excavations at Tell es-Safi/Gath." Pp. 241–62 in *Disaster and Relief Management - Katastrophen und ihre Bewältigung.* Edited by A. Berlejung. Tübingen: Mohr Siebeck, 2012.

———. "Philistine Gath after 20 Years: Regional perspectives on the Iron Age at Tell es-Safi/Gath." Pp. 133–53 in *The Shephelah during the Iron Age: Recent Archaeological Studies.* Edited by O. Lipschits and A. M. Maeir. Winona Lake: Eisenbrauns, 2017.

———. "The Rephaim in Iron Age Philistia: Evidence of a Multi-Generational Family?" Pp. 289–97 in *"Vom Leben umfangen": Ägypten, das Alte Testament und das Gespräch der Religionen Gedenkschrift für Manfred Görg.* Edited by S. Wimmer and G. Gafus. Münster: Ugarit Verlag, 2014.

———. "The Tell es Safi/Gath Archaeological Project 1996–2010: Introduction, Overview, and Synopsis of Results." Pp. 1–88 in *Tell es Safi/Gath I: The 1996—2005 Seasons, Part I: Texts.* Edited by A. Maier. Wiesbaden: Harrassowitz Verlag, 2012.

Maeir, Aren, and Esther Eshel. "Four Short Alphabetic Inscriptions from Late Iron Age IIa Tell es-Safi/Gath and their Implications for the Development of Literacy in Iron Age Philistia and Environs." Pp. 69–88 in *"See, I will bring a scroll recounting what befell me" (Ps 40:8): Epigraphy and Daily Life from the Bible to the Talmud: Dedicated to the Memory of Professor Hanan Eshel*. Göttingen: Vandenhoek & Ruprecht, 2014.

Maeir, Aren, and Louise Hitchcock. "Absence Makes the *Hearth* Grow Fonder: Searching for the Origins of the Philistine hearth." *Er-Isr* 30 (2011): 46–64.

———. "'And the Canaanite was Then in the Land'? A Critical View of the 'Canaanite Enclave' in Iron I Southern Canaan." Pp. 209–26 in *Alphabets, Texts and Artifacts in the Ancient Near East: Studies Presented to Benjamin Sass*. Edited by I. Finkelstein, T. Römer, and C. Robin. Paris: Van Dieren, 2016.

Maeir, Aren, and Joe Uziel. "A Tale of Two Tells: A Comparative Perspective on Tel Miqne-Ekron and Tell es Safi/Gath in Light of Recent Archaeological Research." Pp. 29–42 in *'Up to the Gates of Ekron:' Essays on the Archaeology and History of the Eastern Mediterranean in Honor of Seymour Gitin*. Edited by S. Crawford and A. Ben-Tor. Jerusalem: Israel Exploration Society, 2007.

Maeir, Aren, Louise Hitchcock, and Liora Kolska Horwitz. "On the Constitution and Transformation of Philistine Identity." *OJA* 32.1 (2013): 1–38.

Maeir, Aren, Brent Davis, Liora Kolska Horwitz, Yotam Asscher, and Louise Hitchcock. "An Ivory Bowl from Early Iron Age Tell es-Safi/Gath (Israel): Manufacture, Meaning and Memory." *World Archaeology* 47.3 (2015): 414–38.

Maeir, Aren, Stefan Wimmer, Alexander Zukerman, and Aaron Demsky. "A Late Iron Age I/Early Iron Age IIA Old Canaanite Inscription from Tell eṣ-Ṣâfi/Gath, Israel." *BASOR* 351 (2008): 39–71.

Malafouris, Lambros. *How Things Shape the Mind: A Theory of Material Engagement*. Cambridge: MIT Press, 2013.

Malpas, Jeff. *Place and Experience: A Philosophical Topography*. Cambridge: Cambridge University Press, 2007.

Marom, Nimrod, Noa Raban-Gestel, Amihai Mazar, and Guy Bar-Oz. "Backbone of Society: Evidence for Social and Economic Status of the Iron Age Population of Tel Reḥov, Beth Shean Valley, Israel." *BASOR* 354 (2009): 55–75.

Master, Daniel. "The Renewal of Trade at Iron Age I Ashkelon." *Er-Isr* 28 (2011): 111–22.

———. "Trade and Politics: Ashkelon's Balancing Act in the Seventh Century B. C. E." *BASOR* 330 (2003): 47–64.

Mazar, Amihai. "Archaeology and the Biblical Narrative: The Case of the United Monarchy." Pp. 29–58 in *One God—One Cult—One Nation: Archaeological and Biblical Perspectives*. Edited by R. Kratz and H. Spieckermann. Berlin: De Gruyter, 2010.

———. "Archaeology and the Bible: Reflections on Historical Memory in the Deuteronomistic History." Pp. 347–69 in *Congress Volume Munich 2013*. Edited by C. Maier. Leiden: Brill, 2014.

———. "The Debate over the Chronology of the Iron Age in the Southern Levant: Its History, the Current Situation, and a Suggested Resolution." Pp. 15–30 in *The Bible and Radiocarbon Dating*. Edited by T. Highman and T. Levy. London: Equinox, 2005.

———. "Excavations at Tell Qasile, 1982–1984: Preliminary Report." *IEJ* 36 (1986): 1–15.

———. *Excavations at Tell Qasile, Part One*. Jerusalem: Hebrew University, 1980.

———. *Excavations at Tell Qasile, Part Two*. Jerusalem: Hebrew University, 1985.

———. "The Iron Age Chronology Debate: Is the Gap Narrowing?" *NEA* 74.2 (2011): 105–11.

———. "Iron Age Dwellings at Tell Qasile." Pp. 319–36 in *Exploring the Longue Durée: Essays in Honor of Lawrence E. Stager*. Edited by D. Schloen. Winona Lake: Eisenbrauns, 2009.

———. "The Ladder of Time at Tel Rehov: Stratigraphy, Archaeological Context, Pottery and Radiocarbon dates." Pp. 193–255 in *The Bible and Radiocarbon Dating*. Edited by T. Levy. London: Equinox, 2005.

———. "Qasile, Tell." Pp. 1207–1212 in *NEAEHL*. Volume 4. Edited by E. Stern. Jerusalem: Israel Exploration Society, 1993.

———. "Rehov, Tel." Pp. 2013–18 in *NEAEHL*. Volume 5. Edited by E. Stern. Jerusalem: Israel Exploration Society, 1993.

———. "Rehob." Pp. 221–30 in *The Oxford Encyclopedia of Bible and Archaeology*. Edited by D. Master. New York: Oxford University Press, 2013.

———. "Religious Practices and Cult Objects during the Iron Age IIA at Tel Rehov and Their Implications Regarding Religion in Northern Israel.", *Hebrew Bible and Ancient Israel* 4 (2015): 22–55.

———. "Tel Beth-Shean: History and Archaeology." Pp. 239–71 in *One God—One Cult—One Nation: Archaeological and Biblical Perspectives*. Edited by R. Kratz and H. Spieckermann. Berlin: de Gruyter, 2010.

———. "Tel Rehov in the Assyrian Period: Squatters, Burials, and a Hebrew Seal." Pp. 265–80 in *The Fire Signals of Lachish: Studies in the Archaeology and History of Israel in the Late Bronze Age, Iron Age, and Persian Period in Honor of David Ussishkin*. Edited by N. Na'aman and I. Finkelstein. Winona Lake: Eisenbrauns, 2011.

Mazar, Amihai, and Nina Panitz-Cohen. "It is the Land of Honey: Beekeeping at Tel Rehov." *NEA* 70.4 (2007): 202–19.

Mazar, Amihai, and Shmuel Ahituv. "Inscriptions from Tel Rehob and Their Contribution to the Study of Writing and Literacy During the Iron Age IIA." *Er-Isr* 30 (2011): 300–16.

Mazar, Benjamin. "En Gedi." Pp. 401–03 in *NEAEHL*. Volume 2. Edited by E. Stern. Jerusalem: Israel Exploration Society, 1993.

———. "The Excavations at Tell Qasile." *IEJ* 1 (1950–1951): 61–76; 125–40; 194–218.

———. "Gath and Gittaim." *IEJ* 4 (1954): 227–35.

———. "The Stratification of Tell Abu Hawam on the Bay of Acre." *BASOR* 124 (1951): 21–25.

Mazar, Eilat. *The Palace of King David: Excavations at the Summit of the City of David: Preliminary Report of Seasons 2005–2007*. Jerusalem: Shoham Academic Research and Publication, 2009.

———. *Preliminary Report on The City of David Excavations 2005 at the Visitors Center Area*. Jerusalem: Shalem Press, 2007.

———. *The Summit of the City of David Excavations 2005–2008*. Volume I. Jerusalem: Shoham, 2015.

Mazar, Eilat, David Ben-Shlomo, and Shmuel Ahituv. "An Inscribed Pithos from the Ophel, Jerusalem." *IEJ* 63.1 (2013): 39–49.

Mazzoni, Stefania. "Crisis and Change: The Beginning of the Iron Age in Syria." Pp. 1043–60 in *Proceedings of the First International Congress on the Archaeology of the Ancient Near East*. Edited by P. Matthiae. Rome: Universita degli Studi di Roma, 2000.

McAdams, Robert, and Hans Nissen. *The Uruk Countryside: The Natural Setting of Urban Societies*. Chicago: University of Chicago Press, 1973.

McCarter, P. Kyle. "The Apology of David." *JBL* 99.4 (1980): 489–504.

———."The Historical David." *Interpretation* 40.2 (1986): 117–19.

———. *I Samuel*. New Haven: Yale University Press, 1980

———. *II Samuel*. Garden City: Doubleday, 1984.

McCarter, P. Kyle, Shlomo Bunimovitz, and Zvi Lederman. "An Archaic Baʿl Inscription from Tel Beth-Shemesh." *TA* 38 (2011): 179–93.

McKinny, Chris. *My People as Your People: A Textual and Archaeological Analysis of the Reign of Jehoshaphat*. New York: Peter Lang, 2016.

Meadows, A. R. "Pausanias and the Historiography of Classical Sparta." *The Classical Quarterly* 45.1 (1995): 92–113.

Megill, Allan. *Historical Knowledge, Historical Error: A Contemporary Guide to Practice*. Chicago: University of Chicago Press.

Michaelian, Kourken *Mental Time Travel: Episodic Memory and our Knowledge of a Personal Past*. Cambridge: MIT Press, 2016.

Millard, Alan. "In Praise of Ancient Scribes." *BA* 45.3 (1983): 143–53.

———. "Only Fragments of the Past: The Role of Accident in Our Knowledge of the Ancient Near East." Pp. 301–19 in *Writing and Ancient Near Eastern Society: Papers in Honour of Alan Millard*. Berlin: de Gruyter, 2005.

———. "Scripts and Their Uses in the Twelfth–Tenth Centuries B.C.E." Pp. 405–12 in *The Ancient Near East in the Twelfth–Tenth Centuries B.C.E.* Edited by G. Galil, A. Gilboa, and A. Maeir. Münster: Ugarit, 2012.

Miller, Max. "The Moabite Stone as a Memorial Stela." *PEQ* 106.1 (1974): 9–18.

Miller, Robert. *Oral Tradition in Ancient Israel*. Eugene: Cascade Books, 2011.

———. "The Performance of Oral Tradition in Ancient Israel." Pp. 175–96 in *Contextualizing Israel's Sacred Writings: Ancient Literacy, Orality, and Literary Production*. Edited by B. Schmidt. Atlanta: SBL, 2015.

Minchin, Elizabeth. Homer and the Resources of Memory: Some Applications of Cognitive Theory to the Iliad and Odyssey. Oxford: Oxford University Press, 2001.

Misgav, Haggai, Yosef Garfinkel, and Sa'ar Ganor. "The Ostracon." Pp. 243–57 in *Khirbet Qeiyafa: Vol I. Excavation Report 2007–2008*. Edited by Y. Garfinkel and S. Ganor. Jerusalem: Israel Exploration Society, 2009.

Milstein, Sara. *Tracking the Master Scribe: Revision through Introduction in Biblical and Mesopotamian Literature*. Oxford: Oxford University Press, 2016.

Moles, John. "Ἀνάθημα καὶ κτῆμα: The Inscriptional Inheritance of Ancient Historiography." *Histos* 3 (1999): 44–53.

Momigliano, Arnaldo. "Ancient History and the Antiquarian." *Journal of the Warburg and Courtauld Institutes* 13 (1950): 285–315.

———. "The Historians of the Classical World and Their Audiences: Some Suggestions." Pp. 361–76 in *Sesto contributo alla storia degli studi classici e del mondo antico*. Volume 1. Roma: Edizioni di storia e letteratura, 1980.

———. "Historiography on Written Tradition and Historiography on Oral Tradition." Pp. 211–20 in *Studies in Historiography*. London: Weidenfeld & Nicolson, 1966.

Moran, William. *The Amarna Letters*. Baltimore: Johns Hopkins University Press, 1992.

———. "Gilgamesh." Pp. 557–60 in *The Encyclopedia of Religion*. Edited by M. Eliade. New York: MacMillan, 1987.

———. "The Syrian Scribe of the Jerusalem Amarna Letters." Pp. 146–68 in *Amarna Studies: Collected Writings*. Edited by J. Heuhnergard and S. Izre'el. Winona Lake: Eisenbrauns, 2003.

Morrison, James. "Memory, Time, and Writing: Oral and Literary Aspects of Thucydides' *History*." Pp. 95–116 in *Oral Performance and its Context*. Edited by C. J. Mackie. Leiden: Brill, 2004.

Morrison, John, John Coates, and Boris Rankov. *The Athenian Trireme: The History and Reconstruction of the Ancient Greek Warship*. 2nd edition. Cambridge: Cambridge University Press, 2000.

Mroczek, Eva. *The Literary Imagination in Jewish Antiquity*. Oxford: Oxford University Press, 2016.

Münger, Stefan, and Thomas E. Levy. "The Iron Age Egyptian Amulet Assemblage." Pp. 740–65 in *New Insights into the Iron Age Archaeology of Edom, Southern Jordan*. Edited by T. Levy, M. Najjar and E. Ben-Yosef. Los Angeles: Cotsen Institute of Archaeology, 2014.

Murray, Oswyn. "Herodotus and Oral History." Pp. 16–44 in *The Historian's Craft in the Age of Herodotus*. Edited by N. Luraghi. Oxford: Oxford University Press, 2001.

Bibliography

———."Herodotus and Oral History Reconsidered." Pp. 314–25 in *The Historian's Craft in the Age of Herodotus*. Edited by N. Luraghi. Oxford: Oxford University Press, 2001.

Na'aman, Nadav. "Aribua and the Patina-Hamath Border." *Orientalia* 71.3 (2002): 291–95.

———. "Biblical and Historical Jerusalem in the Tenth and Fifth–Fourth Centuries BCE." *Bib* 93 (2012): 21–42.

———. "The 'Conquest of Canaan' in the Book of Joshua and in History." Pp. 218–81 in *From Nomadism to Monarchy: Archaeological and Historical Aspects of Early Israel*. Edited by I. Finkelstein and N. Na'aman. Jerusalem: Israel Exploration Society, 1994.

———. "The Date of the List of Towns that Received the Spoil of Amalek (1 Sam 30:26–31)." *TA* 37 (2010): 175–87.

———. "David's Sojourn in Keilah in Light of the Amarna Letters." *VT* 60 (2010): 87–97.

———. "Hezekiah's Fortified Cities and the LMLK Stamps." *BASOR* 261 (1986): 5–21.

———. "Ḥirbet ed-Dāwwara—A Philistine Stronghold on the Benjamin Desert Fringe." *ZDPV* 128 (2012): 1–9.

———. "The Inheritance of the Sons of Simeon." *ZDPV* 96.2 (1980): 136–52.

———. "In Search of the Reality Behind the Account of David's Wars with Israel's Neighbours." *IEJ* 52.2 (2002): 200–24.

———. "Ittai the Gittite." *BN* 94 (1998): 22–25.

———."The Judahite Temple at Tel Moza near Jerusalem: The House of Obed-Edom?" *TA* 44 (2017): 3–13.

———. "Khirbet Qeiyafa in Context." *UF* 42 (2010): 497–526.

———. "The Kingdom of Judah in the 9th century BCE: Text Analysis Versus Archaeological Research." *TA* 40 (2013): 247–76.

———. "The Kingdom of Judah under Josiah." *TA* 18.1 (1991): 3–71.

———. "Memories of Canaan in the Old Testament." *UF* 47 (2016): 129–46.

———. "The Northern Kingdom in the Late Tenth-Ninth Centuries BCE." Pp. 399–418 in *Understanding the History of Ancient Israel*. Edited by H. Williamson. London: British Academy, 2007.

———. "Population Changes in Palestine Following Assyrian Deportations." *TA* 20 (1993): 104–24.

———. "Royal Inscriptions and the Histories of Joash and Ahaz, Kings of Judah." *VT* 48 (1998): 333–49.

———. "Saul, Benjamin, and the Emergence of 'Biblical Israel,' Part II." *ZAW* 121 (2009): 342–48.

———. "Sources and Composition in the History of David." Pp. 170–86 in *The Origins of the Ancient Israelite States*. Edited by V. Fritz and P. Davies. Sheffield: Sheffield University Press, 1996.

———. "Sources and Composition in the History of Solomon." Pp. 57–80 in *The Age of Solomon: Scholarship at the Turn of the Millennium*. Edited by L. Handy. Leiden: Brill, 1997.

———. "The Shephelah According to the Amarna Letters." Pp. 281–300 *in The Fire Signals of Lachish: Studies in the Archaeology and History of Israel in the Late Bronze Age, Iron Age, and Persian Period in Honor of David Ussishkin*. Edited by I. Finkelstein and N. Na'aman. Winona Lake: Eisenbrauns, 2011.

———. "Three Notes on the Aramaic Inscription from Tel Dan." *IEJ* 50 (2000): 92–104.

———. "Was Khirbet Qeiyafa a Judahite City? The Case Against it." *JHS* 17.7 (2017): 1–40.

Nagy, Gregory. "Herodotus the *Logios*." *Arethusa* 20 (1987): 175–84.

Namdar, Dvory, Alexander Zukerman, Aren Maeir, Jill Citron Katz, Dan Cabanes, Clive Trueman, Ruth Shahack-Gross, and Steve Weiner. "The 9th Century BCE Destruction Layer at Tell es-Safi/Gath, Israel: Integrating Macro- and Microarchaeology." *Journal of Archaeological Science* 38.12 (2011): 3471–82.

Naveh, Joseph. *Early History of the Alphabet: An Introduction to West Semitic Epigraphy and Palaeography*. Jerusalem: Magnes, 1997.

Nicolai, Roberto. "The Place of History in the Ancient World." Pp. 13–26 in *A Companion to Greek and Roman Historiography*. Volume 1. Edited by J. Marincola. Malden: Blackwell, 2007.

———. "Thucydides' Archaeology: Between Epic and Oral Traditions." Pp. 263–85 in *The Historian's Craft in the Age of Herodotus*. Edited by N. Luraghi. Oxford: Oxford University Press, 2001.

Niditch, Susan. "Hebrew Bible and Oral Literature: Misconceptions and New Directions." Pp. 1–18 in *The Interface of Orality and Writing: Speaking, Seeing, Writing in the Shaping of New Genres*. Edited by A. Weissenrieder and R. Coote. Tübingen: Mohr Siebeck, 2015.

———. *Oral World and Written Word: Ancient Israelite Literature*. Louisville: Westminster John Knox, 1996.

Nielsen, Eduard. *Oral Tradition: A Modern Problem in Old Testament Introduction*. London: SCM Press, 1954.

Niemann, Hermann Michael. "Neighbors and Foes, Rivals and Kin: Philistines, Shepheleans, Judeans between Geography and Economy, History and Theology." Pp. 243–64 in *The Philistines and Other "Sea Peoples" in Text and Archaeology*. Edited by A. Killebrew and G. Lehmann. Atlanta: SBL Press, 2013.

Niemann, Hermann Michael, and Gunnar Lehmann. "Zwischen Wüste und Mittelmeer: Qubur al-Walaydah und seine Umgebung in Südwest-Palästina." *Die Welt des Orients* 40.2 (2010): 216–43.

Nietzsche, Friedrich. "On the Uses and Disadvantages of a History for Life." Pp. 57–124 in *Untimely Meditations*. Edited by D. Breazeale. Cambridge: Cambridge University Press, 1997.

Noth, Martin. *The Deuteronomistic History*. 2nd edition. Translated by J. Doull and J. Barton. Sheffield: JSOT Press, 1991.

Nyberg, Henrik. "Das textkritische Problem des Alten Testaments, am Hoseabuche demonstriert." *ZAW* 52 (1934): 241–54.

O'Brien O'Keeffe, Katherine. "The Performative Body on the Oral-Literate Continuum: Old English Poetry." Pp. 46–58 in *Teaching Oral Traditions*. Edited by J. Foley. New York: MLA, 1998.

Ofer, Avi. "'All the Hill Country of Judah': From a Settlement Fringe to a Prosperous Monarchy." Pp. 92–121 *From Nomadism to Monarchy: Archaeological and Historical Aspects of Early Israel*. Edited by I. Finkelstein and N. Na'aman. Jerusalem: Israel Exploration Society, 1994.

———."Hebron." Pp. 606–09 in *NEAEHL*. Volume 2. Edited by E. Stern. Jerusalem: Israel Exploration Society, 1993.

Olivier, Roy. *Holy Ignorance: When Religion and Culture Part Ways*. Oxford: Oxford University Press, 2014.

Ong, Walter. *Orality and Literacy*. London: Routledge, 1982.

———. "Oral Residue in Tudor Prose Style." *PMLA* 80.3 (1965): 145–54.

Oren, Eliezer. "Ethnicity and Regional Archaeology: The Western Negev Under Assyrian Rule." Pp. 102–05 in *Biblical Archaeology Today, 1990*. Edited by A. Biran and J. Naveh. Jerusalem: Israel Exploration Society, 1993.

———. "Haror, Tel." Pp. 580–84 in *NEAEHL*. Volume 2. Edited by E. Stern. Jerusalem: Israel Exploration Society, 1993.

———. "Sera', Tel." Pp. 1329–35 in *NEAEHL*. Volume 4. Edited by E. Stern. Jerusalem: Israel Exploration Society, 1993.

———. "Ziglag: A Biblical City on the Edge of the Negeb." *BA* 45.3 (1982): 155–66.

Osborne, Robin. "Archaic Greek History." Pp. 497–520 in *Brill's Companion to Herodotus*. Edited by E. Bakker, I. de Jong, H. van Wees. Leiden: Brill, 2002.

———. *Greece in the Making: 1200—479 BC*. 2nd edition. London: Routledge, 2009.

———. "Relics and Remains in an Ancient Greek World Full of Anthropomorphic Gods." *Past and Present* 206 (2010): 56–72.

Óskarsdóttir, Svanhildur (ed.), *Egil's Saga*. Translated by B. Scudder. New York: Penguin, 2002.

Panitz-Cohen, Nava, and Amihai Mazar (eds.). *Excavations at Tel Beth-Shean 1989–1996, Volume III: The 13th-11th Centuries BCE (Areas S and N)*. Jerusalem: Israel Exploration Society, 2009.

Panitz-Cohen, Nava, Robert Mullins, and Ruhama Bonfil. "Northern Exposure: Launching Excavations at Tell Abil el-Qameḥ (Abel Beth Maacah)." *Strata* 31 (2013): 27–42.

Parker, Simon. *The Pre-Biblical Narrative Tradition: Essays on the Ugaritic Poems Keret and Aqhat*. Atlanta: Scholars Press, 1989.

Pennebaker, James, and Amy Gonzales. "Making History: Social and Psychological Processes Underlying Collective Memory." Pp. 171–93 in *Memory in Mind and*

Culture. Edited by P. Boyer and J. Wertsch. Cambridge: Cambridge University Press, 2009.

Perdue, Leo. (ed.). *Scribes, Sages, and Seers: The Sage in the Eastern Mediterranean World*. Göttingen: Vandenhoeck & Ruprecht, 2008.

Person, Raymond. "Biblical Historiography as Traditional History." Pp. 73–83 in *The Oxford Handbook of Biblical Narrative*. Edited by D. Fewell. Oxford: Oxford University Press, 2016.

———. *The Deuteronomistic History and the Book of Chronicles: Scribal Works in an Oral World*. Leiden: Brill, 2010.

———. *The Deuteronomic School: History, Social Setting, and Literature*. Atlanta: SBL Press, 2002.

———. "The Role of Memory in the Tradition Represented by the Deuteronomistic History and the Book of Chronicles." *Oral Tradition* 26.2 (2011): 537–50.

———. "Scribe as Performer." *JBL* 117.4 (1998): 601–09.

Pioske, Daniel. *David's Jerusalem: Between Memory and History*. New York: Routledge, 2015.

———. "Material Culture and Making Visible: On the Portrayal of Philistine Gath in the Book of Samuel." (forthcoming).

———. "Memory and its Materiality: The Case of Early Iron Age Jerusalem and Khirbet Qeiyafa." *ZAW* 127.1 (2015): 78–95.

———. "Mizpah and the Possibilities of Forgetting." Pp. 245–57 in *Memory and the City in Ancient Israel*. Edited by D. Edelman and E. Ben Zvi. Winona Lake: Eisenbrauns, 2014.

———. "Prose Writing in an Age of Orality: A Study of 2 Sam 5:6–9." *VT* 66.2 (2016): 261–79.

———. "Retracing a Remembered Past: Methodological Remarks on Memory, History, and the Hebrew Bible." *Bib Int* 23.3 (2015): 291–315.

Polak, Frank. "The Book of Samuel and the Deuteronomist: A Syntactic-Stylistic Analysis." Pp. 34–73 in *Die Samuelbücher und die Deuteronomisten*. Edited by C. Schäfer-Lichtenberger. Stuttgart: Kohlhammer, 2010.

———. "Book, Scribe, and Bard: Oral Discourse and Written Text in Recent Biblical Scholarship." *Prooftexts* 31 (2011): 118–40.

———. "The Discourse Structure of the Mesha Inscription: 'I-Style,' Intonation Units, and Oral Performance." Pp. 407–27 in *Marbeh Hokmah: Studies in the Bible and the Ancient Near East in Loving Memory of Victor Avigdor Hurowitz*. Edited by S. Yona. Winona Lake: Eisenbrauns, 2015.

———. "Epic Formulas in Biblical Narrative: Frequency and Distribution." Pp. 435–88 in *Actes du Second Colloque International "Bible et Informatique: Méthodes, Outils, Résultats" (Jérusalem 9–13 Juin 1988)* Edited by R. F. Poswick. Geneva: Slatkine, 1989.

———. "The Oral and the Written: Syntax, Stylistics and the Development of Biblical Prose Narrative." *JNES* 26 (1998): 59–105.

———. "Style is More than the Person: Sociolinguistics, Literary Culture and the Distinction Between Written and Oral Narrative." Pp. 38–103 in *Biblical Hebrew: Studies in Chronology and Typology*. Edited by I. Young. London: T&T Clark, 2003.

Pollock, Sheldon. "The Cosmopolitan Vernacular." *The Journal of Asian Studies* 57.1 (1998): 6–37.

———. "India in the Vernacular Millennium: Literary Culture and Polity 1000—1500." *Daedalus* 127.3 (1998): 41–74.

———. *The Language of the Gods in the World of Men: Sanskrit, Culture, and Power in Premodern India*. Berkeley: University of California Press, 2006.

———. "Pretextures of Time." *History and Theory* 46 (2007): 366–83.

Porter, James. "Ideals and Ruins: Pausanias, Longinus, and the Second Sophistic." Pp. 63–92 *Pausanias: Travel and Memory in Roman Greece*. Edited by S. Alcock, J. Cherry, and J. Elsner. Oxford: Oxford University Press, 2001.

Powell, Barry. *Homer and the Origin of the Greek Alphabet*. Cambridge: Cambridge University Press, 1991.

———. "Homer and Writing." Pp. 3–33 in *A New Companion to Homer*. Edited by I. Morris and B. Powell. Leiden: Brill, 1997.

Powell, J. Enoch. *The History of Herodotus*. Cambridge: Cambridge University Press, 1939.

Pretzler, Maria. *Pausanias: Travel Writing in Ancient Greece*. London: Duckworth, 2007.

———. "Pausanias and Oral Tradition." *Classical Quarterly* 55 (2005): 235–49.

Pritchett, W. Kendrick. *Pausanias Periegetes*. Volume II. Amsterdam: J. C. Gieben, 1999.

Provan, Iain, V. Philips Long, and Tremper Longman III. *A Biblical History of Israel*. Louisville: Westminster John Knox, 2003.

Rainey, Anson. *Canaanite in the Amarna Tablets: A Linguistic Analysis of the Mixed Dialect Used by the Scribes from Canaan*. Volume 2. Leiden: Brill, 1996.

———. "The Northwest Semitic Literary Repertoire and its Acquaintances by Judean Writers." *Maarav* 15.2 (2010): 193–206.

———. "Publish it Not as Gath." *IEJ* 54.1 (2004): 100–104.

———. "Syntax, Hermeneutics and History." *IEJ* 48 (1998): 239–51.

———. "Ziklag." Pp. 984–85 in *Interpreters Dictionary of the Bible Supplement*. Edited by K. Crim. Nashville: Abingdon, 1976.

Rainey, Anson, and Steve Notley. *The Sacred Bridge*. Jerusalem: Carta, 2006.

Redford, Donald. *Akhenaten: The Heretic King*. Princeton: Princeton University Press, 1984.

———. "Scribe and Speaker." Pp. 171–202 in *Writing and Speech in Israelite and Ancient Near Eastern Prophecies*. Edited by E. Ben Zvi and M. Floyd. Atlanta: SBL, 2000.

Reich, Ronny, and Eli Shukron. "A Fragmentary Palaeo-Hebrew Inscription from the City of David, Jerusalem." *IEJ* 58 (2008): 48–50.

Rendsburg Gary, and William Schniedewind. "The Siloam Tunnel Inscription: Historical and Linguistic Perspectives." *IEJ* 60.2 (2010): 188–203.

Rendtorff, Rolf. "Beobachtungen zur altisraelitischen Geschichtsschreibung anhand der Geschichte vom Aufstieg Davids." Pp. 428–39 in *Probleme biblischer Theologie*. Edited by H. Wolff. München: Chr. Kaiser, 1971.

Rhodes, P. J. "Documents and the Greek Historians." Pp. 56–66 in *A Companion to Greek and Roman Historiography*. Volume 1. Edited by J. Marincola. Malden: Blackwell, 2007.

Richardson, Seth. "The Many Falls of Babylon and the Shape of Forgetting." Pp. 101–42 in *Envisioning the Past Through Memories: How Memory Shaped Ancient Near Eastern Societies*. Edited by D. Nadali. London: Bloomsbury, 2016.

Richelle, Matthieu. "Elusive Scrolls: Could Any Hebrew Literature Have Been Written Prior to the 8th Century BCE?" *VT* 66 (2016): 1–39.

Ricoeur, Paul. *La Mémoire, L'Histoire, L'Oubli*. Paris: Éditions du Seuil, 2000.

———. *Memory, History, Forgetting*. Translated by K. Blamey and D. Pellauer. Chicago: University of Chicago Press, 2004.

———. *Time and Narrative*, Volume I. Translated by K. McLaughlin and D. Pellauer. Chicago: University of Chicago Press, 1984.

———. *Time and Narrative*, Volume III. Translated by K. Blamey and D. Pellauer. Chicago: University of Chicago Press, 1988.

Rigeny, Ann. "Plenitude, Scarcity, and the Circulation of Cultural Memory." *Journal of European Studies* 35.1 (2005): 11–28.

Roche-Hawley, Carole, and Richard Hawley. "An Essay on Scribal Families, Tradition, and Innovation in Thirteenth-Century Ugarit." Pp. 241–64 in *Beyond Hatti: A Tribute to Gary Beckman*. Edited by B. Collins and P. Michalowski. Atlanta: Lockwood Press, 2013.

Rodriguez Mayorgas, Ana. "History and Memory in Roman Thinking about the Past: *Historia* and *Memoria* in Republican Literature." *Quarderni di Storia* 83 (2016): 51–76.

Roediger, Henry, Franklin Zaromb, and Andrew Butler. "The Role of Repeated Retrieval in Shaping Collective Memory." Pp. 138–70 in *Memory in Mind and Culture*. Edited by P. Boyer and J. Wertsch. Cambridge: Cambridge University Press, 2009.

Rollston, Christopher. "The Khirbet Qeiyafa Ostracon: Methodological Musings and Caveats." *TA* 38 (2011): 67–82.

———. "Scribal Education During the First Temple Period: Epigraphic and Biblical Evidence." Pp. 84–101 in *Contextualizing Israel's Sacred Writings: Ancient Literacy, Orality, and Literary Production*. Edited by B. Schmidt. Atlanta: SBL Press, 2015.

———. "Scribal Education in Ancient Israel: The Old Hebrew Epigraphic Evidence." *BASOR* 344 (2006): 47–74.

———. *Writing and Literacy in the World of Ancient Israel: Epigraphic Evidence from the Iron Age*. Atlanta: SBL Press, 2010.

Routledge, Bruce. "A Fishy Business: The Inland Trade in Nile Perch (*Lates nil Soticus*) in the Early Iron Age Levant." Pp. 212–33 in *Walls of the Prince: Egyptian Interactions with Southwest Asia in Antiquity*. Edited by T. Harrison. Leiden: Brill, 2015.

———. "The Politics of Mesha: Segmented Identities and State Formation in Iron Age Moab." *JESHO* 43 (2000): 221–56.

Rubin, David. *Memory in Oral Traditions: A Cognitive Psychology of Epics, Ballads, and Counting-Out Rhymes*. New York: Oxford University Press, 1995.

Russom, Geoffrey. "Historicity and Anachronism in *Beowulf*." Pp. 243–61 in *Epic and History*. Edited by D. Konstan and K. Raaflaub. Malden: Wiley-Blackwell, 2009.

Saebø, Magne. "Fascination with 'History'—Biblical Interpretation in a Century of Modernism and Historicism." Pp. 17–30 in *Hebrew Bible / Old Testament: The History of Its Interpretation. Volume III/1: From Modernism to Post-Modernism (The Nineteenth and Twentieth Centuries)*. Edited by M. Saebø. Göttingen: Vandenhoeck & Ruprecht, 2013.

Sammons, Benjamin. *The Art and Rhetoric of the Homeric Catalogue*. Oxford: Oxford University Press, 2010.

Sanders, Seth. *The Invention of Hebrew*. Champaign: University of Illinois Press, 2009.

———. "What was the Alphabet For? The Rise of Written Vernaculars and the Making of Israelite National Literature." *Maarav* 11.1 (2004): 25–56.

———. "Writing and Early Iron Age Israel: Before National Scripts, Beyond Nations and States." Pp. 97–112 in *Literate Culture and Tenth-Century Canaan: The Tel Zayit Abecedary in Context*. Edited by R. Tappy and P. K. McCarter. Winona Lake: Eisenbrauns, 2008.

Sapir-Hen Lidar, Guy Bar-Oz, Yuval Gadot, and Israel Finkelstein. "Pig Husbandry in Iron Age Israel and Judah: New Insights Regarding the Origin of the 'Taboo.'" *ZDPV* 129 (2013): 1–20.

Sass, Benjamin, Yosef Garfinkel, Michael Hasel, and Martin Klingbeil. "The Lachish Jar Sherd: An Early Alphabetic Inscription Discovered in 2014." *BASOR* 374 (2015): 233–45.

Sasson, Jack. "On Idrimi and Šarruwa the Scribe." Pp. 309–24 in *Studies on the Civilization and Culture of Nuzi and the Hurrians*. Edited by M. A. Morrison and D. I. Owen. Winona Lake: Eisenbrauns, 1981.

Saussy, Haun. *The Ethnography of Rhythm: Orality and its Technologies*. New York: Fordham University Press, 2016.

Schäfer-Lichtenberger, Christa, ed. *Die Samuelbücher und die Deuteronomisten*. Stuttgart: Kohlhammer, 2010.

Schiffman, Zachary. *The Birth of the Past*. Baltimore: Johns Hopkins University Press, 2011.

Schmid, Konrad. *The Old Testament: A Literary History.* Translated by L. Maloney. Minneapolis: Fortress, 2012.

Schmidt, Brian. "Memorializing Conflict: Toward an Iron Age 'Shadow' History of Israel's Earliest Literature." Pp. 103–32 in *Contextualizing Israel's Sacred Writings: Ancient Literacy, Orality, and Literary Production.* Atlanta: SBL Press, 2015.

Schniedewind, William. "The Geopolitical History of Philistine Gath." *BASOR* 309 (1998): 69–77.

———. *How the Bible Became a Book: The Textualization of Ancient Israel.* Cambridge: Cambridge University Press, 2004.

———. *A Social History of Hebrew: Its Origins Through the Rabbinic Period.* New Haven: Yale University Press, 2013.

Schwartz, Barry. *Abraham Lincoln and the Forge of National Memory.* Chicago: University of Chicago Press, 2000.

———. "Culture and Collective Memory: Comparative Perspectives." Pp. 619–29 in *The Handbook of Cultural Sociology.* Edited by J. Hall. London: Routledge, 2010.

———. "Where There's Smoke, There's Fire: Memory and History." Pp. 7–40 in *Memory and Identity in Ancient Judaism and Early Christianity: A Conversation with Barry Schwartz.* Edited by T. Thatcher. Atlanta: SBL, 2014.

Seger, Joe. "Halif, Tel." Pp. 553–59 in *NEAEHL.* Volume 2. Edited by E. Stern. Jerusalem: Israel Exploration Society, 1993.

———. "The Location of Biblical Ziklag." *BA* 47.1 (1984): 47–53.

Shai, Itzhaq. "Philistia and the Philistines in the Iron IIA." *ZDPV* 127.2 (2011): 119–34.

———. "The Political Organization of the Philistines." Pp. 347–60 in *"I Will Speak the Riddles of Ancient Times:" Archaeological and Historical Studies in Honor of Amihai Mazar on the Occasion of His Sixtieth Birthday.* Edited by A. Maeir and P. Miroschedji. Winona Lake: Eisenbrauns, 2006.

———. "Understanding Philistine Migration: City Names and Their Implications." *BASOR* 354 (2009): 15–27.

Shai, Itzhaq, and Aren Maeir. "Pre-*LMLK* Jars: A New Class of Iron IIA Storage Jars." *TA* 30 (2003): 108–23.

———. "The Late Iron IIA Pottery Assemblage from Stratum A3." Pp. 313–64 in *Tell es Safi/Gath I: The 1996–2005 Seasons, Part I: Texts.* Edited by A. Maeir. Wiesbaden: Harrassowitz Verlag, 2012.

Shai, Itzhaq, and Joel Uziel. "The Whys and Why Nots of Writing: Literacy and Illiteracy in the Southern Levant During the Bronze Ages." *Kaskal* 7 (2010): 67–83.

Shai, Itzhaq, Haskel Greenfield, Johanna Regev, Elisabetta Boaretto, Adi Eliyahu-Behar, and Aren Maeir. "The Early Bronze Age Remains at Tell es Safi / Gath: An Interim Report." *TA* 41 (2014): 20–49.

Shai, Itzhaq, Jeffrey Chadwick, Eric Welch, Jill Katz, Haskey Greenfield, and Aren Maeir. "The Early Bronze Age Fortifications at Tell es-Safi/Gath, Israel." *PEQ* 148.1 (2016): 42–58.

Shai, Itzhaq, David Ilan, Aren Maeir, and Joe Uziel. "The Iron Age Remains at Tel Nagila." *BASOR* 363 (2011): 25–43.

Shai, Itzhaq, Aren Maeir, Yuval Gadot, and Joe Uziel. "Differentiating Between Public and Residential Buildings: A Case Study from Late Bronze Age II Tell es Safi/ Gath." Pp. 107–33 in *Household Archaeology in Ancient Israel and Beyond*. Edited by A. Yasur-Landau, J. Ebeling, and L. Mazow. Leiden: Brill, 2011.

Shanske, Darien. *Thucydides and the Philosophical Origins of History*. Cambridge: Cambridge University Press, 2007.

Shavit, Alon. "Settlement Patterns of Philistine City-States." Pp. 135–64 in *Bene Israel: Studies in the Archaeology of Israel and the Levant during the Bronze and Iron Ages in Honour of Israel Finkelstein*. Edited by A. Fantalkin and A. Yasur- Landau. Leiden: Brill, 2008.

Sherratt, Susan. "Archaeological Contexts." Pp. 119–40 in *A Companion to Ancient Epic*. Edited by J. Foley. Malden: Blackwell, 2005.

———. "The Ceramic Phenomenon of the 'Sea Peoples,': An Overview." Pp. 619–44 in *The Philistines and Other "Sea Peoples" in Text and Archaeology*. Edited by A. Killebrew and G. Lehmann. Atlanta: SBL Press, 2013.

———. "Homeric Epic and Contexts of Bardic Creation." Pp. 35–52 in *Archaeology and Homeric Epic*. Edited by S. Sherratt and J. Bennet. Oxford: Oxbow, 2017.

———. "'Reading the Texts': Archaeology and the Homeric Question." *Antiquity* 64 (1990): 807–24.

Shiloh, Yigal. *Excavations at the City of David*. Volume I. Jerusalem: Hebrew University, 1984.

Simpson, R. Simpson, and J. F. Lazenby. *The Catalogue of the Ships in Homer's Iliad*. Oxford: Oxford University Press, 1970.

Singer, Itamar. "The Philistines in the Bible: A Short Rejoinder to a New Perspective." Pp. 19–28 in *The Philistines and Other "Sea Peoples" in Text and Archaeology*. Edited by A. Killebrew and G. Lehmann. Atlanta: SBL Press, 2013.

Singer-Avitz, Lily. "Khirbet Qeiyafa: Late Iron Age I in Spite of It All." *IEJ* 62.2 (2012): 177–85.

———. "Khirbet Qeiyafa: Late Iron Age I in Spite of it All—Once Again." *IEJ* 66.2 (2016): 232–44.

———. "The Relative Chronology of Khirbet Qeiyafa." *TA* 27 (2010): 79–83.

Smend, Rudolf. "Gunkel und Wellhausen." Pp. 21–40 in *Hermann Gunkel (1862–1932)*. Edited by E. Waschke. Neukirchen-Vluyn: Neukirchener Verlagsgesellschaft, 2013.

———. "In the Wake of Wellhausen: The Growth of a Literary-critical School and Its Varied Influence." Pp. 472–92 in *The Hebrew Bible/Old Testament: The History of*

Its Interpretation. Volume III/1. Edited by M. Saebø. Göttingen: Vandenhoeck & Ruprecht, 2013.

Smith, Mark S. "Biblical Narrative Between Ugaritic and Akkadian Literature: Part I: Ugarit and the Bible." *RB* 114.1 (2007): 5–29.

———. "Biblical Narrative Between Ugaritic and Akkadian Literature: Part II: Mesopotamian Impact on Biblical Narrative." *RB* 114.2 (2007): 189–207.

———. *The Memoirs of God: History, Memory, and the Experience of the Divine in Ancient Israel*. Minneapolis: Fortress, 2004.

———. *Poetic Heroes: Literary Commemorations of Warriors and Warrior Culture in the Early Biblical World*. Grand Rapids: Eerdmans, 2014.

Snodgrass, Anthony. *The Dark Age of Greece: an Archaeological Survey of the Eleventh to the Eighth Centuries BC*. Edinburgh: Edinburgh University Press, 1971.

Spawforth, Antony. "Symbol of Unity? The Persian-Wars Tradition in the Roman Empire." Pp. 233–47 in *Greek Historiography*. Edited by S. Hornblower. Oxford: Oxford University Press, 1994.

Spiegel, Gabrielle. "History, Historicism, and the Social Logic of the Text in the Middle Ages." *Speculum* 65.1 (1990): 59–86.

———. "*Pseudo-Turpin*, the Crisis of the Aristocracy and the Beginnings of Vernacular Prose Historiography in France." *Journal of Medieval History* 12.3 (1986): 207–23.

———. *Romancing the Past: The Rise of Vernacular Prose Historiography in Thirteenth-Century France*. Berkeley: University of California Press, 1993.

Stager, Lawrence. "Asheklon, Tel." Pp. 1578–86 in *NEAEHL*. Volume 5. Edited by E. Stern. Jerusalem: Israel Exploration Society, 2008.

———. "Forging an Identity: The Emergence of Ancient Israel." Pp. 90–131 in *The Oxford History of the Biblical World*. Edited by M. Coogan. New York: Oxford University Press, 1998.

———. "The Impact of the Sea Peoples." Pp. 332–48 in *The Archaeology of Society in the Holy Land*. Edited by T. E. Levy. New York: Facts on File, 1995.

———. "An Inscribed Potsherd from the Eleventh Century." *BASOR* 194 (1969): 45–52.

———. "The Shechem Temple: Where Abimelech Massacred a Thousand." *BAR* 29.4 (2003): 26–35, 66–69.

Stager, Lawrence, J. Davi Schloen, and D. Master. *Ashkelon 1: Introduction and Overview (1985–2006)*. Winona Lake: Eisenbrauns, 2008.

Steinbock, Bernd. *Social Memory in Athenian Public Discourse*. Ann Arbor: University of Michigan Press, 2013.

Steiner, Margreet. *Excavations by Kathleen Kenyon in Jerusalem, 1961–1967*. Volume III. London: Sheffield, 2001.

Stern, Ephraim. *Archaeology of the Land of the Bible: The Assyrian, Babylonian, and Persian Periods, 732–332 BCE*. Volume II. New York: Doubleday, 2001.

Sternberg, Meir. *The Poetics of Biblical Narrative: Ideological Literature and the Drama of Reading*. Bloomington: Indiana University Press, 1987.

Stewart, Daniel. "'Most Worth Remembering': Pausanias, Analogy, and Classical Archaeology." *Hesperia* 82.2 (2013): 231–61.

Stoebe, Hans. *Das Erste Buch Samuelis.* Gütersloh: Verlagshaus Gerd Mohn, 1973.

Stone, Bryan. "The Philistines and Acculturation: Culture Change and Ethnic Continuity in the Iron Age." *BASOR* 298 (1995): 7–32.

Stott, Katherine. *Why Did They Write This Way?: Reflections on References to Written Documents in the Hebrew Bible and Ancient Literature.* New York: T&T Clark, 2008.

Svenbro, Jesper. *Phrasikleia: An Anthropology of Reading in Ancient Greece.* Translated by J. Lloyd. Ithaca: Cornell University Press, 1993.

Tadmor, Hayim. "Autobiographical Apology in the Royal Assyrian Literature." Pp. 36–57 in *History, Historiography and Interpretation.* Edited by H. Tadmor and M. Weinfeld. Jerusalem: Magnes, 1983.

Tappy, Ronald. "The Depositional History of Iron Age Tel Zayit: A Response to Finkelstein, Sass, and Singer-Avitz." *Er-Isr* 30 (2011): 127–43.

———. "Historical and Geographical Notes on the 'Lowland Districts' of Judah in Joshua xv 33–47." *VT* 58 (2008): 381–403.

Tappy, Ronald, P. Kyle McCarter, Marilyn Lundberg, and Bruce Zuckerman. "An Abecedary of the Mid-Tenth Century B.C.E. from the Judaean Shephelah." *BASOR* 344 (2006): 5–46.

Thareani-Sussely, Yifat. "The 'Archaeology of the Days of Manasseh' Reconsidered in Light of Evidence from the Beersheba Valley." *PEQ* 139.2 (2007): 69–77.

———. *Tel 'Aroer. The Iron Age II Caravan Town and the Hellenistic-Early Roman Settlement.* Jerusalem: Hebrew Union College—Jewish Institute of Religion, 2011.

Thomas, Rosalind. *Literacy and Orality in Ancient Greece.* Cambridge: Cambridge University Press, 1992.

———. *Oral Tradition and Written Record in Classical Athens.* Cambridge: Cambridge University Press, 1989.

———. "Prose Performance Text: Epideixis and Written Publication in the Late Fifth and Early Fourth Centuries BCE." Pp. 162–88 in *Written Texts and the Rise of Literate Culture in Ancient Greece.* Edited by H. Yunis. Cambridge: Cambridge University Press, 2003.

Tigay, Jeffrey. *The Evolution of the Gilgamesh Epic.* Philadelphia: University of Pennsylvania Press, 1982.

Tov, Emanuel. *Textual Criticism of the Hebrew Bible.* 3rd edition. Minneapolis: Fortress, 2012.

———. *Scribal Practices and Approaches Reflected in Texts Found in the Judean Desert.* Leiden: Brill, 2004.

Ulrich, Eugene. *The Dead Sea Scrolls and the Developmental Composition of the Bible.* Leiden: Brill, 2015.

Ussishkin, David. "Gath, Lachish, and Jerusalem in the 9th Cent. B.C.E.—an Archaeological Reassessment." *ZDPV* 131.2 (2015): 129–49.

———. "A Synopsis of the Stratigraphical, Chronological and Historical Issues." Pp. 50–122 in *The Renewed Archaeological Excavations at Lachish (1973–1994)*. Volume I. Edited by D. Ussishkin. Tel Aviv: Tel Aviv University Press, 2004.

Uziel, Joe. "The Development Process of Philistine Material Culture: Assimilation, Acculturation and Everything in Between." *Levant* 39 (2007): 165–73.

Uziel, Joe, and Aren Maeir. "The Location, Size and Periods of Settlement at Tell es-Safi/Gath: The Surface Survey Results." Pp. 173–82 in *Tell es Safi/Gath I: The 1996—2005 Seasons, Part I: Texts*. Edited by A. Maeir. Wiesbaden: Harrassowitz Verlag, 2012.

———. "Scratching the Surface at Gath: Implications of the Tell eṣ-Ṣafi/Gath Surface Survey." *TA* 32 (2005): 50–75.

Varner, Eric. *Mutilation and Transformation: Damnatio Memoriae and Roman Imperial Portraiture*. Leiden: Brill, 2004.

Vatri, Alessandro. *Orality and Performance in Classical Attic Prose: A Linguistic Approach*. Oxford: Oxford University Press, 2016.

Van de Mieroop, Marc. *The Ancient Mesopotamian City*. Oxford: Oxford University Press, 1997.

Van Beek, Gus. "Jemmeh, Tel." Pp. 669–72 in *NEAEHL*. Volume II.

Van Bekkum, Koert. "Coexistence as Guilt: Iron I Memories in Judges 1." Pp. 525–47 in *The Ancient Near East in the 12th–10th Centuries BCE: Culture and History*. Edited by G. Galil, A. Gilboa, A. Maeir, and D. Kahn. Münster: Ugarit Verlag, 2012.

Van Neer, Wim, Omri Lernau, Renée Friedman, Gregory Mumford, Jeroen Poblóme, Marc Waelkens. "Fish Remains from Archaeological Sites as Indicators of Former Trade Connections in the Eastern Mediterranean." *Paléorient* 30.1 (2004): 101–47.

van Oorschot, Jürgen. "Geschichte als Erinnerung und Wissenschaft—ein Beitrag zu ihrem Verhältnis." Pp. 1–27 in *Erzählte Geschichte: Beiträge zur narrativen Kultur im alten Israel*. Edited by R. Lux. Neukirchen-Vluyn: Neukirchner, 2000.

van der Steen, Eveline. "Judha, Masos, and Hayil: The Importance of Ethnohistory and Oral Tradition." Pp. 168–86 in *Historical Biblical Archaeology and the Future: The New Pragmatism*. Edited by T. Levy. London: Equinox, 2010.

Van Der Toorn, Karel. *Scribal Culture and the Making of the Hebrew Bible*. Cambridge: Harvard University Press, 2007.

Van Seters, John. *In Search of History: Historiography in the Ancient World and the Origins of Biblical History*. New Haven: Yale University Press, 1983.

Vansina, Jan. *Oral Tradition as History*. Madison: University of Wisconsin Press, 1985.

Verbrugghe, Gerald, and John Wickersham. *Berossus and Manetho, Introduced and Translated*. Ann Arbor: University of Michigan Press, 2001.

Vermeylen, Jacques. *La Loi du Plus Fort: Histoire de la rédaction des récits davidiques de 1 Samuel 8 à 1 Rois 2*. Leuven, Leuven University Press, 2000.

———. "La maison de Saül et la maison de David: Un écrit de propagande théologic-politique de 1 Sm 11 à 2 Sm 7." Pp. 35–74 in *Figures de David à travers la Bible*. Edited by L. Dorousseaux and J. Vermeylen. Paris: Cerf, 1999.

Vésteinsson, Orri. "Patterns of Settlement in Iceland: A Study in Prehistory." *Saga Book of the Viking Society for Northern Research* 25 (1998): 1–29.

Veyne, Paul. *Did the Greeks Believe in their Myths? An Essay on the Constitutive Imagination*. Translated by P. Wissing. Chicago: University of Chicago Press, 1988.

———. *Foucault: His Thought, His Character*. Translated by J. Lloyd. New York: Polity, 2010.

Visser, Edzard. *Homers Katalog der Schiffe: Die epische Beschreibung Griechenlands in der Ilias*. Teubner: Stuttgart and Leipzig, 1997.

Von Dassow, Eva. "Canaanite in Cuneiform." *JAOS* 124 (2004): 641–74.

———. "What Canaanite Cuneiformists Wrote: Review Article." *IEJ* 53.2 (2003): 196–217.

Von Rad, Gerhard. "The Beginnings of Historical Writing in Ancient Israel." Pp. 166–204 in *The Problem of the Hexateuch and Other Essays*. Translated by E. W. Dicken. London: SCM Press, 1964.

———. "Offene Fragen im Umkreis einer Theologie des Alten Testaments." Pp. 289–312 in *Gesammelte Studien zum Alten Testament*. Volume 2. München: C. Kaiser, 1973.

———. *Old Testament Theology*. Volumes 1 & 2. Translated by D. M. G. Stalker. Louisville: Westminster John Knox, 1962–65.

Wagner, Volker. "Die סרינים der Philister und die Ältesten Israels." *ZAR* 14 (2008): 408–33.

Waerzeggers, Caroline. "The Babylonian Chronicles: Classification and Provenance." *JNES* 71 (2012): 285–98.

Walbank, F. W. *A Historical Commentary on Polybius*. 3 Volumes. Oxford: Clarendon Press, 1957–79.

Waters, K. H. *Herodotus the Historian: His Problems, Methods, and Originality*. 2nd edition. London: Routledge, 2014.

Weitzman, Steve. "Crossing the Border with Samson: Beth-Shemesh and the Bible's Geographical Imagination." Pp. 266–80 in *Tel Beth-Shemesh: A Border Community in Judah, Renewed Excavations 1990–2000: The Iron Age*, Volume I. Edited by S. Bunimovitz and Z. Lederman. Tel Aviv: Emery and Claire Yass Publications, 2016.

———. "The Samson Story as Border Fiction." *Bib Int* 10.2 (2002): 158–74.

Wellhausen, Julius. *Prolegomena to the History of Israel*. 3rd edition. New York: Meridian, 1961 [1882].

West, Stephanie. "Herodotus' Epigraphical Interests." *The Classical Quarterly* 35.2 (1985): 278–305.

———. "Sesostris Stelae (Herodotus 2.102–106)." *Historia: Zeitschrift für Alte Geschichte* 41.1 (1992): 117–20.

White, Hayden. *Metahistory: The Historical Imagination in Nineteenth-Century Europe*. Baltimore: Johns Hopkins Press, 1975.

Wiener, Malcolm. "Homer and History: Old Questions, New Evidence." Pp. 3–33 in *Epos: Reconsidering Greek Epic and Aegean Bronze Age Archaeology*. Edited by S. Morris and R. Laffineur. Liège: Université de Liège, 2007.

Willesen, Folker. "The Philistine Corps of the Scimitar from Gath." *JSS* 3.4 (1958): 327–35.

Williams, Ronald. "Scribal Training in Ancient Egypt." *JAOS* 92 (1972): 214–21.

Wilson, Ian. *Kingship and Memory in Ancient Judah*. New York: Oxford, 2017.

Winter, Jay. "Sites of Memory." Pp. 312–24 in *Memory: Histories, Theories, Debates*. Edited by S. Radstone and B. Schwartz. New York: Fordham University Press, 2010.

Wright, G. Ernest. "Fresh Evidence for the Philistine Story." *BA* 29 (1966): 70–86.

Wright, Jacob. *David, King of Israel, and Caleb in Biblical Memory*. Cambridge: Cambridge University Press, 2014.

Wycherley, R. E. "Pausanias and Praxiteles." *Hesperia Supplements* 20 (1982): 182–91.

Yasur-Landau, Assaf. *The Philistines and Aegean Migration at the End of the Late Bronze Age*. Cambridge: Cambridge University Press, 2010.

———. "The Role of the Canaanite Population in the Aegean Migration to the Southern Levant in the late Second Millennium BCE." Pp. 191–97 in *Materiality and Social Practice: Transformative Capacities of Intercultural Encounters*. Edited by J. Maran and P. Stockhammer. Oxford: Oxbow, 2012.

Yates, Francis. *The Art of Memory*. London: Routledge, 1966.

Yerushalmi, Yosef. *Zakhor: Jewish History and Jewish Memory*. Seattle: Univerity of Washington Press, 1996.

Zorn, Jeffrey. *Tell en-Nasbeh: A Re-Evaluation of the Architecture and Stratigraphy of the Early Bronze Age, Iron Age and Later Periods*. Ph.D. dissertation. University of California, Berkeley, 1993.

Zukerman, Alexander. "Iron Age I and Early Iron Age IIA Pottery." Pp. 265–312 in *Tell es Safi/Gath I: The 1996–2005 Seasons, Part I: Texts*. Edited by A. Maeir. Wiesbaden: Harrassowitz Verlag, 2012.

Zukerman, Alexander, and Itzhaq Shai. "'The Royal City of the Philistines' in the 'Azekah Inscription' and the History of Gath in the 8th Century BCE." *UF* 38 (2006): 729–78.

Zumthor, Paul, and Marilyn Engelhardt. "The Text and the Voice." *New Literary History* 16.1 (1984): 67–92.

Index of Ancient Sources

Index of Modern Authors

Index of Select Subjects